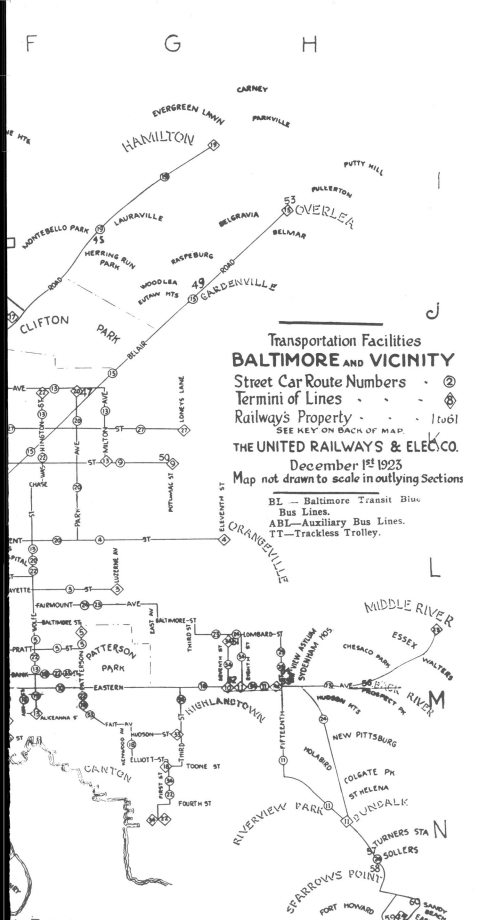

Transportation Facilities
BALTIMORE AND VICINITY

Street Car Route Numbers · ②
Termini of Lines · · · ⑧
Railway's Property · · · 1 to 61
SEE KEY ON BACK OF MAP.

THE UNITED RAILWAYS & ELEC. CO.

December 1st 1923
Map not drawn to scale in outlying Sections

BL — Baltimore Transit Blue
Bus Lines.
ABL—Auxiliary Bus Lines.
TT—Trackless Trolley.

KEY — United Railways Property

22	Madison Avenue	CJ
23	Druid Hill Avenue	CJ
24	Retreat Street	CJ
27	Cumberland Street	CK
29	Oak Street & 25th Street	DJ
38	Washington Boulevard	CN
39	Brooklyn	DN
41	York Road	EI
42	Light Street	EN
45	Harford Avenue	FI
47	Gay Street & North Avenue	FK
50	Potomac Street	GK
51	Lombard Street	GL
52	Eastern Avenue & 8th Street	GM
56	Back River	HM

Power Stations

2	Owings Mills	AI
3	Belvedere Substation	AI
12	Nunnery Lane Substation	AL
21	Druid Hill Avenue Substation	CJ
31	Lombard Street Substation	DM
43	Light Street Substation	EN
46	Harford Avenue Substations	(2) FK
55	Eastern Avenue Substation	HM
56	Back River	HM
58	Bear Creek Substation	HN
60	Bay Shore	HN

Terminal Property

1	Emory Grove	AI
13	Ellicott City	AM
18	Lakeside	DI
20	Guilford Station	DI
28	Callow Avenue	CJ
44	Curtis Bay	EN
53	Overlea	HI

Car Storage Yards

2	Owings Mills	AI
4	Belvedere	AI
35	Car Storage Yard	CM
54	Eastern Avenue & 15th Street	HM

Miscellaneous

7	Gwynn Oak Park	AJ
8	Stone Quarry	AJ
9	Walbrook Junction & Loop	CI
16	Mt. Washington Station	CI
23	Druid Hill Avenue Store Room	CJ
25	Storage Yard — McCulloh Street	CJ
26	Cumberland Street Garage	CK
30	Charles Street Garage	DK
32	Lombard Street Trouble Station	DM
33	Car Shops	CM
34	General Store Room	CM
36	Sand Drying Plant	CM
37	Athletic Field	CM
40	Govans Loop	EI
48	Caroline Street Trouble Station	FL
49	Gardenville Loop	GJ
57	St. Helena Loop	HN
59	Bay Shore Park	HN

Car Route Numbers
(Those with star (*) are also all-night car lines.)

1	Gilmor Street-Guilford Avenue
2	*Carey Street-Fort Avenue
3	Linden Avenue
4	*Edmondson Avenue-Monument Street
5	Pimlico, Pikesville, Emory Grove and West Arlington
6	*Curtis Bay-Fairfield Extension
7	*York & Frederick Roads
8	Towson & Catonsville
9	Wilkens Avenue
10	*Roland Park-Highlandtown
11	Lakeside-Dundalk
12	*John Street-Westport
13	*North Avenue
14	Ellicott City
15	*Gay Street-Belair Road
16	*Madison Avenue
17	St. Paul Street-Gorsuch Avenue-Waverly and Guilford Branches
18	Pennsylvania Avenue
19	*Harford Road
20	*Orleans Street
21	Preston-Caroline Street
22	Canton-Wolfe Street
23	Back & Middle Rivers
24, 26	*Sparrows Point-Bay Shore
25	Mt. Washington
27	Federal Street-Columbia Avenue
29	*Boulevard
30	Fremont Avenue
31	Garrison Boulevard
32	Woodlawn-Howard Park
33	Hudson Street
34	Third Avenue
35	Hillsdale

Merry Christmas, ~~Dave~~ Dad!
Love from ~~Rachel~~ Betty Lynn
and Larry
~~2002~~ 2014

THE HISTORY OF
BALTIMORE'S STREETCARS

Formerly published as *Who Made All Our Streetcars Go?*

Michael R. Farrell

with additional material by
Herbert H. Harwood, Jr. and Andrew S. Blumberg

GREENBERG
PUBLISHING COMPANY, INC.

Greenberg Publishing Company, Inc.
7566 Main Street
Sykesville, Maryland 21784
(410) 795-7447

First Edition

Manufactured in the United States of America

Greenberg Publishing Company, Inc. publishes the world's largest selection of American and European toy train publications as well as books on Marx, Aurora, Buddy L, pressed steel and firefighting toys. For a complete listing of current Greenberg publications, please call 1-800-533-6644 or write to Kalmbach Publishing Company, 21027 Crossroads Circle, Waukesha, Wisconsin 53187.

Greenberg Shows, Inc. sponsors *Greenberg's Great Train, Dollhouse and Toy Shows*, the world's largest of its kind. The shows feature operating train layouts, dollhouses, and collectible toys. Shows are scheduled along the East Coast each year from Massachusetts to Florida. For a list of our current shows please call (410) 795-7447 or write to Greenberg Shows, Inc., 7566 Main Street, Sykesville, Maryland 21784 and request a show brochure.

Greenberg Auctions, a division of Greenberg Shows, Inc., offers nationally advertised auctions of toy trains and toys. Please contact our auction manager at (410) 795-7447 for further information.

ISBN 0-89778-283-6

Library of Congress Cataloging-in-Publication Data

Farrell, Michael R.
    The History of Baltimore's streetcars / by Michael R. Farrell.
      p. cm.
    Updated ed. of: Who made all our streetcars go?, 1973.
    ISBN 0-89778-283-6 : $45.95
      1. Street-railroads--Maryland--Baltimore--History.   I. Farrell,
Michael R. Who made all our streetcars go? II. Title.
HE4491.B37F35 1992
388.4' 6' 097526--dc20   92–8474
                                              CIP

Front cover: Semi-convertible No. 5858 turns on the Smallwood Street loop between Pratt and Lombard Streets on the No. 8 line during a Baltimore Chapter NRHS excursion, August 13, 1950. (Charles M. Wagner, Lee H. Rogers Collection)

Back Cover: Looking north on Eutaw Street from near Camden Station, we see semi-convertible No. 5858 laying over during a Baltimore Chapter NRHS excursion, August 13, 1950. The Bromo Seltzer tower can be seen up the street and also the painted advertising for the late, lamented WB & A Electric Railroad. (Charles M. Wagner, Lee H. Rogers Collection)

When this work was first published in 1973,
the author, Michael R. Farrell, dedicated it to

LOUIS C. MUELLER

who gave freely of his time and his collection and
played a crucial role in making this book a reality.

The Editorial Committee preparing the present version
now dedicates the revision to

MICHAEL R. FARRELL
1925-1976

whose countless volunteer hours of dedicated research and writing
gave us this valuable history.

It seems particularly appropriate that Mike Farrell's birth was announced in the United Railway's house organ, *Transit Topics,* January 1926: Motorman M. Farrell, Roland Park Line, is the proud daddy of a little baby boy.

This brief note was all the United ever had to say about Mike; however, in the present book he wrote at considerably greater length about the United.

An accountant by profession, he became a skilled amateur photographer; this interest led him to join the Baltimore Chapter of the National Railway Historical Society. He contributed articles to the *Bulletin* of the Society and other railfan journals. Later on, he became a member of the Baltimore Streetcar Museum, where he served as Treasurer and Trustee.

Mike was married to Norma Jean Shelby in 1962. They had two children — Julie and Stephen. He died on March 23, 1976 after a brief illness.

His major work was clearly the Baltimore street railway history, a project of the Baltimore Chapter of the National Railway Historical Society. While much of the preliminary study had been done by other Chapter members, it required six years of painstaking research and two more of writing and rewriting to bring the work to completion. The original title, *Who Made All Our Streetcars Go?,* indicates his intent to deal with the people involved as well as the

technical aspects — to appeal to average Baltimore residents as well as railfans.

This book represents probably the most ambitious project ever undertaken by the

Baltimore Chapter. Mike's dedication as a volunteer author was the key factor which made it possible. The Chapter owes him a debt which can never be repaid.

CONTENTS

ACKNOWLEDGMENTS 6

INTRODUCTION 7

THE HISTORY
(1859-1992)

FIRST THERE WAS CITY PASSENGER 12

ODEN BOWIE TIGHTENS THE REINS 22

DRUID HILL WAS THE MAGNET 26

AN IRON WEB 34

THE LINES CALLED FRICK 41

THE MINOR COMPANIES 44

PROFESSOR DAFT AND HIS MOTORS 52

"RAPID TRANSIT" COMES TO TOWN 59

SHOWERS OF ELECTRIC SPARKS 69

AFTER YEARS OF CHANGE, A LULL 74

AND THEN THERE WERE THREE 81

FROM OUT OF THE NORTH 86

AT THE END OF A LINE 91

THE 76 MILLION DOLLAR DEAL 96

THE UNITED 102

BUILT TO LAST 112

A FATEFUL FIFTEEN YEARS 117

A VALIANT TRY — BUT 126

BANKRUPT! 136

A LAST BRILLIANT FLARE 142

LOST STREETCARS AND PART-TIME MOTORMEN 152

UNDER AN ASPHALT BLANKET 158

THE CLOSING DAYS 162

GHOSTS OF STREETCARS PAST 168

NEW MANAGEMENT AND A METRO 174

THE STREETCAR COMES FULL CIRCLE 182

PRESERVING THE PAST 190

FULL-COLOR PICTORIAL HISTORY OF BALTIMORE STREETCARS 201

STREETCAR VIGNETTES

IT TOOK MORE THAN CARS 218

THE STORM 226

THE ACCIDENT 232

THE TRESTLE 236

OF PARKS AND PARTIES 240

CARRYING THE MAIL AND EXPRESS 249

"THE HOODOO CAR" 252

THE FOLKLORE OF THE STREET RAILWAY 256

RANDOM NOTES FROM BYGONE DAYS 260

THE ART OF ABANDONMENT 266

THE LEMMING STRAIN WAS STRONG 272

BRILL SEMI-CONVERTIBLES 278

ARTICULATED UNITS AND PERMANENTLY-COUPLED TRAINS 285

THE PETER WITT CARS 290

ROSTERS

THE BALTIMORE STREETCAR MUSEUM
  HISTORIC EQUIPMENT ROSTER 200

PASSENGER CAR ROSTER
  UNITED RAILWAYS & ELECTRIC CO./BALTIMORE TRANSIT CO.
  1922-1963 294

GLOSSARY 296

BIBLIOGRAPHY 300

INDEX 303

ACKNOWLEDGMENTS

FROM THE PREVIOUSLY PUBLISHED
WHO MADE ALL OUR STREETCARS GO?

It would have been virtually impossible to put together this book without the assistance of a number of people.

Among those to whom the author is especially indebted is John S. Thomsen, who not only served as editor but also performed a multitude of tasks (ranging from raising the necessary funds to taking photographs) over and above the normal editorial duties. Louis C. Mueller, who has spent a lifetime in assembling a remarkable collection of streetcar photographs and reference material, gave freely of his time and of his collection, which forms the nucleus of this book. George F. Nixon, Baltimore's best-known rail historian, also provided valuable help in various phases of the project.

A large measure of credit for the publication of this history must go to Henry S. Wells, Jr., who kept the idea alive over the years, and to his father, Henry S. Wells, Sr., who passed away before it came to fruition but left a wealth of information to those who followed.

Of course, the book would have remained another unpublished manuscript were it not for the generosity of those members and friends of the Baltimore Chapter, NRHS, who supplied the funds to make it a reality.

Charles N. Marshall, attorney for the Baltimore Streetcar Museum, not only gave of his professional services, but offered many constructive suggestions which have been incorporated into the final version.

David M. Novak, while serving as technical advisor, also searched out many of the older photographs.

Charles W. Whittle took rough sketches of the various lines and turned them into first-rate maps.

Alfred C. Haynes, of *The Baltimore Sun*, lent his skills to give the text and captions a professional touch.

Charles R. Lloyd used his extensive knowledge of the graphics field in coordinating typesetting and reproduction.

Kenneth Briers added immeasurably by lending photographic equipment as well as giving advice on techniques.

A special word of thanks goes to the representatives of industries and institutions who assisted in obtaining photographs: Wilbur Hunter and Paul Amelia, of the Peale Museum; Samuel Hopkins and P. William Filby, of the Maryland Historical Society; Harold A. Williams, Bradford Jacobs, William Bernard, and Clement Vitek, of *The Baltimore Sun;* James M. McGarry and Louise Crowningshield of the General Electric Company, Schenectady, New York; Vernon F. Strickland, of the Baltimore Gas and Electric Company; Mrs. Jean Walsh, of *The Catonsville Times;* Mrs. Johnson of the Reference Department and several dozen persons of the Maryland Room of the Enoch Pratt Library, from pages to former department head Miss Elizabeth Litsinger, who untiringly located obscure publications and dusty newspaper files.

Contributions of photographs have been credited in the captions, and others whose efforts fell into a particular area are mentioned in the notes.

Over the years, I have endeavored to keep a listing of the many, many persons from whom I have obtained information relative to the Baltimore street railways. To fully describe their contributions would take half of the book. Therefore, they are merely listed below, with an apology to anyone who has been inadvertently missed: Robert Base, Charles F. Buschman, James E. Dalmas, Ralph E. Edwards, John V. Engleman, Donald Flayhart, James Genthner, Clyde Gerald, Gary Haigley, George W. Hilton, Shelley Hopkins, Carl P. Hughes, John Hutchins, Robert W. Janssen, P. Edward Kaltenbach, J. Randolph Kean, Anthony Kopecni, Max Krueger, Robert Krueger, Daniel Lawrence, Colonel John Merriken, Louis F. Meyer, Kenneth Morse, Roland Nuttrell, John S. Phelps, Robert Reuter, J. Kenneth Roberts, Lee Rogers, Gilbert Sandler, Fred Scharnagle, John S. Sloan, Daniel Sohn, Walter Sondheim, Helen S. Thomsen, George J. Voith, Edward White, David Williams, Ill, and Richard J. Zeller.

Last, but not least, I wish to thank my wife, Norma Jean, who has helped in many ways, especially in typing the final manuscript, and my children, Julie and Stephen, who helped make the layout work less tedious.

Michael R. Farrell
Catonsville, Maryland
March 14, 1973

INTRODUCTION

FROM THE PREVIOUSLY PUBLISHED
WHO MADE ALL OUR STREETCARS GO?

In the spring of 1940, I joined the Baltimore Chapter of the National Railway Historical Society. At one of the earliest meetings I attended it was suggested that the Chapter undertake the project of compiling a history of the Baltimore street railways. Now, in 1973, I have been asked to write an introduction to this history. Surely no one can accuse the Chapter of rushing through this project hastily or unadvisedly.

In the beginning, World War II put a stop to any progress on the history. Subsequently a History Committee was set up under Chairman George Nixon. Later on, Donald Flayhart and Henry Wells, Jr. each served as chairman and helped to keep the project alive. A considerable amount of data was collected and drafts of some sections were compiled. However, the real turning point came when prime responsibility for the history was assigned to Michael R. Farrell. He has spent about six years of methodical and painstaking research, as well as drawing on the combined knowledge of dozens of other Chapter members. An additional two years have been spent in writing and rewriting the manuscript, selecting photographs, and laying out the format of the book.

It might appear that street railways form a rather minor, if interesting, facet in Baltimore history. However, this is far from accurate. In the earliest years of development, the turnpike roads and other highways formed the spokes along which the city grew. Within four years of the arrival of the horse car in Baltimore, suburban lines extended to Towson and Catonsville. By the close of the century, almost every principal road had its paralleling street railway. Real estate sales prospered, and suburban developments sprang up along almost all of these routes; the land between these spokes generally retained its rural character. It was not until after World War II, with the overwhelming popular reliance on the automobile, that the pattern set by the old turnpikes and street railway routes really faded into oblivion.

In one sense, this history is long overdue. The last comprehensive published account of local street railway history appears to be that of William House, prepared in 1909 on the 50th anniversary of street railway operation in the city. This was included as a chapter in the Baltimore history edited by Clayton Colman Hall. Incidentally, the Hall work, published in 1912, seems to be the most recent overall history of the city.

On the other hand, there are two reasons why the long delay in publishing the book now seems rather fortunate. First, the morning of November 3, 1963 marked the end of streetcar operation in Baltimore and thus signaled the end of an era. It is now possible to view the entire span of surface street railway operation and present the story in a single volume. Secondly, Mr. Farrell seems particularly suited to write this narrative for the diverse groups toward which it is aimed.

Mike Farrell has been interested in Baltimore street railways over a long period. As a talented photographer, he was also well qualified to select and arrange the photographs, many of which he supplied himself. He is an authority on many of the technical aspects of streetcars and is acquainted with almost every railfan in the area. At the same time his viewpoint is somewhat different from that of the typical railfan. He can understand the outlook of the old-time Baltimorean who may wish to read an account of the cars and routes he once rode but would only yawn at a record of the different numbers carried by each car at various times. Thus he seems particularly suited to follow a middle path which will appeal to diverse groups of readers.

On the one hand, this book is designed for the railfans and other students of transit history, who are interested in the entire industry. At the same time, it is intended to provide a serious documented account, which will make a significant contribution to Baltimore history. Finally, it is hoped that the book will be sufficiently informal and readable to appeal to all those interested in Baltimore nostalgia.

The book is organized in three principal sections. The first one, roughly half of the text, consists of a chronological history of Baltimore street railways from the first horse car up Broadway in 1859 through the last day of rail operations in 1963; it even includes mention of plans for a forthcoming rapid transit system. This is followed by Selected Short Subjects, a group of self-contained chapters on special topics, such as the blizzard of 1899, the Guilford Avenue elevated, the Brill semi-convertible cars, etc. Each of these chapters may be read by itself without loss of continuity. The third section consists of Notes and Comments, documenting and supplementing all of the preceding chapters.

The book concludes with a glossary, bibliography, and index.

Such a history as this has involved hundreds of names and dates and numerous technical details. Several knowledgeable collaborators have read the manuscript and supplied corrections and clarifications. Nevertheless it seems inevitable that some errors will remain. As chairman of the Publications Committee of the Chapter, I have had primary responsibility for final editing of the manuscript and for arranging for its publication. This task has only been possible to complete through the cooperation of many individuals. I am very grateful to the officers and members of the Baltimore Chapter for their continuing support, especially to those who participated in the Publication Loan to provide the funds necessary for printing this book. A particular vote of thanks is due to the other members of the Publication Committee: Ralph E. Edwards, David M. Novak, and Charles R. Lloyd, as well as the author. Mr. Lloyd's technical background and business contacts in the printing field were vital to the successful completion of the project. Valuable assistance in proofreading was given by Alfred C. Haynes and John Hutchins; the former was also helpful in sharing his expertise in matters of style. George M. Lotz, the artist who designed the dust jacket (for the first edition), deserves special thanks for devoting time and effort far beyond the call of duty. Many of the historical facts were checked in the Eisenhower Library of the Johns Hopkins University; particular thanks are due to the staff of the Audio-Visual Collection.

I am most grateful to the Baltimore Streetcar Museum and to its president, James E. Dalmas, for close cooperation in many phases of the project. Both the Museum itself and several individual members played an important role in assuring the success of the Publication Loan.

Finally, I want to express my deep gratitude to all members of my family for their interest and support in this project, despite the time which my participation involved. I am particularly grateful to my wife, Helen, for assistance in proofreading and editing and for acting as a sounding board for hundreds of questions and problems which arose.

It is certainly a pleasure to see this long-time project finally approaching an end. This fulfills one of the principal aims for which the Baltimore Chapter was organized. It is our hope that this book will lead to more historical publications by other Chapter members.

John S. Thomsen
Baltimore, Maryland
May 1973

INTRODUCTION

THE HISTORY OF BALTIMORE'S STREETCARS

When the first edition of this book was published in 1973 as *Who Made All Our Streetcars Go?,* it appeared that, in fact, streetcars had "gone" forever from Baltimore. The last car in revenue service had made its final trip in 1963 and planning was underway for the first leg of what was intended to be a comprehensive city-wide subway system.

In the decade following publication, the first segment of a new "heavy rail line," much of it a subway, was designed and constructed, and, in November 1983, operation started between the northwest suburbs and the center of the city. An extension to that line was completed a few years later and a further subway extension is scheduled to go into service about 1994.

The steadily increasing cost of heavy rail, particularly those portions constructed as subways, stimulated consideration of what were considered in Europe to be modern trams, but quickly became known in North America as "light rail vehicles," a term now used world-wide. Baltimore was one of a number of cities to find light rail an acceptable alternate, at least for certain lines, and, in 1992, service started on the first increment of a 22-mile light rail line, running north and south, from Hunt Valley,

through the center of the city to Glen Burnie. Streetcars, albeit larger and more sophisticated, had returned.

It is fitting that this renascence coincides with the decision to publish a new edition of this book. From the first horse cars of 1859 to the first PCC cars of 1936, Baltimore had been in the forefront of rail mass transit and, with 425 miles of track, had been the site of one of the nation's more significant streetcar systems. Now, the story continues, with the city being among the first in the United States to adopt the "new" light rail.

In addition to containing new material on both the heavy and light rail systems, a number of pages of color photos and a revised chapter on the Baltimore Streetcar Museum, the book has been updated where necessary, existing black-and-white photography expanded and a few errors remaining after the second printing corrected. The book has also been completely reset. Otherwise it remains as it was: Mike Farrell's book.

This edition was prepared under the direction of Kenneth A. Maylath. The chapters on heavy and light rail were written by Herbert H. Harwood, Jr. and the revised chapter on the Museum by Andrew

S. Blumberg. Photo selections were coordinated by Harry G. Gesser. Copy editing was provided by Herbert Harwood and Harry Gesser. Others contributing were LeRoy E. Gerding, Jr., Richard H. Hutzler, Robert W. Janssen, James L. Larduskey, Jr., Charles R. Lloyd, Kenneth E. Spencer, John S. Thomsen, Henry S. Wells, Jr., and Paul W. Wirtz.

At Greenberg Publishing Company, graphic artist Brian Falkner designed the book's cover and layout; senior artist Maureen Crum prepared the artwork for the cover; graphic artist Jackie Leister finalized the book's design, assisted by Wendy Burgio and Rick Gloth; proofreader Donna Price checked the manuscript for accuracy and coordinated final preparations; editorial assistant Richard M. Watson typed in the many additions and corrections; staff photographer Bill Wantz supplied new prints and stats; and managing editor Samuel Baum provided overall support.

Paul W. Wirtz
Executive Vice President
Baltimore Streetcar Museum
Baltimore, Maryland
May 1992

BALTIMORE CHAPTER NRHS

The Baltimore Chapter of the National Railway Historical Society was organized in 1936 and included members interested in all phases of railroading. During the streetcar era, the local Baltimore Transit Company was naturally a favorite with Chapter members. The NRHS "Special Car" sign appeared on numerous charter trips over all parts of the system; on the last night of the operations, the Chapter special

car covered the entire remaining trackage. Following this tradition, the Chapter enjoyed preinaugural trips over Baltimore's new Metro Rail Line in 1983 and 1987 and the new Central Light Rail Line in 1992.

The group meets monthly and welcomes new members. For further information, please write Baltimore Chapter, NRHS, P.O. Box 100 Lutherville, Maryland 21094-0100.

Sometime in the late 1890s, a car of BCPR's Hall Springs line heads west on Fayette Street near the present-day Fallsway. Looming in the background is the famous 1828 Shot Tower, one of Baltimore's most renowned landmarks. (Mettee Studio, BSM Collection)

THE HISTORY
(1859-1992)

THE PLAY'S THE THING
NOT THE PARKING

After the theatre, which?
The street car at the playhouse door or
The search for your car parked three blocks away.

After all the play is the thing, not the parking problem.
You can think about the acting and not your automobile when you

Ride the Cars

Taken from one of a series of UR & E newspaper advertisements published in 1926, this illustration, which ran April 19th, shows the intersection of Eutaw and Fayette Streets on a rainy night with Ford's Theatre brilliantly lit in the background. (Drawing by Willem Wirtz)

FIRST THERE WAS CITY PASSENGER

The marble shaft of the Battle Monument was bathed in the harsh yet eerie glare of smoking torchlights placed along the iron railing in front of the Court House. A man was engaged in lighting additional ones. A speaker was taking a last look at his notes, which promised to provide a red-hot oration. In Monument Square itself, a considerable crowd of Baltimoreans had gathered.

Suddenly, a clamor arose from the gloom beyond the circle of light. A band of ruffians came forward, seized a torch, and tossed it into the crowd. One by one, those remaining were uprooted and lofted into the square. The meeting broke up in pandemonium.

This was the atmosphere in Baltimore on March 25, 1859, during the discussion on the granting of a horse car franchise. These were frenzied days, to say the least, and the birth of the horse cars was not an easy one. That the city needed public transport was beyond question, for Baltimore was growing. The census of 1860 showed a population of 214,000, compared with 169,000 in 1850. The thickly populated section extended roughly to Fremont Street on the west, Mount Vernon Place on the north, Broadway on the east, and around the harbor to Federal Hill on the south. There were, of course, other built-up enclaves, such as the Pratt Street section around Mount Clare and the Hanover-Hamburg-Ostend Streets area.

To get around town the well-to-do had their own conveyances. Most others walked. It is true that there were hackney coaches which operated on a basis similar to the taxicabs of today; yet the fares charged by the hackneys were too high to make them readily available to the average person. Some idea of the rates is manifest from the fact that fifty cents was charged to carry one person to any of the railroad stations, with an additional charge of fifty cents when the coach was sent especially from the stables. (At that time, the wage of a laborer was only about one dollar a day.) A traveler's guide of the period advised its readers to make sure to settle the matter of fare before setting foot in the hackney.

The first feeble attempt at mass transportation came on May 1, 1844, when the omnibus made its debut in Baltimore. Like the hackneys, it too failed to offer a solution. The omnibus was uncomfortable and slow, but, more important, it did not offer the comprehensive service which was urgently needed.

Another answer to the problem began to be bruited about the town in the early 1850s. In New York, and elsewhere, people were riding in something called horse cars. These were not too different in appearance from the omnibuses, except that the horse cars ran on rails, making it possible for the animals to pull larger and heavier loads.

As early as March 24, 1854, a petition was presented to the City Council, asking permission to operate a horse car line along Baltimore Street from Franklin Square to Broadway, then over to Canton. A simple enough request, except at that time the Monumental City was coming under the control of gangs of thugs. The Native American, or "Know-Nothing" party, was rising to power in the city, and political considerations were to cause a delay of five long years before construction was allowed to begin. To complicate matters further, the omnibus people were politically powerful, so competition was staved off by the tactic of insisting that the horse car question was of such importance as to require a popular referendum, which, of course, never quite came about.

Promoters of the various street railway ventures had the problem of courting both the state Legislature at Annapolis (for incorporation) and the City Council in Baltimore (for an ordinance authorizing the use of streets). In theory, the state ukases carried more weight, but in practice, the City Council seemed easier to influence. In 1858, a horse car bill was introduced in the Legislature at Annapolis, where it died.

The scene of action then returned to the City Council. By March 1859, four different horse car ordinances had been introduced in that body. Of these, two (the Thomas-Latrobe and the omnibus proprietors' bills) were pretty much in limbo; only the Brooks-Barnum and Travers bills retained substantial support. The last two were quite similar, and both provided for a comprehensive railway system covering the built-up portion of the city fairly adequately — not simply one or two lines.

However, in final form these bills differed in three important respects:

1. The fare from any one part of the city to any other was fixed at four cents in the Travers ordinance and three cents in Brooks-Barnum.

2. The Travers proposal specified a $20 per car per year license fee payable to the City; Brooks-Barnum called for a flat payment of $20,000 per year for the complete system.

3. The five grantees in the Travers bill (William H. Travers, William G. Browning, William de Goey, Robert Cathcart, and Joshua G. Sumwalt) were not substantial capitalists in a class with the Brooks-Barnum group. Chauncey Brooks was a recent president of the Baltimore & Ohio Rail-

The Battle Monument in Monument Square as it appeared about 1863. The Court House, with its iron railing, is just out of the picture, behind the trees at right. (The Peale Museum)

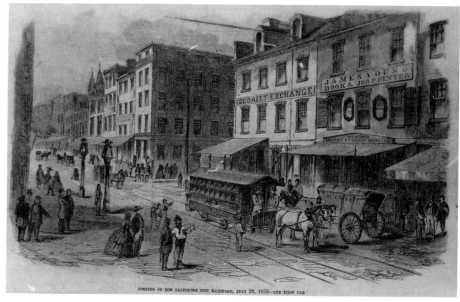

OPENING OF THE BALTIMORE CITY RAILROAD, JULY 20, 1859—THE FIRST CAR

This drawing is reputed to be based on a photograph taken on the first day of horse car operation, although there are some oddities. The car is running eastbound on the westbound track, which possibly could be explained, but it also differs greatly in appearance from some accounts of the original equipment. (BSM Collection)

road, and Zenus Barnum was the former owner of the famous Barnum's Hotel.

Thus, on the face of the two proposals, the Brooks-Barnum bill appeared to give the City the better deal. However, its opponents contended that the three-cent fare was only a ruse and was insufficient to maintain the operation successfully. On March 15th, the Travers ordinance passed the City Council and was sent to the Mayor.

The Mayor of Baltimore at that time was Thomas Swann, another former Baltimore & Ohio Railroad president. He had successfully turned to politics as a Know-Nothing candidate, playing his hand so astutely in this politically volatile period that he was subsequently elected Governor on the Union (Republican) ticket and still later went to Congress as a Democrat. (Throughout the rest of the nineteenth century, politics was closely intertwined with

street railway affairs; two other governors, Bowie and Brown, both played leading roles.)

On March 23rd, Mayor Swann surprised almost everyone by vetoing the Travers ordinance. He conceded the necessity of a four-cent fare and expressed some doubts (rather strangely, in light of his alternative proposal) that even this would be sufficient. However, he urged a revised Travers

A year or so after the Blue Line began operation in December 1862, one of its tiny, bob-tailed cars proceeds down Lexington Street, between North (Guilford Avenue) and Calvert Streets. The route was changed to run down Calvert, past Battle Monument, in 1869. (The Peale Museum)

During 1859, when this building served as the Baltimore City Hall, it was the scene of hot and heavy arguments over the granting of a horse car franchise. Today, as for many years, it houses the Peale Museum. (Michael R. Farrell)

An omnibus of the 1880s taking the Madison Athletic Club football team and rooters to a match. This was a charter vehicle belonging to the Geo. Kinnier Bus Company, 1182 McElderry Street, and is somewhat larger than those which were in competition with the horse cars. (Enoch Pratt Library, Mrs. Mabel L. Knight)

ordinance in which the street railway grant would be tied to a park plan of his own.

Swann proposed that a five-cent fare be charged from terminus to terminus, with one-fifth of the gross receipts going to the City. This tax would be applied to the acquisition and maintenance of public parks and to the completion of a 250-foot-wide boundary avenue around Baltimore. The City was to retain the right to lower the fare one cent by eliminating the park tax after the park and the avenue had been paid for. The Mayor stressed the following advantages for his proposal:

1. Five cents was the standard railway fare in other cities and was adequate for the success of the operation.

2. The City would be assured a share of the profits, which would provide means of obtaining a city park and a grand thoroughfare.

3. The fare was convenient, no special tickets being needed.

4. The City retained the option of reducing the fare.

A perusal of the newspapers of the day provides an insight into the reactions of the press. The *American* had no comment, though one observer suggested, "Let expressive silence muse its praise." (sic) This paper was soon to claim credit for suggesting the park tax. A correspondent to the *Patriot* argued that five cents was little enough to pay for a ride and that others could walk. The *Exchange* observed, "Mr. Swann has contrived to astonish everybody." It felt that experience supported a five-cent fare, but that the park tax could not help the promoters and would only reduce patronage. The *Sun* (which is the principal source for this section) had always been violently opposed to the Travers ordinance. It stated in an editorial, "We express unqualified antagonism to such a proposition. And, if it is possible that so flagrant an imposition can be carried into effect, it will prove a source of universal dissatisfaction in every respect." The paper went on to say that the tax would fall on the working man and that the park plan should stand on its own merits.

The *Clipper* was somewhat in agreement, commenting that, while the park was a desirable object, the proposed tax was questionable, being a tax on the people

rather than the grantees. "The people have a right to ask serious reconsideration." The *Republican* generally condemned Swann's veto, bringing out an interesting point. "Its (Swann's proposal) verbosity and stupidity are themes which (Swann's) old admirers seem to take a malicious pleasure in exposing. The astute idea, upon which the mayor particularly glorified himself, in suggesting the proposed increase of fare, is especially funny. The company could not get along with a fare of four cents, but if you make the fare five cents, and give the extra cent to somebody else, they will go swimmingly. The extra cent may possibly keep a good many persons from riding the cars, but that will only make them last longer, and of course benefit the company. Most admirable logic! . . . eminently worthy of the great patron of the Know-Nothings."

Needless to say, the Baltimore citizens, who were easily excited by any issue, eagerly joined in the controversy. However, despite all opposition, the Travers supporters had the votes. A new Travers bill, modified to meet the Mayor's wishes, passed the Council on March 25th, the same night on which the Monument Square

A political cartoon, of the period when Swann was serving as mayor, appropriately enough has his supporters cavorting in an omnibus. Swann's mark would be left more permanently on the horse cars. (Maryland Historical Society, Baltimore)

mass meeting was broken up. The ordinance was signed by Mayor Swann on March 28, 1859. Now, five years and four days after the bickering had begun, Baltimore had authorized the construction of a street railway system with the provocative provision that 20 percent of the *gross receipts* (not net profit) would go to the City for its park system.

One might reasonably expect that things would now go more smoothly. However, the complications were only beginning. All the suspicions of lack of capital among the five grantees were soon confirmed when the word got around town that they had sold the franchise to a Philadelphia group headed by one Jonathan Brock as little as a week after the Travers ordinance had been signed.

Now the public seethed with anger. The transfer to foreign capitalists (and northerners at that!) was denounced from the pulpit, on street corners, in barrooms, and naturally in the press. Baltimore had already acquired the sobriquet of "Mobtown" and was adding to its reputation for violence as the Know-Nothings roamed the streets. Election day disturbances were routine; the November 1859 elections were later held to be void because of fraud and violence; the city would soon become the scene of the first bloodshed in the War Between the States. Surprisingly, though, no violence occurred as a result of the franchise transfer.

Jonathan Brock, Conrad Grove, and the other Philadelphians agreed to use Baltimore labor and otherwise attempted to pacify the populace for the nonce. However, Brock and his partners were not out of the woods. Basically, the story was this: The franchise granted by the City contained certain provisions that in theory would enable the City government to supervise the railway company's operations and local investors to subscribe for stock. The rapid transfer of control to the Philadelphians and subsequent developments showed

these provisions unenforceable. Yet, the city government held a trump card. The railway company, now generally referred to as the City Passenger Railway, had never been incorporated. Only the state legislature could grant this imprimatur. The Brock group was in control, but legally it was on unsure ground.

Nevertheless the new owners proceeded promptly with plans for construction. On May 17, 1859, an agreement was reached with the omnibus operators. By the terms of the settlement, the proprietors were to retain their stages, horses, and harness and to receive $83,875 for their stable property. On the same day, a contract for the construction of the horse railway lines was awarded to William S. Shoemaker. Ground breaking took place on the lower end of Broadway on the 24th.

While it would only cause confusion to go into the precise routings, a brief outline of the system is in order at this point. The original trackage was to extend from the intersection of Broadway and Thames Street, up Broadway to Baltimore Street, then across that thoroughfare to the extreme western limits of the city, just beyond Smallwood Street. Additional trackage would be laid from Baltimore Street up Greene Street and Pennsylvania Avenue to North Avenue; up Eutaw Street and Madison Avenue, again to North Avenue; and up Gay Street to the city boundary, near Baltimore Cemetery.

There would also be a line from North Avenue, down Charles Street to Read Street, and then via Read, Calvert, Lexington, and North Streets (now Guilford Avenue) to Baltimore Street; from this point it was planned to extend through the financial district and over various streets to reach the extreme eastern city line at Canton. A South Baltimore route would run via Hanover, Montgomery, Light, and Marshall Streets to terminate at Ferry Bar on the Middle Branch of the Patapsco (just east of the present Hanover Street bridge).

Citizens' Railway horse car, westbound on Fayette Street, passes Barnum's City Hotel at Calvert. The omnibuses parked in front of the hotel probably transported guests to the railroad stations. In foreground, the single track on Fayette Street crosses City Passenger Railway tracks as they diverge to go around the Battle Monument. The photo was taken ca. 1875-80. The Equitable Building occupies the site today. (The Peale Museum)

Additional trackage was authorized, but never constructed, on Fayette and Lombard Streets.

Construction had been under way only about ten days when, on June 2nd, a crowd showed up at Broadway, between Pratt and Lombard, asking for jobs. They were offered the going rate of $1.00 a day, but demanded $1.25. When turned down, they created such a disruption that all work came to a halt. The disturbances lasted for several days before the police got the situation under control.

Ground had also been broken both on West Baltimore Street and Greene Street, but another complication arose when a group of citizens obtained an injunction preventing the company from laying a double track on the portion of Baltimore Street between Sharp and North Street (now Guilford). The merchants were behind this move, believing that the horse cars would injure their businesses. In addition, sentiment against the company arose from various vague notions, including the idea that the track would curl up under the weight of the heavily-laden cars. Even more improbable was the suggestion that the rails would attract lightning, which would bombard Broadway and Baltimore Street with electric bolts from the clouds during every thunderstorm. Rumors like these were widely circulated despite the fact that the Baltimore & Ohio Railroad tracks, for over a quarter of a century, had run right down the middle of Pratt Street.

For the first few days of the trial runs, which began on July 12th, everyone was allowed to ride free, as a good will gesture. This proved a howling success; cars ran with men and boys hanging to the sides when the interiors became full. The practice was continued on other lines as they began running, but the free passage was limited to "ladies and misses."

Regular service from Broadway and Thames Street to Baltimore and North Streets commenced on July 26, 1859. Two days later, a fare of three cents was instituted for the trip. This rate was continued until the Baltimore Street blockade was broken in late October, after which the authorized rate of five cents was charged. An indication of the relative value of money in those days is given by the following prices which were quoted in the *Sun* for Center Market during this general period: beef, 12½ to 18¢ a pound; lamb, 75¢ to $1.25 a quarter; potatoes, 25¢ a peck; strawberries, 6 to 12¢ a quart; butter, 31¢ a pound; and eggs, 15¢ a dozen.

There is evidence that none of the cars which were ordered by the railway were delivered until September 9th. According to the *Sun*, September 10, 1859, the first of thirty cars ordered was delivered on September 9th. The builders, Poole and Hunt of Woodberry, promised four cars per week thereafter until the contract was fulfilled. The cars used in the interim appear to have been secondhand boxlike affairs seating twenty-two passengers, probably brought here from the 5th and 6th Street line in Philadelphia. This seems reasonable enough as President Brock of the Baltimore system had been connected with the Philadelphia company.

Since the company planned to operate several different routes on Baltimore Street, some means for identifying the respective lines was needed. In the earliest days there were no destination signs as such, though most cars carried lettering painted permanently on the sides and front of the vehicles, stating the principal points served. The ordinary way of differentiating one line from another was by the color of the cars used on the route.

This practice was continued as new companies entered the field. Most had different colors for each route, but, of course, there were not enough shades in the spectrum for each line of every company to sport a different hue. Nevertheless, there were some vivid results, including the Frick Lines' salmon, and Baltimore Traction's shocking pink. The Baltimore City Passenger Company's routes were the ones most frequently referred to by the color of the cars; we will go along with popular usage in this regard. Thus the pioneer City Passenger line was the Red Line, which was at first routed from South Broadway to the western end of Baltimore Street.

The initial car was put on the Greene Street line on August 24, 1859. Vehicles on this route were reportedly painted blue; later this was changed to green, which seems more appropriate. The White Line (Eutaw Street to Broadway) commenced service on November 24th. It should be noted that these dates are the ones on which partial operation began; completion of the various lines often took some time. For example, the Red Line cars did not reach the end of track on Gay Street until the fall of 1862.

Friends of jerkwater lines (a term for lightly patronized branches or extensions connecting with main routes) will be interested to note that the White and Red Lines used "transfer cars" — these were smaller than the regulation horse cars — on their extremities for the first eight or nine years. Their drivers also served as conductors; thus the one-man cars of the 1920s were really nothing new.

On October 22, 1859, the railway company, in an appeal of the injunction against laying double tracks on Baltimore Street, was allowed to post a bond of $40,000 and put down the desired trackage. The work was completed on the 28th, and cars began to run through for the first time.

In the winter of 1860, Jonathan Brock went to the Maryland Legislature to ask for incorporation. This precipitated a bitter and violent struggle, in which all the arguments of the previous year were renewed with increased intensity. A lengthy legislative committee hearing produced almost 150 pages of testimony. Despite all opposition the Brock bill coasted through the Senate by a comfortable margin. However, at the crucial stage of proceedings in the House of Delegates, it lost by a single vote.

This setback still left Brock in control of the railway. A compromise which allowed some Baltimore money into the operation was now reached; control was vested in the unincorporated "Baltimore City Passenger Railway Association." A Baltimorean, Henry Tyson, was chosen as president to replace Brock, who still remained on the board as a director. On February 13, 1862, the Legislature finally incorporated the enterprise as the Baltimore City Passenger Railway Company. Soon afterwards, Brock disappeared from the scene, and control of the railway passed into local hands.

One of the conditions of incorporation specified that the projected Charles Street line must be built before the end of the year. This was done, with the line commencing operation on December 2, 1862. In 1869, it was combined with the South Baltimore route, which had started running in October 1860 and had previously been a part of the Greene Street line. It is presumed that at this time the Charles Street cars were painted blue, and the former Blue Line (Greene Street) became the Green Line.

Confusing? Yes, definitely. But, while this mention of the routes may prove difficult to digest by those not too familiar with the area, a look at the map (on page 22) will show why City Passenger enjoyed such a stranglehold on local transportation that, once it became established, it could just drift along with continuing prosperity, even in the face of growing competition, until the challenge of the "rapid transit" lines spurred its management into unwise haste in meeting that new threat.

First and foremost, it had an undisputed monopoly for trackage on Baltimore Street, the most important east-west thoroughfare. Then it had a direct route to Druid Hill Park which the opposition could not equal. Its lines out Pennsylvania Avenue, Gay Street, and later, Harford Road followed important arteries deep into what were then growing suburban areas. The ferry from Locust Point connected with its South Broadway route. Last but not least, after some minor extensions, its cars passed Camden, Calvert, President Street, and Baltimore & Potomac (Union) stations, meeting all of the railroads. It also held sole right to lay tracks on Lombard and Fayette Streets for most of their lengths. These latter franchises were never exercised, but for over a decade competition was limited by their very existence.

Rowdyism on the cars in the earliest days was commonplace, and the patrons took it in stride. A typical incident involved conductor Suter of the Red Line when he ordered a man who was smoking to either stop or go out on the platform. The patron reacted by drawing a revolver. Suter knocked him from the platform with a "billy"; then the ejected rider took a shot at him, which Suter returned. According to the report in the *Sun* of December 29, 1859, the ladies on the car were not alarmed; one called Suter a "trump." The conductors apparently took the duty of protecting passengers seriously — the conductor of car No. 12 on Baltimore Street found a soldier kissing a reluctant girl in his car and wounded him with his brake handle. (From the *Sun*, July 16, 1861.)

NOTES AND COMMENTS:

Much of the text of this and the following chapter was influenced strongly by conversations with John S. Thomsen, whose research includes an extensive compilation of items on the Baltimore City Passenger Railway appearing in the *Sun* between 1859 and 1874.

"MILLIONS FOR DEFENSE. NOT ONE CENT FOR TRIBUTE. MASS MEETING. The citizens, believing that a great outrage upon their rights is being perpetrated by the City Councils, by passing a railway bill allowing five cents to be charged, when an ordinance was before them offering to carry passengers for three cents, therefore desire all citizens in favor of the three cent fare to meet in MASS MEETING, at Monument Square at 6½ o'clock THIS EVENING." This notice, appearing in the *Sun* and other papers on March 25, 1859, brought on the boisterous affair which opens this book. Details were reported in the *Sun, March 26th.

Scharf's *History Of Baltimore City And County* gives the March 24, 1854 date for the first horse car petition.

The story of the organization and early struggles of the Baltimore City Passenger Railway has been pieced together from many sources, of which the *Sun, American,*

Gazette, and *Exchange*, all Baltimore dailies, were the most helpful.

Swann's biography appears in Coyle's *Mayors of Baltimore.* In addition to his part in starting the street railway system and acquiring Druid Hill Park, he is credited with organizing a City Fire Department and beginning the Jones Falls waterworks. The latter included Lake Roland, which was at first called Swann Lake.

A comparison of the two bills and Swann's arguments for the park tax are given in the Mayor's veto message, reported in the *Sun*, March 23, 1859. Press comments on the Park Tax proposal are quoted from a letter in the *Sun*, March 25, 1859.

As finally passed, the Travers bill was City of Baltimore, Maryland, Ordinance 44, March 28, 1859. This set several precedents for future authorizations; the provision that the gauge be "the same as that of ordinary street carriages" led to the "Baltimore gauge" of 5 feet 4½ inches.

Twenty years after the Know-Nothings were at the height of their power, Baltimore was the scene of some of the earliest violence in the railroad riots of 1877. A fair amount of damage ensued, but attempts to burn Camden and Mt. Clare Stations failed.

Those who imagine that an exact change requirement is something new will be surprised to learn of the following item, published in the *Sun* of July 10, 1862: Conductor James Shryock was arrested and charged with assaulting John Carr, who entered his car, tendered a dollar, and asked for change. The conductor stated that he had been ordered not to break dollar notes. Inflation was behind the edict. "The officers of the (railway) company contend that there is no right to compel them to give silver change for notes when the former is ten percent premium, and that as the fare is five cents, those who ride should provide themselves with the proper change or with the tickets which represent that amount."

As to the question of the color scheme of the cars on the Greene Street line, there is some evidence that the vehicles may have originally been painted aquamarine. This would account for conflicting reports in contemporary papers that they were "blue" and "green."

The testimony at the legislative committee hearing appears in *Maryland House Documents*, January session, 1860, Document Z (see also Documents R, AA, and CC). This record provides extensive information on the formation of the City Passenger Railway.

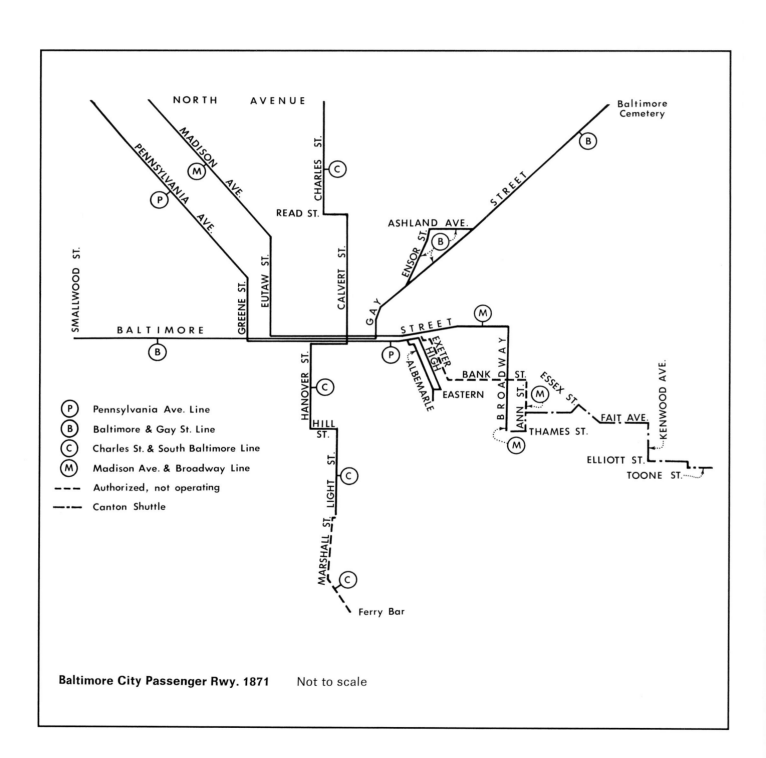

NORTH AVENUE

Baltimore Cemetery

MADISON AVE.

PENNSYLVANIA AVE.

CHARLES ST.

READ ST.

ASHLAND AVE.

STREET

ENSOR ST.

SMALLWOOD ST.

GREENE ST.

EUTAW ST.

CALVERT ST.

GAY

BALTIMORE

STREET

HANOVER ST.

EXETER

HIGH

ALBEMARLE

EASTERN

BROADWAY

BANK ST.

ANN ST.

ESSEX ST.

KENWOOD AVE.

FAIT AVE.

THAMES ST.

ELLIOTT ST.

TOONE ST.

HILL ST.

MARSHALL ST. LIGHT ST.

Ferry Bar

P Pennsylvania Ave. Line

B Baltimore & Gay St. Line

C Charles St. & South Baltimore Line

M Madison Ave. & Broadway Line

— — — Authorized, not operating

—·—·— Canton Shuttle

Baltimore City Passenger Rwy. 1871   Not to scale

ODEN BOWIE
TIGHTENS THE REINS

Despite all the talk of three- and four-cent fares which had echoed through the City Council chambers during early 1859, the street railway company soon found itself in financial troubles. The 20 percent park tax accounted for much of the fiscal difficulties, but it was the Civil War which really complicated matters. Statistics show that, as a result of wartime inflation, the average daily cost of operation per car jumped from $8.54 in 1861 to $18.00 in January of 1865. The company was not only a victim of the depreciation of currency but was also forced to pay a federal internal revenue tax of 1.5 percent of the gross receipts.

The railway's first move was to inaugurate a two-cent transfer charge. The City frowned on this step as one of dubious legality, but did not actively contest it. To further offset rising costs, the City was persuaded to suspend collection of taxes (other than the park tax) and license fees as of February 12, 1864. On March 7th of that year, the Legislature authorized a fare of six cents, with free transfers. As expenses continued to mount rapidly, the company sought further relief from both the City and the State. The Legislature acceded by permitting a four-cent charge for transfers as of March 16, 1865.

A few weeks later, on April 3rd, a seven-cent fare was inaugurated, with transfers reduced to three cents. This was done under the provisions of the recently revised internal revenue act, which raised the rate to 2.5 percent and authorized fare increases to absorb the tax. On October 10, 1871, the internal revenue tax expired and the fare dropped back to six cents, with four cents for transfers. In June of 1874, the City Council reduced the park tax to 12 percent. In exchange for this, the company had to agree to do away with the Slawson fareboxes (these patented devices had

eliminated the need for a conductor) and employ two men on each car.

During this period, the company made several attempts to add to its revenues by offering additional services. Just prior to Christmas of 1860, all-night cars were put on. The combination of a double fare charge and an extremely cold spell put a quick end to the experiment after only one week. As early as 1862, there had been agitation in some quarters to run the cars on Sundays. This had been prohibited by the enabling ordinance. Although many church members opposed Sunday running, other segments of the population clamored for service to Druid Hill Park on their one day off from work. The park had been dedicated on October 19, 1860, but not until March 22, 1867, did the Legislature pass a bill which would allow Sunday operation, contingent on a favorable popular vote. The final result was 10,915 in favor, with 9,152 opposed. On Sunday, April 28th, cars began running on some lines with no untoward events reported.

Prior to May 1870, African-Americans were not allowed to ride inside street railway cars in Baltimore. However, on May 2nd of that year, as a result of a decision by the United States Circuit Court for Maryland, some of the cars appeared on the streets bearing a placard which stated: "Colored persons are allowed to ride in this car." This was never a very satisfactory arrangement. It must be presumed that the company drew a sigh of relief when, as a result of a suit filed by John W. Fields against the Baltimore City Passenger Railway Company, the Circuit Court decided that both races must be allowed to use the same cars. On November 13, 1871, the segregation placards came off, and from that date on all patrons rode together.

The City Passenger franchise put it in a strong position against possible com-

petitors, especially in those days when it was almost unheard of for rival companies to issue transfers between one another's cars. Nevertheless there was no lack of companies willing to compete. The Citizens' Railway obtained a franchise from the City Council as early as 1868 and began service in September 1871; the following year saw inauguration of operation by a new competitor, the Baltimore, Peabody Heights, & Waverly Railway.

Despite its dominant role, City Passenger quickly felt the effect of competition. This was compounded by two other blows, which fell almost simultaneously. The so-called "epizootic" (an epidemic of a type of influenza) swept through horses all over the east in October and November of 1872, with aftereffects lingering until the following summer, causing an estimated loss of $60,000 to the railway. Furthermore, travel generally fell off as a result of the financial panic of 1873. City Passenger, which at best had enjoyed only modest financial success under President Henry Tyson, suddenly found itself operating in the red and under fire from its stockholders. On August 13, 1873, Tyson resigned to become a vice-president of the Erie Railroad. In summing up his administration, he pointed out that the value of the property had increased from $659,624 at the time of incorporation to $1,038,456 in 1873.

On October 14, 1873, ex-Governor Oden Bowie was elected a director and then unanimously chosen as president. Bowie, who was also president of the Baltimore & Potomac Railroad and was destined to head City Passenger for almost a quarter of a century, got off to a rough start. A group of dissident stockholders put up their own slate of directors at the annual meeting held on January 14, 1874 and took over the board by electing four of the seven directors.

The hill boy, with his bucket filled with water or sand, was a familiar sight until the coming of the electric and cable cars. This vehicle ran on BCP Railway's Yellow Line. The sign hung on the side of car reads: "Direct to Druid Hill Park." (Baltimore Sunpapers)

In a closely contested election held the following day, Enoch Pratt was named president over Bowie on the sixth ballot. Bowie's connection with the Tyson administration was a millstone around his neck. The *Sun* summed up the matter in an editorial on January 15th. "(Bowie) labored under the misfortune of having been brought into the service of the company by an administration which had tolerated the abuses and extravagances which had grown up and were so long continued under Mr. Tyson."

Before agreeing to serve as president, Pratt asked for a week in which to investigate the financial affairs of the company. Enoch Pratt was to become a noted philanthropist (much of the research for this book was done at the library which he endowed), but he was first of all a hard-headed businessman. Seven days after his election, he reported to the board that the company's troubles lay in the fare structure and park tax, rather than Bowie management. Under the circumstances, he stated that the presidency would take too much of his time from his other business ventures and threw his support to Bowie. The latter was reelected, but with a salary cut from $5,000 to $4,000 per year. Within a week, other economies were implemented, including a reduction in the force of clerks and salary slashes for those retained.

Bowie went on to become well recognized as an able, but quite conservative, figure in the street railway industry. Under his leadership, the company was paying dividends of 10 and 12 percent, and the stock, which had sold for as low as $11 when he took over, was worth seven times as much by the early 1890s. His stewardship coincided with the years of serious competition. Starting with the early companies which operated what were essentially extensions of City Passenger routes, competitors had by 1874 begun to encroach on its downtown preserves.

NOTES AND COMMENTS:

The average daily cost of running the cars was reported in the *American Railroad Journal*, February 18, 1865.

The *Daily Gazette* of December 12, 1862 noted that, beginning on December 15th, the two-cent transfer charge would be instituted. The reason — "in consequence of the higher price of horse feed at present, and the greater expense tending the working of the road." A report of a joint special committee of the City Council stated that in the opinion of the City Counselor the company had no legal right to make such a charge. The committee, however, advised no immediate action and felt it would be "impolite" to interfere. *Sun,* January 10, 1863.

Scharf's *History Of Baltimore City And County* is the authority for the 1860 all-night operation. This service was not revived until February 9, 1899.

References for the desegregation of the horse cars — *Sun*, May 2 and 10, 1870; November 14, 1871.

This Stephenson car used on BCP Railway's Red Line had odd-looking enclosures for conductors. Its date of construction is conjectural, but is probably not later than mid-1870s. (Museum of the City of New York)

The effects of competition, the "epizootic," and the business panic are detailed in the *Sun*, August 14 and November 13, 1873.

An appraisal of his company's condition by Oden Bowie shortly after his reelection appeared in the *Sun*, February 4, 1874. "The company now owes $100,000 in park tax; many of the cars are dilapidated; the tracks need relaying; and new cars are absolutely necessary."

Perhaps the rarest of all the old photographs
contributed to this book is the only known view of
the "dummy line" in operation in Druid Hill Park.
David Burnette, a North Carolina collector, discovered it among some stereopticon slides. The
view looks west from the hill at the edge of the
present zoo and undoubtedly was taken in the
line's early days. (David Burnette Collection)

The *F. C. Latrobe* No. 1 was built for the
Citizens' Railway by the Baldwin Locomotive Works of Philadelphia. A true "steam
dummy," it was first tested during the fall of
1876. (BSM Collection)

DRUID HILL WAS THE MAGNET

The Park Tax! The Park Tax! Mayor Swann's stubborn insistence on a contribution of 20 percent of the gross receipts collected by City Passenger, to be used for the establishment and maintenance of a park system, was to echo down through the years. Decade after decade, the original company, and all that followed, wailed over the city's hand in their collective fare boxes. Bit by bit, they managed to whittle the levy down to 9 percent by the mid-1880s. They refused to pay it on fares collected outside the city limits, and the courts upheld them. A few fortunate companies, which operated on turnpikes, successfully claimed exemption on this ground.

For all of the gnashing of teeth, many of the companies received quite a boost in their revenues by hauling passengers to the city's park. They were quick to establish a northern terminus on the fringe of the park, and the horse cars early sported large signs reading "to Druid Hill."

The park had barely begun to take shape, when a hue and cry went up for transportation directly to the center of this new playground, which was entirely surrounded by Baltimore County in the year 1859. Strange as it may seem to those unfamiliar with Maryland political subdivisions, the only thing that Baltimore City and Baltimore County then had or still have in common is the sharing of the same name. In all other respects, they are separate and distinct entities. This is important to our story because, until it was incorporated in 1862, City Passenger was operating only by virtue of a franchise granted by the City of Baltimore. Thus, its Madison Avenue line terminated at the county line, North Avenue (often referred to as Boundary Avenue), a good half mile short of the park itself.

The situation was not too inconvenient in fine weather. However, when a sudden thunderstorm blew up, it was another matter entirely. Thus, there came into being a line which, though it operated almost twen-

A plaque affixed to the Madison Avenue gate of Druid Hill Park lists many names prominent in early street railway history. Mayor Swann, Chauncey Brooks, John H. B. Latrobe, and Enoch Pratt are included; but such names as Henry Tyson and Jonathan Brock are among the missing. (Michael R. Farrell)

ty years, is virtually unknown today. Only about a mile in length, it was far more interesting in its operation and equipment than many much longer routes.

The City Park Railway was incorporated as a private venture in 1862 to connect City Passenger's line with the park. However, the company procrastinated in starting construction, perhaps discouraged by the seasonal nature of the operation. Hence, in 1863, the City authorized the Park Commission to construct the line on its own. Due to a lack of funds, this was built from North and Madison Avenues (the connec-

tion with City Passenger) only as far as the edge of the park. City Passenger agreed to operate the line for one year.

Complications arose when a "joker" was spotted in the enabling ordinance, prohibiting the collection of any fares until the road should be constructed almost to the pavilion inside the park. (This meant extending the line to terminate across the road from the present entrance to the zoo.) Though the Commissioners agreed to the extension (which doubled the mileage), City Passenger balked at running the longer line on the original financial terms. A modified agree-

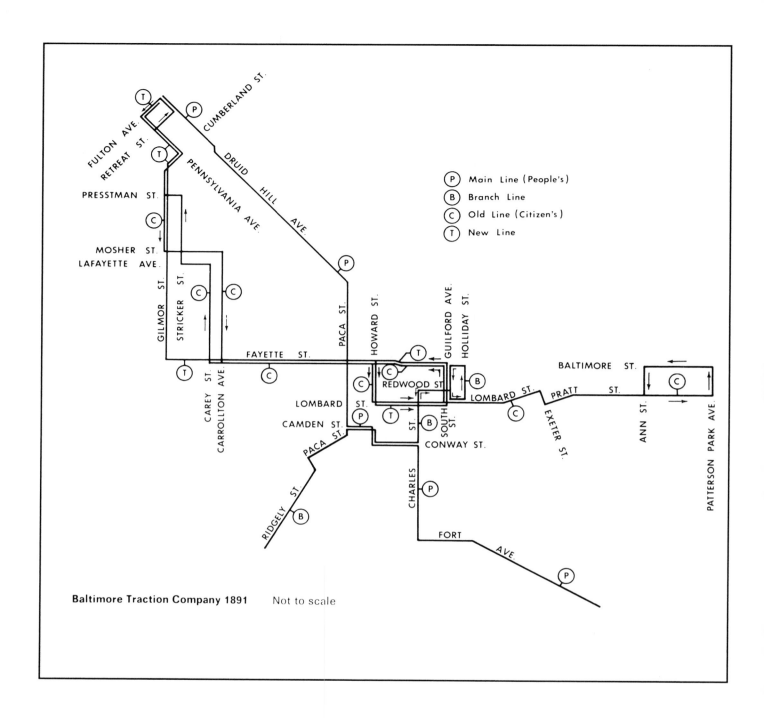

Baltimore Traction Company 1891   Not to scale

Legend:
- (P) Main Line (People's)
- (B) Branch Line
- (C) Old Line (Citizen's)
- (T) New Line

ment was worked out, with operations beginning on May 14, 1864; but the following spring BCPR declined to renew the contract.

Now the Park Commissioners were "stuck" with the orphan. Losing money on horse cars, they soon turned to steam operation. An 0-4-0 tank locomotive (i.e., a combined locomotive and tender with only four wheels — all drivers) was ordered from Grice and Long, of Philadelphia, and put in operating order by the local firm of Hayward, Bartlett and Company. A second

engine arrived in March of 1866. A third engine was acquired in 1869, by which time the first two had "worn out in service." In those days a locomotive used in street railway or similar type of operation was frequently provided with a body resembling a passenger car to avoid frightening horses; hence it was termed a "dummy." While it is not clear whether all of these locomotives were "dummy" types, it is certain that the line was almost universally described as the "dummy line."

Business boomed for a while, but frequent protests were heard against running a railway in the park. After a few years, as profits began to fall off rapidly, the opposition grew, especially against steam operations. In 1873, Citizens' Railway (one of the original companies to compete with City Passenger) was allowed to run its horse cars over the line. The Park Commission Report for 1873 mentions "an arrangement with Citizens' Passenger Railway to work the road,

Enclosed locomotive with passenger compartment rests at Council Grove Station. Note smokestack, "modern" clerestory roof, and ornate trim on building. Such locomotives were made to resemble passenger coaches so as not to frighten horses. (BSM Collection)

giving them the fares earned, and requiring them to make all necessary repairs to tracks."

Records get a bit vague at this point, but it is certain that the tracks within the park were taken up and the iron sold in 1879. From the 1879 report, "The extension of the tracks of the City Passenger Railway from North Avenue to the Madison Avenue entrance to the park coincides with the removal and sale of the iron of the Park Railway." An official explanation, in the reports of the Park Commissioners, was to

have a familiar ring down through the years. "While the latter (City Park Railway) certainly afforded a very great convenience to the public generally, and no doubt increased the number of visitors to the park, it interfered with, more or less, the freest access of carriages."

Some years later, in 1887, Citizens' apparently was allowed to replace the trackage. According to the American, February 20, 1890, Citizens' was permitted by a city ordinance, passed May 4, 1887, to relay the

track in the park from the Chinese station to Council Grove. The company had previously been allowed to extend its line up Druid Hill Avenue to the Chinese station. But this time the line was not a financial success. In 1890, the rails were again out of service, as a part of an agreement whereby cable cars were allowed to loop on park land at the Druid Hill Avenue gate. They were taken up for good in 1895.

Earlier, on January 11, 1882, City Park Railway had officially ceased to exist, City

Although it has lost some of its exotic decor over the years, the Chinese station at Druid Hill and Fulton Avenues at Druid Hill Park stands today in a setting not too unlike that which existed when it was a stop on the "dummy line" more than a century ago. (Michael R. Farrell)

Like the Chinese station, Rotunda, or Orem's, this station dates back to the days of the "dummy line." However, it was moved many years ago to a knoll overlooking Druid Lake. (Michael R. Farrell)

The "dummy line's" Druid Hill Park terminal was the ornate Council Grove pavilion opposite the present zoo entrance. Following years of neglect, the structure was restored to its original appearance in the early 1970s. (Herbert H. Harwood, Jr.)

Central Railway's first cars were bob-tails built by Stephenson in 1881. Wheels were by Baltimore Car Wheel Company. During its first decade, the company did not reach Druid Hill, so it advertised the public squares along the route. (Museum of the City of New York)

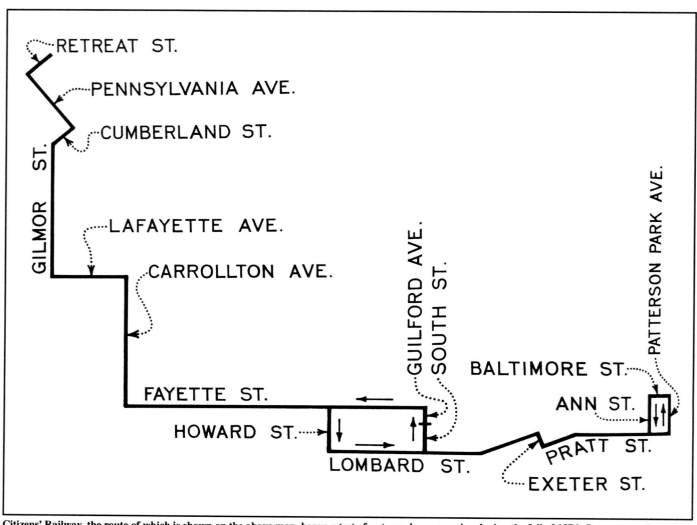

RETREAT ST.

PENNSYLVANIA AVE.

CUMBERLAND ST.

GILMOR ST.

LAFAYETTE AVE.

CARROLLTON AVE.

GUILFORD AVE.
SOUTH ST.

PATTERSON PARK AVE.

BALTIMORE ST.

ANN ST.

FAYETTE ST.

HOWARD ST.

LOMBARD ST.

PRATT ST.

EXETER ST.

Citizens' Railway, the route of which is shown on the above map, began a test of a steam dummy engine during the fall of 1876. It appears to have been the only such operation in Baltimore on a regular street railway line. The experiment probably ended in early 1877.

Passenger having acquired most of its rights; under them the Madison Avenue line was extended to the park entrance. This was a coup for the pioneer company, giving it direct access via the most fashionable and popular route to the park.

Citizens' Railway, which was able to secure authorization to run over the tracks of the "dummy line" in Druid Hill Park, was the chief, albeit distant, rival of City Passenger during the first thirty years of street railway operations in Baltimore. Citizens' tracks ran by a somewhat round-about route from Druid Hill to Patterson Park. Chartered July 9, 1868, it began operations September 18, 1871. This company managed to break City Passenger's stranglehold in the downtown section by running cars on Lombard and Fayette Streets. (City Passenger had held the franchise but never built on these streets.) The

Citizens' line passed close enough to serve the Pratt Street wharves and the Philadelphia, Wilmington & Baltimore Railroad's President Street Station.

Perhaps Citizens' chief claim to fame is that it was the first local company to make an actual trial of a form of locomotion more rapid than horsepower. Its gimmick was a steam engine which was given a sixty-day test beginning in late September 1876. The "dummy line" had used steam power for reasons of economy, but Citizens' operation differed in that the latter company planned to use steam locomotives in order to better running time. Horse cars made the run from Patterson to Druid Hill Park in seventy minutes; this figure was expected to be reduced to fifty-three. Other advantages claimed were the ability to stop on the steepest grade, a smoother start than the horse cars, and quicker stopping due to

a steam brake. There would be no saving in manpower; two men would be required on the engine and attached car, and the same number of hands as employed in the stables would be needed to keep them in good order. Yet, it was believed that the (steam) motor could be operated for less than $16 a day, the estimated cost of running a car with horses.

The little engine, christened *F. C. Latrobe* after the incumbent Mayor, was built by Baldwin at a cost of $3,000. It had 8-inch cylinders, developed 10 to 12 horsepower, and weighed 7,000 pounds. It was said to consume its own smoke, but the only guarantee was that it would be "noiseless" and capable of pulling a fully loaded car up the steepest grades on the line.

Although the full sixty days of testing were carried out, the obituary of the project actually appeared in the *Sun* of October 4, 1876, about a week after the experiment began. "One drawback to the steam motor now in use on the Citizens', is that it is obliged generally with a heavy load, to stop at heavy grades to accumulate steam for the ascent. The motor has a tendency to scare some horses of a scary nature, while others pass it without notice."

A fourth company to be attracted by the magnetic influence of Druid Hill was the one which went so far as to adopt the name Park Railway Company. Strangely enough, it was one company which never reached the park. Soon after being granted a franchise in 1872, its rights were bought by the Baltimore, Peabody Heights & Waverly. Thus it became a part of the so-called Frick lines, forming the city portion of their Waverly line. The right to run up Park Avenue to Druid Hill Park was never exercised.

People's Passenger Railway was incorporated June 28, 1878. Its line went from Druid Hill and North Avenues down through south Baltimore and on to Fort McHenry, with a branch authorized to the Patapsco River at Ferry Bar. By 1889, the reorganized company had dropped the word "Passenger" from its title and acquired stables at Druid Hill and Retreat, as well as near Fort McHenry. Its cars traveled through the business district to City Hall,

and a branch extended southwest to Ridgely Street. In spite of all this expansion, its president was quoted in the *Amercian* of February 6, 1889, as opposing the elimination of bob-tail (one-man) cars. He insisted that the line had not paid one dollar profit in its entire existence.

An interesting memento of this company is preserved at the Enoch Pratt Library in Baltimore. This is a free pass made out to Edward Statler, Jr., a member of the City Council. Accompanying it is a brief note stating that the pass was being returned to the company as Statler wished to accept no favors. The note carries a penciled inscription — "the 9th wonder of the age."

The lure of the park was to attract still one more horse car company. A rather late starter (1881), the Central Railway ran from the Western Maryland Railroad's Fulton Station at Laurens Street, straight across northern Baltimore before taking a right-hand turn at Caroline to end up at the Broadway ferry. Fulton Depot had been established by the steam railroad in 1873 and in its earliest days was responsible for the local version of "the trolley that meets all trains." Handicapped by the high tariff asked for running its passenger trains through the Baltimore & Potomac tunnel to Union Station, the Western Maryland then terminated its passenger service at Fulton.

By an arrangement with the City Passenger Railway, the steam road's patrons were carried to and from the city center by horse cars scheduled to meet incoming and outgoing trains. Soon, the Citizens' cars had taken over this connection. By the time that the Central Railway arrived on the scene, the Western Maryland was running through to Union Station, but there was still some business to be had in carrying passengers from Fulton Depot to north and east Baltimore without encountering the congestion of the business district. This helpful situation enabled the company to limp along, but as the years went by and Fulton Depot became only a way station, the Central strengthened the western end of its route by extending its tracks up Fulton Avenue to Druid Hill Park.

Thus, by the beginning of the Gay Nineties, the dashing Victorian suitor could, if he did not possess his own horse-drawn equipage or a bicycle for two, escort his slim-waisted, long-skirted lady love to the park by no less than four horse car lines. Citizens', People's, and Central all arrived at the Fulton Avenue entrance; City Passenger had its exclusive route up to the more fashionable Madison Avenue gate, its cars laying over in the shadow of that magnificent arch.

NOTES AND COMMENTS:

The principal sources for the history of the City Park Railway are the *Annual Reports Of The Park Commision, 1862-94* and the *Baltimore City Code, 1869.*

The *Sun* of September 30, 1876 gives extensive detail about the Citizens' steam engine. The sixty-day figure for the test of the steam motor was specified in the ordinance which authorized the experiment. However, an account of City Council proceedings (*Sun,* February 21, 1877) indicated that it was still in use during the winter. On March 8, 1877, the *Sun* reported: "The steam motor will appear no

more on the streets. Council having prohibited its use the animal has been withdrawn."

Scharf's *History Of Baltimore City And County* gives the fullest description available of the Park Railway Company. Mention of this company is also found in the *Maryland Journal* (Towson), November 24, 1872, and the *Toronto World,* July 17, 1890.

The routes authorized to People's Passenger Railway are listed in City of Baltimore, Maryland, Ordinance 74, June 28, 1878. First cars ran August 9, 1879. *Baltimore Sun Almanac,* 1880.

The Central Railway was chartered May 6, 1881, according to financial statements which appeared in the *Electric Railway Journal.* The *Sun,* September 21, 1892, reported that the road "opened for business as a horse car line, February 6, 1883."

Some details on service to and from the Western Maryland's Fulton Station can be found in the *Sun,* February 24, 1871, and Williams' *The Western Maryland Railway Story.* The latter claims that the steam railroad owned the street railway tracks from Fulton Station to Pennsylvania Avenue.

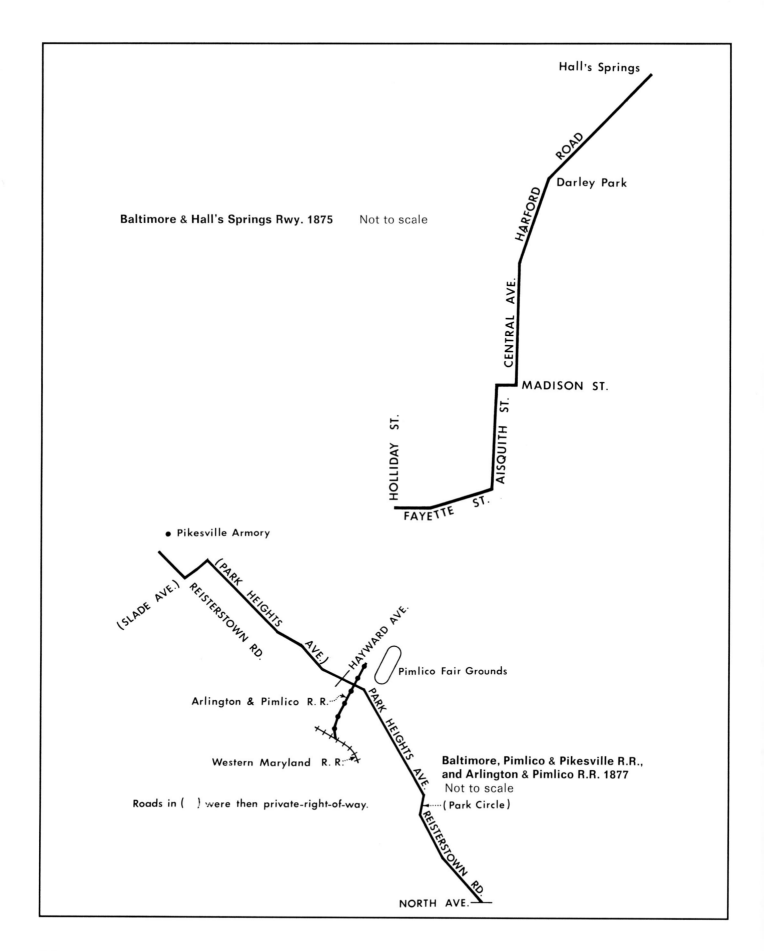

Hall's Springs

HARFORD ROAD

Darley Park

CENTRAL AVE.

Baltimore & Hall's Springs Rwy. 1875   Not to scale

HOLLIDAY ST.

AISQUITH ST.

MADISON ST.

FAYETTE ST.

● Pikesville Armory

(SLADE AVE.)

REISTERSTOWN RD.

(PARK HEIGHTS AVE.)

HAYWARD AVE.

Pimlico Fair Grounds

Arlington & Pimlico R.R.

PARK HEIGHTS AVE.

Western Maryland R.R.

**Baltimore, Pimlico & Pikesville R.R.,
and Arlington & Pimlico R.R. 1877**
Not to scale

Roads in ( ) were then private-right-of-way.

(Park Circle)

REISTERSTOWN RD.

NORTH AVE.

AN IRON WEB

Not everyone, of course, could be served by lines intent on offering a day's outing in the park to the masses from the crowded city. Someone was needed to lay the sinews of metal which would bind to the center of the city the many villages lying athwart the busy roads out of town. The York, Harford, Frederick, Reisterstown, and other bustling turnpikes rapidly began to see the railcars replace stagecoach lines. Even bucolic byways like Windsor Mill Road were early routes for the new type of conveyance. By the end of the 1870s, Pikesville, Towson, Catonsville, Franklintown, and Pimlico were connected to Baltimore by the early strands of an iron web which was to enmesh the entire metropolitan area.

On March 9, 1858, even before City Passenger had been granted its franchise, the Baltimore & Yorktown Turnpike Railway had been incorporated. It has been charged with setting back all local street railways due to its insistence on authority to operate by steam power. In Towson the *Baltimore County Advocate* urged that the company should be made to follow a route through the open country between Hillen and York Roads, away from any traffic potential.

Reincorporation resolved matters in 1862. Work was commenced on the Baltimore & Yorktown Turnpike Railway March 23, 1863, with the cars reaching Govanstown, July 16th. On August 20, 1863, cars began running between the City Hall in Baltimore and Towsontown. Its route had many notable hills, the whole containing hardly any level stretches. Yet this company was unusual in Baltimore in that it operated double-deck horse cars. These were manufactured by Poole & Hunt and used circa 1863-84. In places, as between Monument and Preston Streets, an extra "hill horse" was necessary in addition to the usual pair. Nevertheless the cars are said to have carried upwards of one hundred persons on such occasions as gala theater parties.

Although the line was to become well known as the northern portion of the highly important Towson-Catonsville line of later years, time has obscured some facets of its earliest days. For example, some cars appear to have been routed across North Avenue, then down Charles Street over the tracks of the Blue Line to Baltimore Street. Rates were regulated, but the company attempted to gain a somewhat greater return than the tariff allowed by adding a cent or two to the fare, then giving a rebate coupon for the excess, redeemable only at the company's Baltimore office. The railway figured correctly that a certain percentage of these coupons would never be presented for redemption.

The other end of the Towson-Catonsville line was incorporated in 1860 as the Baltimore, Catonsville & Ellicott's Mills Passenger Railway. Its cars ran from the City Passenger's Red Line, on Baltimore Street near Gilmor, to Stoddard's Hotel west of Catonsville, beginning August 5, 1862. Although there was a connecting stage line to Ellicott City in the earliest days, rails of the BC & EM never reached far beyond Catonsville on Frederick Road. This turnpike, one of the main paths to the west in an earlier day, descended to the flour mills on the banks of the Patapsco by a particularly steep hill, impractical for horse cars. In 1900, cars finally reached the town settled by the Ellicotts, but by another route from Edmondson Avenue to the north.

The eastern terminus of the line was gradually moved toward the center of the city; by July 1883, the cars were running through to Fayette and Liberty Streets. The short gap between this point and City Hall was later closed under the aegis of the Baltimore Union Passenger Railway, and the Catonsville and Towson lines became a single entity.

In 1863, during the midst of the War Between the States, there was incorporated a company which was to become the most written-about line ever to run in this area. The Baltimore & Hampden, considered by many to be the first successful electric railway operation in the country, remained only a paper company for a number of years. Finally constructed in the early 1870s, it was strictly a marginal operation, ill-known even locally, until 1885. In that year, Leo Daft came to town with his electric motor cars, *Morse* and *Faraday*. The operation by electricity was brief, a little more than four years, but the importance of what took place demands a section of its own a little later in the story.

During 1870, two meager operations were chartered. The Baltimore & Hall's Springs and the Baltimore, Calverton & Powhatan railways were much alike at their inceptions, yet their operations present a strong contrast. The former, connecting a minor summer resort with the city, extended from Hall's Springs (adjacent to Herring Run) down Harford Road through the village of Homestead, and on into town. It opened in late 1872. A "transfer car" ran from the outer end of the line to Darley Park (just above Broadway); this was a "shooting park" much favored by the German populace of the city. From the park to town, the single track line unsuccessfully struggled to meet expenses, finally suspending operations when a fire destroyed the car barn and equipment in 1884. Soon afterwards, the company was purchased by City Passenger. As the open country was built up, this line gradually became one of the pioneer company's busiest routes.

So much for success. The Baltimore, Calverton & Powhatan presented the other side of the token. The area west of Walbrook served by the sad little line was always pretty well devoid of potential passengers. Starting from the end of the Red Line, the BC & P ran out Calverton Road

A Baltimore, Catonsville & Ellicott's Mills Passenger Railway car about 1883, in front of ornate gateway which once graced Loudon Park Cemetery on the Frederick Road. Legends on the car show that the line had come under control of the Union Passenger Railway, and was running to downtown Baltimore. This was one of the "large" Catonsville Railway cars which were borrowed for the Daft experiment in Hampden. (Catonsville Room Collection, Catonsville Area branch, Baltimore County Public Library)

In the early twentieth century, Loudon Park Cemetery operated its own private trolley line within the cemetery, using two former City Passenger Railway cars. (The Kenneth Morse Collection, BSM)

Traffic jams on Reisterstown Road were far in the future, when a Patapsco Baking Powder wagon crossed the turnpike as Pimlico & Pikesville Railway horse car waited for riders. The date is about 1885, give or take a few years. The camera looks northwest on Reisterstown Road at Walker Avenue. (Baltimore Sunpapers)

through what later became Walbrook and followed Windsor Mill Road, when not cutting across open country, to the mill town of Powhatan. (The site of Powhatan is today covered by Woodlawn Cemetery). As far as can be ascertained, the Baltimore, Calverton & Powhatan began operation about January 1, 1871. Opposition to the road's Edmondson Avenue extension appeared in the *Sun*, November 19, 1877. (These tracks eventually were laid down by the North Baltimore Passenger Railway.) As early as 1887, the hourly service during "rush hours" led its patrons to ask that another company take over the franchise.

West of Gwynn's Falls there was just no real reason for a passenger railway to exist, but somehow or other the little cars kept running. When, in 1894, Baltimore Traction took over this company, it electrified the portion from the city to Walbrook and

abandoned the rest; even then the line managed to survive in part. The section from Powhatan (Woodlawn) to Lorraine Cemetery was kept intact, running until the first years of the twentieth century, and earning for the Baltimore & Powhatan the dubious distinction of harboring the last horse car line in the metropolitan area.

The Baltimore, Pimlico & Pikesville is another of those companies that was organized to serve a purpose more imagined than needed; later, after being taken over by a larger company, the line gradually developed an intensive traffic as the area which it served became a bedroom for the workers of the emerging metropolis. It was first chartered in 1866, but failure of attempts to acquire the City Park Railway in Druid Hill Park put off any construction until 1871. By 1873, cars were running "at irregular intervals" on what became Park Heights Avenue, between Rogers Avenue

and the present Park Circle. This line was long plagued by the bottleneck of a single track along that portion of its route adjoining Druid Hill Park. Some idea of the unsophisticated way of running a suburban line in those unhurried days is evident in the following item from the Baltimore *Sun*. "Mr. Chenowith, the overseer of the farm, also had the duty of going to Pikesville at 5 a.m. to see that the (horse car) service got started."

So it was in the beginning. In later days, other roads were to be established, which would spin more threads of the web of iron that was to girdle Baltimore and its environs. But, they belong to another era — a time of cables, electricity, consolidations, and franchise disputes — all of the things which were to make these railways, that ran along the streets, the fascinating business which spawned financial giants and put transit moguls among the titans of the nineties.

The first cars of the Yorktown Turnpike Railway were double-deckers built by Poole and Hunt. Photo dates from about 1884, shortly before scrapping. A safety feature was two hand brakes on each platform. At least one car was used for "Jim Crow" service, with the top closed in for use by "colored persons." (Louis C. Mueller Collection)

A mystery vehicle — built by Stephenson about 1891, just after Union Passenger had taken over the York Road line with a promise of "rapid transit." Yet the car was bob-tailed and carried no conductor — note coin chute at window level. It had been used for several years as a horse car, then electrified. (George F. Nixon Collection)

Thus far we have traced the early history from its beginning in 1859 to the financial panic of 1873. During this crisis men might dream that transit could soon become big business, but no one could be sure. The golden era of the streetcars, around the turn of the century, would still have to be prefaced by times during which William House (who rose to become president of United Railways) was working at the most

menial of jobs for the People's Railway. And not taking a day off in years, including Sundays! Times when it was normal for a horse car driver to work a 16- to 18-hour day. Times when one-man operation was really new; the driver of the bob-tail vehicle managed the horses, collected the fares, made change, and opened and shut the rear door. Times when the jingling bells were removed from the harness when passing

down a street where someone was seriously ill.

It was not much fun. It was hard work. Those early men had to take the headlight into the car, in order to relight it when it went out on windy, wintry nights; they had to hitch an extra team to the cars when the snow piled up; they had no shelter at most layover points; but they were pioneers, and blazing the way is never easy.

Former Baltimore City Passenger horse car No. 129 leaves what appears to be Darley Park car house. This car, later a showpiece for United Railways, had been extensively rebuilt in the late 1880s, but is reputed to date back to a much earlier period. The condition of Harford Road and the abundance of electric wires suggest that the shot was probably taken about 1910. (Mass Transit Administration)

NOTES AND COMMENTS:

References for the Baltimore & Yorktowne Turnpike Railway are in the *Towson Advocate*, March 28, July 18, and August 22, 1863.

The *Sun,* August 6, 1945, ran an article on the double-deck cars, quoting from an interview it had published in 1912 with John T. Mackenzie who had been a conductor on the cars. Although the *Towson Advo-cate*, July 25, 1863, described the open upper deck as "affording space for baggage, and an opportunity for passengers to smoke without annoyance to those inside," at least one vehicle later had the top portion enclosed for use as a "Jim Crow" car. *Sun,* November 20, 1872.

The little-known routing across North Avenue is confirmed by schedules listed in the *Daily Gazette*, November 2, 1863, and the *Towson Advocate*, November 6, 1863.

The *Maryland Journal* (Towson), April 27, 1872, brought out in detail the "indignation" which patrons manifested over the use of the rebate coupons. The practice was discontinued, effective July 12, 1883. *Sun,* July 13, 1883.

On a snowy day around 1890, a bob-tail Stephenson car, built about a dozen years earlier, sits alongside of Frick lines (North Baltimore Passenger Railway) stables on McMechen Street, just below North Avenue. (Louis C. Mueller Collection)

The *Towson Advocate*, August 9, 1862, reported the commencement of service to Catonsville, noting that "Omnibuses for Ellicott's Mills will connect with the Catonsville terminus." *Sun*, July 9, 1883. "The cars of the Catonsville Railway are now running hourly from the corner of Fayette and Liberty through to Catonsville." This extension of service, over Union Passenger trackage east of Smallwood Street, made part of the original line into a jerkwater operation. "A transfer car leaves Baltimore and Mount streets every half-hour connecting with through cars (at Smallwood and Frederick road)." *Maryland Journal* (Towson), August 11, 1883.

The Baltimore & Hall's Springs Railway reached Darley Park about November 2,

1872 and Hall's Springs the following December 14th. *Maryland Journal* (Towson) of the dates cited.

After the car barn fire at Darley Park, Baltimore City Passenger Railway, Baltimore Union Passenger Railway, and a Washington street railway company were reported interested in acquiring the route. The D.C. company was said to be "looking toward making it a cable road." This is the earliest mention found of a potential cable system in Baltimore. *Maryland Journal* (Towson), January 31, 1885.

Baltimore Traction acquired most of the BC & P in the fall of 1894, then abandoned the Walbrook-Powhatan portion on October 31st. One segment of the discontinued

trackage apparently was kept in use by the owners of Lorraine Cemetery, and the Gwynns Falls Railway later restored the tracks on Windsor Mill Road between Walbrook Junction and the bridge over the falls. *Sun*, May 14, 1896.

Baltimore, Pimlico & Pikesville references in the *Sun*, September 22, 1866 and April 15, 1867; *Maryland Journal* (Towson), September 6, 1873.

The quote concerning Mr. Chenowith is taken from a letter to the editor of the *Sunday Sun Magazine*, published June 7, 1959. It was from J. Roland Walker, who also identifies his grandfather, P. H. Walker, as the "owner" of the horse car line.

THE LINES CALLED FRICK

In this story of the combining and consolidating of railway companies, the frequent changing of the names of corporate entities can tend to become a bit confusing. Fortunately, it was the usual practice for a company to hold the same name during the years of its independent existence.

One definite exception was the Frick lines. During the twenty-year existence of this outfit, it was known officially as the Park Railway Company, the Baltimore, Peabody Heights & Waverly Passenger Railway, and the North Baltimore Passenger Railway Company. The public got around all of this corporate foolishness by referring to the company as the Frick lines, from an early president. (George Frick was a Baltimore dry goods merchant and served as president of the Baltimore, Peabody Heights & Waverly and other early lines from 1872 to about 1885.) This was unusual. Only occasionally was City Passenger mentioned in print as the Bowie lines, and even rarer was the mention of the Union Passenger as the Perin line. No one ever called People's the Hambleton line, nor Citizens' the Hagerty line, although it would have been justifiable enough as these men certainly were in complete control of the operations.

The Frick lines came into being in 1872, with the passing of an ordinance by the City Council of Baltimore authorizing the Park Railway Company to lay down railway tracks from North Avenue and McMechen, westwardly on McMechen to Bolton, then on Bolton, Dolphin, Park, Howard, Franklin, back on Park again to Saratoga, Charles, and Redwood to South Street. The routing, though roundabout, was a good one, beginning in growing residential sections on the north, passing through the heart of the business district, and ending in the center of the financial area.

But this company never spiked a rail. At almost the same time that it was authorized, the Legislature incorporated the Baltimore, Peabody Heights & Waverly Passenger Railroad. No streets were claimed for the latter company; but the legislation permitted it to construct passenger railways in the city of Baltimore, on all such streets and subject to such conditions as might be designated by the Mayor and City Council.

Upon the passage of this act, the Park Railway Company assigned its rights to the Baltimore, Peabody Heights & Waverly, and the two organizations were consolidated under the latter name. The new company drew its officers from both of the original companies, and operations commenced on the 21st of November 1872.

Another company entered the picture when, on June 7, 1872, the Park Railway was allowed to lay tracks on North Avenue, from John Street eastward to Charles Street, so as to connect with the Peabody Heights & Waverly Railroad of Baltimore County. This county company's cars ran north and east to the present 31st Street and Greenmount Avenue in the village of Waverly. Presumably, through cars were run from 1872 on, though according to Scharf (who is sometimes inaccurate), a consolidation did not take place until December 2, 1876. In any event, the companies always worked in close concert.

The Frick lines were never flamboyant in the manner of Baltimore Traction or as great a financial success as City Passenger. Yet they seem to have held the confidence of the general public and were one of the few early companies to pay any dividends at all. At the time that Edmondson Avenue was being improved from the west side of the Baltimore & Potomac Railroad tracks to Calverton Road, the Baltimore, Calverton & Powhatan held the franchise to run horse cars on that section. Potential passengers wailed at the poor service provided by the Powhatan and asked that the Frick lines be given the route. The Calverton & Powhatan was cut back, with Frick's Edmondson Avenue line (which he had ac-

quired by then) picking up service from Fulton Avenue out to Walbrook, then being developed under the name of Highland Park.

Unlike City Passenger, the Frick lines did not have the exclusive right to all of the streets on which its tracks were laid. The authorizing ordinance set up a committee consisting of the president of the railway, the Mayor, and the City Commissioner to agree on "regulations and the payment of a sum of money" for the right of other companies to run cars on these tracks.

When the Frick lines secured permission to lay their "City Hall loop" on Exchange Place, Holliday, Fayette, and South Streets, it worked to the advantage of both People's Railway and Union Passenger Railway. These companies, among others, used the loop in order to reach the government and financial centers, thereby gaining a logical terminus with a good traffic potential. Trackage rights were apparently willingly granted in many cases, but not always.

On May 1, 1892, the Frick lines came under the control of the Baltimore Traction Company. About the time the Lake Roland Railway was formed, one of Lake Roland's routes was planned to include the portion of North Avenue which was occupied by tracks of the Frick lines. Despite the clause in Frick's authorization which compelled track sharing, Lake Roland had to go to court to win trackage rights. Further west on North Avenue, City Passenger was under no such obligation. The Lake Roland had to construct its own tracks alongside of City Passenger's, and for a half dozen years there were four sets of tracks on this stretch of North Avenue between Division and McCulloh. The only other place in which this situation occurred was on a stretch of Belvedere Avenue near Electric Park, where both the Traction Company and the Baltimore & Northern had separate tracks from 1897 to 1900.

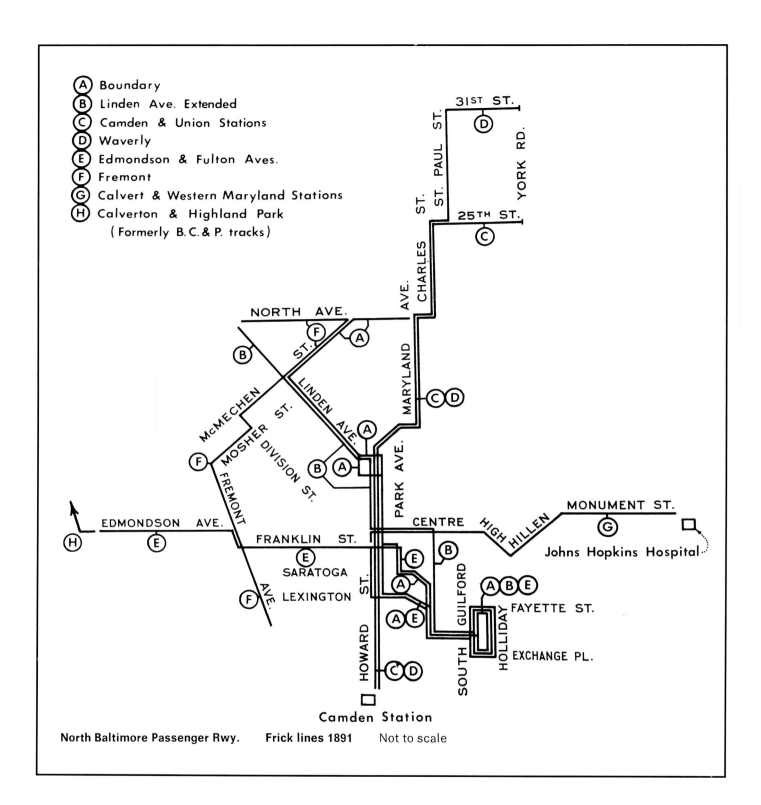

A Boundary
B Linden Ave. Extended
C Camden & Union Stations
D Waverly
E Edmondson & Fulton Aves.
F Fremont
G Calvert & Western Maryland Stations
H Calverton & Highland Park
(Formerly B.C.& P. tracks)

31ST ST.

D

ST. PAUL ST.

CHARLES ST.

25TH ST.

C

YORK RD.

NORTH AVE.

F   A

B

ST.

MARYLAND AVE.

C D

LINDEN AVE.

McMECHEN

MOSHER ST.

DIVISION ST.

A

F

B   A

PARK AVE.

MONUMENT ST.

CENTRE

HIGH HILLEN

G

EDMONDSON AVE.

FREMONT

Johns Hopkins Hospital

H   E

FRANKLIN   ST.

E

B

E

E

SARATOGA

A

AVE.

LEXINGTON

F

A   E

HOWARD   ST.

SOUTH GUILFORD

A B E

HOLLIDAY

FAYETTE ST.

EXCHANGE PL.

C D

Camden Station

North Baltimore Passenger Rwy.   **Frick lines 1891**   Not to scale

Frick lines No. 100, of the Edmondson Avenue line, sits amid pastoral surroundings sometime in the 1880s. The location is not identified, but may be near Edmondson and Fulton Avenues. The dark speck between the horses and the smaller house is a cow! (Baltimore Sunpapers)

NOTES AND COMMENTS:

The first (of the constituent companies that became the Frick lines) to begin operation appears to have been the Baltimore, Peabody Heights & Waverly Railway of Baltimore County, probably in August 1871. *Sun*, August 15, 1871. Other data on the early operation of these lines was gathered from *Baltimore City Code*, 1879; *Sun*, May 5, 1872; A. T. Clark notes.

Conditions of "track-sharing" are spelled out in City of Baltimore, Maryland, Ordinance 27, March 28, 1872 and Ordinance 74, June 7, 1872.

The *Sun*, July 16, 1892 stated that the North Baltimore Passenger Railway "came under control of the Traction Company, May 1, 1892." The *American*, January 31, 1892, reported that the transaction had been consummated the previous day (January 30th). A. T. Clark writing on July 17, 1945 cited railway company records to the effect that April 11, 1892 was the date of the purchase.

The legal aspects of trackage rights on North Avenue are brought out in Koch v. North Avenue Railway, *Maryland Reports*, vol. 75, pp. 222-246 (1892).

Around 1895, Gwynn Oak Park looked like this. The letterboard on Walbrook, Gwynn Oak & Powhatan Railway No. 2 (a Lamokin product) is inscribed "Gwynn Oak Park." The crew stands in the center, the motorman wearing a white hat and the conductor a fedora. (Louis C. Mueller Collection)

THE MINOR COMPANIES

One of the difficulties in trying to compile a Baltimore streetcar history in narrative fashion is that it becomes well-nigh impossible to present all of the companies involved in the order of their appearance. So far, the emphasis has been on giving the genesis of the "city passenger railways" — this being the generic term encompassing all of the companies. Soon, the story will shift to the era of "rapid transit." Running through it is the thread of consolidation, weaving the many companies into the inexorable, final unification.

Before moving on to these developments, it might be well to pause and take a brief glance at some of the companies which came into being before 1900, played varying roles in the transportation story, then quickly faded into the category of forgotten hopes and dreams.

Certainly, about all that the various promoters of the Columbia & Maryland Railway could lay hold of was broken dreams. This company is the best remembered of a complex corporate structure which included the Baltimore & Washington Turnpike and Tramway Company, the Columbia & Maryland Railway Company, and the Maryland & Washington Railway Company — all chartered in 1892 — and the Edmondson Avenue, Catonsville & Ellicott City Electric Railway Company, chartered in 1894. On March 25, 1898, all of these entities were sold at a foreclosure sale to the Maryland Traction Company.

Visualized as an interurban connecting the nation's capital with Maryland's largest city, the system finally saw completion of its route from Washington as far as Laurel. On the Baltimore end it could only claim a short-lived route from Howard and Saratoga Streets to the vicinity of the Baltimore & Potomac Railroad overpass on Franklin Street. This line had a certain claim to fame as the only standard gauge

trackage ever operated by a street railway company in Baltimore. But this, along with the rest of its almost completed standard gauge route to Ellicott City (a total of seventeen miles), was sold to the Consolidated Railway and converted to 5 feet 4½ inches in 1898. The sale marked the end of any construction by this company, even though it was still trying to find a way into Baltimore from the west as late as 1901.

The Columbia & Maryland had another unique distinction; it controlled a steam railroad, the Catonsville Short Line. The Short Line had been built in 1884 as a competitor of the Baltimore, Catonsville & Ellicott's Mills horse car line. It proved successful enough to push the BC & EM into financial difficulties, but the C & M's hopes of integrating it into its transportation empire went a glimmering in 1898, and the Short Line was sold into other hands. As a branch of the Pennsylvania Railroad (after 1968, Penn Central) it survived until the spring of 1972.

The Baltimore, Catonsville & Ellicott's Mills, which has been mentioned previously, was one of the earliest lines. The operation proved reasonably profitable, but a lack of competition resulted in such casual service that the opening of the steam line paralleling its right of way led to a drastic decline in revenues. In 1883, it was acquired by the Baltimore Union Passenger Railway.

Baltimore Union Passenger was to become, through consolidations, one of the titans of local operations; but, until the advent of electrification, it was very small indeed. Chartered in 1881, it commenced operations during the following year with a line from the Light Street wharves westward on Lombard Street and Wilkens Avenue to the vicinity of what was to become the Union Stockyards. In the next few years, the company added two lines up-

town via John Street and Maryland Avenue, as well as one across East North Avenue. By this time, Nelson Perin had arrived in town from Cincinnati; in subsequent chapters it will be seen how, through this company, he became perhaps the dominant figure in Baltimore street railway circles.

On the other hand, the Baltimore & Randallstown Railroad went from mediocrity to early oblivion. Organized in 1872, it was sold on February 3, 1874, according to historian Thomas Scharf. The record is vague, but after that it was probably operated as a branch of the Baltimore, Calverton & Powhatan until 1879. In any event, in July of that year, the Baltimore and Liberty Turnpike Company complained of $450 due for use of its roadway, and the Baltimore & Randallstown's rails were sold to a Virginia company for $31 a ton.

Another line to the northwest, the previously cited Baltimore, Pimlico & Pikesville, had more success. Also chartered in 1872, it managed to survive the Panic of 1873, and was obtained in 1881 by Shirley Jones, et al., at a foreclosure sale. Reorganized as the Pimlico & Pikesville Railroad Company, its tracks ran from Reisterstown Road, near Fulton Avenue, alongside the turnpike as far as what is now Park Circle and then cross country over what became Park Heights Avenue to the Confederate Soldiers' Home in Pikesville (the present State Police headquarters).

It was one of the earliest electrified lines in the Baltimore area. At the time that the wires went up, July 25, 1892, it was closely allied with Baltimore Traction, and its further history is found under that company. The Pimlico & Pikesville was connected with a short line along Belvedere Avenue, from the village of Arlington to Park Heights Avenue. This line replaced service on the Arlington & Pimlico, a steam road built in 1881, which had run

Available evidence indicates that this car was built for the Union Passenger Railway by John Stephenson Company in 1883. Except for being about three feet shorter, the car is an almost exact copy of the earliest Central Railway equipment. Charles Street station served the Northern Central and Baltimore & Potomac steam roads. Delta was the Baltimore & Delta Railroad, later the Maryland & Pennsylvania. (Smithsonian Institution)

One of the few mementos of the Columbia & Maryland is this culvert which dates from the early 1900s near Chalfont Drive on the Ellicott City line. (Michael R. Farrell)

Interior views of early horse cars are virtually non-existent, but this shot of one converted to overhead line car No. 8001 gives some idea of the craftsmanship that went into them. Even surrounded by mundane rope and tackle, workbench, and bare light bulbs, the carlines — roof rafters — reflect precision work done at the Stephenson plant in 1891. (Louis C. Mueller Collection)

a short distance to the north and had connected the Western Maryland Railroad with the Agricultural Grounds, now Pimlico Racetrack.

The Baltimore & Curtis Bay was another company which fell into the Baltimore Traction net soon after it began operating. Electricity was the motive power from the start on May 28, 1892. The route was across the Light Street bridge from Ferry Bar to the Anne Arundel County village of Brooklyn. When operation commenced, cars ran only from the foot of Light Street over the bridge into Brooklyn. During 1893, tracks were extended along Hanover Street in Baltimore, and Patapsco and Curtis Avenues in Brooklyn. Soon after the line became allied with Baltimore Traction, cars were routed northward to a connection with that company's cars at Fort Avenue and Charles Street, effective April 17, 1894. During the fall of that year, the opposite end of the line was extended to the famous (or infamous) Jack Flood's resort on Curtis Bay. Beginning in 1895, the portion of the road across Long Bridge and through Brooklyn and Curtis Bay (also then part of Anne Arundel County) was double-tracked.

The Walbrook Gwynn Oak & Powhatan was also conceived as an electric operation. Construction began April 23, 1894, out Garrison Avenue (later Garrison Boulevard) to the Baltimore & Liberty Turnpike (later Liberty Heights Avenue) to Gwynn Oak Avenue and thence to Powhatan (Woodlawn). Originally there had been a working agreement with the Lake Roland Elevated Railway with which it connected at Walbrook; but, in December, Baltimore Traction secured a majority of the directors of the company. It is perhaps best remembered as the founder of Gwynn Oak amusement park.

The reason for the existence of the Gwynns Falls Railway was the discontinuance of service on Windsor Mill Road between Walbrook and Powhatan, on October 31, 1894. (This had been operated by the Baltimore, Calverton & Powhatan, discussed earlier.) This upset the residents of the vicinity who depended on the cars and who, with a typical reaction for the times, organized their own railway company. By July 4, 1896, it was operating an electric line from Walbrook as far as Gwynns Falls, not quite a mile.

Quite surprising, though, was the type of operation that had originally been planned. When the company was organized, it had been seriously proposed to build the line as a monorail, or "bicycle railway," as the newspapers referred to it. It might be noted here that Edwin Tunis, who had pioneered this type of transportation on Long Island, lived in the immediate vicinity of the line. A short stretch of experimental monorail was set up on the family estate. However, the line was ultimately built and operated as a conventional trolley line, which was absorbed by the Traction Company on October 8, 1897.

Where other companies had been expected to build a line to make a profit, the Baltimore, Canton & Point Breeze expected to earn a profit by not building a line. Its purpose allegedly was to peddle its franchises to some established company. It came into existence in 1892, by which time most of the logical streets for car lines had been preempted. It secured franchises which extended from the Battle Monument out Lexington Street to Bond, and then split towards North Avenue and Canton.

Rather than begin construction, it stalled for time while trying to sell its rights. For once, the railway managements put up a united front and refused to bid. The newspapers had quite a time with the affair, dubbing the Baltimore, Canton & Point Breeze, the "Rams Horn Railway." Two years later, the sale of the franchise was again proposed, but once more the "Rams Horn" failed to make a sale, especially as it was now handicapped by the fact that the time limit for building the line had expired.

Some idea of the newspaper treatment given such items may be gained from the June 7, 1894 issue of the Baltimore *World*, a paper which believed in telling it like it was. "Why do they call it the Ramshorn Railway ordinance? Is it because it is a crooked line, or a crooked scheme, or controlled by crooked people? Where there is a ram's horn, there is a 'but', and there seem to be many in this matter, and there is also wool, and therein may be the connection." By October 1895, George Blakistone of the Central Railway was ready to break the show of solidarity and purchase the franchise. However, the courts ruled that the franchise was indeed void, and the Central took another means of securing a route to Canton.

The Monumental Railway is one line which does not fit readily into either the major or minor categories. Organized in 1880, it began running from Hillen Station to Highlandtown on December 4, 1881, with five well-filled cars. Its story is closely intertwined with the Highlandtown & Point Breeze, which began service between the two communities in its corporate title around the same date or possibly a little earlier. The H & PB was interested in running steam dummies on its line as early as 1882 and was definitely operating them in June 1886, though it is very probable that the company had suspended operation during part of that period.

In any event, the Monumental was sold at auction to a syndicate of Baltimore and Philadelphia financiers on May 8, 1883. At the time, assets included 14 cars, 66 horses, 2 dummy engines, and stables and offices on Eastern Avenue in Highlandtown. The newspaper account mentions: "The purchasers, it is stated, will put money into the enterprise, get new cars, etc., and run the road on business principles. It is claimed that it will be a first class road." The two corporate entities were combined on April 30, 1884, as the Highlandtown & Point Breeze Railway.

The paramount problem that had prevented the company from becoming a first class enterprise was lack of entrée into downtown Baltimore. This was solved in 1886, when permission was granted to extend trackage up Pratt Street, to South, and around the City Hall loop. The old route to Hillen Station was retained as a shuttle service. The new routing encouraged the Philadelphia syndicate headed by William Wharton, Jr., to take over active control, and the Highlandtown & Point Breeze continued successfully until taken over by the Baltimore Union Passenger Railway in February 1892.

NOTES AND COMMENTS:

In the limited space available it is impossible to give a complete picture of the complicated tangle of franchises and corporations which have been lumped under the Columbia & Maryland. Much is not germane anyway since the emphasis has been placed upon what happened, rather than what was projected. Indeed, except for its brief operation of a standard gauge line and its part in delaying the entry of the Washington, Baltimore & Annapolis interurban into downtown, the Columbia & Maryland et al. contributed but little to Baltimore streetcar history. On April 18, 1898, the C & M borrowed a car from one of its Washington affiliates and ran a trial trip on a line beginning at Howard and Saratoga Streets, along Saratoga to Monroe, to Franklin as far as the Baltimore & Potomac overpass. *Sun*, April 19, 1898. Although the paper indicated that the car would commence running regularly on the 19th, it appears doubtful if more than a few more trial runs were made before the line was sold to the Consolidated Railway, which immediately began to wide gauge the trackage.

Baltimore & Randallstown No. 1 was used to illustrate an early 1900s history of the J. G. Brill Company. It points out the difficulty in presenting an exact account of the earliest years. While the article declares that the car was built in 1870, the B & R was not incorporated until 1872; the car probably dates from 1873. (Louis C. Mueller Collection)

What follows is a synopsis of an explanation given by John E. Merriken of the contretemps with the WB & A. One condition of the sale of the Edmondson Avenue, Catonsville & Ellicott City branch to the Consolidated was a commitment that whoever might complete the interurban line to Washington would be granted preferential rights to the route which the original backers had almost completed via Catonsville and Ellicott City. Such preference afforded incentive to other buyers of the remainder (Ellicott City to Washington) of the project. A written agreement was entered into between the United (as successor to Consolidated) and Baltimore Security & Trading Company (the holder of the C & M's old rights) on April 20, 1901 concerning trackage sharing into Baltimore. A few months later, this arrangement was repudiated by the United, which maintained that their former president, Nelson Perin, was without authorization to sign such a contract.

At this same time, construction of a totally independent interurban line was stymied by various natural obstacles at the city line near Westport. This company, the Washington & Annapolis (later WB & A), soon reached an agreement with the United for trackage rights. The Baltimore Security & Trading Company contended this was prejudicial to the interurban line via Catonsville and filed an injunction to bar any concessions to the W & A. The United agreed to retain their option for an interurban "within the family" and on October 7, 1901, incorporated their own Baltimore & Laurel Electric Railway. This appeased the BS & T, but left the W & A stranded in Westport. The latter was forced to form a subsidiary, the Baltimore Terminal Company. This corporation was not able to secure a right of way until April 1906 when, after reaching an agreement to share a few blocks of common trackage with the United on Lombard and Liberty Streets, it was given permission to build to a downtown terminal at Park Avenue and Marion Street. Track construction was completed October 25, 1907, and service via the new Washington, Baltimore & Annapolis Electric Railway commenced April 3, 1908. The Baltimore Terminal Company had the distinction of owning 0.85 mile of single rail laid between the wide gauge track of the United.

The Catonsville Short Line Railroad was completed in 1884 from a station on the south side of Frederick Road, opposite Egges Lane, to a junction with the Pennsylvania Railroad at Loudon Park. Trackage rights allowed the road's trains to run through to Union (Pennsylvania) Station. On June 10, 1895, the line passed into the hands of the Edmondson Avenue, Catonsville & Ellicott City Electric Railway (Columbia & Maryland). Though it was stated that the steam railroad would be turned into an electric line, this never came about. By mid-1898, the Short Line had been sold, along with other C & M properties, and continued in service as a freight carrier until the spring of 1972. *Sun*, June 21, 1883 and August 5, 1897; *American*, June 11, 1895 and June 22, 1898.

Additional notes on the Baltimore, Catonsville & Ellicott's Mills will be found under the chapter, "An Iron Web." On

December 21, 1882, Col. J. C. Holland, president of the company for the previous fifteen years, and two other directors resigned. Two of the replacements were officials of the Baltimore Union Passenger, J. L. Keck and T. C. Robbins. Though it was stressed that the latter gentlemen, while having purchased sufficient stock to control the Catonsville railway, had done so "as individuals, not as officers of the Union," an arrangement was made to run cars over the Union line into downtown Baltimore. *Maryland Journal* (Towson), January 6, 1883. The company not only lost passengers to the Short Line, but the mail contract as well on March 16, 1885. *Baltimore County Union*, March 7, 1885. On January 31, 1887, the fare on the horse cars from downtown Baltimore to Catonsville was cut to ten cents. The BC & EM was sold at public auction, December 15, 1890 to George C. Jenkins, Nelson Perin, John K. Cowen, E. J. D. Cross, and George D. Penniman, stockholders of that company, but also in control of the Baltimore Union Passenger. *Baltimore County Union*, December 20, 1890 and *Maryland Journal* (Towson), December 13, 1890. The road was electrified in 1895. An interesting aside is that John K. Cowen, who is known to have been very interested in Daft's experiments on another BUP holding, the Baltimore & Hampden, was very influential in the Baltimore & Ohio at the time when the decision was made to use electricity on the Belt Line, the first main line railroad electrification. (He became president of the B & O in 1896.)

Additional comments about the Pimlico & Pikesville can be found in the chapter, "An Iron Web." At the time that this road began electric operation, it was single-tracked with passing sidings. Less than four months later, double-tracking was commenced between Park Circle and Pimlico. *Baltimore County Union*, November 12, 1893. This was completed August 23, 1893, but an arrangement was not worked out with the Baltimore and Reisterstown Turnpike Company for double-tracking the Park Circle to Fulton Avenue stretch until June 1897. *Herald*, August 24, 1893 and *Sun*, June 24, 1897.

The Arlington & Pimlico began operation as a steam railroad on May 21, 1881, between Arlington station on the Western Maryland and the grounds of the State Agricultural and Mechanical Association (Pimlico Racetrack). Its successor, the Arlington branch of the Pimlico & Pikesville, was opened for electric operation in June 1893. *Maryland Journal* (Towson), December 18, 1880; *Baltimore County Union*, May 21, 1881 and June 3, 1893.

The Baltimore, South Baltimore & Curtis Bay Railway Company was chartered in 1890. Under an amended charter — Maryland Laws of 1892, ch. 574 — the name was changed to the Baltimore & Curtis Bay Railway. A. T. Clark notes; L. C. Mueller notes; *Maryland Public Service Commission Report*, 1914; *American*, April 18 and November 12, 1894; *Sun*, March 27, 1895.

The information pertaining to the Walbrook, Gwynn Oak & Powhatan and its affiliation with the Lake Roland Elevated and the Baltimore Traction Company was taken from the *American*, April 22, 1894, and various papers for December 1894.

Robert Base was very helpful in piecing together the story of the Gwynns Falls Railway. Other sources included: *American*, November 1, 1894 and July 5, 1895; *Sun*, March 1 and 20, 1895, January 23 and May 14, 1896; *Electric Railway Journal*, April 1897. The *Sun*, May 2, 1895, presented the following explanation (which has been condensed) of the "bicycle electric railway": It is said that the new line to be built here is the first of its kind that will be put into practical operation, although the efficiency of the bicycle electric system has been tested on a road in Bellport, Long Island. The Boynton electric railway system, which is to be constructed, is a combination of the bicycle and trolley roads, with some modifications. The system can be embodied in several forms of construction, but in general principle is a long, narrow, high car, with wheels beneath arranged on a single rail, like the wheels of a bicycle, and a strong grooved beam overhead arranged like a trolley wire. The cars are designed to be forty feet long, divided

into two stories, although a one-story car may be used. They are supported on the single rail by gravity, the guiding beam above being used to prevent them from falling to either side in case they are more heavily weighted on one side than on the other. At curves this guiding beam is moved toward the inner side of the curve. so that high speeds can be maintained. It is claimed that it is impossible for them to "jump" the track unless the structure is broken. Claimed speed is 90 to 100 mph. Electric current is carried in the overhead beam. Advantages claimed are shape of cars makes them lighter and stronger; greater speed and economy, with less construction cost; saving of expense in grading and securing right of way; reduction in cost and wear of rolling stock; saving of friction in rounding curves by substituting bicycle spindles for ordinary car axles; and avoiding the possibility of spreading rails, as in ordinary two-rail track.

Resumes of the doings of the "Rams Horn Railway," including a listing of all routings claimed for the company, appeared in the *Sun*, April 17 and 20, 1894; *News*, April 20, 1894. Central Railway's willingness to buy the franchises, as well as reports of the court decisions, are confirmed by the *News*, October 3, 1895.

The *Baltimore County Union* reported on April 29, 1882 that a committee had gone before the County Commissioners to discuss the matter of steam dummies on the Highlandtown & Point Breeze. The same paper, on June 12, 1886, noted that these vehicles were running; in the *Sunday Sun Magazine*, May 1, 1940, George M. Baier recalled greasing curves between Hillen Station and Highlandtown on Sunday mornings and then firing the boiler of a "donkey engine" running to Point Breeze in the evening. The listing of assets at the time of the auction comes from the *Maryland Journal* (Towson), May 12, 1883. The *Sun*, December 31, 1886 reported the franchise grant for extension of tracks, and the *Baltimore County Union*, February 27, 1892 mentioned "The Union Passenger Railway, which owns the York Road line, has secured control of the Highlandtown & Point Breeze."

The only available photograph of the Baltimore, Calverton & Powhatan shows a car crossing the Windsor Mill Road bridge at Gwynns Falls. The scene typifies the rural nature of the line between Walbrook Junction and Powhatan (Woodlawn). (Enoch Pratt Library, Armistead Webb)

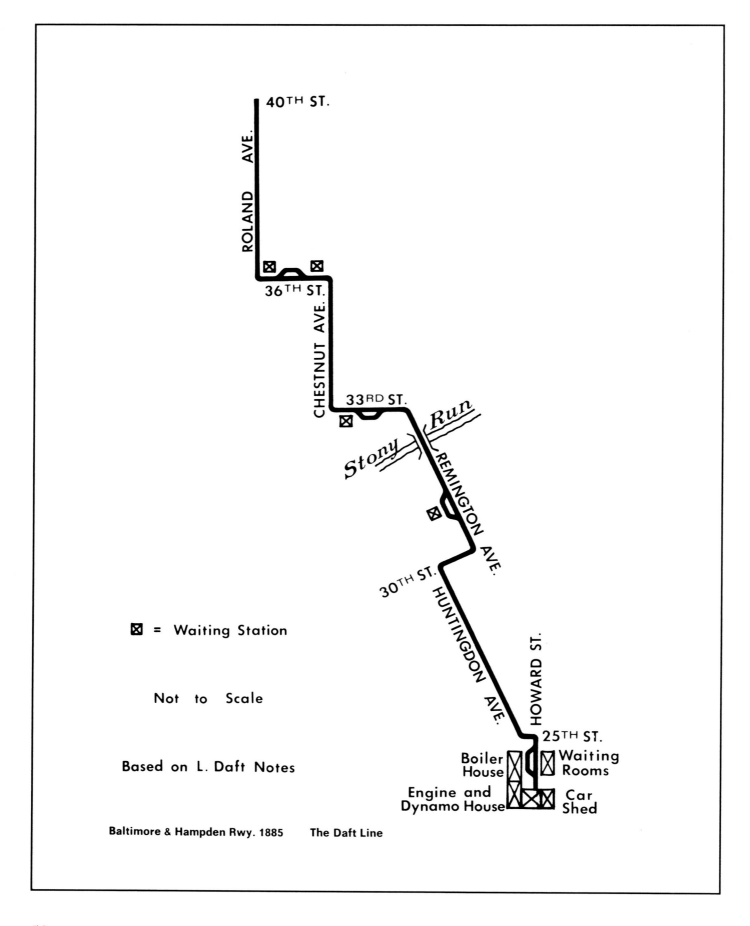

40TH ST.

ROLAND AVE.

36TH ST.

CHESTNUT AVE.

33RD ST.

Stony Run

REMINGTON AVE.

30TH ST.

HUNTINGDON AVE.

HOWARD ST.

25TH ST.

⊠ = Waiting Station

Not to Scale

Based on L. Daft Notes

Baltimore & Hampden Rwy. 1885   The Daft Line

Boiler House

Waiting Rooms

Engine and Dynamo House

Car Shed

PROFESSOR DAFT
AND HIS MOTORS

Except for a quirk of fate, the best remembered of all the early streetcar operations in Baltimore would have remained one of the most obscure. The Baltimore & Hampden operated its first car in March 1876 on a line running from Charles Street and Huntingdon Avenue (now 25th Street) to Roland Avenue and 36th Street, in Hampden. It went its unobtrusive way, attracting little notice beyond an occasional mention of the difficult grades through the Stony Run valley on Remington Avenue, which led the company to attach mules, rather than horses, to its little cars.

All of this changed dramatically in mid-August of 1885 — the exact date is in dispute — when the road discarded its mules in favor of electric motors. This installation, designed by Leo Daft, is generally conceded to represent the first successful commercial electric railway in the United States. It is true that, in Cleveland in 1881, Bentley and Knight had built a short electric line, which was operated by an underground conduit system. However, neither this nor any other early line can be classed as successful. It was not until 1888 that Frank Sprague installed his famous trolley system in Richmond, an event which was to revolutionize the entire street railway industry.

The Baltimore & Hampden operated its third rail system with a fair degree of success for more than four years. When the road was finally returned to animal power, it was probably due more to financial considerations than to operational difficulties. All of this is not to say that Daft's system was better than Frank Sprague's; it was not. Daft just happened to get his running first.

The Hampden experiment came about as a result of what appears to have been a chance meeting between T. C. Robbins,

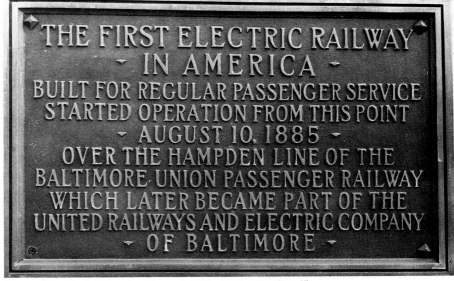

Plaque affixed to Oak Street car house in 1925. (Michael R. Farrell)

general manager of the line, and Professor Leo Daft, who was exhibiting an experimental electric railway at Coney Island. Daft was the founder of the Daft Electric Company, located at Greenville, New Jersey. In 1881, he had become interested in the possibilities of adapting the electric motor to the operation of street railways. After conducting tests at the factory, he took to the road with his ideas. The first stop was at Mount McGregor, near Saratoga, New York, where trial runs were somewhat marred by an accident caused by excessive speed. By 1884, he was showing his equipment to large crowds at the Mechanics Fair in Boston and the Iron Pier at Coney Island. Though carrying large numbers of the curious on these short runs, he was unsuccessful in attracting any serious attention on the part of the horse railway managements until Robbins appeared at Coney Island.

Robbins was impressed. His Hampden line was proving difficult to traverse, even

for the mules, when there was any considerable number of passengers on the cars. According to Robbins, the grades were as steep as 350 feet to the mile, complicated by severe curves.

Daft accepted an invitation to come down to Baltimore in 1885 to view the line, with the thought of equipping it for electric operation. He was not overly enthusiastic with what he found. Still, no other company had shown any interest in this equipment, so he agreed to tackle it.

The hand of Nelson Perin, whose Union Passenger Railway had an interest in the line, might well have shaped the proposition that was made to the Daft Company. The latter was to equip the route with motive power and make the electrical installation, then wait until the road had been in successful operation for a year before receiving compensation. Unfair as this seems, Daft had faith in his system and went along with the terms.

On what appears to be a trial trip in August 1885, a Daft motor car, with a borrowed Catonsville line horse car as trailer, pauses at the top of the slope after the ascent from the Stony Run valley. Location is near the present 33rd and Remington. Some believe that Daft himself is leaning against the motor and that the man at right is T. C. Robbins. (Sam W. Pattison Rea Collection, BSM)

Daft motor car *Faraday* sits outside the Oak Street car house probably soon after its arrival in Baltimore. (Sam W. Pattison Rea Collection, BSM)

The passing siding at Chestnut and 33rd. The raised center rail is clearly visible. Except for the vehicles, the scene today — more than one hundred years later — has not changed very much. (Sam W. Pattison Rea Collection, BSM)

Even then he was not in the clear. The management had second thoughts about the experiment. Some of the directors sought other advice and were told, "The man who undertakes to operate this section by electricity in the present state of the art is either a knave or a fool!" Fearing that they would become a laughingstock, the Baltimore & Hampden directors tried to call off the deal.

Daft hurried to Baltimore. Even though he argued that the cost of failure would fall almost entirely on his company, the day was almost lost until Robbins threatened to quit as general manager if the contract with Daft was not honored. Many years later, Frank Sprague, who was by then recognized as the father of the streetcar, cited this as a case "in which those who are strong in the faith were willing to take great risks." In the same speech Sprague also said, "I believe that this was the first regularly operated electric road in the country."

In the Daft System, ordinary passenger cars were pulled by separate motor cars, which were simply dummy cabs equipped with series motors grouped by commuted fields. They were given names, the first being *Morse,* and succeeding ones, *Faraday* and *T. C. Robbins* and *Keck.* Power was supplied by an Atlas engine connected to two Daft dynamos, which were in series and supplied 260 volts. This voltage was fed into a third rail, located in the center of the tracks and supported by insulators. Bonding was by copper wire, riveted to the web with copper rivets. The arrangement worked well, according to Daft, though there was considerable leakage during severe thunderstorms.

By the end of March 1885, the dynamos, two in number, had been installed at the car barn at Oak Street and Huntingdon Avenue (now Howard and 25th). The first of the motors arrived in May, with a second joining it a month later. By the middle of June, testing was in full swing.

The voltage mentioned above may appear suspect, but this and the other technical data are from an article by Daft in a *Street Railway Journal* of 1904. In the same story he recalls that regular operation began on August 15, 1885. A plaque commemorating the event states that it began on the 10th, while contemporary newspapers indicate scheduled service started the 18th.

Be that as it may, the electric line was quite an attraction. On August 16th, about five hundred people showed up to see the motors run. The regular cars were replaced by larger ones borrowed from the Baltimore, Catonsville & Ellicott's Mills Railway. Even these could not accommodate all who wanted to ride. Many, of course, were drawn by curiosity — nevertheless, a year later the line was averaging around twenty-nine thousand passengers a month. This is not bad for what was strictly a suburban line and is in direct contradiction to the stories that the line was not successful.

The B & H's greatest operating difficulty was in surmounting this Remington Avenue hill. The location often flooded, but Daft maintained that service was not affected, even with the third rail under water for considerable distances. (Sam W. Pattison Rea Collection, BSM)

An inspection party pauses around the corner from Roland Avenue station, near the northern end of the line. Live rail in front of the shelter has been covered with planks as a safety measure. Despite the electrification of the railway, the lamp at left appears to use gas. (Sam W. Pattison Rea Collection, BSM)

Some changes have been made to the Daft trains as can be seen by comparing this photo with those on preceding pages. The motor is the *Faraday*, repainted to match the Baltimore & Hampden Electric Railroad trailer. A trolley pole with its "shoe" has been added, as well as a bracket for an oil headlamp installed at rub-rail height. Photo is uncaptioned but may be in front of Oak Street car house. (Enoch Pratt Library, Smithsonian Institution)

A report of T. C. Robbins shows that between September 1, 1885 and May 20, 1886, the B & H carried 188,591 riders with its electric motors, an increase of 31,907 over those carried by horse cars for a similar period the year previous. Robbins figured that the cost per passenger was 3.01 cents with horsepower, compared to a 1.66 cents cost with electricity.

Another misconception about the Daft operation is that it was lethal to unwary or careless humans. Intensive research fails to turn up a single case to confirm this. Of course, the electricity could provide quite a jolt and did prove fatal to some livestock. To offset this danger to animals, the company placed wooden scantlings around the live rail, somewhat in the manner of modern third rail practice. Within a few months this precaution had been supplemented by an overhead pickup at street crossings. When a car approached a crossing, the motorman raised a lever on the roof which brought a copper sheet into contact with the overhead.

At the end of the prescribed year, the railway company purchased the motors and electrical equipment from the Daft Company and, six months later, placed an order for two improved dynamos. During this period, things looked so promising that the Baltimore & Hampden toyed with the idea of converting the whole operation into an overhead line, using Daft equipment. This was never pursued, and perhaps it was just as well. Frank Sprague was, at about the same time, making his famous Richmond installation, and it was Sprague's inventions that were to prove to be the ultimate method of electrifying the street railways. By the fall of 1889, the Daft electrical equipment was not only obsolete, it was worn out. Rather than spend the money to replace it at a time when the final results were not yet in on which system would prove to be the best, the company reverted to animal power.

The Baltimore & Hampden had long been controlled by the Baltimore Union Passenger Railway, and on June 10, 1891, the B & H was leased to the Union for 999 years, the consideration being a nominal $5 plus the assumption of an indebtedness of $45,000. When, several years later, Union Passenger electrified its Maryland Avenue line with conventional overhead wiring, the Baltimore & Hampden was combined with it, and streetcar service was continued over a slightly altered route until 1949.

The latter half of the 1880s saw experimentation with other types of motive power as well. Prior attempts at running steam engines along the streets had caused that type of locomotion to be written off. Propulsion by compressed air, in the form of the Roberts Noiseless Motor, caused a stir on the Arlington & Pimlico and the York Road Railway, but nothing came of it. City Passenger even invested $500 in an alleged perpetual motion machine.

Much serious consideration, though, was given to the battery car. One model, which was tested on the Baltimore & Hampden at the time of the Daft installation, quietly passed from the scene; but the North Baltimore Passenger Railway was so taken with this type of motive power that it purchased its own battery car in 1887.

This vehicle was built by the J. G. Brill Co. of Philadelphia, and the electrical installation was carried out by the Electric Storage Battery Company. A large car for its time, it was 16 feet long between bulkheads. The power was supplied by a set of fourteen storage batteries which ran a pair of 7½ hp Sprague motors. The batteries were manufactured locally at the works of the United States Light and Power Company at Centre and Holliday Streets. A top speed of 12 mph was claimed. Among the innovations were an electric bell for warning pedestrians and four 10-candlepower lamps.

The car caused quite a stir when it arrived in town during the middle of February 1888. During testing on the various routes of the North Baltimore Company, it was clocked at a snappy 8 mph across the North Avenue bridge. When the baseball season started, the car was put in regular service on the line to the ball park on York Road. Newspaper reports indicated that it climbed the steepest grades without dif-

ficulty, and stopped and started with more facility and more quickly than a horse car. It made no noise and turned the sharpest curves with ease; horses paid no attention to it. The one drawback mentioned was the weight. On June 1st, it began running on a regular basis, making six or eight trips a day. But its fatal flaw could be read between the lines. The limitations imposed by the batteries made it impractical for continuous service, so it spent most of its time in the McMechen Street car house.

The failure of the battery car in Baltimore was summed up by T. Edward Hambleton during an interview on August 30, 1892. He stated: "I have in my possession one of the finest storage battery cars that was ever built. We cannot make it run, and if you can, I will make you a present of it. It is impossible to run a storage battery line with success from a financial standpoint."

Although this car's fate is uncertain, it was probably destroyed in the fire which leveled the McMechen Street car barn that the Baltimore Traction had likewise inherited when it took over the North Baltimore Passenger Railway.

There was to be one practical application of the storage battery car in the area, though. Years and years of refinement finally developed a vehicle which combined an extremely low weight with roller bearings and more substantial batteries. In the World War I era, two of these were used with a fair amount of success on the Towson & Cockeysville Railway. This company, which never became a part of the city traction system, began operations in 1912 over a single track line from the Towson end of the No. 8 route north to Timonium. However, when the batteries became low, even these improved models often had to be pulled by a team of horses up the final hill into Towson.

NOTES AND COMMENTS:

Much of the material in this chapter was extracted from, or confirmed by, an extensive article, "The Early Days of the Daft Company," written by Leo Daft for the *Street Railway Journal* of October 8, 1904.

"The operation of the Baltimore & Hampden Electric Railway by the Daft motor is pronounced too expensive, and consequently has been discontinued." *Maryland Journal* (Towson), October 5, 1889.

Serious researchers are also referred to the *Sun Almanac*, 1896 and the *National Railway Historical Society Bulletin*, vol. 36, no. 2, p. 18 (1971).

Notes on the motive power: "There are two motors, the *Morse* and the *Faraday*." *Sun*, August 14, 1885. "The latest addition is the *T. C. Robbins*." *Maryland Journal* (Towson), November 21, 1885. "The new motor placed upon the road draws two cars instead of the one drawn by *Morse* and

Faraday." *Maryland Journal* (Towson), December 19, 1885. "Another new motor has been received, making four now on the road." *Baltimore County Union*, December 19, 1885. Edward T. Francis, who has long been interested in the Daft lines, furnished the name of the fourth motor — *Keck*, after J. L. Keck, the president of the B & H.

There are several items to confirm that the Hampden line seems to have used mules, rather than horses, as motive power. This was extremely rare in Baltimore. The *Maryland Journal* (Towson) refers to "mule power" on August 22, 1885 as taking one-third more time than the motors.

The same paper, on June 19, 1886, reported that a pair of mules were pulling a car that ran away on the shuttle which ran between the electric line at 36th Street and Roland Avenue and the village of Sweet Air.

The figure of twenty-nine thousand passengers a month is based upon statistics

printed in the *Baltimore County Union*, July 10, 1886.

Information on the North Baltimore Passenger Railway's storage battery car appeared in the *Sun*, December 27, 1887; February 27, April 7, and May 29, 1888. The interview with Hambleton was reported by the *American*.

The Towson & Cockeysville began operation in 1912 between Timonium and Chesapeake and Bosley Avenues in Towson. By mid-1913, the Towson terminus had been extended south to Washington and Chesapeake, but the line never got any further north than Timonium. The company had two cars during its existence — one was built by Federal in 1912, the other by Brill in 1916. *Electric Railway Journal*, April 20, 1912; January 4 and March 29, 1913; October 28, 1916; *Maryland Public Service Commission Report*, 1923.

"RAPID TRANSIT" COMES TO TOWN

Despite the best efforts of Professor Daft, the horse (or mule) was still the basic factor of street railway operations in Baltimore. As the decade which was to become known as the "Gay Nineties" began, the third rail method of electrical transmission joined the Citizens' steam engine and North Baltimore Passenger's battery car in the vague memories reserved for what might have been.

In other places, newer modes of transportation were already taking over. Pioneered in San Francisco and proven capable in colder climates through operation in Chicago, the cable system was near the zenith of its popularity. Sprague's overhead electrical system was proving so successful in Richmond that other communities were eagerly adopting his techniques.

The Baltimore companies were not blind to the parade of progress marked by the quiet, swift pace of the cable cars or the somewhat noisier and certainly more spectacular passage of the trolleys. As usual, though, the local situation was fraught with complications. City Passenger was dominant in the field. The original company was in no hurry to change motive power. Paying dividends in excess of 10 percent a year, it saw no reason to tamper with the status quo. Reasoning, quite correctly, that new modes of transportation could open a Pandora's box, after which things would never be quite the same, Bowie and his associates marked time.

Overhead electrical transmission and cable propulsion each had serious drawbacks. In addition to prejudice created during the operation of the Baltimore & Hampden by the third rail, the average person still held electricity as an awesome, even fearful force. The newspapers carried stories of sudden death caused by the short-circuiting of a wire — turning such innocent things as electric fans into gruesome death traps. "Blinded by the brilliant flash of flame as a trolley passed along the street" was a recurring, if inaccurate, newspaper heading in stories concerning other cities where streetcars were already in operation.

In addition, the local climate was not propitious for any proposal to string wires over the city streets. While it is almost forgotten today, just before the turn of the century, the streets of any metropolitan area were overhung with literally hundreds of wires. A glance at any photograph of downtown Baltimore, taken during this era, vividly shows the resulting appearance. Electric wires, telephone wires, telegraph wires — these and their corresponding poles presented a crowded haphazard look that the more aesthetically

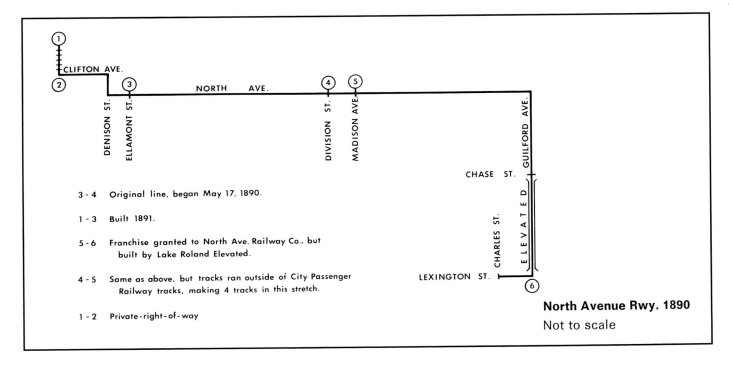

3 - 4   Original line, began May 17, 1890.

1 - 3   Built 1891.

5 - 6   Franchise granted to North Ave. Railway Co., but built by Lake Roland Elevated.

4 - 5   Same as above, but tracks ran outside of City Passenger Railway tracks, making 4 tracks in this stretch.

1 - 2   Private-right-of-way

North Avenue Rwy. 1890

Not to scale

In a well-known, but classic, photograph of Baltimore's cable days, Blue Line train passes Northern Central's Calvert Station. The date is around 1894, and crude electric arc lamps are beginning to replace gas lamps for street lighting. The Baltimore Sunpapers building replaced the station at Calvert and Franklin Streets. (Louis C. Mueller Collection)

inclined of the citizenry frowned upon. A program had been initiated to build "subways" (underground conduits constructed by the city), which the utilities were being required by law to use for their wires. Progress was being made with this project, and the public officials would be sure to look askance at any plan to put additional wires overhead.

The main disadvantage of a cable-powered street railway line was economic in nature. By 1890, it was generally recognized that the percentage of energy consumed in merely moving the cable itself was so large as to make cable cars unfeasible in any except unique situations, like hilly San Francisco and Kansas City. The operating expenses of a cable line were double that of a comparable electric line and capital costs were also considerably higher. The Baltimore operators were

intelligent and, to a man, are quoted as being in favor of electric operations; yet circumstances resulted in both Baltimore Traction and City Passenger constructing extensive systems using the "rope."

"There is much talk of 'rapid transit'; however, the North Avenue Railway is the first to furnish our people with rapid transit." This was in essence the boast of a new company constructed to supply service to the newly developing area called Highland Park, now Walbrook. Its first car ran on May 16, 1890, along North Avenue, from Division Street to 10th Street (now Ellamont Street). The car, a product of Brill, weighed five tons, and its cost of $4,500 included paneling of mahogany and cherry, as well as carpeting on the floor. A comment on street railway thinking of the times is the statement that, while the car

would seat twenty-five, it would be possible to carry one hundred.

Almost as soon as the car began operating, extensions were started at either end of the tracks. To the westward, the line was opened to Ridgewood Park, an amusement park located near what was to become the well-known Mount Holly Casino. The extension to the east was much more ambitious. By January 1891, construction had reached McCulloh Street and North Avenue, and plans were being firmed up for a further extension across North Avenue, and down North Street (now Guilford Avenue) to City Hall. These plans came to fruition through the consolidation of the North Avenue Railway and the Baltimore, Hampden & Lake Roland as the Lake Roland Elevated Railway Company, in May 1892. But that consolida-

The first of Baltimore's short-lived cable operations of the 1890s was the Baltimore Traction Company. Here we see a cable car and trailer on the loop in front of the Chinese station on Druid Hill Avenue. (BSM Collection)

tion comes later, both in a chronological sequence and in the importance of its consequences.

In early 1889, over a year before the North Avenue Railway had put its cars on the streets, two of the early companies, Citizens' and People's, came under control of a syndicate headed by T. Edward Hambleton, of the prominent banking house of Hambleton and Company. Thus, the Hambleton family moved into a leading position in the local transportation field and were to exert a strong influence which lasted long after the final consolidation.

The company which resulted from the joining of Citizens' and People's was The Baltimore Traction Company. Efforts to secure control of Union Passenger in 1889 and of City Passenger in 1891 proved unsuccessful, but the Traction

Company did succeed in bringing a faster mode of transportation to Baltimore, as well as setting in motion the series of mergers which culminated in the combining of all the major lines under one management.

Hambleton's early efforts brought to mind the early days of City Passenger, as, when unable to raise sufficient capital in Baltimore, he turned for assistance to Philadelphians, P. A. Widener and William Elkins. They were well acquainted with cable lines. Soon, the word was all over town that cable cars would be running on the streets of the Monumental City.

There was no real danger that loss of local control over the company, as had happened in 1859, would be repeated. Baltimore Traction was capitalized at $5 million, with the privilege of doubling this amount. In addition to the Hambleton

family, who had controlled the People's line, the new company included among the grantees in its charter: J. S. Hagerty, president of Citizens'; James L. McLane, president of the Frick lines; and Howard Munnikhuysen, president of the Highlandtown & Point Breeze. Another prominent name was that of Postmaster Frank Brown. Some soon dropped their affiliation; for instance, McLane left to head the Lake Roland Elevated in 1892. On the other hand, Brown was elected governor of the state shortly afterward, but returned to become president of Baltimore Traction. The influence of the Philadelphians, Widener and Elkins, soon waned; when they were dropped from the board of directors a few years later, the action caused scarcely a ripple.

Baltimore Traction was committed to "rapid transit." In light of succeeding

The Baltimore Traction Company has been gone since 1897 but its name lingers on, carved in stone atop the former power house on Druid Hill Avenue. (Michael R. Farrell)

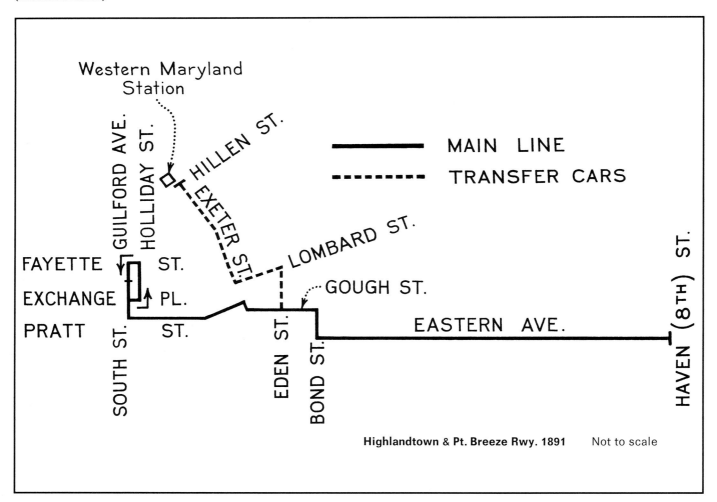

Baltimore's first car built to use the overhead trolley system, on North Avenue Railway. An 1890 Brill, it burned in the Irvington car house fire, May 1898. (George F. Nixon Collection)

events, it bears repeating that there was considerable feeling that the cable road was passé. Hagerty, of Citizens', is quoted as doubting that cable cars would ever appear in Baltimore, with electricity so near to perfection. President Bowie, of City Passenger, stated that his company could not stand the expense of running cars by cable. (Historian George Hilton is of the opinion that Bowie may have changed his mind after studying the costs of electric operation in Boston, perhaps the most unfavorable example.)

But it was T. Edward Hambleton who pinpointed the key to the problem of motive power. Years later, he was to cite earlier statements to the effect that his company would have preferred to use electric cars, but was refused permission to do so by the city authorities. Hambleton's contention is backed up by the fact that City Passenger had to go to court to get permission to begin electrification of its lines, even though an 1890 revision of its charter seemed clearly to authorize the change.

So, if Baltimore Traction was to take the initiative, cable power it had to be. In early March of 1890, ground was broken for a combined power plant and car house. Trackwork began simultaneously. Compared to an electric line, such as the North

Avenue Railway was then constructing, a cable line was a tremendously large and expensive undertaking. Instead of merely laying a pair of rails down the center of a wide roadway, with a series of poles contiguous to the track, Baltimore Traction was faced with the prospect of completely reconstructing a route which was being served with light horse cars. The initial cable car weighed seventeen thousand pounds against ten thousand for the North Avenue's electric vehicle.

Not only did the Traction Company have to dig up the streets, in order to install the conduit through which the cable rope ran, and replace thirty- and forty-pound rails with ones weighing seventy-eight pounds to the yard, it also faced the arduous task of changing the grades at many intersections all along its route, and constructing gutters and sewers to carry off heavy rainfall. Unlike electric lines, which could purchase power, the cable lines also faced the heavy expense of constructing substantial steam power houses in order to move the heavy steel ropes which ran continuously through the conduits.

Some idea of the immensity of these power houses may be found in a description of the original plant and its adjoining

car house (which still stood in 1992) at the southwest corner of Druid Hill Avenue and Retreat Street. The lot extends 210 feet along Druid Hill, and runs 260 feet deep on Retreat, to Francis Street. The cars entered through a center door on Druid Hill Avenue onto a transfer table which extended the full width of the building. Blacksmith shops and a room for washing the cars were adjacent. Next to these was a machine room, 85 x 100 feet, where the cable mechanism was located. To the rear was the boiler room, with a large space adjoining for storage of coal. In the basement were the vaults through which ran the cables themselves. These threaded a series of pulleys and blocks in subterranean alleyways which were 180 feet long. Another large power house, also still standing in 1992, was constructed on Pratt Street near Central Avenue to serve the eastern end of the route.

By October 1890, the first car had arrived. It had been planned to parade the car through town, but its weight precluded this. Instead, the citizens came to view the wonder. Huge compared to the horse cars, it was fully thirty feet long. A brownish-yellow predominated the paint scheme, relieved by white on the lower

Lettering on No. 7, built by Stephenson in 1891, indicates North Avenue Railway's intention of extending trackage into downtown Baltimore via Guilford Avenue, which was carried out by the Lake Roland Elevated Railway. The car's electrical system was furnished by the Baltimore firm of Baxter & Company. It was rebuilt in 1897 to mail car No. 400. (Louis C. Mueller Collection)

panels. The legends "Druid Hill Avenue," "Druid Hill & Patterson Parks," and "Baltimore Traction Company" glistened in gilt lettering.

The interior shone with brightly varnished, contrasting woods, set off by red plush cushions covering the seats. A distinctive feature of the car was the gripman's section. Located at the left-hand side at the front of the car, it was about seven feet by three feet in area. (As there was an opening in the floor to permit operation of the grip lever, this arrangement was anything but warm in the colder weather. The hole in the floor and the open window in front resulted in conditions which have been described as not unlike working in a chimney, with the cold air whipping by.)

The first equipment consisted of twenty cars built at the shops of the Philadelphia Traction Company. A. D. Whitton, chief engineer for the Widener and Elkins cable companies, designed the cars, which contemporary accounts describe as being very similar (except for the grip mechanism) to those run in Philadelphia, Pittsburgh, and other cities under control of the Philadel-

phia syndicate. They were double trucked, with wheels twenty-two inches in diameter.

The speed of the car was necessarily determined by that of the rope or cable. The line was divided into three separate segments with rope speeds as follows: Druid Hill Park to downtown, 8 mph; the downtown section, 6 mph; and the eastern end from the Pratt Street power house to Patterson Park, a snappy 11 mph.

Progress on the construction of the line continued throughout the year. E. D. Smith and Son, the prime contractor, was a Philadelphia firm, again showing the Widener and Elkins influence at this stage of events.

Operations had been planned to begin on May 16, 1891; but, although a test car had run over the entire route two days prior to that date, a hitch in completing the engines in one of the power houses forced a postponement. One week later, on Saturday, May 23rd, regular service was inaugurated. The first car pulled out at 5 a.m. with no special ceremonies. The big day had dawned cloudy, with a bit of rain in the air. Despite the weather, many people had stayed up all night, and the early morning gloom saw them lining the

curbs, eagerly awaiting the sight of a car moving along with no visible means of propulsion.

It seemed that everyone wanted to ride. According to the *American* of May 25th, "Every car was packed to overflowing, from the start of the first car until they stopped at night. It was not possible to carry all the people who wanted to ride." No accurate count of the first day's patronage was possible for twenty-four hours. The personnel at the office could not count the nickels fast enough. When things calmed down a bit, General Manager William House reported that sixty thousand fares were turned in on the big day.

There was an interesting sidelight in connection with the Fort Avenue line of horse cars. These were drawn by the cable cars as trailers to the intersection of Lombard and South, at which point they were disconnected and hitched to horses for the remainder of the trip to Fort McHenry.

That the cable line was a resounding success in attracting patronage was beyond question. Oden Bowie and his fellow directors at City Passenger must have given much thought to combating this, the most

Artist's conception of first Baltimore & Curtis Bay car built by Lewis & Fowler in 1892. One wonders about apparent lack of a controller on the platform and unusual trolley pole base. (George F. Nixon Collection)

serious threat to their company's dominance of over thirty years duration. The new operation practically paralleled their White line, on which patronage dropped alarmingly. But the Traction Company was just beginning the challenge. On November 1st, the *Herald* announced that the Epworth Independent Methodist Church structure had been purchased for the site of the power house for a second route, the Gilmor Street line. Unlike City Passenger, which could not seem to decide which way to move in the matter of propulsion, the Traction Company acted quickly, but always with an eye toward the rapid progress which was taking place in the transportation field.

A subtle hint of an impending change was discernible in Baltimore Traction's

decision to merely convert an old church building to the needs of the power house, rather than construct an elaborate new structure, as had been done for the original line. Trackwork was still substantial, though, with the slot rails weighing sixty-five pounds to the yard, and the track rails seventy-eight pounds. The cars were very similar to the equipage on the Druid Hill Avenue line, except that the colors were Tuscan red with silver striping. The line commenced operations August 30, 1892; but, as early as March 3rd of the following year, an ordinance was introduced to authorize the Traction Company to dispense with cable propulsion and substitute electric motors with a trolley system. The ordinance was not adopted, yet it tends to show what was in the offing.

City Passenger finally made a commitment to convert three lines to cable: the White Line (Madison Avenue to Patterson Park), the Red Line (West Baltimore and Gay Streets), and the Blue Line (Calvert and Charles Streets). After this decision, two years were needed before the new system was ready for service. Hence, even while the old company was putting in its conduits, the fast changing traction picture had placed it in the position of building power installations which were obsolete before they were even completed.

Surprisingly, however, it was not Baltimore Traction or Baltimore City Passenger but the Central Railway which was to be the pioneer in overhead electric operation in the built-up area of the city.

Baltimore City Passenger Railway cable car sits over an inspection pit in a car house — probably Smallwood Street. Fire buckets on posts emphasize constant hazard from fire posed by the storing of wooden cars in wooden buildings. (Louis C. Mueller Collection)

NOTES AND COMMENTS:

A clipping from an 1889 issue of an unidentified Baltimore newspaper, which is preserved in the United Railways and Electric Company scrapbook, estimated that the cost of equipping a ten-mile line for electric cars would be $462,000; a cable line of similar length would cost $803,000 according to the same source. Annual operating expenses were estimated as: electric, $51,891; cable, $101,210.

The North Avenue Electric Railway is described in the *Sun,* May 16, 1890, and *Baltimore County Union,* May 24, 1890. Some idea of the unfamiliarity of the average person with the new mode of transportation fairly seeps from each sen-

tence of the following description of the first car, printed in the *Maryland Journal* (Towson), May 19, 1890. "On the top of each car is a pole, attached to it by flexible springs, tending always to the vehicle, and on the end of the pole a pair of trolley wheels constantly pressed against the electric conductor. The wheels [*sic*] move with the car, contact is made perfect, and thus the electrical fluid conveyed to the motive power of the car. The essential difference between a car of this type and an ordinary horse car is in the trucks, for here the entire machinery is located in a small, compact space entirely hidden from sight beneath the floor. The current from the trolleys pass into two dynamos of 15 horse-

power each, located near the axles, to which the motive power is conveyed by gearing." The reference to a pair of wheels may represent the mistaken idea that both poles were to be raised simultaneously. The reporter also mentions that "the cars operated on the Sprague system" and noted that an overhead wire had been used by the cars at Bay Ridge (a beach south of Annapolis) the previous summer.

The formation of the Baltimore Traction Company was spelled out in detail by the *Sun,* June 21, 1889, and *American,* June 25, 1889.

It was my good fortune to be able to discuss many of the aspects of the cable era in Baltimore with George Hilton while

The area immediately to the south of Druid Hill Park became the center of street railway facilities. City Passenger, Citizens', the Traction Company, Central, and United Railways all had car houses or stables within three blocks of Druid Hill and Fulton. Today, this Traction Street sign is passed by thousands of motorists who do not know that the city once had cable-operated cars. (Michael R. Farrell)

The Baltimore Traction Company's power house presented an ornate frontage to Druid Hill Avenue, but a view of the structure from Retreat Street reveals a plainer face. From this angle it seems more utilitarian in appearance than ornamental. (Michael R. Farrell)

Horse car of Baltimore City Passenger Railway halts in front of Lexington Market, at Eutaw and Lexington, early one Sunday afternoon in 1893. This company had just converted some lines to cable as evidenced by slot between tracks. The Yellow Line, which at this point in time extended from Madison Avenue to Orleans Street, still used animal power. (The Peale Museum)

he was in the process of preparing his monumental work, *The Cable Car In America*. A detailed description of the Baltimore cable operations is given in pp. 457-462 of Hilton's book.

One unresolved question is, why did City Passenger decide to put in a cable system rather than one using electricity as the motive power? My recollection of conversations with Professor Hilton is that he was pretty well convinced that after studying the Boston installation Bowie decided on the cable system. Later evidence appears to have weakened this conclusion, and even John Thomsen, who has gone to great lengths to unravel this particular puzzle, cannot come up with a definite answer.

Thomsen tends to agree with my opinion that political rather than technical factors determined the decision to go with cable. After the die was cast, Bowie was quoted in the *Sun*, August 24, 1892, "... (my) first inclination to use the trolley system was at the suggestion of Mayor Latrobe, prior to the decision of the directors of the company upon the rapid transit system to be placed on any of their lines. Application was made to the City Council for the right to use the trolley system, but the ordinance was never reported out and the company decided to use the cable system. ..."

The description of the power house and car sheds adjoining is from the *Sun*, March 18, 1890; of the first service, *American*,

May 25, 1891. The cable cars were such a sensation that a barkeeper of a prominent club brought out a "cable cocktail." It was reported as being immensely popular. *News,* May 25, 1891.

The *Sun,* August 24, 1892, gave good coverage to the Gilmor Street cable line. While the technical data reported in the *Sun* is undoubtedly reasonably accurate, the *Maryland Journal* (Towson), June 6, 1891, took that paper to task for lauding Baltimore Traction's cable lines, while alleging that the trolley wire was dangerous. The *Journal* cited experience in Boston, Chicago, and Washington in asserting that "the 'danger' is more imaginative than anything else. ..."

SHOWERS OF ELECTRIC SPARKS

Not all Baltimoreans were enraptured by streetcars when they first began to run through the more central parts of town, but the following quote from a letter sent to Mayor Latrobe by Mr. John Henry Keene, Jr., who lived at Preston and St. Paul Streets, was fortunately not a typical reaction:

"This nuisance is not a mere visionary picture, it is a stern reality — a flesh and blood fact with color in its cheeks. It is a system of rapid transit by hissing monsters, often hurled at frightful rates of speed, thumping and bumping at every step. They ascend and descend every grade with Babylonish howls. The air rings with the shrieks of their gongs, and by day and by night, a flesh-creeping, saw-mill buzz, with showers of electric sparks, make their struggling, groaning course through the higways of a densely populated city."

Mr. Keene's consternation was a result of the construction of Central's Railway's electric line, which began operating on September 22, 1892. Though the North Avenue Railway, the Pimlico & Pikesville, and, probably, the Baltimore & Curtis Bay had previously run within the city limits, all of these operations were on the fringes. Central did not enter the downtown area, yet its operation bisected the city from east to west and traversed almost the entire length of Caroline Street on its north-south axis.

Actually, the first cars of the Central Railway were probably guilty of most of the faults that Keene attributed to them. The company promised to make adjustments which would eliminate most of the howling and sparking. The frightful speed was undoubtedly exaggerated; by law the cars were limited to 10 mph. Evidence indicates that this was often exceeded on the outskirts of town; but it is unlikely that the early electric cars often went more than five miles over the limit inside the city, for they could not accelerate rapidly.

The Central had been running horse cars for about nine years when it was reorganized under George Blakistone in 1892 and gained permission to run electric cars. Construction was begun about May 15th, with J. D. Murray handling the trackwork and J. G. White putting up the overhead. Both were New York concerns. Twenty cars were ordered from John Stephenson, each being equipped with two 25-horsepower Thomson Houston motors, with generators and overhead equipment by the same manufacturer. Trucks came from McGuire.

The cars ran on eighty-pound steel girder rails. They were sixteen feet between bulkheads, double-ended, and finished in a deep orange. The seats held twenty-four persons, but the company listed the cars' capacity as ninety. They were manned by a conductor and motorman, clad in neat blue uniforms and caps. The fare was five cents. For their nickels, patrons could expect to make the round trip over the 12½ mile route in 70 minutes. This contrasts with the 128 minutes taken by horse-drawn vehicles. Unlike the cable lines, no trailers were to be hauled, though they were used later on. The old stables on the south side of Preston Street, between Greenmount Avenue and Jones Falls, were enlarged to meet the requirements of the new operation, and a power house was built on the same site.

At the same time that Central Railway was reconstructing its horse car line, plans were evolving to bring the pioneer electric line of the North Avenue Railway Company from the northern reaches of town into the business district. On August 18, 1891, according to the *Baltimore County Union*, the Roland Avenue Electric Company of Baltimore City was incorporated and asked for permission to lay double tracks on Roland Avenue. This company soon disappeared from the records, but most of its incorporators, along with James L. McLane of the Baltimore Traction Company, reappeared as organizers of the Lake Roland Elevated Railway Company. The new company was the result of the merger of the North Avenue Railway and the Baltimore, Hampden & Lake Roland, the latter being a paper entity holding a franchise granted in 1872.

The word "elevated" in the corporate title is somewhat misleading. Only a relatively small portion of the line was planned to be above ground, and that for a special reason. By 1892, almost all of the north-south streets leading into the business sector were already being used by other street railway companies. The logical remaining thoroughfare was North Street (now Guilford Avenue), on which ran the tracks of the Northern Central Railway, connecting its Calvert Station with various yards, sidings, and the railroad's main line to Union Station.

The Lake Roland adopted the previous plan of the North Avenue Railway to leapfrog this stretch with an elevated structure. Originally planned to extend from Chase Street almost to Fayette Street, it was slightly shortened so as to avoid "crossing above grade between the City Hall and the Post Office." This adjustment brought it to street level just north of Lexington Street, and a short spur westward on that street to Charles Street was proposed "to meet the convenience of ladies coming downtown to shop."

There were legal difficulties, both over building the elevated structure and over running a double track up Lexington Street; but a contract for the elevated structure (invariably referred to locally as the trestle, or viaduct) was awarded to the Pennsylvania Steel Company toward the end of June 1892. By December 1st, things had progressed to the point where masonry piers were in place, and work was commencing on the elevated structure itself. At the same time, the power house on Falls Road, at Stony Run, was nearing completion, and about forty cars were stored in the company's shed near Walbrook. These

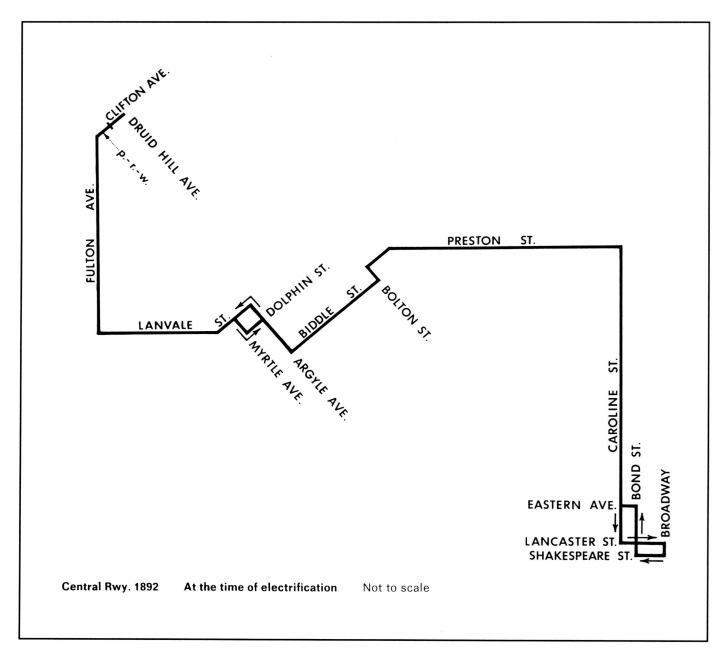

Central Rwy. 1892   At the time of electrification   Not to scale

cars, the American stated, "were undoubtedly the most expensive, largest, and heaviest cars used on any street railway in this city." (They were double-truck Pullman-built cars, bought secondhand from Pittsburgh and among the very few secondhand cars ever purchased locally.)

By early May, workmen were putting the finishing touches on the railway. The elevated proved to be four thousand feet long, double-tracked its entire length, with the trolley wire suspended from poles in the center of the structure. In addition, there was a double-tracked viaduct of about four hundred feet over the tracks of the Bal-

timore & Lehigh Railroad near the power house in the Stony Run valley. (This portion of the route is now Sisson Street and the trestle was replaced by a fill. The Baltimore & Lehigh became the Maryland & Pennsylvania, and was abandoned in 1958.) As originally built, the steelwork of the main elevated structure followed the contour of the land, resulting in a series of dips and rises. In addition, the southbound tracks made sharp curves at the Madison and Centre Street stations.

On May 3, 1893, the first trial run took place, a car leaving North Avenue at 5 p.m. This trip marked the first time in America

that a car had been operated on an elevated line with electric power. (The New York and Sioux City elevateds still used steam dummies.) Several days later, the cars began to run through to Roland Park and Walbrook. Baltimore's "ride in the sky" proved immediately popular.

A little more than a week prior to the running of the first Lake Roland Elevated car, an event had taken place which should have convinced all doubters that electrification was to be the final answer to the question of what mode of "rapid transit" would prevail. At twenty-eight minutes before one o'clock on the afternoon of

Lake Roland Elevated Railway No. 26 was built by Pullman, obtained secondhand from the Duquesne Railway of Pittsburgh. Rather flimsy construction of downtown elevated structure in 1893 was strengthened in 1898 and 1910. (George F. Nixon Collection)

April 27th, the first electric car of the York Road line of the Baltimore Union Passenger Railway reached the center of Towson, thus inaugurating regular thirty-minute service between that point and City Hall in Baltimore.

This event had been presaged on June 1, 1891, when the Baltimore and Yorktown Turnpike Company had conveyed their horse car line to Union Passenger for $75,000. The new owners immediately promised to bring rapid transit to the county seat, but Towsontown waited and fretted for over a year until construction began in the fall of 1892. For a number of years the *Baltimore County Union*, a Towson paper, had campaigned for faster service, plug-

ging, at various stages, battery cars, electric cars, and even the Roberts compressed air car.

By late 1892, Nelson Perin, having conserved his funds while Baltimore Traction and Baltimore City Passenger Railway squandered huge sums on cable lines, had made up his mind. He had consolidated all of his lines, including Baltimore Union Passenger, into a heavily capitalized new corporation, the City & Suburban Railway. When construction commenced on the first of his overhead electric lines, Perin was the toast of York Road; as the winter progressed into spring, adulation turned to invective. York Road was a series of hills, and in order to secure less severe grades, the company decided to reconstruct the entire

line. As the railway actually was controlled by the turnpike company, there was no problem with franchise technicalities. But owners of abutting properties, to say nothing of the county authorities, were considerably upset by the effect on adjacent land and roadways. Particularly during the spring, when inclement weather made the roadway one vast mudhole, did tempers flare.

From an operating standpoint, there were some interesting developments. For a month or so, during the worst period of mud, a steam motor pulled a horse car between Govanstown and Towson. For most of the period, though, a stagecoach served as a connection between the two

Another early view of the elevated shows two cars of the Lake Roland Elevated Railway going in opposite directions. Note the extensive railyards of the Northern Central below, which created the need for the span. (BSM Collection)

suburbs. The electric cars commenced operation on the lower end of the line during the first week of March 1893. Double tracks had been laid as far north as Rodgers Forge, though only one was in use. The first of the new cars to reach Towson arrived on April 2nd, though none ran over the new loop past the Court House for another three weeks.

An event which had taken place the day previous was to be repeated under slightly different circumstances almost seventy-one years later, when the streetcars were replaced by buses. According to the *Baltimore County Union* of April 8, 1893, "The 'Deadwood Stage' that had been running for some months on the York Road made

its final trip on April 1st, the electric cars taking its place the next day. The old stage was gaily decorated for the occasion, and bore on its side this legend: 'Last day of the Deadwood Stage'."

Sic transit gloria mundi!

NOTES AND COMMENTS:

A. T. Clark's notes give September 17, 1892 as the first day of operation of the Central's electric cars; but the *Sun*, September 21, 1892, says that, though experimental trips had been made previously, "The company plans to begin operating (revenue service) tomorrow."

That not everyone shared John Henry Keane, Jr.'s dislike for the electric cars is evident by a paragraph from Frey's *Reminiscences Of Baltimore*, published in 1893. "The effect (of the electric cars) was startling, even to those who know what an excursion-loving people the Baltimoreans are. They thronged the conveyances, men, women and children by the thousand,

crowding the cars. Ten days later, the same line carried a Sunday crowd numbering at least eighteen thousand people."

"Speed on all rapid transit lines in the city is regulated by law. By section 2 of ordinance 19, approved March 2, 1892, the electric cars of the Central line may not run faster than ten miles per hour exclusive of stops." *Sun*, May 6, 1893.

Frey's book, previously cited, gives ninety minutes as the time consumed in a round trip.

According to L. C. Mueller's notes, the first cars operated on the portion of the Lake Roland Elevated Railway between North Avenue and Roland Park on April

23, 1893. The first trip (a trial run) over the elevated structure itself was, as noted, made on May 3rd. *Sun*, May 5, 1893.

Chicago's claim to the first electric elevated railway is discounted due to the fact that its "Inter Mural Railway" seems to have operated entirely within the World's Fair grounds and did not offer transportation to the general public. *Baltimore Sun Almanac*, 1896.

The little-known Sioux City elevated line was described in some detail by Leonard V. Tripp in the February 1966 issue of *Traction & Models*.

Lake Roland Elevated Railway No. 26 on Stony Run trestle, near the present 28th Street. The ravine was later filled in to become the bed of Sisson Street. These strange looking double-truck cars were changed to single truck by United Railways. (George F. Nixon Collection)

To serve their newly-built lines in northeast Baltimore, Central Railway purchased twenty of these eighteen-foot cars in December 1896. (George F. Nixon Collection)

Additional information on the Guilford Avenue elevated is given in the subsequent chapter entitled "The Trestle."

Sources for the story of the purchase of the York Road line by the Baltimore Union Passenger Railway (which, on June 17, 1890, reduced the fare from Towson to Baltimore from twenty-five to ten cents) and its reconstruction as an electric line (using the Thomson-Houston system) include the *Baltimore County Union*, May 24 and June 21, 1890; September 10, 1892; February 12, March 11, and April 29, 1893; *American,* March 14, 1893.

By 1891, when the Baltimore City Passenger Railway petitioned for permission to run electric cars on Baltimore and North Charles Streets, the city authorities were making progress in having overhead utility wires run underground. It is no wonder then that Oden Bowie had to go to court to win permission to put up more wires, even though this act was authorized by the company's charter. (Baltimore Gas and Electric Company)

AFTER YEARS OF CHANGE, A LULL

The two short years spanning the period from late April of 1893 to March of 1895 marked a time of great changes in the Baltimore street railway transportation system, both in method of operation and management.

As previously mentioned, both the Lake Roland Elevated and City & Suburban's York Road line had begun electric operation in the spring of 1893. In rapid succession, the Carey Street (May 15th), Fort Avenue (July 23rd), and the Linden Avenue (September 20th) lines of Baltimore Traction were converted to operation by the overhead trolley, with the upper end of the same company's Fremont Street (now Fremont Avenue) line following suit on November 23rd. Nelson Perin's City & Suburban began running electric cars on three more routes during a five-week period in the summer: on July 30th, Wilkens Avenue; August 9th, Highlandtown; and September 3rd, Maryland Avenue. Two new independent companies began operations with the new mode of propulsion: the Walbrook, Gwynn Oak & Powhatan on October 18th, and the Pikesville, Reisterstown & Emory Grove on December 20th.

The rapid swing to the electric system (Lake Roland Elevated, two lines; City & Suburban, four lines; Baltimore Traction, four lines; plus the two independents) in 1893 contrasts strangely with the opening of the first three City Passenger routes propelled by "rapid transit" that same year. The Blue Line (May 22nd), Red Line (July 23rd), and the White Line (August 20th) of the Bowie system began cable operations at a time when progressive companies all over the country were giving up on this expensive means of transporting patrons.

These three were among the very last cable lines to be constructed in the United States, but they did enable the old company temporarily to stem the flow of riders deserting to other companies. What effect the cost of building the expensive systems, which lasted only about five years, would have on future operations will be seen later on in the discussion of the financial troubles that plagued the United Railways during much of its lifetime.

But this, the ultimate consolidation, was several years in the future. Conversions slowed a bit during 1894, although Baltimore Traction electrified its Edmondson Avenue line (June 20th) and completed the conversion of the Fremont Street line (July 28th). City Passenger finally joined the trend by putting up wires and poles on three of its lines: Harford Avenue (the old Hall's Springs line), April 15th; the Green Line, May 13th; and the Orleans Street portion of the Yellow Line, June 15th.

There was one significant merger in 1895, involving Nelson Perin, the astute president of City & Suburban. Perin stood mutely on the sidelines while the daily papers bandied about the story that the Traction Company was about to take over the Lake Roland Elevated. The latter company had been in financial straits since the end of 1894. Stock held by out-of-town financial interests was in the hands of receivers, who were anxious to unload it. This was supposedly a cut and dried affair; Baltimore Traction would buy control of the Lake Roland, thus gaining two important lines, i.e., the branches to Walbrook and Roland Park, along with the elevated trunk into downtown Baltimore. Then suddenly, in early January 1895, City & Suburban moved in, purchased the stock, and obtained trackage that nicely comple-

mented its lines to both north and west Baltimore. Chalk one up for Perin!

Yet even his hour of victory could perhaps have served as a portent to Perin if he had possessed but a modicum of clairvoyance. This was a game at which two could play, and the drama which had just unfolded foreshadowed that of the coming big consolidation of 1899.

There were two other important incorporations during the brief period. One was the Baltimore & Loreley Electric Railway. Loreley is located at the point east of Baltimore where the Baltimore & Ohio Railroad crosses the Big Gunpowder Falls. Originally planned as part of a scheme to harness the Gunpowder River as a source of electric power for the city, it was later rechristened the Baltimore, Gardenville & Belair Electric Railway in 1896, when it became a part of the plan of George Blakistone and his Central Railway to become a dominant factor in the local transportation picture.

Seemingly less significant at the time was the introduction of a bill into the legislature for incorporation of the Falls Road Railway in February 1894. For the moment, nothing came of this; yet, in the drama that was beginning to unfold, this, the first pang of the yet unborn Baltimore & Northern, could have been another portent. But alas, Nelson Perin, scion of an Ohio banking family, whose mother was known as the "Hetty Green of the West" for her financial wizardry, was apparently not clairvoyant. And, almost certainly, neither he nor anyone else saw any connection between the Falls Road Railway and the Pikesville, Reisterstown, & Emory Grove — that little line which George Webb was building out in the far northwest reaches.

Long body overhang, combined with short single-truck, of Lake Roland Elevated Railway No. 13, must have provided some bouncy, but interesting, rides over the Guilford Avenue elevated. This eight-bench car was built by Lewis & Fowler about 1893. (Louis C. Mueller Collection)

City and Suburban No. 294 is representative of the first electric cars on the York Road line. It is reported to have been built by Stephenson in 1895, and is very similiar to that builder's 1891 horse cars. The suspicion is that it is an older car refitted for operation by electricity about 1893. (Louis C. Mueller Collection)

After five hectic years of the conversion of horse car lines to either cable or electric operation, the year 1895 saw a lull, with only one line changed over. The reason for this was quite simple. Except for a few branches and unimportant outlying lines, there was not anything left to convert from animal power. Still, on March 3rd of that year, an event took place which was to have

far-reaching effects. On that date, Baltimore Traction, to the surprise of no one, replaced the cable cars on its Gilmor Street line with electric streetcars. Only two and one half years after the installation of a cable system, with all its attendant expense, the Traction Company was writing it off as an expensive miscalculation. It was now clear to all that City Passenger had three

costly mistakes on its hands in its Red, Blue, and White lines, on all of which the rope had been installed not even two years previously.

On October 4, 1896, the Druid Hill Avenue line of Baltimore Traction was changed from cable to electricity. With the conversion of this, the first cable line in

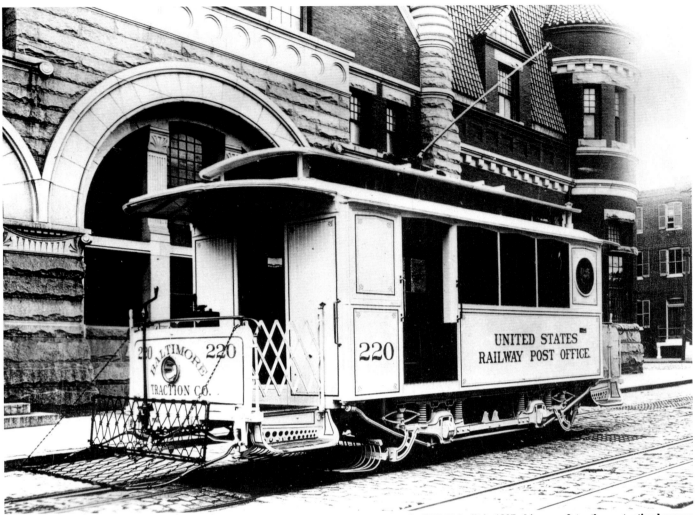

Traction Company mail car No. 220 was acquired from Lewis & Fowler as a passenger car in 1893. Rebuilt in 1897, this car refutes the contention by some that mail cars were not allowed to have a doorway giving access to the mail compartment from platform. The cable slot on Druid Hill Avenue was no longer necessary by the late 1890s. (George F. Nixon Collection)

Baltimore, the Traction Company was now an all-electric operation. Coming generations would pay dearly for the experiment. The power houses were converted to electric generating plants, the cable cars received electric motors, and the tracks could be used for the new equipment. Still, none of these makeshifts were really efficient, and the open cable slots especially caused endless annoyance until the last of them was removed early in the twentieth century.

The year 1896 saw the entry of two new companies into the field. They provide a study in contrasts. One, the Falls Road Electric Railway, which had been incorporated two years previously, received scant attention, for certainly few foresaw the influence that it would have on

Baltimore's street railways. The other, the Shore Line Railway, was widely heralded as having tremendous potential, but turned out to be a magnificent disappointment. Unlike the Falls Road line, which forms a vital part of the coming saga of the Baltimore & Northern, the Shore Line story can be told in a few brief paragraphs.

It must represent one of the greatest miscalculations of potential patronage ever made locally. Built in the early summer of 1896, its almost 4½ miles of double track ran from a connection with Baltimore Traction near the present Bush and Ridgely Streets, through Westport (where an associated company owned land), and down Waterview Avenue (then called Fish House Road) to Shore Line Park, located on the

present grounds of the Harbor Hospital Center.

Baltimore Traction had a strong interest in the road and acquired it outright on July 1, 1897. Service had commenced on May 31st of the previous year; but Shore Line Park, which had been expected to eclipse the tremendously popular Riverview Park of rival City & Suburban, never lived up to expectations. Its clientele did not mix well with the patrons of other resorts along the Patapsco, and there was constant friction on the open cars. However, as the years went by, the line developed its own set of patrons and eventually showed a modest profit until industrial pollution and silting befouled the once beautiful Middle Branch of the Patapsco.

The trucks make the difference. Lewis & Fowler 1892 electric car towers over ex-horse car trailer, even though their bodies are approximately the same dimensions. (George F. Nixon Collection)

In United Railways livery, No. 1270, a former Baltimore Traction nine-bench car, waits for crew in front of the Madison Avenue car house. (Louis C. Mueller Collection)

Glyndon Viaduct.
3-12-08

There are no known photographs of the Pikesville, Reisterstown & Emory Grove, but this view of the company's bridge at Glyndon shows that, considering the times, construction was fairly substantial. No reports have survived to tell of the difficulties encountered in climbing the steep ramp from the Butler Road. This 1908 photo shows a United Railways car. (George F. Nixon/ LeRoy E. Gerding, Jr. Collection)

Cable trailer No. 220 sits on a transfer table at Brill prior to delivery to Baltimore City Passenger Railway in 1892. Unlike White and Red Line trailers, which had been transformed into grip cars, those of the Blue Line were converted to electric cars in 1897. (George F. Nixon Collection)

The Howard Park car house of the Walbrook, Gwynn Oak & Powhatan, as it appeared about 1925. Ironically, the flanking billboards advertise the Dodge Brothers autos and General tires. (Robert L. Krueger Collection)

NOTES AND COMMENTS:

Although the cable lines of City Passenger took no longer to construct than had Baltimore Traction's, the years of indecision about what mode of "rapid transit" would be used had hurt the company's image. "A man in a play at one of the theaters in Baltimore was supposed to have been asleep 25 years. The first question he asked on waking up was: 'Is Bowie's cable line finished yet?' The audience saw the point and applauded vigorously." *Baltimore County Union*, November 26, 1892.

Nelson Perin was born October 31, 1853 in Cincinnati. His father was a successful banker. His mother was said to be "gifted with business ability of a high order, and after the death of her husband, largely increased the value of the estate by careful and judicious investments." Perin became interested in the street railways of his native city in 1874. Three years later, he married Ella Keck, the daughter of the builder

of the Baltimore Union Passenger Railway. Becoming associated with the Union line in 1880, Perin, about 1888, moved to Baltimore. At the time of his death in 1904, he was a director of the Union Trust Company, Continental Trust Company, Mercantile Trust and Deposit Company, Maryland Telephone Company, and the Calvert Bank. Described as being of medium height, with a rather heavy though finely proportioned build, he often sported a derby and affected a mustache. Aside from his active business affairs, Perin was noted as a yachtsman and social leader. Of Ella Perin it was said, "Her entertainments are marvels of refined and novel effects, and it is due to her brilliant mind that many new forms of entertainment have been evolved in the society of Baltimore since she has been in the foremost ranks of entertainers." *Baltimore Its History And People,* C. C. Hall, editor; *American,* January 13, 1895.

By Laws of Maryland, 1896, ch. 248, the name of the Baltimore & Loreley was changed to the Baltimore, Gardenville & Belair Electric Railway. By indenture dated December 10, 1896, between Simon J. Martenet and the Baltimore, Gardenville & Belair, the railway company received trackage rights on the Baltimore and Jerusalem Turnpike (Belair Road). A. T. Clark notes.

According to A. T. Clark notes, "The South Baltimore Company, which was the owner of a large tract of land in Westport, petitioned the County Commissioners of Baltimore County and received their approval, September 23, 1895 to put down a double track railway. Certificate of incorporation dated January 23, 1896, recorded Lib. 2, vol. 121, in the office of the Secretary of State at Annapolis, Maryland." Further details on the Shore Line Railway are found under the chapter, "Of Parks and Parties."

AND THEN THERE WERE THREE

Although there were still a few tributary lines which managed to sustain an independent or quasi-independent existence, the period from June 1897 to January 1898 saw the consolidation of all the important operations in Baltimore into three major companies.

Nelson Perin benefited by the first move. On June 7, 1897, Baltimore Traction and City & Suburban were merged into one corporation known as the Baltimore Consolidated Railway Company. Capital stock was in the amount of $10 million. Traction Company shares were exchanged at a valuation of 84 percent of par while City & Suburban stock was accepted at full par value, $50 a share. The trackage of the new system totaled 191 miles. It was planned to take advantage of Perin's consummate skill in building up his company by using primarily the City & Suburban cars for the operation. Besides the sale of surplus cars, other advantages of the combination would materially reduce the administrative overhead and eliminate the expense of purchasing power (from the Baltimore & Ohio), which had been a practice of the Traction Company.

Out of local pride, one might regard an item in the *Philadelphia Stockholder*, January 2, 1895, saying pre-rapid-transit Baltimore equipment "bordered on the grotesque," as an exaggeration. One might, that is, until seeing this photo of Baltimore Traction No. 291, taken August 9, 1893. The lettering reads "Druid Hill Park and Fort McHenry," but car is probably operating on the Ridgely Street line. Almost certainly, it had once belonged to People's Railway. (Library of Congress)

Separate operation of the individual lines ceased June 30th, and soon afterward an old Baltimore tradition began to fade. From the earliest times, cars of the various routes had been painted in different colors. The Consolidated planned to redo all of its cars in the same hue, a Tuscan red. Destination signs were provided; but, without route numbers to aid in telling on which line a car was operating, consternation was registered by the man in the street. With the number of identical red cars increasing, the *American* of October 20, 1898 published this mournful piece of doggerel:

"All cars look alike to me!
York road or Waverly!
Jumped on a car, thought I was right —
Never got home, till late last night!
All cars look alike to me!"

It might be expected that any combination containing such forceful personalities as Nelson Perin and T. Edward Hambleton could not function without friction. Surely enough, the first annual meeting of the Consolidated Railway, scheduled for January 1898, promised to be a lively affair. There was no doubt that Perin and his associates, especially the Jenkins family, dominated the new company. It was reported that Hambleton was to be "retired" from the directorate of Consolidated. Seeing the weakness of his position, Hambleton severed his connections; but a few years later, he reappeared on the streetcar scene with Maryland Electric Railways. However, much was to change in the interim.

Oden Bowie had died in December 1894, and, under Walter C. Franklin, the Baltimore City Passenger Railway Company began moving to extend its influence outside of the city proper. On the first day of September 1897, the pioneer company acquired the bonds of the Baltimore, Middle River & Sparrows Point Railway, which had built about 8½ miles of track from Highlandtown out Eastern Avenue to Middle River. City Passenger did not buy the stock of the company, which remained nominally independent. While Baltimore City Passenger Railway had no physical connection with the Baltimore, Middle River & Sparrows Point, the purchase of the bonds (which were secured by a mortgage on the property) prevented the Consolidated, which did have a connection at Highlandtown, from acquiring the line. City Passenger's purchase of the Central Railway in 1898 allowed through service

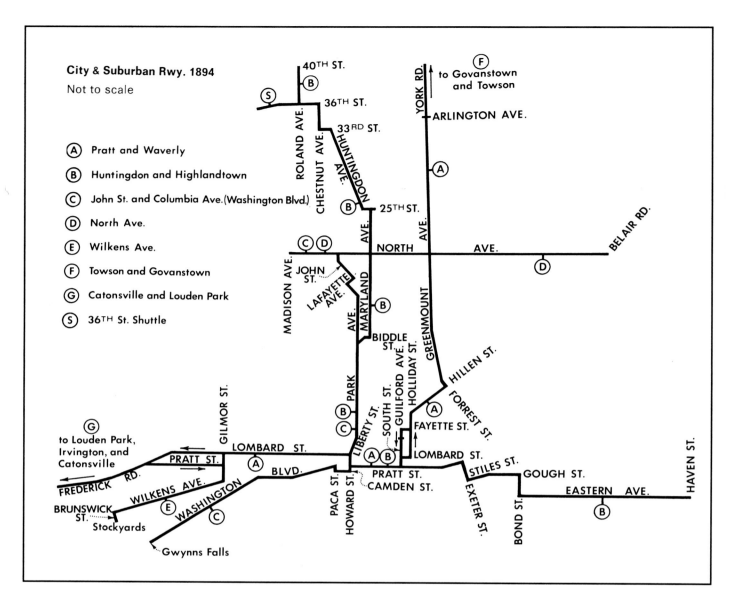

City & Suburban Rwy. 1894
Not to scale

(A) Pratt and Waverly

(B) Huntingdon and Highlandtown

(C) John St. and Columbia Ave.(Washington Blvd.)

(D) North Ave.

(E) Wilkens Ave.

(F) Towson and Govanstown

(G) Catonsville and Louden Park

(S) 36TH St. Shuttle

by way of the latter's Fairmount Avenue trackage, which began on September 17, 1898. A planned junction with City Passenger's Green Line was not effected, but the acquisition did provide the basis for the United Railways trackage on Highland Avenue from Eastern Avenue to Toone Street.

A more far-reaching event was City Passenger's absorption of the Central Railway in January 1898. Formal transfer of Central Railway stock to Baltimore City Passenger Railway took place February 14, 1898; the purchase included the Baltimore, Gardenville & Belair Electric Railway, which was the Belair Road extension of Central Railway, as well as the Baltimore & Jerusalem Turnpike Company (the present Belair Road from North Avenue to the Harford County boundary).

The Central Railway, built as a horse car line in the early 1880s, had been revitalized under George Blakistone in 1892. Since that time, the original line from Fulton Avenue to the Broadway ferry had been electrified, and important branches constructed eastward out Fairmount Avenue, and northward on the Belair Road as far as Gardenville. Central had two barns (on Preston near Jones Falls and at Preston and Potomac), as well as a power plant at the former location. It also owned a structure at the Druid Hill Avenue (between Fulton Avenue and Retreat Street) end of its original line. Both this and its Jones Falls barn were used at this point in time mostly for storage and repairs. This was not an incidental acquisition; City Passenger paid $600,000 for the property, double the par value of the stock.

One additional move in this sequence was a less complicated one. On October 21, 1897, the Baltimore & Northern Electric Railway merged with the Falls Road Electric Railway. This took place a mere three days after operations had begun over the affiliated lines and actually represented only a combination of mutual interests. The capital stock of the new corporation (which retained the corporate title Baltimore & Northern) was $1 million. The new company issued one share of new stock for each share of the Falls Road Company and one share for each five of the original Baltimore & Northern. Also under the control of the new management was the Pikesville, Reisterstown & Emory Grove.

So, in the dreary days of late winter 1897-98, the dozens of companies, which

UNION STATION

710 E. Baltimore Street.

In this photo the site of the present Pennsylvania Station is occupied by a station built in 1885 as a replacement for the original structure built in 1873. Blue Line horse cars were within three years of being replaced by cable cars. The vehicle furthest down ramp is a U. S. Mail wagon. (George F. Nixon Collection)

The combining of Baltimore Traction and City & Suburban into the Consolidated Railway in 1897 made possible a continuous routing across North Avenue from Walbrook to Gay Street. Some cars turned off at Washington Street. No. 409, shown at Druid Hill Avenue car house, is an 1897 Brownell "accelerator." (Louis C. Mueller Collection)

had been formed over a half century to transport the citizens of Baltimore, had been narrowed down to a triumvirate vying for control of the 350-odd miles of trackage. Popular opinion favored competition as a good thing, but recognized that the companies would not be content until

one could enjoy the fruits of monopoly. City Passenger was still a very viable operation. Nelson Perin was in control of Consolidated and the chief suitor for the pioneer company; yet his well-laid plans were in danger of going awry on the very eve of their culmination, due to the

tempestuous antics of the upstart Baltimore & Northern. As the days waxed into spring, then summer, and waned with the coming of autumn, all Baltimore knew that City Passenger's corporate existence was to be short-lived; but who would claim the prize?

Retreat Street car house, shown about 1925, was typical of wooden car barns. A small portion of the structure is incorporated in today's MTA facility. (Robert L. Krueger Collection)

This City & Suburban Railway postal car was built for passenger service by Lewis & Fowler in 1893, and rebuilt for mail service in 1897. Comparison with Baltimore Traction postal car in preceding chapter shows that the Traction Company's car, built by the same company in the same year, received much more extensive modifications. (Louis C. Mueller Collection)

NOTES AND COMMENTS:

Details of the merger between Baltimore Traction and City & Suburban can be found in the *News,* May 10, 1897, and *American,* June 8, 1897.

Background for Perin-Hambleton affair — *News,* January 19, 1899.

Various newspapers of September 2, 1897 and December 16, 1898 cover the Baltimore, Middle River & Sparrows Point purchase.

Details of Central Railway Acquisition in the *Sun,* February 15, 1898; L. C. Mueller notes; and *Herald,* January 16, 1898.

The genesis of the Baltimore & Northern was quite complicated. According to a list compiled by Charles Pielart for the *Baltimore City Code,* 1906, the B & N had absorbed the Electric Light & Railway Company, Falls Road Electric Railway, and Maryland Traction Company. The Pikesville, Reisterstown & Emory Grove had acquired, along the way, the Baltimore & Pikesville Railroad Company, Pikesville & Reisterstown Turnpike Company, and Baltimore & Reisterstown Turnpike Company.

The very last horse car in the Baltimore area sits in front of Lorraine Cemetery gate about 1902. (Enoch Pratt Library)

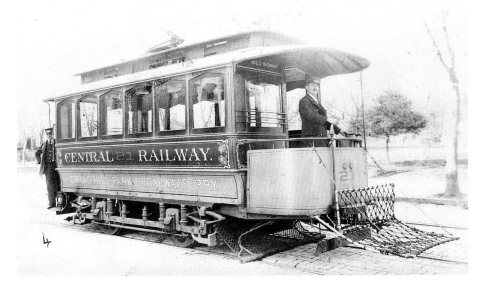

Central Railway electric car, built by Brill in 1893, was provided with a "lifeguard," invented by George Blakistone and very similair to those still being used on PCC cars when service ended in 1963. The "lifeguard," just ahead of the truck, is in tripped position here. (Louis C. Mueller Collection)

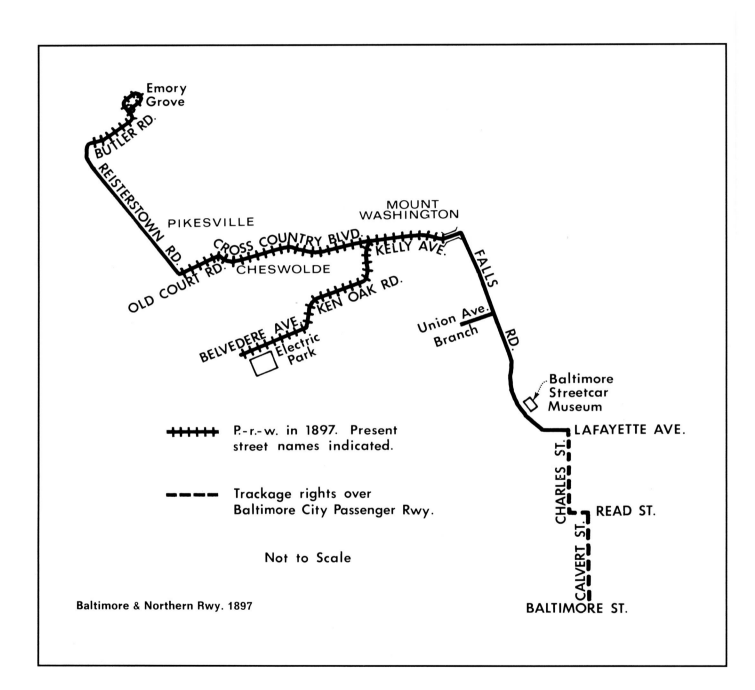

Emory
Grove

BUTLER RD.

REISTERSTOWN RD.

PIKESVILLE

MOUNT
WASHINGTON

CROSS COUNTRY BLVD.

KELLY AVE.

OLD COURT RD.

CHESWOLDE

FALLS RD.

KEN OAK RD.

BELVEDERE AVE.

Union Ave.
Branch

Electric
Park

Baltimore
Streetcar
Museum

LAFAYETTE AVE.

CHARLES ST.

READ ST.

CALVERT ST.

BALTIMORE ST.

+++++++ P.-r.-w. in 1897. Present
street names indicated.

— — — — Trackage rights over
Baltimore City Passenger Rwy.

Not to Scale

Baltimore & Northern Rwy. 1897

FROM OUT OF THE NORTH

"George Webb is well known as a promoter," stated an advertisement inserted in the *Herald* during 1898 by one who was less than enchanted with one of Webb's projects. His talent in this not ignoble field was displayed on many occasions, but Webb's most spectacular promotion was in helping to parlay an insignificant suburban line into the prime mover for the consolidation of all the Baltimore streetcar companies.

Like William House, Webb started at the bottom. In his case, this meant the offices of one of the steam railroads, the Baltimore & Ohio. He then moved to the Western Maryland, where he soon advanced to a responsible position in connection with the sale of land in the northwest suburb of Arlington. This suburb was being boomed, not only by the railroad but also by the expanding trolley lines, and it is reported that Webb had had something to do with Baltimore Traction's acquisition of the Pimlico & Pikesville.

All during the 1890s (and into the early years of the twentieth century), there was talk of connecting the expanding interurban system of south central Pennsylvania with Baltimore. Then, as now, the Reisterstown Road takes off through the hills and valleys of Baltimore County toward the Pennsylvania border, in the general direction of Hanover and Gettysburg. Actually, the Pennsylvania companies never got any further south than Hanover, quite a few miles to the north. Yet, these plans undoubtedly figured in the thoughts of the builders of the little trolley line, called after the towns which it served, the Pikesville, Reisterstown & Emory Grove. While awaiting its role in bigger things, the PR & EG served as a feeder to the Traction Company, with which it connected at Pikesville.

The records show that it was rather well constructed, indicating an eye toward larger things. Single tracked, with passing sidings, it followed a straight, albeit hilly,

path alongside the turnpike as far north as Reisterstown. There it bent northeastward along Dover (now Butler) Road, passing over the Western Maryland tracks, just before terminating a short distance beyond at the Methodist camp meeting ground known as Emory Grove.

Henry Parr, who had been a director of Baltimore Traction, was president of the line, while Webb served as general manager. They made a good team, but it was the latter whose name was most often in the papers, hence better known to the general public. As the prospects of the Pennsylvania to Baltimore interurban ebbed and rose, then ebbed again with no tangible results, the Pikesville, Reisterstown & Emory Grove turned to more realistic plans.

Demonstrating a knack for making the right decision (which was to be the keynote of their traction operations), the Parr-Webb combine had constructed their line as "wide gauge" (5 feet 4½ inches). Thus they were in a position to run their cars on any of the Baltimore systems. Talks were begun with the idea of taking the Emory Grove cars straight through to downtown Baltimore via the Traction Company's trackage. Baltimore Traction's annual reports acknowledge that the larger company gave serious consideration to this plan. For some reason, though, the arrangement fell through, but not before the PR & EG had purchased some large, interurbanlike coaches to supplement their small open cars.

So, here was the Emory Grove with the classiest and fastest cars in Baltimore, and no proper place to run them or passengers to fill them. Emory Grove camp ground offered good summer business, but the roundabout BT and PR & EG routing was in no position to compete with the Western Maryland, which offered less frequent, but far faster, steam car service to this section of Baltimore County. Parr and Webb quickly moved to find a solution. The sources of patronage lay closer to Baltimore, so they

decided to find a way of their own into town from out of the north. Piece by piece, their plans appeared in the Baltimore newspapers. They were shrewd enough to divulge only what was necessary, so for a while it looked as if they were in over their heads. All of their plans seemed to leave them at a disadvantage with Baltimore Traction and/or City & Suburban. Yet Mr. House and Mr. Perin were soon to learn that they had been "taken."

The big problem was to find a way into town. First, a new company, the Falls Road Railway, had been formed to build a line northward, from Lafayette Avenue out Falls Road. At Mt. Washington, it would swing west across country to Electric Park, where it would be able to connect with the Baltimore Traction Company's tracks. At its southern end, it would run a block along Lafayette Avenue to Maryland Avenue, where, presumably, it would feed the City & Suburban line into town. This was in May 1896. Quite possibly feeling that, at its worst, the new company would act as a feeder, the larger companies offered little protest to the franchise.

This prize safely in hand, Webb and Parr blithely acquired additional private right of way beyond Mt. Washington. At Arlington Junction, a branch split off from the Electric Park line to connect with their Pikesville, Reisterstown & Emory Grove Railway. City & Suburban's Perin was concerned enough by now to try to work out an agreement whereby passengers would transfer to his line for the trip south at Falls Road and 3rd (now 36th) Street. This offer was declined by the new company, which at about this time changed its name to the Baltimore & Northern Railway.

Still, Parr and Webb seemed to have reached an impasse. True, they now had a connected route of their own from Emory Grove to Maryland and Lafayette Avenues. Along the way, they had even, perhaps surprisingly, reached an amicable agreement with the Northern Central Railway

Baltimore & Northern's Falls Road car house in the late 1890s. Sitting in the doorway is B & N No. 24, purchased by the Pikesville, Reisterstown & Emory Grove from Laclede in 1896. This combine was later converted to parlor car *Chesapeake*. (Robert W. Janssen Collection)

with respect to building an overpass across the steam road's tracks at Mt. Washington. Still, they were about two miles north of the center of the city and on the far side of the Northern Central and Pennsylvania yards (which it was impractical to leapfrog with a bridge), and all possible city streets seemed to have been preempted by other streetcar companies.

The solution, when announced, was remarkably simple. The Baltimore & Northern applied for a track extension of an additional block along Lafayette, to Charles. City Passenger had its Blue Line tracks on Charles, and the B & N would use them to get to the very heart of downtown Baltimore. Simple, but nevertheless startling. Conservative, aloof City Passenger aligning itself with this brash new upstart! Oden Bowie was dead, and the new president had no compunction about doing a little horse trading.

Actual operation of the Baltimore & Northern provided a feature unique among local traction companies. While B & N cars operated over the entire line, they were manned by City Passenger crews from Charles and Lafayette to Calvert and Baltimore Streets. Northbound, crews again changed when the big yellow cars left the Blue Line trackage.

Webb got plenty of newspaper space for this coup, but City Passenger retained tacit control over operations on the southern end of the line. This was clearly illustrated during the furor over the use of patented collection boxes. These were little locked containers carried by the conductors, into which the passenger inserted his nickel, causing a bell to ring. Many of the conductors resented this as an affront to their honesty, and the newspapers gave the story quite a play when the Central Railway put them into use. Despite the commotion,

Webb decided that they would be used on the Baltimore & Northern cars. This announcement came at a time when Walter Franklin of City Passenger was out of town. Upon returning, he exploded: "The Baltimore & Northern can do as they please north of Lafayette Avenue, but there will be none of those boxes used on our tracks." Webb hastily backed down, and the boxes went into use only as far south as Charles Street and Lafayette Avenue.

Test runs were made over the entire line October 15, 1897, in order to meet the date (set down in the franchise) when operations must commence. Regular schedules began on the 18th. The northern end of the route (the old Pikesville, Reisterstown & Emory Grove) was still single track, though more passing sidings had been added.

There were no signals at first, but in a couple of weeks, the Mt. Washington

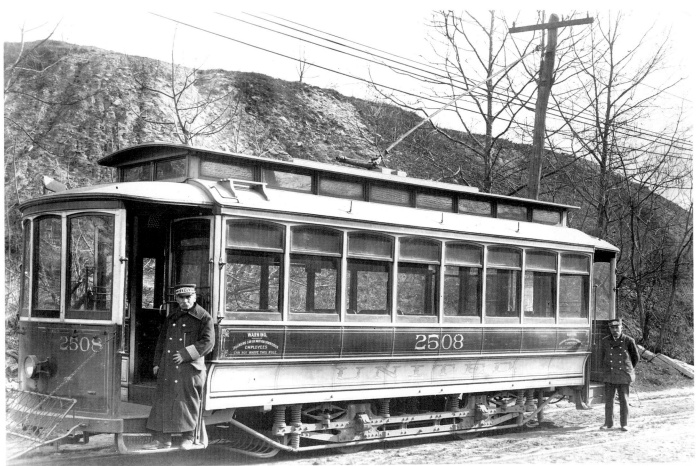

Many ex-Baltimore & Northern cars were unpopular with the United and were quickly sold or converted to other uses. No. 2508 had been the former's No. 41, built by Laclede in 1898. Scene appears to be on Falls Road, in the vicinity of Mt. Vernon Mill; car may have been in use as a tripper to the mills. (Maryland Historical Society, Baltimore)

viaduct was protected by a system of flags by day and lanterns by night. (This was occasioned by the fact that, due to sharp curves at both approaches to the single-tracked bridge, two cars would sometimes enter upon the span at the same time, and one would have to back off. Later, colored light signals were installed.) It appears that most of the stretch from Reisterstown Road and Electric Park over to Mt. Washington and thence down Falls Road was double tracked, though there may have been several thousand feet of single iron on the private right of way between Arlington Junction and Pikesville.

It is interesting to note that, while the original equipment (carried over from the Pikesville, Reisterstown, & Emory Grove) was on the small side, most of the B & N cars were of substantial proportions, which fitted with its interurban-like operations. Many of them had separate smoking, express, or baggage sections. Practically all of its cars in use during the colder seasons had vestibules at both ends to protect the motorman from the weather. These vestibules would play a part in the great argument relative to the comfort of motormen which arose in 1899. The center aisle on the B & N open cars was another feature not often offered locally.

Not every one was pleased with the Baltimore & Northern. Robert Poole, head of the large Poole & Hunt foundry in Woodberry, objected that the company had cut corners in building its Union Avenue line. Actually, it had literally "stolen the street" to put in this short spur to the Gambrill Mills, having completed the entire line over one weekend so that no one could obtain a court injunction to prevent the work. Poole's objection was that heavy wooden poles were placed in front of his property, rather than the smaller iron ones used in the city.

One detractor, in a letter to the editor, called it a "gutter line." This was an unfair comment. Although it can be argued that much of the Baltimore & Northern should never have been built, and it must be admitted that several sections did not last too long after the consolidation, the company did many things in fine style. For its trackage within the city limits nine-inch girder rail, weighing eighty-six pounds to the yard, was used. Along Falls Road it laid seventy-two-pound, six-inch "T" rail, with sixty-pound "T" rail being standard elsewhere. To many it had the most impressive car house ever to have graced the city. The brick barn on Falls Road, with a circular tower containing a clock, was certainly far more graceful than the substantial monstrosities of concrete which the United Railways specialized in, though City Passenger's Victorian car house on Madison Avenue had a special charm of its own.

In the days of cobblestone and dirt streets, sprinkler cars were operated over many routes to settle the dust. No. 1748 was built at the B & N shop by mounting a 2,250-gallon tank on a flatcar. The car was inherited by the United Railways, and this photo is one of a series taken for valuation purposes, ca. 1914. (Louis C. Mueller Collection)

NOTES AND COMMENTS:

Summaries of Webb's biography appear in the *News,* December 9, 1898 and April 1, 1901, and (shortly after his death) the *Electric Railway Journal,* vol. 54, p. 265 (1919).

Some idea of the scope of operations planned north of Reisterstown is contained in the *Sun,* July 3, 1894, and *The Philadelphia Stockbroker,* January 2, 1895.

A. T. Clark in his notes appears satisfied that the line was of substantial construction.

While the Pikesville, Reisterstown & Emory Grove line established a connection with the Pimlico & Pikesville (*American,* March 19, 1895) and, according to a notice put out by the PR & EG on June 8, 1895, through service was then being offered to Retreat Street, the junction at Pikesville was removed (probably when the Bal-timore & Northern was constructed) and the 692-foot gap in the vicinity of Druid Ridge Cemetery was not replaced until after the big consolidation. *American,* August 19, 1899.

The large interurban-like coaches were four 27 foot 7 inch cars built by Laclede; all of these had express compartments. One finished its career as a regular passenger car; the others were rebuilt into a parlor car, a funeral car, and an express car. *United Railways & Electric Co., Inventory Of Cars,* December 31, 1903.

Those interested in following the planning and construction of the B & N are referred to: *American,* February 28 and June 6, 1896; *Baltimore County Democrat,* December 1896 issues; *Herald,* January 16, 1898; *News,* May 18, 1896, October 16 and 18, 1897; *Sun,* October 21, 1897.

The patented collection boxes, which were known as Merlin safes, measured 7¾ inches long, 2½ inches thick, and 3 inches wide. They were introduced on Central Railway, December 29, 1897. Webb announced January 6, 1898 that they would be used on the B & N cars, but less than a week later had backed down. *Herald,* December 29, 1897 and January 1, 1898; *American,* January 6 and 12, 1898; and *News,* February 12, 1898.

The attorneys for the B & N insisted that the injunction against track laying on Union Avenue applied only to the south side of the street (the side nearest to Poole's property). In any event, the Union Avenue branch remained single-track until it was abandoned half a century later. *Herald,* September 11, 1897; *Sun,* November 8, 1897; *American,* September 1, 1897.

AT THE END OF A LINE

Why was the Baltimore City Passenger Railway so desirable a property? Though it was far less volatile than the Baltimore & Northern, or the new Consolidated Railway combine of City & Suburban and Baltimore Traction, the City Passenger Railway had nevertheless been actively improving its position during these hectic years. Since the death of Oden Bowie, Walter Franklin had been quietly making changes that were once again pushing the oldest company far to the forefront in the Baltimore street railway field, despite all that its competitors could do.

During a span of three years, its net income varied relatively little and stayed within the range of 8 to 12 percent of the gross. In a comparable period, Baltimore Traction's net fluctuated widely — from 1 to 10 percent. From $780,000 in 1892, City Passenger's gross receipts had risen to over $1 million in the fiscal year of 1895, at which time it was operating twenty-six miles of electric trackage and twenty-two miles of cable. Its approximately 150 powered cars were equally divided between motor and grip vehicles. Its last horse-powered line had been converted to electricity in 1895.

Therefore, of the days during which plans were being formulated to convert all of the company's routes to electric power, the month of June 1896 would seem to be a good point at which to view the manner in which the largest company ran its operations.

City Passenger had recently opened a new barn and repair shop on the north side of Cumberland Street at Pennsylvania Avenue, across from the old horse car facilities. Here an unusual occurrence was taking place. The seventy-five cable grip cars were being converted into open trail cars, while the closed cars which had been used for this purpose received the new Broadway type of grip, thus reversing the roles of the vehicles. The new grips were installed on the front platform; as the cars had already been refitted with heavy Peckham trucks, this

was actually an interim step until the same cars would be wired for electricity. This conversion gives some idea of the company's thorough way of planning.

The company had always been noted for its skilled wood craftsmen. Almost from the beginning, its vehicles had been periodically rebuilt to incorporate the latest improvements in car design. Not only did this show up in the financial reports — in 1893 the saving appears to have been 25 percent of the cost of identical new equipment — but the quality of workmanship was so high that it is almost impossible to tell when, or by whom, the two cars extant today were originally built.

The cable power houses were located at Eutaw Street below German (now Redwood) Street; Charles Street above Lanvale Street; and Baltimore Street near Aisquith Street. (The last two stood in 1992.) The electric power station was at Light and Heath, at which location the cars of the Orleans Street (Yellow) line were also housed. The White Line barn, adjacent to the Madison Avenue gate of Druid Hill Park, had recently been doubled in capacity (to fifty cars). The Red Line had two barns, at Baltimore and Smallwood Streets and at North Avenue and Gay Street. A wooden structure at Darley Park (Harford Road at Broadway) had been constructed to shelter the cars of the Hall's Springs line at the time that City Passenger had taken over that company in June 1885.

For those interested in minutia, the City Passenger Railway still ran one horse car in June 1896, though it could hardly be called a line. This solitary car ran on Ann Street, from Bank to Thames Streets, on days when the Broadway Market was open and during market hours only; but plans were being finalized for new trackage on Aliceanna Street. When this was laid (the Green line used it as part of a new routing to Canton), the horse car had made its last trip through the city streets. The very last horse car in the metropolitan

area, though, was on a former segment of the Baltimore, Calverton & Powhatan, and operated between Powhatan and Lorraine Cemetery into the first decade of the twentieth century.

By 1897, City Passenger was making plans for expansion. Except for the acquisition of the bankrupt Hall's Springs Railway in 1885, Bowie had been content to stay with the routings obtained in the earliest days. By law it was not allowed to acquire any paralleling line.

During the summer of 1897, the company obtained control of the Harford Road Turnpike Company with the object of extending its Hall's Springs line out that roadway. On September 1st, as previously noted, it purchased the bonds of the Baltimore, Middle River & Sparrows Point. This seemed a strange move, for there was no physical connection at the time; as the stock was not acquired, City Passenger did not actually control the property. The franchise did contain authority to build to Sparrows Point (which was to prove valuable in the future), but as of the date the railway was obtained, it consisted of a double track from Highlandtown to Back River, with single track to Middle River.

It had opened on June 1, 1895 as an independent company, later coming under the influence of the Alexander Brown combine. The routing followed Eastern Avenue Road for much of its length, and served the popular bathing resorts of Back and Middle Rivers. It had originally terminated near the Back River bridge at the almost forgotten Fairy Grove Park, located north of Eastern Avenue.

Meanwhile, back in the city, plans were being completed in 1898 for the conversion of City Passenger's Red and White cable lines to electricity. Oden Bowie's reasoning for putting in the cable had been demonstrated by the difficulties encountered by the company when it decided to convert the Blue Line to overhead

Both the nine-bench open car and Madison Avenue car house are decked out for the 50th anniversary of the street railways in Baltimore — 1909. Lower portion of the building still stood in 1992, but the many-turreted upper stories are long gone. The car operated on the Columbia Avenue (now Washington Boulevard) line. (Louis C. Mueller Collection)

Green Line car No. 463 of Baltimore City Passenger Railway sits on tracks separating Druid Hill Park from Madison Avenue car house, on part of two-block stretch that was once Baltimore's "shortest line." This Laclede ten-bench car rode on a Peckham 9 AX extra long truck. (George F. Nixon Collection)

electric operation. The city authorities had refused permission to put up the necessary poles on Charles Street, although a revision of City Passenger's charter authorized it to use any power that any other company was employing on the streets of Baltimore. As City Passenger was already using electricity on some lines and as Baltimore Traction, Central Railway, and City & Sub-

urban, among others, had been running trolleys for some years, the Court of Appeals ruled in the company's favor.

At the time that the final conversion commenced in late 1898, it was obvious that City Passenger had almost reached the end of the line as an independent organization. Therefore the company, in order to conserve the stockholders' money, decided

against any expensive power plant construction. It merely enlarged its Light Street plant and began installing electrical equipment in its cable power houses on a piece-meal basis. This resulted in the unusual situation of electric and cable cars running on the same route, as the electric cars were put in service a few at a time and the cable cars withdrawn on the same basis.

NOTES AND COMMENTS:

Baltimore City Passenger Railway's gross receipts were (in thousands of dollars): 780 (1892), 794 (1893), 942 (1894), 1,058 (1895). These figures are from *Street Railway Journals* of the period and were included among a wealth of statistical material furnished by J. Randolph Kean. BCPR paid a 9 percent dividend in 1892; 11 percent in 1893; 8 percent in 1894; 12 percent in 1895. Baltimore Traction paid 1 percent in 1892, nothing in the other years. City and Suburban Railway's dividends were 1 percent in 1893 and 1895, 2 percent in 1894. *News,* April 10, 1897.

Soon after acquiring the Baltimore & Hall's Springs Railway, City Passenger

improved most of the line by putting down a second track. *Sun,* June 10, 1885. This was not possible on the part of Fayette Street between Gay and Aisquith Streets, so permission was gained to lay a track on Aisquith between Fayette and Baltimore Streets. Eastbound cars then proceeded by way of Baltimore Street to Aisquith to the old B & HS line. Westbound cars followed the same routing as formerly. *Sun,* October 19, 1887. Additional information on both the Baltimore & Hall's Springs Railway and the Baltimore, Middle River & Sparrows Point Railway is to be found elsewhere in this book.

The *Sun,* November 6, 1897, in commenting on the decision to introduce electric cars on the Red and White Lines said, "The charter of City Passenger authorizes it to use any power that any other company uses on the streets of Baltimore and a recent decision of the Court of Appeals ruled that the city could not refuse the company permission to erect poles to operate its lines by electricity." This decision was given in legal proceedings caused by the city authorities refusing to grant permission to the company to put up poles on Charles Street. The Court of Appeals opinion is given in Hooper v. City Passenger, *Maryland Reports,* vol. 85, pp. 509-516 (1896-97).

Pratt Street, looking west, early in the twentieth century. Twelve-bench Brill open cars were new in 1902. The row of buildings beyond the Ericsson line steamer, front on Light Street, which was considerably widened shortly after photo was made. The Uneeda Biscuit building and many of its neighbors to the west stood until 1972. (The Peale Museum)

Located at Eutaw and Lombard Streets, another famous Baltimore Landmark, the Bromo Seltzer Tower, dominates the scene as No. 17 car makes its way north along Eutaw at Baltimore Street in the first decade of the twentieth century. (Mettee Studio, BSM Collection)

THE 76 MILLION DOLLAR DEAL

By the fall of 1898 the drama of the struggle for the control of the street railways of Baltimore was well into the final act. There were three principal players. Col. Walter Franklin of City Passenger could play an enviable role, going daily to his office in the many-turreted headquarters up by Druid Hill Park, secure in the knowledge that whatever happened his company could hardly lose. City Passenger, again the dominant company and operating at a good profit, was ready to sell when the price was right.

Nelson Perin, of the Consolidated Railway, was playing it cautiously, as usual. He had been stalking City Passenger from a distance, lying back for the right moment to make his move. This posture did not sit too well with a number of the other Consolidated stockholders, who were becoming impatient with all the waiting. Michael Jenkins was their spokesman, but Perin held a tight rein.

A third member of importance in the cast had previously been cloaked in relative obscurity, at least as far as the local streetcar operations had been concerned. This was Alexander Brown, of the banking house of Alex. Brown & Sons. Although previously playing a large role in obtaining control of lines in Pittsburgh, St. Louis, and Newport News, Brown had generally remained in the background of the newspaper stories as Henry Parr and George Webb moved the Baltimore & Northern into a prominent place in Baltimore's transportation picture. But, now that the hour was at hand for the crucial decision, it was Brown who took over the starring role.

By mid-October 1898, though the principals denied it, the papers were full of rumors that a final consolidation was near at hand. At this time, the Consolidated was the largest of the properties with 818 cars running over 181 miles of trackage. City Passenger was about half this size with 407 cars and 103 miles of tracks, though it must be remembered that it had the more profitable lines. The Baltimore & Northern had about forty miles and fifty-three cars, a normal proportion for a line with so much suburban traffic. On this basis, it might be assumed that the contest was to be between City Passenger and the Consolidated, if anyone was to have the monopoly.

Actually, this was not the case, as City Passenger, by reason of legal complications, could not acquire (for consolidation purposes) any parallel lines. The other companies were under no such restriction. Well aware of this, Perin apparently felt that he could bide his time, trying to beat the City Passenger people down, then picking up the Baltimore & Northern (and its affiliate, the Baltimore, Middle River & Sparrows Point) at a bargain price. The B & N roads operated only in the suburbs, depending on trackage rights over City Passenger to enter downtown.

Therefore, quite a few people, even in the financial community, were rather surprised at the turn of events on December 8, 1898. Early in the day, rumors began to circulate that something definite was taking place, as City Passenger stock climbed up and up. From 78¼, it went to 88. At the same time, Consolidated rose to 29⅛. Soon, the real story began to make the rounds; it was not Consolidated but little Baltimore & Northern which had bought out City Passenger at a price of $90 a share.

There were many who wondered at the wisdom of paying such a price, but the *Herald* of December 12th briefly explained the situation, "As to Alexander Brown — he is a bold operator, and he went into the deal to protect his roads. He holds the bonds of the Baltimore & Northern, and he could not get rid of them. He also holds the stock of the Baltimore, Middle River & Sparrows Point Railroad (while the BCPR owned the bonds). . . . If the Consolidated had obtained control of the City Passenger, these roads would have been practically worthless, not more than fifty cents on the dollar."

An insight into the attitude of the financial community towards the deal may be found in the following observations credited to Hambleton & Company, a financial institution with prior experience in the local street railway industry. It appeared in the *Herald,* December 10, 1898. "The feature of the week was the coup d'etat of the managers and friends of the managers of the Baltimore & Northern Railway Company, who while the Consolidated people were discussing the subject and trying to beat the City Passenger people down in price, stepped in and captured the prize, if prize it may be, at $90 per share (par 25). While the price paid seems high, it is to be supposed that the purchasers know what they are about, and that they have some plan in contemplation whereby the purchase may prove profitable."

The transaction, which was dramatic in its suddenness, nevertheless had a bit of the cloak and dagger business to it. Perin's associate, Michael Jenkins, vigorously disagreed with the shrewd one's conviction that the stock was not worth more than $85. It was indicated later that some large Consolidated stockholders would have paid close to $100 a share to control City Passenger. They explained that they did not look upon the stock as having that value when the concern was managed independently, but felt that it would be worth all that and more too if the two systems should become one, giving to them a virtual monopoly of street railway traffic in and around Baltimore. (Without its City Passenger trackage rights, the B & N would be isolated in the suburbs.)

With so strong a feeling among some of his associates, Perin could not move as freely in making decisions as was his wont. The way that things worked out proved that Perin seldom swerved from his course unless it served his purpose to do so.

Parade at turn of century backs up streetcars on Baltimore Street. Though by now obsolete, the cable slot is still in place, presenting an impediment to horse-drawn vehicles. Trackage seems to be holding up well under the heavy electric cars. (The Peale Museum)

On that fateful December 8th, Jenkins went to Philadelphia to attend a meeting of the Northern Central Railway, in which he had holdings. Knowing that negotiations were pending, he called his office upon arriving in Philadelphia. He was told that there had been no inquiries made for him. He was understandably surprised when, soon afterwards, he was handed a telegram stating that City Passenger had been sold to Brown's syndicate. Though Jenkins and other Consolidated's stockholders fumed, it was for naught. Perin had spoken.

Some of the fuming of the Consolidated's stockholders appeared in the *Herald,* December 12, 1898. "The Consolidated people are inclined to blame the representatives of the City Passenger people, for taking Mr. Perin's word that $90 would not be paid for the stock. They hold

that Michael Jenkins, the other member of the committee, should have been consulted. . . . It is claimed if Mr. Jenkins had been telephoned that the deal was about to be declared off, he might have gone to the office of City Passenger for a talk, and might have bought the road."

If the Consolidated people were unhappy, this was not the case with City Passenger backers. The stock which they sold for $90 a share, had been available only a few months previously for $62.

So, now there were but two companies. The Consolidated Railway and the City Passenger/ Baltimore & Northern situation was a standoff, an impasse, a draw. After all the excitement, the ultimate combining of all the lines under one management was strictly anticlimactic. During the eight weeks following the agreement of Decem-

ber 8th, items periodically appeared in the newspapers that the amalgamation of all the lines was imminent. Finally, on January 25, 1899, the two survivors agreed to unite, with Consolidated stock being acquired for $37.50 a share. Thus, there was no merger in the usual sense, rather Brown's syndicate had bought out both City Passenger and Consolidated and formed a new company.

The new arrangement went into effect on April 1, 1899, a date which perhaps would have a certain significance for future riders. There was no particular rejoicing on the part of the patrons generally when the United Railways & Electric Company came into being; they tended to feel that the public would have received better service with two companies in the field than with one corporation controlling all of the street railway lines.

This car is typical of electric vehicles on Baltimore City Passenger Railway's Green Line just before the consolidation of 1899. Probably built by City Passenger in the 1880s, it was first a horse car before conversion to electricity. Part of the historic collection, it was presented by the Baltimore Transit Company to the Maryland Historical Society at Irvington Loop on July 11, 1954. The motorman is Carvey G. Davis. (BSM Collection)

Even before the final agreement had been signed, the *News,* on February 4, 1899, summed up the feeling pretty well, as follows:

"The street railways of the city are about to be consolidated into a single system. The total capitalization will be $76 million. It may be safely asserted, in the light of past experience, that the actual market value of these securities will, either immediately, or within a short time, aggregate an amount not very far from the actual capitalization. In other words, the street railways of Baltimore are now worth, or will be worth in a short time, something like $70 million.

"Yet, it is very safe to say that the whole system — tracks, power houses, machinery, electrical construction, rolling stock and all — could be duplicated for a much less sum than $20 million. What does the difference represent? What will the new company own that is worth the other $50 million? The obvious answer is a public franchise."

The *World* was even more outspoken, stating on December 9, 1901, "United Railways has a capitalization of $76 million, based on a $12 million investment. Of course, $64 million may be what is known as watered stock."

Another point of view was presented to the Public Service Commission, during the valuation case which was heard in 1926. The following is a summary of a report in the *Electric Railway Journal* for January 9th of that year. The final consolidation differed from the usual consolidation — in which two or more companies pool their stock and issue to the stockholders of the constituent companies agreed amounts of stock in the new company — in that one company acquired the other two by outright purchase of stock in the others.

One of the best remembered vehicles is the funeral car *Dolores*. The casket was placed behind plate glass over the front truck; the two "picture windows" above allowed passersby to view floral tributes. (Mass Transit Administration)

As late as August 1893, Baltimore City Passenger Railway was operating this ancient horse car on its Hall's Springs line. It would be two more years before the route was converted to electricity. (Library of Congress)

As to the prices paid, the article went on to say:

"The question of whether the purchase of these stocks at the price paid was a prudent one was answered, from the company's point of view at least, by the fact that the syndicate, formed to take over the stocks thus acquired, was very largely oversubscribed; that many of owners of stocks, who had an opportunity to withdraw the cash chose rather to put the cash back into the syndicate; and, finally that allotments in the syndicate sold on the Baltimore Stock Exchange at a premium of 14 percent. The company argued from this that, judged by the standards of the day, the investment must have been regarded as a prudent and wise one. The company showed in this way a total investment of $69 million, exclusive of any allowance to the promoters or any profit to the final syndicate, but including a profit of between 5 and 6 percent to the purchasers of the first of the large companies."

Looking rather forlorn, United Railways No. 2213, formerly Baltimore City Passenger Railway horse car No. 338, sits on shop trucks. The car had last seen service on the No. 22 Wolfe Street line, the old Central Railway route to Canton. It would end up as a yard shifter. (Louis C. Mueller Collection)

It should be noted that the various figures quoted above are somewhat misleading. The authorized capitalization was indeed $76 million — half in stock and half in mortgage bonds. However, this amount was not all issued immediately at the time of the consolidation. The 1899 issue of *Poor's Manual Of Railroads* reports issuance of $13 million in common stock and

$14 million in preferred (most of which was promptly exchanged for an equal amount of income bonds). Slightly over $19 million of the mortgage bonds had been issued, and about another $14 million were reserved to retire the outstanding bonds of predecessor companies as they matured. Hence, the securities actually issued totaled just over $60 mil-

lion. (In the next annual issue of *Poor's,* this total had risen to almost $65 million.) Thus, the consolidation might more precisely be described as "the $60 million deal." In any event, if the replacement costs quoted above can be accepted as roughly accurate, the capitalization would seem to be greatly inflated.

NOTES AND COMMENTS:

It may be remembered that the *Sun* had vigorously opposed giving control of City Passenger Railway to the original grantees back in 1859. Somewhere along the way, though, publisher A. S. Abell had jumped on the bandwagon, for the *Herald,* December 9, 1898, listed his estate as one of the largest holders of Baltimore City Passenger Railway stock.

City Passenger's legal dilemma was spelled out in the *American,* December 25, 1898. "City Passenger cannot acquire for

consolidation purposes a parallel line. This is true, but the Consolidated is not so hampered. It can buy the stock of City Passenger Railway, and absorbing the lines of that company, operate them in unison with its own."

Even before the street railway consolidation became effective, it was reported: "Mr. Alexander Brown, and the other gentlemen associated with him in the syndicate which controls all the street railways in Baltimore, have purchased all the properties of

the three electric light companies in the city. It is a cash deal and it is reported that the price to be paid is about $3 million." *Sun,* February 1, 1899. A consolidation of the street railways and the electric companies never came to fruition, though.

The final consolidation, through purchase of the Consolidated stock by Alex. Brown interests, is reported in the *American,* January 26, 1899.

Many lines were temporarily shortened after the great fire of February 1904, but service was resumed as soon as the rubble was cleared from the streets. No. 17 route car heads west on Baltimore Street, even while the roadbed is impassible to other traffic. Gutted Continental Trust, later Mercantile Trust, building looms in background. (Maryland Historical Society, Baltimore)

THE UNITED

As one result of the consolidation, Nelson Perin realized his goal of becoming the head of a united system of Baltimore street railways. His satisfaction was tempered by the fact that, for once, he was not in complete control. The old Baltimore & Northern combination of Henry Parr and George Webb, plus Alexander Brown, were figuratively standing on the front platform advising Perin of the proper point on which the controller should be set. Predictably enough, there was a disagreement, and Perin stepped down after only one year. Despite a rumor that he was going to return and regain control with the backing of his old Ohio cronies, he never again had any official connection with the United. He died in 1904 at the age of fifty-one.

Most of the events of his administration had a very definite connection with those which had occurred prior to the consolidation. On Friday, February 3, 1900, part of the old dream of the Columbia & Maryland et al. came to reality when the line from Ellicott City was finally finished along Edmondson Avenue, and the cars ran over it to Charles and Lexington Streets. The "cutoff" between Catonsville Junction and Stoddard's then was used only by mail and express cars. In July of the same year, the Consolidated Railway's trackage on Schroeder Street was finally put to use with an extension eastward over Dolphin Street to the Mt. Royal Station of the B & O. Also, another service of the United began on October 2nd of the same year, when the funeral car *Dolores* made her initial trip. A landmark of horse and cable car days passed out of existence on the day before Halloween, when the buildings at Druid Hill and Fulton went up in flames.

Perin was succeeded by old friend George Webb, with Henry Parr and Alexander Brown once more choosing to remain in the background. For once, Webb picked the wrong time to assume the limelight. The United was not enjoying anything like the financial success that had

John Mifflin Hood was the third president of the United Railways, but he came to fame beforehand as head of the Western Maryland. The City of Baltimore immortalized Hood in bronze for his part in revitalizing the steam road in which the municipality had a sizable financial interest. (Michael R. Farrell)

been predicted for it. Elimination of duplicate lines was not expedient politically; the only real discontinuance of service was on the old Baltimore & Northern route along Falls Road, south of 36th Street. The public was clamoring for more new cars, and the expected permission to institute a charge for transfers proved elusive. With debt service running to 46 percent of gross income, the financial picture was a bleak one. Dividends were being paid, but subsequent ones would have to be passed.

Devastation caused by the Waverly car house fire in 1906. Cars in background were salvaged, but forty-seven others, including two mail cars and two sprinklers, fueled the flames, leaving this twisted mass of trucks, dashers, and assorted metal fittings among the charred beams. (Robert E. Base Collection)

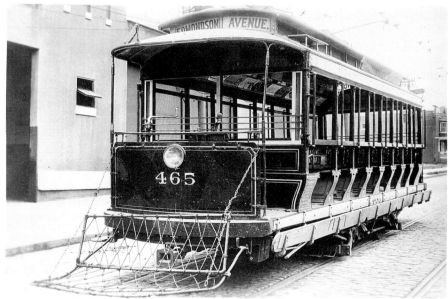

No. 465, a nine-bench St. Louis Car Company product, sits in front of the Edmondson Avenue car house. Illuminated destination sign etched in clerestory glass was an early attempt at easier visual route identification. (Louis C. Mueller Collection)

Catonsville-bound No. 816, an 1898 Brill convertible, passes beneath workman on tower on horse-drawn line car. The scene appears to be Eutaw and Lombard Streets, about 1902. (Louis C. Mueller Collection)

A Brill 1898 convertible with windows installed for winter service. In the warmer months, only the thin white posts and metal bars remained in place. No. 2117 is about to enter Baltimore Traction Company's ex-cable barn on Druid Hill Avenue, which required little alteration to handle electric cars. (Louis C. Mueller Collection)

One bright spot was the opening of the Carroll Park shops, which enabled the company to effect substantial savings by doing all major car repair and remodeling work at one location.

Carroll Park shops were built in 1900-01. There were two main buildings containing a total of eight "bays." Only brick and steel were used in the construction, except for the wood-covered roofs. The buildings fronted on Columbia Avenue (now Washington Boulevard) for about 1,000 feet, and extended southward for about 475 feet. Baldwin and Pennington were the architects. The complex is still in use by the Mass Transit Administration.

Like Perin, Webb soon resigned. While he was to become active elsewhere in traction, electric light, and telephone companies, he never again served the United though, like Perin, he maintained his residence in Baltimore.

The third head of the United was well-known in the transportation industry, although his prior experience was in steam railroading. John Mifflin Hood moved into the post in 1903, soon after resigning as long-time head of the Western Maryland Railroad (later "Railway"). Though he died after less than four years at the helm, he seemed on the way to duplicating the phenomenal success that he had achieved in the metamorphosis of the Western Maryland from a second-rate carrier to one of the showpieces of eastern railroading.

During Hood's administration, the United's trackage was extended out beyond Walbrook to Windsor Hills, and the line to Sparrows Point began operation.

One of the major events in Baltimore history took place during Hood's tenure, the great fire of February 1904. This conflagration, which completely destroyed most of the city's downtown area, incidentally played havoc with the present recreation of the city's street railway history. In 1901, the railway company's main offices had been moved from Druid Hill Avenue to the Continental Building, at Baltimore and Calvert Streets. When the "fireproof" Continental went up like a torch, some of the offices were removed to the old People's Railway building, also on Druid Hill Avenue, but many of the old records had helped feed the flames.

Whenever possible, the early street railway operators preferred to purchase cars with longitudinal seating. These provided more standing room for handling the maximum number of passengers with the minimum number of cars. Interior shown is of a 1902 Brill double-truck car, No. 3828, now in the BSM Collection. (Michael R. Farrell)

For the United, though, more than records were lost. The Pratt Street power house on Dugan's Wharf was badly damaged. The structure itself was salvaged, but it was weeks before the power plant was serviceable. Even with the makeshift arrangements, using auxiliary substations and older generating stations, service through the downtown section was weeks getting back to normal. Even lines such as Fremont Avenue, far from the burnt area, were out for almost a week because of the power shortage. Some method of additional financing was imperative, but the company was so heavily mortgaged that even railway financiers used to taking high risks steered shy of it.

Hood passed away just as the problem was being resolved, and the mantle passed to William A. House, he of the Horatio Alger mold. Though not born to poverty — he was the son of a successful coal merchant — Billy House started at the lowliest positions with the People's line and worked his way up, through successive consolidations, to general manager of Baltimore Traction, the Consolidated Railway, and

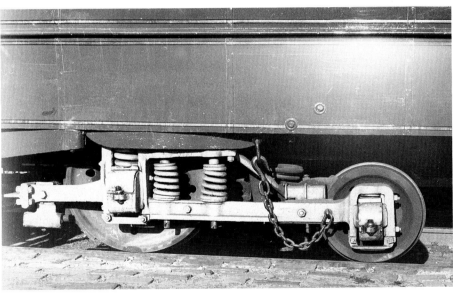

To many people, red and cream No. 5565 typifies *The* Baltimore streetcar. Bought from Brill in 1914, this type was similiar to previous semi-convertibles, but the first to have fully-enclosed platforms with mechanically-operated doors and folding steps. As a result, the end wall of the bulkhead, containing the main entrance and emergency exit door, could be supplanted by a large open archway extending from side to side of the car. (Enoch Pratt Library)

Among experiments tried around the turn of the century was the maximum-traction truck. These featured one large and one small wheel. The object was to provide more traction by placing more weight on the motorized larger wheel. It failed, due to a tendency of the small wheel to derail at switchwork. (Michael R. Farrell)

the United Railways. Next came a vice-presidency with the United, and finally, at this trying time, he took over the top position, at the relatively young age of forty-six.

Just prior to the transition, the Waverly car house went up in flames in the last of a series of car house fires. Due to the poor condition of the York Road, coupled with frozen hydrants, the fire department was hindered in getting a fast start on the blaze. When dawn came on that cold January 10,

1906, the United counted not only the loss of the structure but also fifty-six cars completely destroyed or badly burned. Strenuous efforts by the employees saved all of the twenty-eight new semi-convertibles in the building, or the loss would have been substantially greater.

This proved to be the ebb tide of the company's early financial troubles, for in August an agreement was reached with Maryland Electric Railways which was to

put the United on a reasonably sound financial footing. This savior was not really a new organization. It was an offshoot, incorporated in 1898, of the old Columbia & Maryland/Maryland Traction outfits. Though the Washington-Baltimore interurban plans were dormant, the company, by 1901, controlled the Baltimore, Halethorpe & St. Denis electric railway franchise and the operating steam railroad known as the Catonsville Short Line and also held the rights (never exercised) for construction of

Between 1900, when the old horse car building burned, and the time that Park Terminal was built, the southwest corner of Druid Hill and Fulton presented this appearance. In center are screen-sided American open cars. Photo was taken July 17, 1909. (Louis C. Mueller Collection)

a line on the Philadelphia Road, from the city line to Harford County.

In 1904, Maryland Electric Railways was raising the specter of competition which the United had thought was vanquished for good in 1899. However, the threat subsided when Maryland Electric found that, in addition to its pledge to pave streets from curb to curb and to accept the 9 percent Park Tax, its franchises or easements would likewise be taxable.

Taking a new tack, Maryland Electric had its charter revised to increase its capital stock authorization to $1.2 million. This, in turn, could be further increased to a practically unlimited amount. Amongst its directors were Edwin C. Baetjer, who was to become well-known in the United's legal affairs, and Frank S. Hambleton, thus bringing back the Hambleton name to the local traction field. By August 7, 1906, things had reached a point where the *American* could state: "The United and Maryland Electric Railways managements

are in close accord, and the last named can do under its new charter rights many things which the United itself could not do."

Following the 1904 fire, money was needed for four essential purposes. These were described in an article in the *Electric Railway Journal* of March 24, 1906, and may be summarized as follows:

1. Relaying and repairing of track. This was being and would continue to be done by the railway company itself, out of earnings.

2. The purchase of new and repairing of old equipment. Purchase of new equipment was being carried out through equipment trusts, with satisfactory terms being obtained for the certificates.

3. The building of new and repairing of old car houses and buildings.

4. The extension to and development of that portion of the suburbs of the city now unsupplied with lines.

A start on items 3 and 4 was financed (as reported in the United's Annual Report of

1906) through the issuance of $8 million in first mortgage 5 percent, twenty-five-year bonds by the Maryland Electric Railways. The proceeds were earmarked to be used only "for the purpose of acquiring by purchase, construction or otherwise: car houses, terminal stations, power houses, excursion resorts, cars, rolling stock, railway extensions, tracks, rights of way, franchises, and such other buildings, structures, or additions to the system of the United Railways and Electric Company as would be necessary to the operation thereof, and approved by the trustees under the mortgage."

This property was to be leased to the United at an annual rental equal to 6 percent of actual cost. The United further agreed to pay as rental, beginning in 1910, 1.5 percent per annum on the amount of the outstanding bonds. This was to be used as a sinking fund to retire these bonds and was to be credited toward the purchase price of the property by the United.

This is the architect's drawing of Park Terminal, opened in 1910. This massive structure still stands, and with ample evidence of the important role it once played. (BSM Collection)

New cars were a prime consideration, and instead of the former car trusts, a special sinking fund, limited to ten years, was set up to provide for them. The first fruit of the agreement was an order for forty double-truck, semi-convertible, high-speed cars, placed with Brill on November 24, 1906. An additional order, with the same company, for forty more cars of this same type, was entered on February 1, 1907. All of these cars were to be equipped with multiple-unit control for use on the new Bay Shore Park line. Two sweepers and ten plows, ordered at about the same time, were put in service during the winter of 1906-07.

Thus, 1906 saw not only an easing of the United's financial situation but also the inauguration of service to its most popular resort, Bay Shore. The new bathing spa, located on the salt water of Chesapeake Bay and served by an interesting extension of the Sparrows Point line, was opened to the public on August 11, 1906.

NOTES AND COMMENTS:

It is not entirely clear exactly when cars first used that portion of the route which the Columbia & Maryland had partially completed along Edmondson Avenue. When the Baltimore Consolidated Railway purchased the C & M rights of way in the Baltimore area (in the spring of 1898), Consolidated quickly finished work on the Oella to Catonsville Junction segment, at the same time pushing trackage through the woods from the end of its Catonsville line up to the junction. As the Patapsco River bridge was not finished until July 12, 1899, shuttle cars ran from the east bank of the river to Catonsville (Frederick Road) beginning December 22, 1898. *American,* December 22 and 23, 1898. Kenneth Morse and other sources indicate that through ser-

vice over what became the Ellicott City route began in February 1900; however, items in the *News,* June 15, 1899 and *American,* June 16, 1899 suggest that this service may have actually begun June 15, 1899. The No. 8 line was not extended from its Frederick Road terminus to Catonsville Junction until February 21, 1911.

Robert S. Brooks, a veteran residing at the Confederate Soldiers Home in Pikesville, passed away in August 1898. In those days of dirt roads the difficulties of conveying the body to Loudon Park Cemetery prompted his comrades to charter a car from the Consolidated Railway for this purpose. The company removed the backs from four seats. placed smoothly-hewn boards covered with black cloth across the

benches, and secured the coffin with hooks. The minister, undertaker, and his comrades occupied the remaining seats. Such makeshift arrangements ended when the United built its funeral car. According to a company brochure, *Dolores* could be chartered at rates ranging from $20 for burials within the city limits to $25 if the cemetery was far out on one of the suburban lines.

The question of a transfer charge is brought out in the 1912 *Annual Report Of The United Railways* — "at the time of the consolidation (1899), the city charter provided for a five-cent fare with three-cent transfers. Immediately after the consolidation, the Legislature passed a law providing for a five-cent adult fare with the

There is not a streetcar in sight in this view of Pratt and Light Streets about 1915, but the United Railways' power house is busy generating power, if the smoke rising from the stacks at left can be taken as evidence. An Ericsson steamship, preparing to leave for Philadelphia, is doing its share to darken the sky. As United generated all the power necessary for public transportation at this site, air pollution was concentrated in a non-residential area. Note that the wagon wheels are directly on the streetcar tracks. The wide gauge of the Baltimore trackage provided a smoother ride for the wagon drivers. (The Peale Musuem)

condition that the company abolish all charges for transferring with connecting lines within the city."

As to the matter of cars, a letter to the *World,* published December 6, 1901, commented: "Don't you think that it is about time that this company should get some new cars? The ones that it has have been painted so much that they won't take any more paint, and are falling to pieces."

The *Electric Railway Journal,* June 4, 1921, reported that the United's payments for interest charges during 1900 had been 46 percent of gross income. This had been reduced to 34 percent by 1911 and to 18 percent in 1920.

References to Carroll Park shops are in the *American,* August 14, 1900 and *Street*

Railway Journal, vol. 21, pp. 508-514 (1903).

Some of Hood's problems upon taking over the presidency of the United appeared in print in the form of tributes appended to the *Memoirs Of John M. Hood,* published after his death.

Company records from the period after 1904 were hard to come by, except for those preserved by George F. Nixon and Louis C. Mueller. Many remaining records may be found in the library of the BSM. The only items of real help which I could locate through the MTA were a handful of sketches and maps from the Baltimore City Passenger cable era.

In addition to the references cited in the text, the United's *Annual Report* for 1910 gives a brief resume of the financial

problems faced between 1900 and 1906. Not only was the company not paying dividends on its common stock; after the February 1904 fire, the UR & E stopped paying interest on its income bonds. The arrangement with Maryland Electric Railways included a provision for funding the income bond coupons falling due between June 1906 and December 1910 with 5 percent funding bonds. Things had been so difficult for the United that, a year prior to the agreement with Maryland Electric, in replying to a query as to whether the Washington, Baltimore & Annapolis interurban was interested in acquiring the United, George T. Bishop, president of the WB & A, replied: "The United is rather too heavily loaded with mortgages for us to seriously consider such a proposal at this time." *Sun,* August 10, 1905.

Street peddlers ply their wares at steps of private car Lord Baltimore, during stop on inspection tour after 1904 fire. Built for Consolidated Railway in 1899 by Brill, car had maximum-traction trucks, was painted olive green. (Enoch Pratt Library, J. E. Henry)

One of much admired twelve-bench open cars, built by Brill, sits alongside the Roland Park car house. The type of destination sign on hood dates photo to about 1902. (George F. Nixon Collection)

A good example of why city fathers insisted that street railway companies put down wide-gauge trackage which could be shared by private carriages. Tram rail offers much more inviting pathway than cobblestones still in place. Scene is on West North Avenue, July 20, 1907. Poles in devilstrip probably date from Lake Roland Elevated Railway days. Grand Opera Company was presenting Verdi at Gwynn Oak the following day. (Nixon/Gerding Collection)

BUILT TO LAST

The skein of Maryland Electric Railways continued to be interwoven with the United Railways until 1935, when both corporations were superseded by a reorganized company, the Baltimore Transit Company. The most lasting memento of both early companies will probably be the car houses. Seven of these were constructed in the period from 1907 to 1912. Six have outlived the streetcar service for which they were built and, although converted to other uses, still survived in 1992 and appeared as substantial as when they were put in service.

All were designed by the noted Baltimore architect E. Francis Baldwin, who had previously done the Carroll Park shops, many notable stations and structures for the Baltimore & Ohio (including the Mt. Royal station and present B & O Museum roundhouse), as well as commercial and religious buildings in the city.

The first of these structures to be opened was at Edmondson Avenue and Poplar Grove Street on May 19, 1907. This made surplus the old car barn, erected by the Frick lines, at Edmondson and Fulton, and it was closed on September 21st of the same year. About two weeks later, on October 5th, the former Baltimore & Northern power house on Falls Road was destroyed by fire. The following day, the new car house at North Avenue and Gay Street was put into use, followed by Belvedere Avenue on November 30th, and York Road on February 24, 1908. The latter replaced the old Waverly car barn, a half mile to the south, which had burned in 1906.

Next to come, in July 1908, was the structure at Lombard and Haven Streets in Highlandtown. In 1910, the ornate Park Terminal, combining car house facilities with company offices, was opened; the last of the modern, fireproof car houses, Montebello, on Harford Road, was completed in 1912.

The residents of the stretch of North Charles Street between North Avenue and

The tops of early semi-convertibles were remarkably uncluttered. Wires run from the trolley bases across the clerestory roof on their way to controller and motors. Other visible wiring is for lighting system. Step and catwalk provided support for crewmen when making emergency repairs. (Nixon/Gerding Collection)

25th Street succeeded in having the tracks removed from that thoroughfare in May of 1907, but the new financial structure allowed construction of many miles of new trackage to offset this small loss. On the first day of July in 1908, the "cut-off" between Eastern Avenue and Dundalk Junction saw its first service, replacing the old routing to Sparrows Point by way of Riverview. On October 9th, the former Blue Line was extended out St. Paul Street and University Parkway, giving an alternate route to Roland Park. Another lengthy extension was opened to Halethorpe in Baltimore County on November 19th.

Extensions continued in 1910, when the East Monument Street line was pushed out

to Loney's Lane (now Edison Highway); in 1911, the Fremont Avenue line spanned the Baltimore & Ohio tracks by way of a new overpass on Hamburg Street, and the Curtis Bay line was routed up Light Street. The final new trackage put in operation during House's administration were the rails up Callow Avenue which were used by the John Street line and a second track between Woodlawn and Gwynn Oak Park.

In 1901, the United decided to concentrate its steam generating equipment at O'Donnell's Wharf (south of Pratt Street and Market Place). By 1905, the United Railways (which also was supplying some power to the electric company) was unable to generate sufficient power to handle the

Almost everything is gone now. Streetcar, tracks, poles, cobblestones — even the houses have vanished since this No. 13 line car shared North Avenue, east of Linden, with horse-drawn vehicles, on June 15, 1907. The Brill semi-convertible was then two years old. (Nixon/Gerding Collection)

The terminus of the No. 17 line until the 1920s was Greenmount Avenue and 31st Street. Hunter destination signs on these 1914 Brills read northbound, "Union Station — St. Paul St."; southbound, "Camden Station — Light St. Wharves." (Louis C. Mueller Collection)

Much of the early maintenance of way equipment appears remarkably unsophisticated today. Yet this Gherky rail grinder, in service at the present Roland and 41st on March 19, 1910, had the advantage of being easily removed from track to allow the passage of revenue cars. (Nixon/Gerding Collection)

unusual demand of the Christmas holiday season and its one hundred heavy new semi-convertible cars. Even the placing back into service of the closed-down Gilmor, Carey, and Preston Street power houses did not solve the problem. To meet the emergency, the railway company engaged the Ericsson Line steamship *Lord Baltimore* as an adjunct for supplying steam to the Pratt Street generating plant.

Three events occurred during William House's tenure (1906-17) which were to have far-reaching effects, each in a different way. In 1909, the State Roads Commission began paving operations; as the years went by, the railway was to find itself in many disputes with this agency. The following year, the Public Service Com-

mission came into being, thus putting the company under a state regulatory body for the first time. The real disputes with both of these were in the future, but 1915 saw the United being confronted by another force. This was the motor vehicle, in the guise of the jitney. Most of the jitneys really offered unfair competition; their effect will be seen a little later on.

Another event of the era with far-reaching ramifications was the first use of electric power transmitted from Holtwood on the Susquehanna River. By 1922, when the Pratt Street power house was sold, the company was entirely out of the electrical generating business and completely dependent on power purchased from the Consolidated Gas, Electric Light and Power

Company of Baltimore (later Baltimore Gas & Electric Company).

There were other changes, too. In 1910, on Christmas Day, the first "pay-as-you-enter" (soon abbreviated to P.A.Y.E.) cars were put into service. A campaign, begun prior to the turn of the century, began to be implemented in earnest when, under the prodding of the PSC, the company started the task of enclosing the platforms of all its cars with permanent vestibules. Another humane touch was the furnishing of a seat for the motorman. Still, he was required to get up from his wooden stool whenever his car entered the downtown area where traffic was heavy.

Another link with the past came to an end on December 31, 1912, when the Gaither

Edmondson Avenue, the first of the modern fireproof car houses, had a certain massive charm in its early years. Neither it nor any of the other concrete structures ever suffered a serious fire, so they served their intended purpose well. (Robert E. Base Collection)

Express service was discontinued. The Baltimore & Northern had experimented with the delivery of packages in 1898, but it took James H. Gaither to make a success of this service. Originally, his horse-drawn wagons had connected Ellicott City with the Catonsville terminus of the City & Suburban Railway. By July 1899, he had made arrangements to run express cars over the United's lines to Ellicott City and Towson, as well as over the old B & N route up to Emory Grove. As of that date, Gaither's Express was running three round trips daily to Ellicott City and two each to Towson and Emory Grove.

The operation proved so successful that on May 29, 1900, the Gaither City & Suburban Express Company was organized, with United Railways officials in executive capacities and Gaither as general manager. The streetcar company furnished the cars and supplied the power. From a warehouse, located at the triangle where Lombard, Liberty, and Howard Streets came together, and served by trackage on which passenger service had been discontinued, seven express cars operated over many of the United's outlying lines.

There was a dispute with the Baltimore and Frederick Turnpike Company concerning this service to Ellicott City and some complaint from patrons on the regular cars over delays caused by loading and unloading freight cars along the lines. Nevertheless the operation managed to survive a dozen years before being discontinued, at which time the cars were turned over to the maintenance of way department, with one surviving as late as 1963.

William House resigned in 1917 to serve the government during the war and was succeeded by Thomas A. Cross as president. Like his predecessor, Cross had worked his way up, starting with the North Avenue Railway in 1890 as a lineman. In 1898, he became superintendent of the overhead lines for the Consolidated Railway, general manager of the United in 1907, and vice-president in 1911. In the spring of 1920, Cross was replaced in turn by C. D. Emmons.

NOTES AND COMMENTS:

Trolley Topics, May 1930 contains a biography of Thomas Cross.

The P.A.Y.E. cars put in service on December 25, 1910 were the first Baltimore cars to be specifically built for this type of operation. *Electric Railway Journal,* October 15, 1910. However, on January 1, 1910, the company had put into service, on the Pennsylvania Avenue line, thirty-two older Brill semi-convertibles which had been altered in the company shops to allow pay-as-you-enter operation. The main modification required was the lengthening of the platforms from an even 5 feet to 5 feet, 8½ inches. *Electric Traction Weekly,* January 8, 1910.

Gaither's Express service reported in the *News,* July 19, 1899. The court case of Baltimore & Frederick Turnpike v. United Railways is covered in detail in *Maryland Reports,* vol. 93, pp. 138-149 (1901). Gaither's seven cars consisted of two Lewis & Fowler passenger cars rebuilt in 1899, a Laclede rebuilt in 1900, and four 1903-04 shop-built cars. L. C. Mueller notes.

A FATEFUL FIFTEEN YEARS

The life span of the streetcar in Baltimore was 104 years (until its rebirth as light rail in 1992), but in the brief period between 1915 and 1930 the cars fell from the pinnacle and were well on their way to oblivion, though their demise was to be a lingering one.

It is doubtful if anyone in those days realized just how close the streetcar was to being written off as a viable transportation factor in Baltimore. Certainly the utterances of the company officials, as late as the 1950s, were positive in stating that rail vehicles would continue to serve the more heavily traveled routes during the foreseeable future. Even the lightly patronized lines, it was thought, would continue in service as long as they proved economically feasible — until major track reconstruction was necessary.

Therefore, no one suspected the chain of events that was to be set in motion when, in February 1915, there appeared on the streets of Baltimore something called a "jitney." This was basically a truck body upon which was mounted a set of crude benches.

In those days of relatively high unemployment, the idea quickly spread. Soon, there were hundreds of the vehicles, cruising the streetcar routes and "pirating" the United's patrons. At first, regulations were nil. Crowding people on every inch of available space and not bound by routes or schedules, the jitneys rapidly caused a sharp decrease in the streetcar company's revenues.

Turnover in ownership of the jitneys was rapid, because they were not really profitable. This factor, combined with the

City and railway officials gather around private car *Maryland,* just prior to inauguration of service over the Hanover Street bridge in 1917. (Louis C. Mueller Collection)

One of Baltimore's first group of Birney cars loads at Charles and Hamburg terminus during 1920. Despite assignment of an extra man to throw switch, change poles, give out transfers, etc., rush-hour congestion due to narrow doorway slowed service. Newsboys, some barefoot, sold many a paper to riders during the streetcar era. (George F. Nixon Collection)

gradual imposition of regulations by the Public Service Commission, would undoubtedly have led to the eventual death of the craze. The United could not play this waiting game, however. A new threat of competition was arising, as responsible parties made advances to the city fathers for the establishment of a more elaborate bus system, featuring better equipment.

In July 1915, the United Railways and Electric Company created two subsidiaries. The first of these was the City Motor Company, which was to operate jitneys in direct competition with the freelancers. Between July 1st and 24th, three routes were established, all of which ran to the intersection of Howard and Lexington Streets, the heart of the shopping district. The outer extremities of the lines were at Patterson Park Avenue and Preston Street, Baltimore Street and Highland Avenue, and Payson Street and Edmondson Avenue. As the jitney fad waned, the City Motor routes were phased out only a little more than a year after they were begun.

The second subsidiary was a different proposition, though. The name chosen for it was — curiously enough — the Baltimore Transit Company. Its task was to run substantial buses on what was termed "an auxiliary service of a luxurious nature." Routed up swank Charles Street from the intersection of Redwood, they "landed," as the newspapers phrased it, at University Parkway. Though this bus operation lost money during its early days (official sources indicate $93,000 in 3½ years), the company did not discontinue it as it had the jitneys.

Nevertheless, the line was considered a fluke. Most people still rode the streetcars, so it was good news when the private car *Maryland*, with soon-to-be-Mayor Broening at the controls, inaugurated service over the new Hanover Street bridge on January 21, 1917. The old route to Brooklyn and Curtis Bay had fallen into disrepute when, on April 8, 1913, a car, headed towards town, derailed and plunged into the murky Patapsco, resulting in the death of a passenger. Two years later, a fire on the old bridge had sealed its fate. No one questioned the lack of a physical connection between the new route and the Westport line under the bridge.

The entry of the United States into World War I brought a tremendous increase in patronage on all of the lines, but particularly those serving the shipyards. A large number of trailers were put into service on the Fort Avenue line; these were 1898 Brownell cars which had been in storage. The most extensive innovation was near the lower end of the Sparrows Point route, where a new branch with a loop and prepayment station was constructed to serve the Bethlehem shipyards there. The new installation included an interlocking tower, protecting the main Sparrows Point streetcar trackage, as well as that of the Pennsylvania Railroad. Though primarily

Diminutive as it appears, and despite solid tires and exposed gas tank, original Charles Street bus was a vast improvement over the "jitneys." Photo was taken in late 1950s. In January 1965, this bus was presented to the Smithsonian Institution by the BTC. Lettering "Baltimore Transit Co." refers to a United Railways subsidiary later merged into the Baltimore Coach Company. (J. Kenneth Roberts Collection, BSM)

Early double-deck bus with open top was styled after New York's Fifth Avenue vehicles. This one was brand-new in 1922, when officials took a trial spin on upper Charles Street. (George F. Nixon Collection)

The United's Randallstown trackless trolleys, apparently just arrived in town. They promised much, delivered little. The company complained of expenses far in excess of estimates due to the bumpy condition of Liberty Road. When these vehicles expired after only ten years, no tears were shed. (Louis C. Mueller Collection)

intended to carry war workers, the extension was not completed until June 29, 1919.

Other innovations of the wartime period included the use of the highly unpopular skip-stop plan and the employment of women as conductors for the first time. It was generally conceded that their performance was highly satisfactory. Accordingly, the company let it be known in January 1919 that any of the 120 to 125 "conductorettes" who wished to might remain in the company's employ. Given new blue uniforms in November 1919, to replace the former unflattering khaki ones, members of the distaff sex remained in service until the end of the streetcars. Reduced to a handful by natural attrition at the start of World War II, their number was substantially increased during that conflict, when they were allowed to motor the cars for the first time.

In January 1920, the streetcars took on a strange new look. A Garrison Boulevard car was experimentally painted completely in "Allentown Red" with no contrasting trim. Labeling the test a success, the company during the next month announced that all cars would henceforth emerge from the paint shop in this shade (between a cherry and a vermilion). The former scheme of

dull red, with yellow striping, was abandoned. The company figured that it saved $10 per car, but Baltimore's leading streetcar historian, George Nixon, recalls his first glimpse of the cars in their unrelieved red paint with one word, "Horrible!"

At about the same time it was also decided that "lifeguards" on the cars would sufficiently protect the public; hence the iron and rope fenders which had been affixed to the fronts of the vehicles were removed. These lifeguards were wooden slat platforms tripped by a person or animal who was knocked beneath a car. When this occurred, the platform dropped to track level and prevented the victim from being mangled by the wheels.

All during the twenties a new breeze was blowing in the Baltimore transportation field. In May of 1920, the waiting station at Howard and Franklin, opened in 1905, was closed. July 1922 saw the Charles Street bus line so well patronized, that it was decided to put double-decker buses on the route. The following year the summer cars were permanently withdrawn from service.

In April of 1925, most of the East Fayette Street buses were acquired from independent operators, implementing a suggestion of the PSC that the United operate sup-

plemental service. (A handful of independents continued on this route until 1949.) As the twenties drew to a close, more and more familiar cars were retired. In March 1927, the funeral car *Dolores* was placed in storage, and on November 9, 1929, the railway post office cars were retired, the new post office then under construction having no facilities to handle them. Within the next few years, the company phased out the "pay cars," used to carry the payroll to the men on duty and to collect daily receipts from the car houses for deposit in the banks.

Probably the most nostalgic event of the decade was the closing of the popular amusement park, Riverview. The midway and casino were dismantled and much of the shoreline extended by fill; the Western Electric plant (now also closed) then rose on the site of the "Coney Island of the South."

Another innovation of the 1920s were those hybrid vehicles using electric power picked up from wires but running on rubber tires over regular roadways — the trackless trolleys. Their use was authorized by the PSC on December 18, 1922, and the company was granted a franchise by the City Council of Baltimore to run them on

Trailer No. 7002 on arrival in 1920. The one hundred units purchased bore a strong resemblance to 1924 Peter Witts but, of course, had no motors. Always handicapped by lack of cars powerful enough to pull them, trailers lasted barely ten years. President Emmons brought the basic design from the Boston system, where he had served until 1919. (Louis C. Mueller Collection)

Essential as they were when the snow piled high, few things about the street railways were as useless as a sweeper in the summertime. Here, No. 3224 lazes away the summer in Gardenville yard. (George J. Voith)

a route out Liberty Road from Gwynn Oak Junction to Randallstown.

Strange as it may seem in this present day (though rapid transit lines are rekindling the idea), real estate promoters in the twenties still thought it most desirable to have a rail line serving their properties. Not a few of the horse car lines had come into being for this reason, and, in 1892, the Lake Roland Elevated Railway had been built in order to connect the embryo Roland Park with downtown Baltimore. This idea persisted down to the time when the Guilford community was being developed, the line out St. Paul Street from 31st Street to Bedford Square being subsidized to serve the area.

When a new rail line to Randallstown was proposed, the United balked, however. The company felt that the potential did not justify the expense. A compromise was reached: trackless trolleys would be used. The developers felt that the stringing of the overhead would give an air of permanence to the operation and agreed to guarantee a portion of the losses. Three vehicles were acquired from J. G. Brill and used for about ten years, by which time the equipment was just about worn out.

Like the earlier Daft third rail line, the experiment appears to have been neither a success nor a failure. Still, when buses were put on the line in June 1932, it marked the first time that internal combustion engines had replaced electricity as a means of propulsion on the Baltimore system.

It was wartime, and, as was the case in many industries, women were replacing men who had departed for the armed forces. Whereas women served only as conductors in World War I, here we see a complete crew aboard a semi-convertible being trained under the watchful eye of an instructor, ca. 1943. (Transit Topics, BSM Collection)

NOTES AND COMMENTS:

As indicated in the United's *Annual Report,* 1916, the railway company determined that neither the jitneys nor the Charles Street bus line "could be operated at a profit with a five-cent fare." The claim of a $93,000 loss on the Charles Street line was reported in the *Evening Sun,* December 17, 1918.

According to George Nixon's notes, the Fort Avenue trailers were single-truck, eight-window, closed-body Brownell cars from which the motors had been removed. At the same time, forty-five double-truck, open-platform, semi-convertibles of 1912 vintage were assigned to Fort Avenue.

The Sparrows Point shipyard branch is fully described in the *Electric Railway Journal,* vol. 55, pp. 930-935 (1920). The article is illustrated with photographs and drawings.

Though women were not allowed by company rules to motor cars until World War II, a mention of a woman at the controls first appears on January 14, 1919 in the *Star.* Her name is unknown. Mentioned only as conductorette No. 6753, she was moving the car a few feet during switching over at the end of the No. 17 line, Light and Conway. For some reason she was unable to stop, and the car went through a switch and up Light Street. It hit a wagon loaded with tobacco before being halted by a pas-

serby, one C. J. Slattery, who stopped the car by pulling the trolley from the wire.

The company had been considering double-deck buses as early as August 1921, and by that December was ready to adopt them on the Charles Street line, contingent upon being allowed to charge a ten-cent fare to riders on that route. *Evening Sun,* August 5, 1921 and *Sun,* December 1, 1921.

The comprehensive story of Baltimore's early trackless trolleys can be obtained from the following sources: *Sun,* December 7 and 17, 1921; *Electric Railway Journal,* vol. 60, p. 760 (1922) and vol. 64, pp. 18-19 (1924); *Maryland Public Service Commission Report,* 1920.

During World War I, the United attempted to handle the peaks brought about by shift changes at Sparrows Point shipyard by putting down a new spur line with a prepayment station. Streetcars took care of the bulk of the workers, but Pennsylvania Railroad commuter trains at left handled a significant number of riders to Highlandtown and on to Union Station. (Nixon/Gerding Collection)

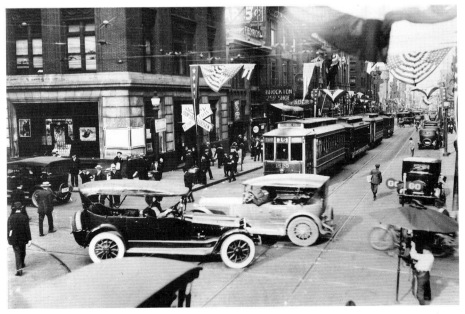

Baltimore Street was decorated for World War I Victory Loan drive when this picture was taken, May 28, 1919. Crossbuck sign on pole at Calvert Street intersection advises: "Victory Loan. Stop, look, LOOSEN." Another sign of the times is that for Brockton $2.50 shoes. The first three approaching streetcars are: 1918 semi-convertible, 1902 twelve-bench open car, another 1918 semi-convertible — all by Brill. (The Peale Museum)

"The Block," Baltimore Street east from Holliday, about 1917. Though the glow of neon was in the future, light bulbs outlining many signs and rococo ornamentation of Lubin's Theater give a hint of what was to come. A Brave Little Indian, billed as a "big western drama," was the featured film. Part of Gayety Theatre sign is visible behind the whiteway lamppost. (The Peale Museum)

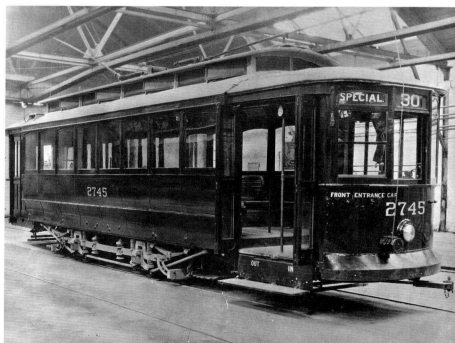

United Railways officials had little faith in the Birneys and, in 1921, rebuilt some 1904 Brill-built vehicles as one-man safety cars. The experiment was not very successful and most wound up on the Preston Street and other secondary lines. (Louis C. Mueller Collection)

Artist's conception of a rainy evening in Baltimore-town in 1926. The scene is Park Avenue and Liberty and Fayette Streets. Cars ran one after another and, once aboard, passengers could relax in a warm and comfortable atmosphere, leaving worries about slippery streets and rush-hour traffic to the motorman. Today, we have the marvel called the Jones Falls Expressway — ah progress! (UR & E Company, Willem Wirtz)

Baltimore tried several variations of the Birney cars. All proved impractical due to the slowness in loading and unloading caused by narrow doorway used for entrance and exit. Here, in what appears to be an experiment, No. 4006 is equipped with treadle-operated rear exit. None of the cars lasted ten years in Baltimore. (Louis C. Mueller Collection)

At least sixteen streetcars can be counted running up and down Howard Street through the remains of a wet snow, sometime around 1915. View is south from Mulberry Street, with the Baltimore Bargain House looming in the background. Pollack's and Stewart's, plus other firms such as Cohen and Hughes, Hirshberg Art Co., Schusters' Mattress factory, and the Sterling and Archer laundries, have vanished from Howard Street. Streetcars, in the form of modern light rail vehicles, returned to Howard Street in 1992 after more than fifty years. (Enoch Pratt Library)

A VALIANT TRY — BUT

In 1930, the United was headed by Lucius Storrs who had been brought in to try to stave off financial disaster. In that year, he made a valiant try to rejuvenate the streetcar system; but, though no one yet really believed it, it was too late. Storrs' gesture was the purchase of 150 new steel cars, which became known as Peter Witts, after the man who designed their interior arrangements.

The cars were roomy, comfortable, and fast — when they had room to operate. This was the key to the situation. When the number of private automobiles increased, as it inexorably did, any type of mass transportation vehicle was invariably slowed in the tangle of traffic. Private right of way (where the streetcars were completely separated from other traffic) was rare within the city limits, and while there had once been considerable "reserved" right of way, (where the cars ran adjacent to the roadway or in a median strip), this had substantially decreased as the population expanded into the suburbs. On Frederick, Belair, Harford — road after road — the tracks were moved to the center to widen the roadways, causing the streetcars to compete with automobiles along the entire route.

It is not the purpose of this book to delve too deeply into what might have been. Suffice it to say that, except for the Guilford Avenue elevated line (which was not really long enough to qualify), there was never constructed in Baltimore, or even seriously contemplated, any means of rapid transit in the modern sense (before Metro in the 1980s and light rail in the 1990s).

In Mayor William S. Broening's second administration (1927-31), there was some talk of building a new railroad bypass on an elevated structure over Pratt Street and diverting some of the north-south streetcar lines into the then-to-be-vacated Howard Street tunnel. This idea died aborning.

During 1921, many plans were put forth to use the existing surface tracks for express service. Abortive attempts on the Gilmor Street-Guilford Avenue and Towson-Catonsville lines, with certain cars stopping only at intersecting lines, failed when it was found that, despite the attempted scheduling, the "expresses" invariably caught up with the locals. Similar schemes on Druid Hill Avenue and St. Paul Street were also unsuccessful.

On the other hand, in the decade following World War I, the United seems to have quite innocently pursued a course in selection of vehicles which led patrons to desert in droves. The company's annual reports during the twenties show an ever increasing loss of patrons, which led to increases in fares to maintain the *status quo*. The company was further squeezed by the rapidly rising wages paid to motormen and conductors in the years during and following the war.

It will be readily agreed that it is much easier to see the picture in retrospect. Even with this advantage, it is difficult to speculate as to whether a different course would have had a different result in the long run.

Still, it should be borne in mind that the company did have certain alternatives in providing for vehicles in which to transport the riders. From 1905 until 1919, the United Railways and Electric Company purchased a total of 885 new passenger cars. The details of these vehicles are outlined elsewhere; but, briefly, they were considered among the most modern cars of their day. While the design remained basically the same, refinements were constantly made so as to provide the riders with the advantages of the advancing technology.

Beginning in 1920, the company decided that in order to offset increasing costs of transportation, especially the rising wage scale, some method of decreasing the number of platform men was essential. The first result of this decision was the purchase of one hundred trailers. In October 1919, Charles D. Emmons came to Baltimore from the Boston Elevated, succeeded Thomas A. Cross (who became Chairman of The Board) as president in 1920, and served as a catalyst to set off experiments right and left. While later efforts with articulated cars were reasonably successful, the early attempts (trailers and express runs) proved to be fiascoes. The 1920 trailer trains were said to be very difficult to get moving and almost impossible to stop.

Trailers in Baltimore were really nothing new, as most of the cable lines had used them during the rush hours, and the early electric cars had pulled them as well. They did reduce the crew of a two-car train by one, but unfortunately there were not enough cars on the property capable of hauling trailers. The cost of adding more powerful motors to existing cars led to a hunt for other methods of dealing with the problem.

The *Sun* of March 23, 1930 saw as the chief defect of a trailer train the fact that, even if one car of a two-car train were loaded and ready to go, it could not start until the other was loaded. The same article mentioned that the company was experimenting with a small motor attached to the truck of the trailer. The cost was over $3,000 a car and, as the trailers were removed from service only a year later, the project could not have been very successful.

Baltimore then tried the short, single-truck Birney cars. These were most unpopular, with wooden slat seats like the trailers and other spartan accommodations. It was also necessary, due to their limited capacity, to run more of these to carry the same number of riders as on the larger cars which they replaced. At the same time, since no rear door was provided, congestion at the front platform held down their efficiency.

Public transportation alternatives around 1925. Open-top, double-deck bus with steps at rear gets underway at Charles Street at Sun Square. Smaller Park Avenue bus is southbound. Articulated unit on No. 15 line is about to cross Baltimore Street intersection. Even at this early date, the practice of using Belgian blocks or bricks only adjacent to rails or specialwork is in evidence. The Hub department store, stretching an entire block on Charles Street, was later replaced. (BSM Collection)

Early on a snowy morn in 1921, rebuilt 1904 Brill car sits on transfer table at Carroll Park in all its awful all-red glory. This is very likely the first of these cars to be rebuilt for one-man operation. (George F. Nixon Collection)

No. 4522, a sister car of No. 2745, is pictured here at Maryland Avenue and Preston Street. The paint scheme is apparently orange. The bumpers, fenders, and grille of automobile at left may appear somewhat "quaint," but they would not crumple on a slight impact. (Robert L. Krueger Collection)

Prosperity was just around the corner? Not in 1930, but the United was making an attempt to recover lost riders with 150 modern steel cars. Peter Witt No. 6004 passes the spanking-new Baltimore Trust (Maryland National) building on a sunny Depression morning. The ground floor windows in the skyscraper fronted a Pennsylvania Railroad ticket office and advised passersby of Pullman and air-rail service. The group at Redwood Street stands in middle of street, "protected" while waiting for southbound car by a safety zone consisting of stanchions and chains. (Louis C. Mueller Collection)

The next idea was to convert some of the older single-truck cars to one-man operation. Again, one-man operation was not new to Baltimore. It had been used in horse car days, and electric cars had been run by one man on some of the jerkwater lines as early as the 1890s. However, in previous usage the rear platform had merely been locked up; the new plan called for extensive modernization of the cars, including installation of air brakes and deadman controls. Again, this did not prove to be the ultimate solution.

Another attempt (and the most successful) at cutting costs was the construction of the articulated units. Two older cars were spliced together, a hollow drum permitting passage between the sections. By this method, two men could perform the work which would require a crew of four — two motormen and two conductors — if single cars were used. Despite their somewhat awkward look, these cars moved fairly well in the traffic of the day. Because fares were collected while in motion by the conductor stationed at the front of the second car (the Peter Witt system), these units could swallow up large crowds rapidly. Their fatal flaw was the inability to disconnect the two cars. Unlike the multiple-unit trains, or even the unpowered trailers, which could be uncoupled and dropped off at a convenient car house during slack periods, the articulated cars were not versatile.

The year 1924 saw a feeble attempt to acquire new vehicles, when two cars were purchased for experimental purposes. These were early versions of the Peter Witt design, generally similar to the 150 acquired in 1930. One important difference was the fact that the 1924 cars were equipped for multiple-unit operation, although there was no through passageway as in the articulated units. To even the casual observer, the early cars could easily be identified by their front ends, which were more like the semi-convertibles in that they had three windows set at angles. The later Witts had flat fronts, and a double slanted windshield. The experimental cars, both as multiple and single units, were pronounced successful (every car tested in this period was invariably pronounced a success), but financial conditions precluded exercising of the company's option to purchase an additional forty-eight cars.

And the company was in financial difficulties — serious difficulties. Throughout its existence, the United had suffered from a lack of money to carry out necessary projects. A crisis had existed as early as 1904, when the Baltimore fire seriously disrupted revenues. This had been alleviated by the agreement with Maryland Electric Railways Company, which was able to fund projects that the United's credit restrictions would not permit it to finance directly. The arrangement had worked well for over twenty-five years, allowing the purchase of new cars and construction of many power houses, substations, and similar necessities. By 1928, the Maryland Electric Railways had become a completely controlled subsidiary and, along the way, had absorbed the few remaining "paper companies" which were not a part of the United itself. These included the Sparrows Point, Halethorpe, and Carney lines.

There had always been one specter lurking in the background of the financial affairs. The piper had never been completely paid for those halcyon days when cable and electric lines were being built with reckless abandon, and the day of recompense was drawing nigh. Things were so bad in December 1926, that the company tried to conserve power by not heating the cars during the morning and evening rush hours. The company explained that it felt the body heat of the passengers would keep the vehicles at the required 45-degree temperature.

For those interested in the intricate financial details, a letter put out by the financial house of Nelson, Cook and Company, of Baltimore, in the fall of 1928, spells out the problem succinctly.

Briefly, on November 1, 1929, a $1.5 million Baltimore Traction bond issue fell due. This was followed in March 1930 by $2.5 million of unsecured notes; in October 1931, by $2.8 million of Maryland Electric bonds; and in March 1932, by $1.3 million of Central Railway bonds. Thus, the very considerable sum of approximately $8 million fell due in a period of about 3½ years. In prior years, the company had managed to take care of the outstanding obligations of its predecessor companies as they matured; but at this point Nelson, Cook and Company concluded: "These sums cannot be obtained to refund unless the company's credit is restored now."

Much of the financial woe was credited to a decision of the Court of Appeals of Maryland, which had allowed a return of but 6.26 percent on investment. After protracted investigations, it had been established shortly before that the value of the company's property was $75 million. As a result of all this, the company's most active securities had declined in market value in excess of $11 million, with the average decline being about 20 percent. The setting of a 6.26 percent return rate had resulted in a further drop of $2.25 million in a few weeks.

Essentially, all of this meant that it was difficult to obtain new money, and that funds which were obtained probably cost from 1 to 2 percent more in annual interest rate than they would have otherwise. This would amount to many millions of dollars paid out in interest over a period of years, money that might instead have gone for new equipment.

The United soon scored two important points in its battle to secure a better return on investment. First, a change in the allowance for depreciation worked to the company's advantage; then, in early 1930, the United States Supreme Court ruled that the company was entitled to a return of 7.5 to 8 percent on its present fair value. This meant that the company could charge a higher rate of fare, and soon a base rate of ten cents went into effect.

While all this was going on, Lucius Storrs, who had been serving as managing director of the American Electric Railway Association, was brought in as executive chairman of the United in April 1929. He took over the leadership of the company without a shakeup of local officials, though Emmons resigned as president the following year.

Six months after Storrs arrived, the start of the Great Depression was signaled by the stock market crash. The new leader soon showed his mettle. In November, a new plan of financing the looming bond redemptions was devised. In connection with this, and in the teeth of the deepening depression, the United ordered 150 new streetcars at a cost of $2,550,000 in March 1930.

As noted earlier, these new steel cars (one hundred from Brill and fifty from Cincinnati Car) were of the Peter Witt design. While the details of the Peter Witt varied from city to city, its distinguishing feature was a center door exit with a conductor stationed just forward of it. A passenger boarded at the front entrance; if he sat in the forward section, he paid his fare just before leaving the car; if he took a rear seat, he paid as he passed the farebox. In either case there was no delay in taking on a crowd at a busy intersection. The same principle was applied to the articulated units, where the conductor was stationed at the front of the second car.

The Baltimore Peter Witts were also suitable for one-man operation and were used exclusively in this manner after a brief initial period. Thus, ironically, the prime feature of the design was virtually ignored. However, there were numerous others. Passenger comfort was enhanced by leather bucket seats, quiet operation, and door arrangement for quick loading and unloading. Fast acceleration and braking enabled them to hold their own easily in high-speed traffic.

It was a gallant effort, a valiant try; but it came too late. Conditions beyond the company's control, a financial depression that staggered the imagination, would soon spell finis for the United itself, despite all the innovations and economies that Storrs and his people could effect.

It must be concluded that these 1924 experimental Peter Witts were a mistake. Only two were purchased and they were seldom used. (Louis C. Mueller Collection)

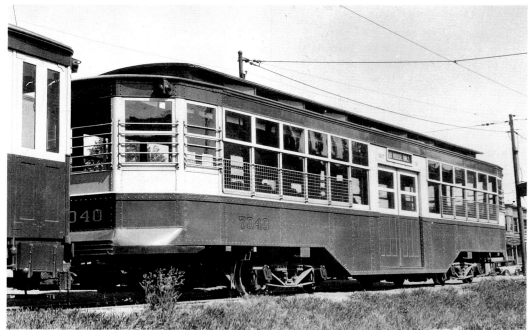

No. 7040, a steel trailer built by Brill in 1920, had an ungainly appearance, even in colorful paint scheme used after 1927. Its original solid red color was even worse. (Louis C. Mueller Collection)

Schoolgirls board Brill-built Peter Witt car on early fall morning in 1930. Dash sign reads "The New Baltimore Streetcar. The utmost in Comfortable, Safe, Smooth Riding." (Robert L. Krueger Collection)

This 1938 Brill trackless trolley somehow seems smaller than one remembers. Towards the end, Brills were largely restricted to the No. 21 Preston Street route. (Mass Transit Administration)

The Cincinnati Car Company built this Peter Witt in 1930. Vehicles made excellent time across the Hanover Street bridges on way to Fairfield and Curtis Bay. Complicated overhead wiring was made necessary by the draw span located at this point. (George J. Voith)

NOTES AND COMMENTS:

Harry S. Sherwood in an article entitled "The Railroads and the City," which appeared in the *Evening Sun* of May 18, 1929, touched on the possibilities of streetcars using the B & O's Howard Street (Belt Line) tunnel if it should be vacated by the railroad, which would construct a new line across Pratt Street. Had all of this come about, the result might have given Baltimore a trolley subway similar to Philadelphia's. "With the B & O tunnels freed from use by railroads, streetcars coming in from Belair and Harford roads, and other sections, could be led into the Belt Line Tunnel and brought down Howard Street with considerable increase in speed. The Washington, Baltimore & Annapolis cars could be led into the tunnel south of Camden Station, and could continue through the tunnel to sections north of the city, to some of the sections now served by the Northern Central. A station might be built by this road on Howard Street between Saratoga and Franklin."

From 1916 to 1920, streetcar riding, despite the fare increase, rose regularly and at a greater annual rate than during the preceding five years. But, from 1920 to 1929, car riding decreased at an annual rate of about 2.5 percent a year. The number of passengers carried, as well as the number of miles and cars operated, by coincidence, were very close to being the same in 1916 as in 1929, with passengers carried in 1916 numbering 199 million against 193 million in 1929. On the other hand, expenses had more than doubled, from $4,567,000 to $9,690,477. *Sun,* February 25, 1930.

Thirty-three Birney cars built by J. G. Brill were put on the Fremont Avenue line, July 1, 1920. Details of these cars and the group of "improved" Birneys purchased in 1921 can be found in the following issues of the *Electric Railway Journal*; vol. 56, p. 246 (1920); vol. 57, p. 1005 (1921); vol. 58, pp. 400-401 (1921).

According to L. C. Mueller, fourteen 20-foot 9-inch closed, single-truck, eight-win-dow Brownell cars were remodeled as one-man, prepayment cars in 1922. They were restricted to the Lorraine, Druid Ridge, Lakeside, Westport, Carney, Gorsuch Avenue, and Ferry Bar jerkwater lines. By October 1, 1933, all of these cars, numbered 4701-4714, had been scrapped.

At one time, the PSC had required the railway to equip all of its cars with thermometers. This requirement had been dropped because light-fingered riders kept making off with them.

A rather different look at the company's financial problems was written by H. L. Mencken for the *Evening Sun* of September 28, 1931. This was reprinted in the October 1931 issue of *Trolley Topics.*

The opinions of the Maryland Court of Appeals and the U. S. Supreme Court on the rate of return are given in *Maryland Reports,* vol. 155, pp. 572-613 (1928) and *Supreme Court Reporter,* vol. 50, pp. 123-139 (1930).

Brill 1910-12 semi-convertibles at rest in Putnam Street yard, west of Monroe Street and Washington Boulevard, July 1, 1931. Economies of Depression years are evident in casual refinishing of mashed-in dasher of No. 5420. (A. Aubrey Bodine Collection, the Peale Museum)

Howard and Lexington Streets in 1934. The No. 10 line car carried riders from Roland Park to Highlandtown by way of Pratt Street and Eastern Avenue. United Railways bus competed with independent operators on Fayette Street to Highlandtown. Safety zone "protects" group awaiting approaching Sparrows Point two-man car. The Central Light Rail Line now carries riders from Baltimore County to Anne Arundel County through this intersection. (The Peale Museum)

BANKRUPT!

In 1929, Lucius Storrs became president of the United. In 1930, he authorized the company's purchase of the 150 Peter Witt cars. In 1933, the United went bankrupt. Everyone knew that the payments due on the new cars were a big drain on the United's slim treasury. Therefore, Storrs plus new cars equaled bankruptcy. Right? Wrong!

Strange as it may seem, if the company had only been able to raise the money to purchase more new cars, it might well have staved off financial collapse. This paradox is explained in a report to the court when the receivers sought permission to pay an installment on the Peter Witt cars. Because of the savings involved as a consequence of the large weight differential of the new cars compared to the older vehicles, as well as the one-man operation principle, the 150 cars were responsible for the saving of $400,000 a year. This was far in excess of the 6 percent interest, plus depreciation.

But the difficult times, combined with the poor financial shape of the company, made it impossible to borrow the necessary money. Starting in 1928, large scale economies were begun in the operating department. In each succeeding year, the cost reductions cut deeper. As another paradox, service to the public was reduced very little — on some lines it was actually improved. Again, this is explained by the fact that the Peter Witt cars made possible faster schedules with fewer cars and less manpower.

Another means of easing the financial strain on the railway was effected by the City of Baltimore. The municipal authorities finally realized that the company could no longer stand the drain of a 9 percent park tax (originally 20 percent, the tax had been reduced to 9 percent by 1882). In 1932, a new arrangement was made which cut the park tax to 3 percent and added, as a sop, a net income tax of 20 percent in the unlikely event that the company again became a profitable operation. It was quite a surprise when this actually came to pass, as it did during the unusual days of World War II, and it caused all kinds of complications.

Despite all the efforts in cutting costs and expenses, the company, beginning in July 1931, went into the red with monotonous regularity, month after month. In 1932, income fell short of expenditures by almost $2 million. Soon after the new year dawned, attorneys for the General Electric Company, which held a number of the company's notes, went into Federal Court to petition for receivership. This was granted, and on January 6, 1933, the United Railways and Electric Company was officially declared bankrupt!

Bankruptcy, as it turned out, was just what the company needed to get back upon its feet. The economies previously put in force were, of course, continued, while others, normally impossible, could be effected under the circumstances. Not the least of these was the suspension of bond interest payments.

The rejuvenation of the company was put in the hands of two men appointed as receivers by the court. One, William H. Meese, was the plant manager of the Western Electric's Point Breeze works. The other was Lucius Storrs. Thus Storrs was placed in a position to leave an indelible mark on the company. Already, he was well known, not only for his purchase of new cars, but also for his leading role in obtaining the fare increase to ten cents during the early days of the depression.

Incidentally, under prodding from the court, the company instituted a trial fare reduction to two tokens for fifteen cents, in January 1934. It was calculated that, to offset this 25 percent cut in fares, the company would have to attract an additional 98,000-odd riders per day. The actual increase was barely half this number, so the trial was quickly abandoned.

The period of receivership lasted for the relatively brief period from January 6, 1933 to July 9, 1935. The corporation emerged from bankruptcy, not only with a new capitalization of about $50 million, rather than the previous $85 million, but also with a new name — the Baltimore Transit Company. Again, it is not the purpose of this book to present an involved financial record of the companies that ran the streetcars. Still, it would be remiss not to enable those interested in such matters to follow the broad outlines of the financial picture.

Fortunately, the *Sun* of September 1, 1935 presented a comprehensive article on the subject, from which the following excerpts are taken:

"Nowhere in the annals of the municipal transit companies can one find record of a company being subjected to such a thorough financial renovation as the United Railways & Electric Company — now the Baltimore Transit Company — received at the hands of its first-line bondholders. They made a bold, clean sweep of an antiquated financial structure which had hung like a millstone around the neck of the company for years. By a plan of reorganization — considered by legal authorities as worthy of the appellation 'unique,' — the committee representing the bondholders squeezed the company free of water, induced the mortgageholders to postpone their expectation of financial return to some unnamed date in the future, and set up a revamped structure which — if there is any hope for street railways at all — has the soundest chance to get on a profitable basis that any company has enjoyed in many moons. When the new directors took over the Baltimore Transit Company a few weeks ago they took over a debt-free organization. Not only that, they took over a balance sheet that ought to gladden the hearts of any corporate directors. Instead of the capital obligations running far in excess of the actual value of the property — as they had done for so many years — . . . the

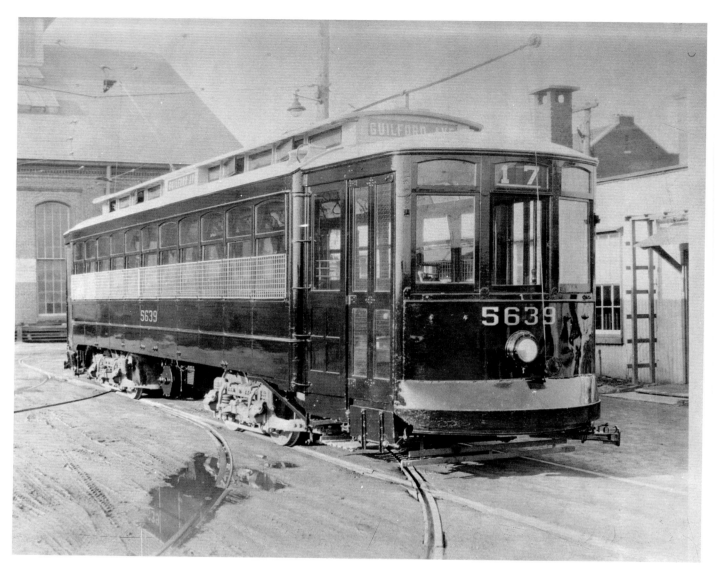

This is how the semi-convertibles looked in the solid red paint scheme used from World War I to 1927. The only contrast was provided by roof, trucks, and window screens. (Louis C. Mueller Collection)

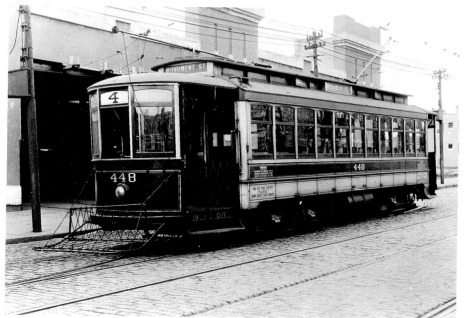

Until 1930, the 885 Brill semi-convertibles bought between 1905 and 1919 were the workhorses of the Baltimore fleet. Beginning in 1912, when No. 448 was delivered, cars started carrying illuminated route numbers. At first, dark numerals were etched on white frosted glass; later, this was reversed so that the background was dark, the numbers clear. (Louis C. Mueller Collection)

Double-deck bus leads a semi-convertible past Pennsylvania Station in late twenties; by now autos are beginning to dominate the street scene. (Louis C. Mueller Collection)

exact reverse is true of the new company; the present value of the used and useful property exceeds its capital obligations by a good many million dollars . . . .

"In their work of reorganization, the first-line bondholders were completely and compellingly realistic. They knew that the bondholders could never again have any honest expectation of a return on their investment until the properties were placed on an income basis — that is to say, on a basis that, after providing for all operating expenses and the reserves adequate to cover retirements and depreciation, will produce a surplus sufficient to cover interest requirements.

"Because there was no earthly way of telling when the tide of prosperity would again flow heavily enough in the com-

pany's direction to produce such an agreeable situation, the reorganization committee took no chances by loading down the structure with a new burden of fixed charges. They gave the old holders debentures and preferred stock, and made future payments dependent upon earnings, save for a small block of less than a million dollars of obligations, on which they provided an unconditional annual payment of $46,000 — the sole fixed obligation of the company. They added, however, that the interest should be cumulative, on a scale, and the dividends on the preferred stock cumulative — to which nobody, in the circumstances, could object."

The company was "debt-free" in the sense that the old bondholders, who

formerly expected to receive fixed interest payments on certain dates, now owned stock and debentures, which, of course, depended on profitable operations for a return on investment.

Lucius Storrs became the first president of the new BTC but retired in April 1936. He was succeeded by Executive Vice President Bancroft Hill, who headed the Company until June 1945. A native of Baltimore, Hill had held the position of Harbor Engineer for the City before joining the United as Consulting Engineer in 1925. He was the last president of the system while it remained under local control and played an important role in the acquisition of more than two hundred streamlined PCC cars.

NOTES AND COMMENTS:

The savings effected by the use of the Peter Witt cars (referred to in the article as "Baltimore-type cars") were reported by Mark S. Watson in the *Sun,* May 21, 1933.

A "Park Tax" of 20 percent on gross receipts was one of the conditions imposed in the original horse car franchise. This was reduced to 12 percent in 1874 and to 9

percent in 1882. For the next fifty years, the rate remained unchanged; but, with the company facing receivership, a new city ordinance passed in 1932 reduced the Park

Twenty years of service as a utility car for the maintenance of way department had changed Gaither's express car surprisingly little. Shortly before being scapped in 1937, it served as a convenient backrest for the shopman during his lunch hour. (Louis C. Mueller Collection)

The street railway plays the good neighbor. When the covered county bridge at Ellicott City burned on June 7, 1914, a footwalk allowed the United's bridge to be used for pedestrian access across the Patapsco River. (George F. Nixon Collection)

Tax to 3 percent, with a clause inserted for a 20 percent net income tax on any future earnings. "When the company attained unprecedented prosperity (during World War II) the net income tax failed to materialize because of certain arbitrary deductions permitted in the 1932 ordinance and because of other, questionable, deductions made by the company." The BTC finally settled with the city for $550,000, the major portion of which, it was said, was to adjust differences pertaining to the net income tax. *Evening Sun,* November 15, 1944 and *Journal Of The City Council,* May 6, 1946, pp. 1407-8.

Much of the financial woe of the company during this period was summarized in the feature "Our Yesterdays" which appeared in the *Evening Sun,* January 6, 1958, twenty-five years after the company went bankrupt.

Articulated unit No. 8141 curves through sidewalk track adjacent to Belvedere car house. This particular car was made in 1926 by butting together two semi-convertible cars. Multiple-unit trains were more versatile. (Louis C. Mueller Collection)

Snow-clearing operations always intrigued recorders of railway history. This was North and Maryland Avenues. Expensive photographic equipment was not a prerequisite. This photo was made with a "box" camera. (Robert W. Janssen)

No. 4 streetcars, bound for Windsor Hills, are tied up on Charles Street, between Centre and Hamilton, as chains are adjusted on stalled automobile. Strange as it may seem, the trolleys had relatively little trouble climbing snow-covered hills such as this. Their heavy weight, plus a liberal use of sand, accomplished the feat. This incident occurred during 1935, the last year that the fixed-wheel streetcars would "impede" the free-wheeling autos on this stretch. On December 31st, the No. 4 line was cut back to a loop via Saratoga, Charles, and Lexington. (A. Aubrey Bodine Collection, the Peale Museum)

A LAST BRILLIANT FLARE

The state of the streetcar industry in Baltimore, after the time of World War I, might be compared to a guttering candle in a drafty room. As America was becoming enmeshed in its love affair with the automobile, the winds of change often reduced the lure of the trolley to a flickering flame seemingly on the verge of being extinguished. The spark of life, which had shone so brightly in the days of City Passenger and Baltimore Traction, burned low. During the 1920s and early 1930s, the distaste of the public for the spartan Birney cars and trailers caused it to gutter low, gasping for life, while the carbon monoxide of the buses spread from Charles Street — to Monroe Street, to Canton, to Middle River, to Glyndon.

There was to be one last flare of brilliance, though. Just at the time when Baltimore Transit was emerging from bankruptcy, the powers in the streetcar industry decided that the way to win back the fickle public was by beating the bus boys at their own game. All of the carbuilders, save Brill, pooled their talents in designing a vehicle which would be the last word in comfort, convenience, and speed. The moving force behind the innovations consisted of the leaders of the street railway companies. Therefore, the new car which evolved came to be known as the Presidents' Conference Committee car, or PCC.

Many of the mechanical and electrical changes had been perfected in the earlier cars, such as the 1930 Peter Witts in Baltimore and the "Master Unit" cars in several other cities. These streamlined PCCs featured smooth, rapid acceleration, but what most impressed the public was the exterior design.

The impact of the streamlined design is illustrated by experience at the Baltimore Streetcar Museum. At first, many of the guides were distressed that not a few of the younger visitors (those who had never ridden a streetcar) referred to the PCC in the

It was a cold day in December 1944, when PCC No. 7409, newly delivered, prepared to swing past the traffic tower at North and Charles. Turrets of the North Avenue Market loom above Taney Place, once a park with trees and grass, now paved over for automobiles. This scene is much different today. (Louis C. Mueller Collection)

collection as a bus. Yet, when it originally went into production, the PCC certainly bore little resemblance to the buses of that period. So, on second thought, it could only be assumed that these babes were paying the PCC the ultimate compliment, since imitation is said to be the sincerest form of flattery. In all the ensuing years, the designing geniuses in Detroit have failed to get away from the basic appearance of this streetcar designed way back in 1935.

Baltimore was among the earliest of the cities to show an interest in the PCC, but the first deliveries went to Brooklyn, New York. Not long after, the first car (No. 7023) arrived here from the St. Louis Car Company. The Transit Company promptly put it on a loop over portions of two lines to familiarize the personnel and the public with the new equipment.

Cars Nos. 7023-7027 were the first in regular service, on the No. 31 — Garrison

Boulevard line. The date was December 1, 1936. Since the No. 31, in an unusual arrangement, took over the No. 13 line across North Avenue on Sundays, the new cars also served on that line once a week. The remainder of the new cars, Nos. 7001-7022, also from St. Louis, quickly followed. Just before Christmas, on December 20th, PCC operation began on the No. 25 Mt. Washington route.

These twenty-seven cars were to be the only ones purchased from St. Louis. The rest of the PCC fleet came from the Pullman-Standard Car Manufacturing Company. In addition, BTC purchased one Brilliner, No. 7501, the J. G. Brill Company's own answer to the PCC. It was very similar in appearance and quite possibly the smoothest riding car ever to run in Baltimore.

The public was genuinely excited by the startling change. People began to ride the cars again, just to see what they were like.

Photographer Bodine's ingenuity shows in his use of the mirror at the center exit of a St. Louis PCC car to obtain unusual picture of door well. "Ice-cube tray" lighting diffusers are behind mirror. (A. Aubrey Bodine Collection, the Peale Museum)

Sitting in a comfortable leather seat, fingering switches on control console, operator of the late 1930s was a far cry from his brothers who had stood exposed to the elements on the open platforms of early electric cars. Some things had not changed much over the years, though. Uniform is very like those worn at turn of the century. (A. Aubrey Bodine Collection, the Peale Museum)

Close-up of modern Clark Equipment Company truck on St. Louis PCC No. 7023, the first of the streamlined cars to run in Baltimore. (A. Aubrey Bodine Collection, the Peale Museum)

Head-on view of the BTC's only Brilliner, acquired in 1939, gives one the feeling that Brill design was more functional than esthetically pleasing. (George J. Voith)

Newly refurbished double-trucked flatcar No. 3713 belies its forty-odd years in work service when photographed in 1948. Oil lamp tied to cab was safety precaution on rare occasions when the car was run at night. (George J. Voith)

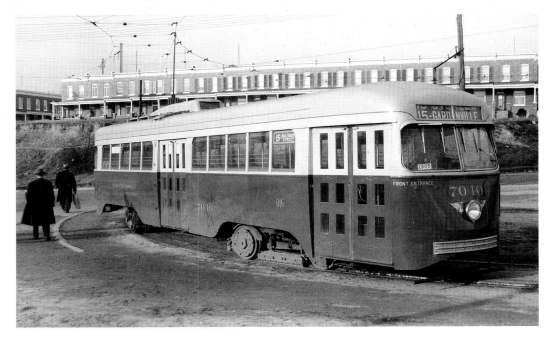

No. 7040, built by Pullman-Standard in 1940, sits at West Baltimore Street loop, ready to begin return run to Gardenville. Block number — 1505 — at lower left of front window was metal plate picked up by operator at beginning of run. (George J. Voith)

This was Charles Center on February 7, 1941. Single-ended semi-convertible of No. 4 line makes turn from Charles into Lexington past the Fidelity Building. A corner of O'Neill's is at left. Further down the street are United-Whalen, Kay Jewelers, Wyman Shoes, and Lexway Theater. Beyond the Gas and Electric Company building is a billboard advertising Free State Beer. Keith's was showing *Back Street*. Loew's Century featured a rerun of *Gone With the Wind*, with "nothing cut but prices." (A. Aubrey Bodine Collection, the Peale Museum)

A LAST BRILLIANT FLARE 147

No. 7302, once numbered in the 7000 series as one of the first lot of St. Louis PCCs, sits at Belvedere loop. The car still had blinker doors and the original type of windshield wipers. The streamlined cars were Baltimore's first with powered wipers. (Enoch Pratt Library, Burridge Jennings)

No. 7501, Baltimore's one and only Brilliner, makes a stop on York Road, when the car still had wheel skirts and circular glass in doors. Despite boxy look, some thought the car's heavy weight provided a better ride than the PCCs. *New Moon*, a Romberg operetta, was playing at City College. (Louis C. Mueller Collection)

After years of red rear-entrance cars, and yellow front-entrance ones, the PCCs were a throwback to the colorful streetcars of yesteryear. The lower portion was Alexandria blue (practically a dark green) and the belt rail orange; from there to where the roof soffit boards were located on the older cars, cream paint was used, set off by a pearl gray roof. There was liberal use of chrome, including the anti-climbers, standee straps, seat handholds, and the "wings" alongside the headlight. The color scheme was chosen as the result of a contest among the students at the Maryland Institute.

Among the mechanical features were rubber-sandwich wheels and magnetic brakes; but the public principally noted the operator's console, his foot-operator accelerator (rather than the old hand controller), brake and dead-man controls, the comfortable green upholstered seats, and the indirect lighting. One boy, just entering his teens, was particularly fascinated by the light diffusers which looked for all the world like ice-cube trays set into the headliner.

The Transit Company found various scenic places throughout the area as convenient backdrops to pose buses. In this 1939 photo, articulated "one of a kind" No. 1019 looks ungainly, yet it negotiated turns such as the one from the steep hill northbound on Cathedral Street into narrow Mulberry Street with ease. (BSM Collection)

While this is primarily a book about streetcars, it would be remiss not to mention a very unusual bus that the company tried out about 1939. It was forty-seven feet in length and seated fifty-eight riders. This was a "Super-Twin," built by the Twin Coach Company, and the company claimed that it could turn the sharpest corners as easily as the smaller buses. A turning radius of about thirty-four feet was achieved by means of "synchronous turning of the front and rear pairs of wheels, the latter taking an angle opposite to the front pair and tracking in the same path." The vehicle was articulated, with four wheels with dual tires at the center. Company literature described the power supply thus: "equipped for operation as a diesel-electric unit, having a 175 horsepower Hercules engine attached to an electric generator in the rear compartment. Propulsion was through two 125 horsepower motors placed under the floor, beneath each half of the coach."

Downtown just after World War II, a No. 14 line car prepares to turn onto Park Avenue from Lexington. Painted lines in street warned of swing of car body. Keith's Theater was torn down for a parking garage; most of the buildings behind the semi-convertible were demolished in connection with the construction of Charles Center. (Robert W. Janssen)

Trackless trolley peeking into photo from left made tracks on Howard Street obsolete. The company often removed unneeded rail at its convenience, as this crane is doing at Lombard Street. (Robert W. Janssen)

Some cars served a number of purposes over the years. This one was built in 1904 as a dump car, later converted to a weed sprayer as shown here. It then became reel car numbered 3551. (Louis C. Mueller Collection)

NOTES AND COMMENTS:

Detailed technical articles on the PCC are found in *Transit Journal,* vol. 80, pp. 216-232 (1936).

A good insight into Baltimore's attitude toward the PCC cars can be gained from the *Sun,* September 1, 1935 and the *Baltimore Transit Company Annual Report* for 1940. Various issues of *Transit Topics* and *Trolley Topics* from 1936 through World War II contain data on the cars and their performance.

Herbert G. Frank, Jr. gives an excellent description of the Brilliners in the *National Railway Historical Society Bulletin,* vol. 23, no. 4, pp. 26-31 (1958). Baltimore's

No. 7501 was one of only thirty standard Brilliners to be built.

My favorite cars were the St. Louis PCCs and I have often wondered why the Baltimore Transit Company swung over completely to the Pullman-Standard models. According to John V. Engleman in the *Live Wire* (newsletter of the Baltimore Streetcar Museum), vol. 5, No. 2 (1972), "the Pullman cars were of superior construction, but lacked some of the fancy frills of the St. Louis cars." John notes that the lower portion of the original paint scheme was Alexandria blue, not Alexander. Most issues of the *Live Wire* contain much tech-

nical and other information on various Baltimore cars. The copy alluded to gives, in detail, the many color combinations applied to the streamlined cars over the years.

The "ice-cube trays" referred to were absent in the Pullman-Standard cars, which used bull's-eye lenses for interior lighting. These cars also had a single longitudinal seat along the side of the car between the doors, rather than the individual cross seats of the St. Louis cars. Outwardly, the St. Louis vehicles had more rounded front and rear ends, a rubrail, and several strips of molding at roof level, which readily distinguished them from the Pullmans.

8 MAIN TYPES
OF TRANSIT VEHICLES
and How to Use Them

1 **GREEN CARS**
Front Entrance, Center Exit

Pay as you enter at *front* of car; then please move *back* in car and leave by *center* exit. To leave car, pull cord to signal motorman. Then step down one step and doors open automatically when car stops.

2 **YELLOW CARS**
Front Entrance, Center Exit

Pay as you enter at *front* of car; then please move *back* in car and leave by *center* exit. To leave car, push button to signal motorman, stand on treadle step, and doors open automatically when car stops.

3 **YELLOW CARS**
Front Entrance, Rear Exit

Pay as you enter at *front* of car; then please move *back* in car and leave by *rear* exit. To leave car, push button at your seat or on left jamb of rear door, then stand on treadle.

4 **RED CARS**
Rear Entrance, Front Exit

Pay as you enter at *rear* of car; then please move *forward* and leave by *front* exit. At some transfer points, transfer passengers *only* may enter Red Cars at front and present transfers to motorman.

5 **RED 2-CAR or 3-CAR TRAINS**—*Rear Entrance, Front Exit*

Pay as you enter at *rear* of either car; then if in first car please move *forward* and leave by *front* exit. In second or third cars leave by rear door.

6 **YELLOW ARTICULATED TRAINS**—*Front Entrance, Center Exit*

Enter at *front* of train *only*; leave by *center* exit *only*. Pay fare as you pass conductor at center of train—either in moving back to occupy rear car, or as you move from front car to leave by center exit.

7 **TRACKLESS TROLLEYS**
Front Entrance, Center Exit

Pay as you enter at *front* of trolley; then please move *back* in car and leave by *center* exit. To leave car, pull cord and stand on treadle. Door opens automatically when trolley stops.

8 **MOST BUSSES**
Front Entrance, Center Exit

Pay as you enter at front of bus; then please move *back* in bus and leave by *center* exit. To leave bus, pull cord to signal operator and stand on treadle.

During World War II many who were not used to riding public transit were thrown onto the cars. Gas rationing was largely responsible, but the influx of war workers added to the crowds. New riders were often confused by the six different types of cars, hence this guide. (Transit Topics)

LOST STREETCARS AND PART-TIME MOTORMEN

At 5:39 a.m., March 6, 1938, the trackless trolley returned to Baltimore in a pilot operation on the No. 21 route. Not that the Baltimore Transit Company was not completely satisfied with its new streamlined streetcars — rather, this was in anticipation of future developments; the City was improving things for the automobile again.

In 1936, when the Orleans Street Viaduct (spanning Calvert Street, Guilford Avenue, the Fallsway, and Bath Street) opened, rail traffic had not only been banned from it but also from the existing rail trackage on Orleans Street. The viaduct was a part of a new free-wheel traffic artery, planned by the City of Baltimore, which would run west from Philadelphia Road (Pulaski Highway) across Orleans Street, the new viaduct, Franklin Street, Monroe Street, Wilkens Avenue, and into Washington Boulevard. This resulted in removing the Nos. 4, 23, and 26 lines from portions of Franklin Street, as well as replacing the No. 3 cars with buses. In conjunction with the latter switchover, the wide grass plots in the center of Wilkens Avenue were replaced by asphalt divided by a narrow slab of concrete.

Now the City was constructing another major improvement, the long-delayed Howard Street extension. This involved extending Howard several blocks northward from Richmond Market (near the Fifth Regiment Armory), tunneling under Mt. Royal Avenue, and building a new bridge over Jones Falls and the Pennsylvania Railroad to North Avenue and Oak Street (now Howard). As a part of this project, the City decreed that the trackage on the old portion of Howard Street had to go.

Rather than go for buses, as it had on Orleans Street, the Company opted for trackless trolleys. As noted above, they were first tried out on the No. 21 (Preston Street) line, which coincidentally was rearranged so that it approximated the old Central Railway routing. Twenty-two vehicles were purchased for this initial conversion — eleven from Mack, ten from Brill, and one from General Motors Corporation. The G.M.C. was an "all-service vehicle" — the only one of its kind ever to run in Baltimore. This could either operate as an ordinary trackless trolley, or provide its own power by means of a gasoline engine driving an electric generator.

The new equipment worked well. By the time the red brick roadway on Howard Street had been completed, thirty new Pullman trackless trolleys were ready to take over the No. 27 (Preston Street-Morrell Park) line. Forty additional Pullman-built units joined the fleet when the No. 10 (Roland Park-Highlandtown) line went trackless on April 14, 1940; the route was revised to make use of the new Howard Street bridge.

Residents of the upper portion of Roland Avenue objected to the planned conversion. This would have meant the No. 29 streetcars continuing to operate on their reserved trackage in the median strip, while the new trackless vehicles ran on the rather narrow roadways to either side. Since the Company was not yet quite ready to convert the No. 29, it agreed to terminate the No. 10 at a loop around the Roland Park Water Tower, just south of University Parkway. To provide sufficient connecting service, the No. 24 Lakeside jerkwater was extended south from the Roland Park car house on Upland Avenue to the Water Tower. As this was considered a temporary arrangement, tracks were not run into the loop, resulting in streetcars laying over in the middle of busy Roland Avenue.

In addition to the Nos. 10 and 27 lines, streetcars on the Nos. 23, 25, 26, and 32 lines were rerouted off Howard Street. A "take one," listing service changes effective January 1, 1939, notes: "In order to cooperate with the plans of the City's Traffic Committee, and with the approval of the PSC, several transit lines will be rerouted to *facilitate the movement of free-wheel vehicles in congested areas."* (Author's emphasis)

Thirty more Pullman trackless trolleys arrived in 1942, marked for the No. 29 line conversion. However, due to wartime conditions, the overhead fixtures and copper trolley wire were not obtainable, so the vehicles were divided among the three existing routes. Six more Pullmans arrived in 1944. (Sixty-two purchased from Brill in 1947 and 1948 were the last to be built for Baltimore.)

For streetcars, the year 1938 was both good and bad. On April 3rd, the portion of the No. 5 line north of Manhattan Avenue in Pimlico was replaced by bus. In conjunction with the conversion of the No. 27 line to trackless, rail service on the No. 12 (John Street-Westport) line was discontinued on the last day of the year. However, this loss was partly offset by extending the No. 17 streetcar route from Camden Station to Westport to take over the lower portion of the old No. 12.

It was a good year for riding. During the summer, one could travel back and forth, transferring when desired, from 7 p.m. to 1 a.m. for only one ten-cent adult fare. All year long, from 10 a.m. to 4 p.m. on weekdays and all day Sundays, round trips cost only fifteen cents with the use of the two-trip slips, which had been introduced in January 1937.

On July 2, 1939, forty new PCCs were acquired to provide base service on the No. 8 (Towson-Catonsville) line. This move provided modern equipment on the company's heaviest route. Like all future deliveries, these cars came from Pullman-Standard.

Rail service held its own going into the 1940s. The portion of the old No. 10 line from Highlandtown to Point Breeze had been retained as a streetcar route, with the No. 20 designation. In early 1941, preparations for the coming war effort brought a curtailment of bus conversions. In the same year, the Fairfield loop extension was built to serve the heavy influx of shipyard and other war workers. In the months just prior to Pearl Harbor, 108 more PCCs were put in use on the Belair Road, Harford Road, Woodlawn, Pimlico, Rolling Road, and Edmondson Avenue lines. Eighteen more of these cars arrived for the No. 6 Curtis Bay line on December 21, 1941, and seven for the No. 29 "Roland Park-Boulevard line" the following February 2nd.

Although the war prevented the delivery of other cars on order, there were an even two hundred streamlined cars on the property now. For some time past, the company had been storing the older cars as they had become surplus, rather than scrapping them. Thus, it was in a much better position to handle the wartime boom in patronage than had been the case in World War I, when there was practically no reserve.

Soon, old red 5200s which had not been seen in years, as well as 8100 and 8500 series articulated cars, began to come out of storage. The No. 23 streetcar line from Grundy Street to Back River was discontinued. It had stopped several miles short of the Glenn L. Martin aircraft plant in Middle River, to which through service was urgently needed for war workers. For this purpose buses were now pulled off other lines, resulting in the discontinuance of some bus routes and the drastic curtailment of many others. Among the casualties was the "A" line, whose double-deckers ran up Charles Street for the last time on December 27, 1942. Though some, at least, reappeared on the Monroe Street line in 1945, the war service had just about worn them out, and they never returned to Charles Street.

Skip-stops returned to the local scene in 1943, by which time the manpower shortage was so severe (despite the large number of women taken on to replace employees who had gone into the service) that part-time operators were hired for rush-hour

A Towson-bound streetcar passes the Peale Museum — between trolley and bus — during final days of operation. The Peale building had served as Baltimore City Hall in 1859 when the horse car question was being debated. At the time photo was taken, discussions were being held in present City Hall — just out of picture to right — relative to abandonment of all streetcar service. (James A. Genthner)

To turn PCC and Peter Witt cars on the dead-end Stadium spur, it was necessary to back them down to Gorsuch Avenue, where they were wyed, and made the return trip in reverse up Loch Raven Road, as shown. Emergency controls at rear of cars made this a relatively simple operation. (Robert W. Janssen)

periods. The newspapers made a big splash on several occasions when inexperienced motormen missed a switch, taking the surprised patrons on an unexpected tour before finding the way back to the normal path.

The Paradise Avenue loop on Frederick Road was constructed in 1944, the same year that the company received seventy-five more Pullman-Standard PCC cars,

the very last Baltimore streetcars to be placed in service. They were similar to previous deliveries, except that most of the brightwork was painted in gray or black due to wartime shortages of certain metals.

When the war ended in 1945, the skip-stop plan was discarded, and the cars again stopped at every corner. However, perhaps

Pullman-Standard No. 7407, delivered in 1944, was one of the last group of streetcars purchased by the BTC. This car made the very last run in the early morning hours of November 3, 1963. The restored car is shown on Baltimore Streetcar Museum trackage in 1972. The use of a cardboard route number in conjunction with roller destination sign was a fairly common Baltimore practice. (Joseph F. Hasener, Jr.)

the two big events of the year were the acquisition of a block of BTC stock by American City Lines (which was affiliated with Roy Fitzgerald's National City Lines) and the retirement of John Brooke Duvall, Sr., as of December 31st. Mr. Duvall, who at retirement was serving as vice-president and general manager, had been with the company for forty-eight years, having started as a motorman for the Baltimore City Passenger Railway way back in 1897, when cable cars were still in use.

NOTES AND COMMENTS:

Just prior to the opening of the Orleans Street (or Bath Street) viaduct, the Baltimore Transit Company placed in racks in its vehicles a "take one" folder which included the following statement: "The re-routing of both the No. 4 and No. 6 lines was required by the Federal Government, which furnished a portion of the funds for building the viaduct on condition that streetcars be removed from approaches to the viaduct and that only buses be operated over it."

Transit Topics, September 1937 issue, contains an article on Baltimore's first "modern" trackless trolleys. A short, but comprehensive, history about trackless trolley operation in Baltimore by James Genthner appeared in the *Sunday Sun Magazine* of March 7, 1965. Incidentally, the hybrid vehicles were seldom, if ever, referred to locally as "trolley buses."

The *Sun,* September 12, 1943, is the basis for statement relative to failure to use the 30 Pullman trackless trolleys delivered in 1942 on the No. 29 line.

According to a BTC "take one" notice — "Discontinuance of the No. 12 line will make room on Park Avenue for any lines which may be shifted from Howard Street."

Assignments of PCC cars are based on George Nixon's notes — Evolution of PCC Assignments (by lot).

No. 5842, one of a group of fifty semi-convertibles built by Brill in 1919 for the U.S. Emergency Fleet Corporation and leased to the United, is running along the shore of Chesapeake Bay in August 1947. These cars, which became known as the "red rockets," served the Sparrows Point shipyard and steel mill on weekdays and carried the crowds to Bay Shore on Sundays and holidays. Sign on dasher reads "Swim Bay Shore Park." The overhead feed wire with tap to the trolley wire shows up clearly. (George J. Voith)

The coming of the single-end Peter Witt and PCC cars made terminal loops almost mandatory, but on a few lines double-ended cars still laid over in the center of the street. These one-man semi-convertibles wait for scheduled departure times on 25th, at Greenmount. (Robert W. Janssen)

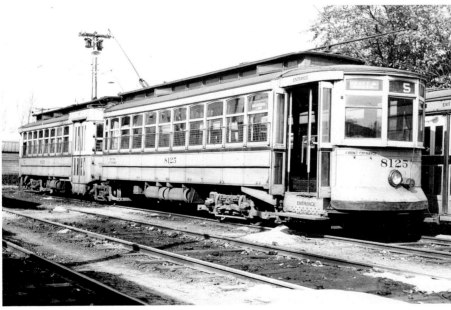

This trackage on Lafayette Avenue west of Charles was originally used by Baltimore & Northern cars to reach the Baltimore City Passenger Railway route to downtown. It later served as northern terminus for the No. 30 route. No. 5439 was purchased from Brill in 1910, No. 5456 in 1912. According to available records, both were converted to one-man, single-end operation in 1931-32. Yet, No. 5439 is an enigma; it obviously has two trolley poles. (George J. Voith)

Articulated unit No. 8125, rebuilt in 1930 from two semi-convertibles, was often idle unless needed to handle rush-hour or special event crowds. (Louis C. Mueller Collection)

As soon as word got around that a line was to be discontinued, fan trips were planned to tour the routes. This excursion was part of a "Farewell Trip to Lakeside, Roland Park, Gorsuch Avenue, and Bedford Square" on Sunday, June 15, 1947, over a year and a half before the demise of the No. 2 route. Here, No. 5201, built by Brill in 1906, lays over at Fort McHenry gate. This car did not ordinarily run on the Fort Avenue route, but the fans preferred the oldest cars on the property. (George J. Voith)

Shopmen look on in cavernous Park Terminal as the motorman readies No. 5550 for the last run on the No. 11 Bedford Square route. (George J. Voith)

UNDER AN ASPHALT BLANKET

When peace came, the street railways of Baltimore, having done an excellent job under extreme wartime handicaps, remained the most important factor in the public transportation picture. While some lines had been turned over to trackless trolleys and others to buses, the total trackage figure in 1945 was about three-quarters of the four hundred-odd miles that had been in operation at the time of the 1899 consolidation; this was partly due to additional construction in the early years of United Railways.

However, two unconnected events would result in the elimination of all but two routes by 1958. Traffic expert Henry Barnes came to town from Denver, and National City Lines obtained control of the Baltimore Transit Company. Under the combined onslaught of Barnes and National City Lines, the streetcar tracks (save only the No. 8 and No. 15 lines) which still connected all areas of metropolitan Baltimore were, in the period between June 1947 and September 1958, covered under a blanket of black asphalt much the same as the tracks had been buried under a mantle of snow during the blizzard of 1899. The tar was only an inch or two deep, but it represented no temporary blockade as had the snowstorm.

Barnes was quoted as saying that the only thing which he had against streetcars was that they traveled in the streets. Stranger that he was, possibly he did not realize that the wholesale postwar paving over, for automobile traffic, of such extensive private rights of way as those along St. Paul Street and Roland Avenue, was merely duplicating that done previously on Belair Road, Frederick Road, Greenmount Avenue, and many, many other places. (Barnes added Edmondson and Dundalk Avenues.) This, coupled with the destruction of the Guilford Avenue elevated structure and the Huntingdon Avenue viaduct, eliminated any small advantages that might yet have remained to the streetcar riders.

In defense of Barnes, it must be admitted that he did a good job on what he considered to be only temporary expedients. In the prevailing view, the salvation of the city was to be the expressways. The real culprits in the strangulation of downtown Baltimore were the city administrations, which from the days of Thomas Swann on, looked upon the street railways as a means of filling the municipal coffers, rather than as arteries to Baltimore's heart, whose deterioration would threaten the existence of the entire city.

If one had to pick a single year as the most interesting, out of the 104 that the streetcars roamed the streets of Baltimore, the choice could well be 1945. Random recollections would include: two attractive young women, the crew of an old red 5200 car that creaked and groaned its way up the steep hill on University Parkway; a yellow articulated car making the turn at Gay and Baltimore; semi-convertibles almost everywhere you went, sporting Lakeside, Conkling & Toone, Bedford Square, along with dozens of other destinations on their Hunter signs; multiple-unit trains rocketing along the private right of way in the middle of Dundalk Avenue on their way to Sparrows Point; Peter Witts rushing along Falls Road, easily pacing the automobile traffic; St. Louis-built PCCs, blinker doors ajar, sitting on the loop adjacent to Belvedere car house while laying over at the end of the No. 25 and No. 31 routes; Pullman-Standard PCCs crowded to the doorwells, holding down the city's longest and busiest run, Catonsville to Towson. The cars still carried the crowds to every section of Baltimore and its environs, but representatives of the bus manufacturers were busily preparing to launch a "modernization" program on an unsuspecting city.

The initial blow fell on a fine Sunday in June 1947. The scene at St. Paul and 25th Streets early that sunny morning seemed much the same as it had the previous after-

noon. Stretching eastward were the same yellow bricks, mellowed with age, their regular geometric design pierced by double streetcar tracks whose burnished rails caught the glint of the morning sunlight.

St. Paul Street, by contrast, presented the appearance of a patchwork quilt. Again, there were two sets of tracks, but these were set off by several courses of bricks, in varying red and bluish tints. On either side of the trackwork, the paving was dull black asphalt, or stone-flecked macadam. The switches had been set for St. Paul by the owl car on the No. 17 line. A precise diagram of the poles and overhead wires was etched on the roadways by shadows. At least one person passing by would reflect that nothing in the scene seemed changed from the way it had been for as long as he could remember.

But something intangible was different. In vain he glanced toward Greenmount Avenue to see a No. 1 line car laying over there. St. Paul Street, which the No. 1 cars shared with the Nos. 11, 17, and 29 lines, presented an equally vacant appearance. Not a single streetcar was in sight. For the first time in three-quarters of a century, cars did not run past St. Paul and 25th Streets. Quickly, the man walked away. He was young and knew little of the city's transportation history. Little did he realize that the plans of Nelson Perin, George Webb, and Alexander Brown were being fulfilled, almost half a century late. Four rail lines were being reduced to one. Next thing you knew, they would be charging for transfers.

There were numerous casualties on that sunny June 22, 1947. The No. 17 (Gorsuch Avenue-Westport) line was dismembered among three bus lines. The No. 1 (Guilford Avenue-Gilmor Street) line was cut back to Fayette and Gay Streets, its route over the trestle being taken over by the No. 8, which was routed off lower Greenmount Avenue. Little No. 24, the Lakeside line, was terminated at Lake Avenue. This separated it from a physical connection with the rest of the system, and for 2½ years its solitary car was locked up in a cage at night, after shuttling back and forth on the lonely route during the daylight and early evening hours. Bus service replaced the cars on the No. 29 (Roland Park) route. The No. 11 (Bedford Square) branch of the No. 1 line became part of the No. 11 bus line.

Nine months later, on March 21, 1948, the No. 6 streetcar line, from Monument and Kresson to Curtis Bay, received replacement buses. On May 9th, a concerted effort on the part of local contractors resulted in the paving over of almost all car tracks on West Baltimore Street during a single weekend. The exception was one block used in conjunction with the Pearl Street loop. As a result of this, all streetcars came off Baltimore Street. The No. 16 (Madison Avenue) cars were replaced by buses, and the No. 20 cut back to its prewar jerkwater operation between Highlandtown and Point Breeze. Also truncated were the No. 15 to Fayette and Pearl Streets and the No. 19 to Hanover and Lombard Streets. Lines No. 1, 2, 18, and 26 were rerouted over Fayette Street.

In June, the No. 33 from West Arlington to Pratt and South Streets went to bus, as did its companion No. 5 line. In connection with this move, the No. 33 trackage from Gwynn Oak Junction to Belvedere car house was taken over by a branch of the No. 32; also the No. 32 line was rerouted to Pennsylvania Avenue (instead of Linden, Whitelock, and Druid Hill) above North Avenue. On August 1, 1948, the shortened No. 1 line was taken over by trackless trolleys, one week after the remaining Point Breeze jerkwater segment of the No. 20 had become a part of a new bus line carrying the same number.

All of these changes had taken place in the thirteen months between June 1947 and the end of July 1948. In December 1948, the No. 2 (Fort Avenue) line saw trackless trolleys take over. The month previous, there had been an unforeseen change in routing. During switching operations on the Pennsylvania Railroad, near Calvert Station, a gondola car jumped the track and struck a footing of the elevated structure, putting it temporarily out of service. This forced the No. 8 cars to revert to the old Greenmount Avenue routing. In several months the el was repaired, and the Towson-Catonsville line resumed using it. This

When the No. 26 Sparrows Point route trackage was torn up, this overhead line car was used in the dismantling, then left to await its fate at the end of the private right of way. At least one railfan acquired the street railway virus from contact with car. (Mrs. Mary Krueger)

lasted only until December 31, 1949, when it was closed for good. In May 1950, it was dismantled, thus ending the fifty-eight-year existence of Baltimore's "sky-ride."

April 1949 saw the discontinuance of only one branch line and the abandonment of most of the No. 25. On the 24th the cars made their last trip down the steep hill on Union Avenue to the mills at Jones Falls. That year's most significant change, though, was the discontinuation of streetcars on that portion of the old Baltimore & Northern (the No. 25 line) between Mt. Washington and Camden Station, on the same day that the Union Avenue branch went.

Five lines were phased over to the rubber-tired vehicles in 1950, and another major line was drastically curtailed in length. On January 29th, the lonesome little Lakeside shuttle finally succumbed. Its lone car was dismembered on the spot, and there are those who are sure that portions of it, dumped into the inspection pit at Lake Avenue, will remain buried for all time under the new pavement.

March 5th saw the No. 34 (Eastern and Oldham to Conkling and Toone) abandoned, and the No. 30 (Fremont Avenue) line ran its last streetcars on the 26th. The diesel buses took over on what remained of the B & N line (the Key Avenue shuttle and the Belvedere Loop-Mt. Washington seg-

ment) September 14th, but the year's largest trackage abandonment was the cutback of the Sparrows Point line. Streetcars were taken off the section between Fayette and Pearl Streets and Highlandtown, so that only the portion from "the Point" to Pratt and Grundy in Highlandtown remained in use after July 29th. At the same time, PCCs took over the base service on the line, and the semi-convertibles ran only when there were insufficient streamlined cars available.

NOTES AND COMMENTS:

The abandonments of June 1947 were a result of a PSC order the previous year, permitting total or partial conversion of about half the BTC routes. *Maryland Public Service Commission Report,* 1946, pp. 114-120.

There was at least one court contest attempting to enjoin the BTC from abandoning almost 50 percent of its track mileage and substituting buses for streetcars. The following statements are extracted from the opinion rendered January 14, 1948, in an appeal from a decision of the Circuit Court of Baltimore City in the case of Warren v. Fitzgerald, *Maryland Reports,* vol. 189, pp. 480-481 and p. 490 (1947).

"As appears from the bill, testimony and the opinion below, the case was originally based largely upon charges of fraud on the part of Transit Company's directors. The charges of fraud involved alleged 'domination' of Transit Company by National City Lines, Inc., a 'holding corporation' which owns almost 30 percent of the preferred and common stock of Transit Company and also owns stock of local transportation companies in many other cities, and alleged contractual and financial relations between National, 'its local operating companies' and certain 'supplier corporations' whereby National was furnished 'money and capital' by the 'supplier corporations', used this 'money and capital' to secure control of, or financial interest in, 'local transit systems' and purchased and caused its 'operating companies' to purchase 'tires, tubes, petroleum products and buses' from the 'supplier corporations.' This mention of the charges of fraud need not be elaborated or made more definite or even more accurate. At the argument appellants stated that the charges of fraud had not been proved and were abandoned. No question of fraud, actual or constructive, is stated in appellants' brief. . . .

"Transit Company's trolley lines do not constitute an independent department of its business. They are part — still the greater part, if the proposed 'conversion' is fully carried out — of an integrated whole which comprises both cars and buses. Its lines to be abandoned are not an integral part of its property, essential for the transaction of its business; they are, in the judgment of its directors, obsolete parts, to be replaced by substituted parts to make a better, integrated whole."

The St. Louis cars originally had metal blinker doors which in opening slid inward into the doorwells. These were later replaced by wooden doors which opened by folding into position outside the car body. The reason for the change is said to have been for safety reasons in case of an accident. At about the same time, the rigid safety bars across the windows on the curb side of the cars were removed.

After the line was cut back on June 22, 1947, the No. 1 cars continued east on Fayette to Gay, south on Gay to Baltimore Street, and across that street to Carrollton Avenue, then north to Fayette, where it rejoined the former route. With the removal of streetcars from Baltimore Street, the No. 1 line used Fayette in both directions to Eutaw, where it turned southward to take over the territory formerly served by the truncated No. 19 line.

For those interested in all the highly intricate routing changes which were made in this period (and earlier days), *Baltimore Streetcar Routes,* published by Kenneth Morse in 1960, is highly recommended. Comparing the listing with my own research on the routes, by means of city directories, newspaper accounts, company maps and records, Public Service Commission rulings, etc., discloses very few differences. This is all the more remarkable when it is realized that Mr. Morse, who was from Cleveland (and had published some interesting books on that city's street railway), did not have the advantage of knowing the Baltimore system as a native.

This cartoon, by Edmund Duffy, appeared in the *Sun* shortly after World War II at the time the Baltimore Transit Company announced plans to convert more than half of its streetcar lines to buses. It seemed even more appropriate in 1963. (Louis F. Meyer Collection, BSM)

THE CLOSING DAYS

One looks in vain for some cheerful note in the closing days of streetcar service. The first big strike in Baltimore's transportation history occurred in 1952, lasting from January 10th to the 29th. One result of the settlement was the institution of a two-cent charge for transfers, ending over fifty years of free transfer privileges throughout the city. The inconvenience of this strike was as nothing compared to that of 1956, which stretched from January 30th to April 26th. The 1956 stoppage was not finally ended until the property had been seized by the State of Maryland.

Meanwhile the parade of discontinuances, which by the end of the 1950s would see only the No. 8 and No. 15 lines still running, continued its dreary course. In June 1952, the No. 18 (Pennsylvania Avenue) route was converted, resulting in the closing of the huge Park Terminal car house. On August 8th, the No. 9 (Ellicott City) line discontinued its remaining through car service to downtown Baltimore. In October, the No. 31 Garrison Boulevard route was combined with the No. 19 to run through to Harford Road. The Fort Howard shuttle went out in the same month, the heavy crosstown No. 13 North Avenue route in January 1954, and the No. 35, the well-known and picturesque jerkwater line from Walbrook Junction through Dickeyville to Lorraine Cemetery in February of that year. The No. 35 Lorraine line was the last example of independent street railway ownership in Baltimore. Built as the Lorraine Electric Railway, it began operation on August 20, 1907 from Lorraine Cemetery to Dickeyville. Since United Railways cars and crews were leased from the beginning, and through service was given, beginning July 1, 1916, to Walbrook Junction, many do not realize that it did not become a part of the unified Baltimore system until sometime in the early 1930s.

In September 1954, the No. 4 Edmondson Avenue line to Walbrook Junction was combined with the No. 15 out Belair Road to Overlea. On the same date, the No. 14 from Rolling Road to downtown Baltimore was converted to bus. Three semi-convertibles (Nos. 5706, 5745, and 5748) were left to serve the then-isolated No. 9 route between Catonsville Junction and Ellicott City, with its extensive private right of way through the woods and its own bridge over the Patapsco River. On June 18th of the following year, this final remnant was also converted and the last of the old Brills disappeared from service. (No. 5748 is still preserved at the Seashore Trolley Museum at Kennebunkport, Maine.)

September 1955 saw the last day of rail service on the No. 32 Woodlawn route. The No. 19 Harford Road service went out on June 19, 1956, along with the Walbrook-Windsor Hills branch of the No. 15. On August 31, 1958, the remainder of the No. 26 from Highlandtown to Sparrows Point was changed to bus. This eliminated one of the most interesting pieces of trackage on the system, mostly private right of way with a long bridge over Bear Creek. Only two car lines remained, the No. 8 and No. 15. Somewhat surprisingly, the last trackless trolley disappeared in June 1959, predeceasing the streetcars by more than four years.

Not only had the lines shrunk to two, the cars themselves had undergone a transformation. There may be some, particularly those who remember only the last few years of operation, who think the following is overdone; but to one who returned to Baltimore in late 1963, just before the end, the splendid streetcars of his youth presented a ramshackle look — derelict might be a better word. No longer did they display the attractive predominantly green and cream paint scheme. Instead they now roamed the streets in a particularly unappealing solid orange-yellow shade. It was

not too far-fetched to liken them, with their battleship gray roofs, to misshapen pumpkins, caught by an early winter frost, trolley poles reaching upward like so many withered, blackened vines.

As the cars passed by, their once smooth metal bodies showed evidence of many encounters with other vehicles. Where not hastily repaired or still mashed in, they sported large advertising signs, front, sides, and rear. Often these overflowed their allocated spaces, sprouting outsized replicas of soft drink bottle caps, and other unlikely items, with little regard for taste.

There are some who regret that National City Lines did not repaint at least one of the streetcars in the attractive two-tone green effect being applied to the buses at that time. On the other hand, perhaps it was just as well. With the deterioration of the cars, the effect might well have been that of a floozie who attempts to repair the ravages of time with mascara, rouge, and bright lipstick.

Inside, the change was even more striking. Some windows could not be raised; others rattled in their frames; bell ropes were broken; in many places the rubber flooring had worked loose, rising in humps; there was often a gap of several inches between the sets of doors at front and center, letting in the wintry air; and some of the roofs leaked. One long ride on a No. 8 car was spent in the fascinating observation of a light fixture, whose bulb shone brightly through a bull's-eye lens almost completely filled with rainwater.

So, in one sense, there was no real surprise when it was announced that the streetcars would end service with the owl runs on November 3, 1963. The trolleys were suffering from a terminal illness, and, much as an animal which broke a leg back in the horse car days, were being dispatched because they had outlived their usefulness.

This car is shown on the Highlandtown loop between Haven and Grundy Streets, which since July 1950 had been the western end of the No. 26 line. (James A. Genthner)

After reaching Eastern Avenue, the No. 26 line cars passed under the Pennsylvania and Baltimore & Ohio railroads, then skirted the City Hospitals grounds (now the Francis Scott Key Medical Center). Safety pylon shown was among the last in the city, removed September 1958. Traffic requirements had taken out three hundred of them in five years. (George F. Nixon Collection)

The "red-rockets" were only a memory when this PCC passed Dundalk in 1958, but the right of way remained much the same as when constructed a half-century earlier. (James A. Genthner)

The old meets the new. Someone with a sense of history posed a bus from the No. 29 line with a semi-convertible still running on the Lakeside line. Streetcars had operated on the latter for over a half a century; replacement buses lasted only a very brief time. The photo was taken at Roland and Lake Avenues. (Baltimore Sunpapers)

This short block of track, located within a new housing project on Ashland Avenue east of Ensor, was probably the only bit of private right of way in the inner city. Photo was taken about time of abandonment of No. 19 route, which then shared this trackage with No. 15 line. (Robert W. Janssen)

No. 2145, one of the last group of trackless trolleys purchased, sits at Carroll Park sometime in the 1950s. Its destination sign — Washington Boulevard and Fremont Avenue — was not a cut-back point but the intersection where No. 30 route coaches turned off in order to reach the storage yard. (Mass Transit Administration)

NOTES AND COMMENTS:

The 1952 transfer charge lasted only until a base fare increase was granted in July.

The issuance of free transfers for use between cars of competing companies was extremely rare. The first known instance of this began during August 1893 at the crossings of the Central Railway and the Lake Roland Elevated Railway at Guilford and Preston Streets and at North and Fulton Avenues. At the end of each quarter, officials of the two companies met, exchanged coupons, and divided equally the residue of fares collected by one company over the other. *Herald,* August 16, 1893 and *St. Louis Globe-Democrat,* March 11, 1895.

About a year and a half after the big consolidation, the United Railways, on July 1, 1900, put a more liberal system of free transfers into effect. The keynote was that transfers would be given at any point where lines intersected. Exceptions would be in effect where a passenger could return in the general direction from which he had come, and at terminal points from one line to another. *Herald,* June 29, 1900.

The No. 16 line included the trackage out East Baltimore Street and down to the foot of Broadway. Thus, with it went service on the route used for the first horse cars in July 1859.

The combining of the No. 19 and No. 31 routings resulted in one of the strange quirks in scheduling wherein the No. 19 buses, on Sundays only, ran from Carney to a terminus at Eutaw and Baltimore Streets, rather than continuing on to the far northwest reaches of town. The sequence of events began in 1929, when the United Railways was struggling to cut expenses. Noting that the No. 31 route had been established primarily to carry weekday shoppers and commuters from Arlington, West Arlington, Forest Park, and Walbrook to downtown without the necessity of transferring, the company decided that Sunday service was unnecessary. Consequently,

With smashed headlight and dented dasher, No. 7308 sits idly over pit at York Road car house while the rest of the fleet fulfills the waning hours of service on November 2-3, 1963. Somehow the askew "Not in Service" sign seems superfluous. (James A. Genthner)

Another product of the Pullman-Standard line, No. 7086, was caught as it prepared to swing into Fayette Street from Holliday. That loaf of bread helps to hide some unrepaired dents. (James A. Genthner)

No. 5318 was bumped off the Catonsville line with the arrival of the PCC cars in July 1939. The outbreak of war in Europe two months later moved the company to keep the car in storage rather than sending it to the scrap yard. After Pearl Harbor, the car went back into service, but the reprieve ended in 1945, and here it sits, paint peeling, metal rusting, waiting its final trip. (George J. Voith)

Shopman throws switch as Pullman-Standard-built No. 7076 prepares to enter Belvedere car house not long before that facility was abandoned in February 1960. The Food Fair across the street was featuring franks at forty-nine cents a pound. (James A. Genthner)

the No. 31 line took over the branch of the No. 13 line running between Walbrook Junction and Preston and Milton on the first day of the week. Service on the portion of the No. 31 south of North Avenue (on Madison Avenue and Eutaw Street) was considered to be adequately handled by the No. 16 cars, which shared the same trackage. Some-

time later, the No. 31 took over the Wolfe and Aliceanna branch of the No. 13 instead. When the No. 19 and the No. 31 were combined, the former followed the old No. 31 route into northwest Baltimore, except on Sundays.

Data on the routing changes is based on Kenneth Morse's *Baltimore Streetcar Rout-*

ings; L. C. Mueller and George F. Nixon notes; conversations with Louis F. Meyer; *City Directories;* various newspaper files; and company maps and literature.

During the early 1950s, a few PCC cars carried a paint scheme of orange below the belt rail, light green in the window area, and white roof.

Catonsville Junction, the western terminus of the No. 8 Line. PCC No. 7111 awaits departure time for the long run to Towson in August 1963. The building was still standing in 1992. (Herbert H. Harwood, Jr.)

The northern terminus of the No. 8 Line was on Washington Avenue in Towson, immediately east of the 1854 County Court House. No. 7106 laid over on an October evening in 1963. (Herbert H. Harwood, Jr.)

GHOSTS OF STREETCARS PAST

On November 2, 1963, the people of Baltimore rediscovered its streetcars. All kinds and classes of people wanted to take one final ride. The regular patrons discovered that they were sharing the cars with old-timers who reminisced of Riverview and five-cent fares, young suburbanites taking their toddlers out for a ride on the vehicles which the parents had forsaken as soon as they had acquired a driver's license, and inevitably that group of persons who are generally classed under the heading of railfans.

There was the usual desire to ride the last car. For the purists, this was the last regularly scheduled car, No. 7084, which pulled in at 5:25 a.m.; but the very last trip was one chartered by a group of fans on No. 7407, which entered the car house at Irvington at 6:34 a.m.

There were also many others riding charter cars that last fateful day and night, at least some of whom hoped to achieve the "honor" of being last, including fans from out of town. One such group, including members of the Baltimore Chapter NRHS, aboard car No. 7083, met the last regular car at the Towson end of the No. 8 line at 6:00 a.m. on the 3rd. The two PCCs were coupled together, draped with the appropriate black bunting, and run as a train to the York Road car house, backing in shortly before 6:30, when the power was to have been turned off. The aforementioned group on No. 7407, however, left the Irvington car house, looped at the Irvington loop on Frederick Road, and returned, thus achieving the "honor."

Both the No. 8 and No. 15 lines were discontinued on the same night, and all of the above cars operated on the No. 8 route, thereby giving it the honor of being the very last line to operate in Baltimore. This is a bit ironic as the No. 15 (through being combined with the No. 4) was descended from the Baltimore City Passenger Railway Company, which had run the very first horse cars over 104 years previously, and

the Baltimore, Calverton & Powhatan, which had operated the last horse car. On the other hand, the No. 8 was a lineal descendant of the Towson and Catonsville lines, which were considered as being merely feeders to City Passenger. Another ironic twist was that a desire to make Baltimore Street (in conjunction with Fayette) one-way was the determining factor in eliminating the streetcar lines; and it had been opposition to track on Baltimore Street which had come close to crippling the original horse car operation.

For all of the memories cherished by the last-day riders, it is doubtful that any realized just how well the No. 8 line epitomized the "city passenger railways" of Baltimore. The variety of vehicles used on the route over the years was remarkable. Bob-tailed and double-deck horse cars, little single-truckers, convertibles, and semi-convertibles, trailers, articulated units, Peter Witts, PCCs, even the Brilliner — the Towson-Catonsville route had seen them all.

In addition to these ghosts of streetcars past, much of the lore of days gone by could be brought to mind by merely gazing out of the window as the cars made the long, long trip from the Baltimore County Court House to Catonsville Junction.

The start at Towson was from Washington Avenue in front of the Court House, which was contemporary with the building of the line. Soon, the car crossed Susquehanna Avenue at York Road, where only the abutments remained of the railroad bridge which had been the cause célèbre in a "war" between the narrow gauge predecessor of the Ma & Pa and the proprietors of the horse car line. The undulating roadway from here to Govanstown bore little resemblance to the quagmire which had caused all the commotion when Nelson Perin was grading the route in preparation for electrification.

The massive concrete car house at York Road and Arlington Avenue boded well to

stand as a monument for all time to the engineering skill, if not the architectural taste, of the United; but a few blocks to the south, at 36th Street, there was no trace left of the wooden car barn which had gone up in flames on that cold January morning in 1906. A little further there were crossovers at the site of old Oriole Park, where the streetcars once had stood waiting in the midst of busy Greenmount Avenue traffic until the baseball game was over. At North Avenue, Greenmount Cemetery, where visitors to its many graves had provided a steady source of fares in the early days, was one of the few places along the line that had changed but little.

The car soon was downtown, turning past City Hall at Holliday and Fayette Streets. This had been the terminus of the York Road line until Perin had extended it to connect with the Catonsville cars. The specialwork was still in place at Guilford Avenue, and a reflex glance northward looked in vain for the elevated line, gone thirteen years. Ducking beneath the underpass at the budding Charles Center, the car tracks were flanked by Belgian block paving, reminiscent of the days when smooth macadam was considered too slick for the horses' hoofs. Almost every cross street in this area had formerly carried cable or horse cars painted in the vivid shades of the rainbow — now there were only buses in identical paint schemes.

On out toward west Baltimore, the neighborhoods grew rather shabby; Franklin and Union Squares had seen better days; it was a far cry from an earlier time when the Catonsville cars carried many of the city's elite to these very same houses. There was still a turnout at Smallwood Street, but the old car barn once located there had been replaced by a filling station. The route along Frederick Road through the old village of Millington was much the same; the foundations of an old bridge which had once spanned Gwynns Falls were a mute

The last days. Like many another railfan, Jim Genthner was out with his camera recording the last days of the streetcars. While only this photo was taken on November 2, 1963 — that gloomy day of lowering clouds — all photos on these pages are of the No. 8 line as the end rapidly approached. No. 7072 runs in middle of York Road at State College station (now Towson State University). Many years ago, this stretch was private right of way. (James A. Genthner)

No. 7398, a car marked Paradise Avenue, waits for light at Fayette and Liberty. Miller Bros. still stood at right, while the Blaustein Building and Hamburger's rise in the background. (James A. Genthner)

No. 7069 pauses while its motorman surveys clearance. The Vermont Federal Building was under construction; the Omni Inner Harbor Hotel now occupies the vacant lot. (James A. Genthner)

No. 7382 runs on a stretch of snow-covered private right of way north of Frederick Road. This trackage was put down at the turn of the century to connect Ellicott City with the No. 8 route. (James A. Genthner)

All cars on these two pages are by Pullman-Standard. No. 7398 dates to 1942, No. 7103 to 1944. All others were built in 1941. Numbering was by make of electrical equipment — Nos. 7001-7147, General Electric; Nos. 7301-7428, Westinghouse. No. 7337 above is shown at Frederick and Augusta, one block east of Irvington loop. (James A. Genthner)

No. 7094 and No. 7103 meet at Catonsville Junction. The latter, chartered for a farewell trip, sports unique — in Baltimore — sliding rear windows. (James A. Genthner)

No. 7135 pulls into sand-littered Overlea loop. Like most Baltimore cars, it served on many different lines — in this case, the Nos. 30, 4, 14, 26, and 15 routes, in that order. (James A. Genthner)

Frederick Road tracks have already been covered with asphalt as small group gathers to watch removal of cars from the dilapidated Irvington car house in August 1964. (James H. Genthner)

reminder of the floods that had played havoc with the line in this vicinity in its earliest days. Mount Olivet Cemetery was pretty much unchanged. However, at Caton Avenue the Carroll Station building of the Baltimore & Potomac, where steam train connections had once been made, had been replaced by a stairway to a trackside platform, served only by a few commuter trains.

The old Fairview Inn had been replaced by a church; but the same ancient wall, with its intricate ironwork, still enclosed Loudon Park. In times gone by, the horse cars had been so crowded with visitors to its cemetery plots that they ran more frequently on Sundays than during the week, so that the Sabbath was no day of rest for the horses. However, its two private streetcars had ceased running a generation previously.

Irvington, the last of the brick car houses in service, had only a few more hours of activity remaining, while beyond, Irvington Loop, behind which had once been stored large numbers of semi-convertibles and articulated cars, now sat empty and forlorn. Paradise Loop, a product of the war not long past, would handle the buses, but houses completely covered the site diagonally opposite where there had been

A sad scene to behold by those who appreciated the 104 years of streetcar service in Baltimore unfolded in August 1964, at Irvington car house, as workers cut traction motors from trucks and piled them haphazardly alongside a disused sandbox. (Michael R. Farrell)

located (almost a century previous) the earliest of all the parks established by the various streetcar companies, Catonsville Railway Park.

Almost everyone in Catonsville could remember when the tracks on the far side of town had run adjacent to the north side of the roadway, for that was hardly a dozen years past. Far fewer could recall that Stoddard's was once the end of the line; that was prior to the turn of the century,

before the rails were laid through the half mile of woods up to Catonsville Junction. At the Junction, a fairly new shelter, constructed of reclaimed paving blocks, stood in the loop (and still stands in 1992). There was no waiting Ellicott City car on which to continue the trip westward.

Verily, in 1963, one might wonder what all the fuss over building streetcar lines had been about. Three-quarters of a century earlier, a tremendous amount of money and

effort had been spent here in building a route that was to extend to Washington. The final result was a picturesque little line reaching only just beyond the Patapsco; now even that was merely a gradually diminishing pathway, still strewn with ballast, but with only an occasional rotting tie or rusty spike left to show for all the money that had been expended.

NOTES AND COMMENTS:

A non-sentimental description of the last runs appears in the *Sun,* November 4, 1963. John Engleman is the authority for the pull-in time of car No. 7407, which is preserved at the Baltimore Streetcar Museum.

In 1859, the original company had been served with an injunction preventing them from putting down double tracks on the stretch of Baltimore Street between Sharp and North (Guilford) Streets.

At Oriole Park at 29th Street there was no siding. The waiting cars stood on the southbound main line, with regular cars switching to the northbound tracks above 30th Street, and proceeding against automobile traffic until crossing back to the southbound tracks in the vicinity of 28th Street. Municipal Stadium, built in 1922 on 33rd Street, was served by a spur off the

No. 17 trackage. This extended from Gorsuch Avenue up what is now Loch Raven Boulevard to about 36th Street. The trackage was later used by trippers to City College and Eastern High. For stadium events, through cars were operated from points on the No. 17 and No. 19 lines. Double-ended cars could reverse by using a crossover near 36th Street, but Peter Witt and PCC cars had to back down Loch Raven for about a half a mile and onto Gorsuch. Here they were wyed, and again proceeding in reverse, backed up to 36th Street. (All single-end Baltimore cars had an emergency controller and brake at the non-operating end.) They were thus placed in the proper direction to head homeward with the departing crowds. By the time that Memorial Stadium was built on the same site, streetcar service was no longer offered. Ironically, however, in

1992 the new Central Light Rail Line now serves the equally new Oriole Park at Camden Yards.

Catonsville Railway Park covered an irregularly shaped tract between Frederick Road and Edmondson Avenue, just west of what is now Edmondson Ridge Road. G. M. Hopkins, *City Atlas Of Baltimore, Maryland And Environs,* vol. 2, 1877.

As the years passed after the last streetcar ran in Baltimore, most of the old No. 9 right of way from Stonewall Road to the Patapsco was gradually reclaimed by nature or fell victim to progress. The "deepcut" east of Oella may still be seen, along with the abutments of the Patapsco River bridge.

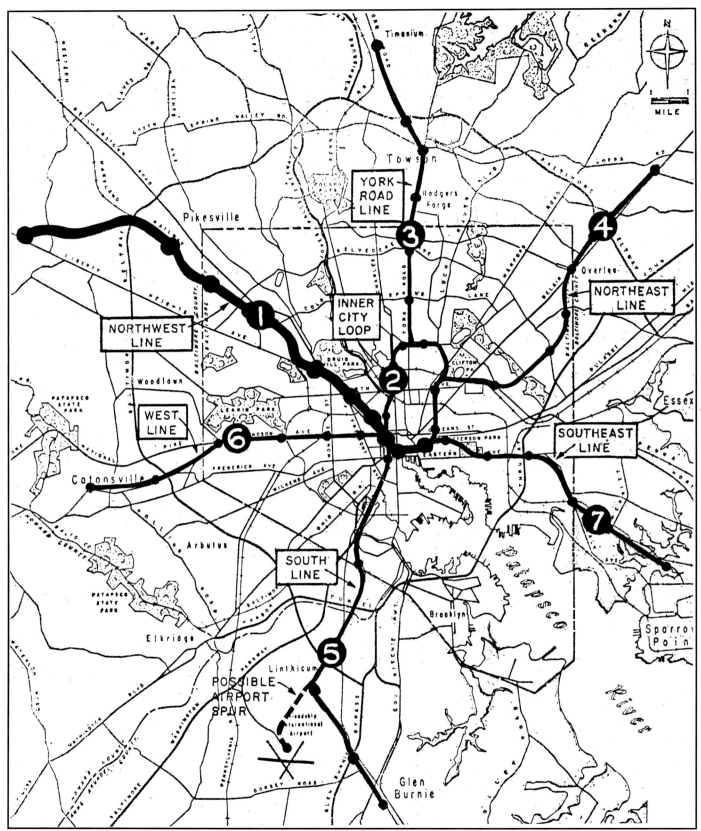

The original 1965 rapid transit plan proposed by the Parsons, Brinckerhoff engineering firm. The numbers shown for each line indicate the construction priority recommended by the consultants. The present Metro line roughly follows the "first priority" Randallstown route (labeled "Northwest Line" on the map), but terminates in Owings Mills. (Baltimore *News American* map; Robert L. Krueger Collection)

NEW MANAGEMENT
AND A METRO

By Herbert H. Harwood, Jr.

Hardly had the power been switched off on Baltimore's last two streetcar lines than the stirrings of a revival of electric rail transit began. The process would be slow, erratic, and sometimes agonizing; eventually, however, the city would again boast an active (albeit somewhat disjointed) system of tracks, overhead wire, and third rail reaching from downtown in four directions. Baltimore's extensive streetcar system had been pushed into oblivion by its own economics and by the automobile. But, by the mid-1960s, it was becoming clear that the auto itself needed to be tamed. Too much urban and suburban space and too much money were being consumed by concrete and asphalt, and all of it seemed to serve only to create more congestion. Added to that was the even more serious problem of the decay of downtown, as businesses and residential population were dispersed outward.

In 1964, Maryland's Regional Planning Council followed the lead of Washington, the San Francisco Bay area, Atlanta, and Philadelphia's New Jersey suburbs by commissioning a comprehensive rapid transit study for Baltimore. The engineering consulting firm of Parsons, Brinckerhoff, Quade, and Douglas was hired for the job, and its report was released in November 1965. By then, most urban transit planners had long since dismissed the streetcar as obsolete, but believed that high-speed, high capacity subway/elevated systems — what was later called "heavy rail" — were appropriate for very large cities, while buses could handle all other public transit duties.

Accordingly, the Parsons, Brinckerhoff report proposed an ambitious seventy-two-mile subway system for Baltimore consisting of six spokes radiating from downtown to:

- Northwest Baltimore-Pikesville-Randallstown

- Towson-Timonium, via York Road

- Glen Burnie and Friendship Airport (now Baltimore-Washington International Airport)

- Catonsville, via Edmondson Avenue

- Dundalk-Sparrows Point, via Eastern Avenue

In addition, most of these spokes were to be connected by a seventh line consisting of an inner-city loop subway serving north Baltimore, Memorial Stadium, and Johns Hopkins Hospital. These were Baltimore's traditional heavy traffic corridors, so it was no coincidence that the proposed rapid transit system was essentially a reincarnation of the city's old streetcar trunk lines, plus the former Baltimore & Annapolis Railroad's route to Glen Burnie. The difference was that now they were to be moved under or over the streets and transformed into high-speed (and highly expensive) subway routes.

Recognizing the construction disruption and particularly the cost (which in 1965 was estimated at $700 million), the consultants suggested building the system in a series of steps spread out over many years. They would start first with the Randallstown spoke, followed by the loop route, then — by 1985 — the Towson-Timonium line.

But for the Baltimore of 1965, even this much was too expensive and too far-sighted. No one rushed into immediate action, and the next several years were spent in inconclusive discussions and counter-proposals. One of these was to adopt the Westinghouse-sponsored "Skybus" system of small, fully automated rubber-tired vehicles running on an elevated or surface-level concrete guideway.

As this debate was going on, the entire environment for city transit was changing dramatically. The world of Oden Bowie, Nelson Perin, and the other nineteenth century street railway entrepreneurs had vanished years before. Through the 1960s, many large city transit systems were still in private hands, but rising costs and ever-diminishing patronage made profitable operation increasing difficult — and eventually impossible. Finally (but all too slowly in some cases), local governments and their taxpayers reluctantly recognized that subsidies or outright public ownership was inevitable if their public transportation was to be preserved.

Almost always a financial beachcomber, the Baltimore Transit Company was a prime example of these woes. Indeed, its last two streetcar lines partly owed their longevity to the company's inability to pay for replacement buses and conversion costs, such as street repaving. The 101 buses that finally retired the trolleys in 1963 had to be financed through a back-door subsidy involving relief from gross receipts taxes and repaving costs, plus state acquiescence to a five-cent transfer charge. The first formal step toward public ownership was taken on January 1, 1962, when the state created the Metropolitan Transit Authority (MTA), which in turn absorbed the transit regulatory functions of the Public Service Commission. A year and a half later, the MTA was given power to purchase or condemn operating bus companies. (When the Maryland Department of Transportation was formed in 1971, the MTA was moved into the new agency and renamed the Mass Transit Administration — still "MTA.") Prodded by a crippling transit strike in 1968, the MTA moved to acquire the Baltimore Transit Company; on April 30, 1970, the deed was done and "MTA" stickers were pasted over the "BTCo" on

The western end of the Charles Center subway terminal begins to take shape alongside Baltimore Street at Hanover in May 1982. The now-vanished Tower Building, a longtime Baltimore landmark, still dominates the distant scene. (H. H. Harwood, Jr.)

Baltimore's buses. The last nominal vestige of the traction era was gone.

It was a mixed blessing. With the city's transit system now an arm of the state, it inevitably was the victim of bureaucratic procedures and the unpredictable political gyrations of city, county, state, and federal governments. But to the good, it stabilized a deteriorating situation and allowed access to public funds for services and equipment. And with the subsequent takeover of the major suburban bus companies (completed by 1973), it unified the operation of the region's transit facilities and integrated them with any systems planned for the future — such as rapid transit.

In early 1971, not long after the Baltimore Transit takeover, MTA Administrator Walter Addison (ironically a former highway planner) brought the 1965 Parsons, Brinckerhoff plan back to life. As a first step, the transit agency proposed building a twenty-eight-mile rapid transit line starting in Owings Mills, passing through Pikesville and downtown Baltimore, and continuing southeast through Glen Burnie to Harundale and Marley in

A Metro train rests between runs in the quiet of the Charles Center terminal. (Chris Alexis)

Anne Arundel County. As planned earlier, it would be a full-scale "heavy rail" operation using conventional subway construction techniques and equipment. It also was to be built to standard gauge (4 foot 8½ inches) — for all practical purposes, a first in Baltimore's city transit history.

The route through northwest Baltimore followed a heavy traffic corridor, although it was not really the city's heaviest. Rather, it was picked partly for political reasons, and partly because construction could be quicker and cheaper than other routes. Major sections of the line would use existing railroad rights of way and the median strips of expressways. It was hoped that the first segment — 8½ miles between Charles Center and Reisterstown Plaza — would be operating by late 1978.

That date turned out to be five years too optimistic, but at least a positive start was made. The key to the project was generous funding from a then-sympathetic federal government, which ultimately paid 80 percent of the cost of what was called "Section A." Initial government approval came in October 1972, and afterwards things began to move — although in fits, starts, and sidesteps. Ceremonial groundbreaking took place on October 10, 1974 at Eutaw Place and Preston Street, near the state office complex, with speeches by Governor Marvin Mandel, Baltimore Mayor William Donald Schaefer, and various federal and transit agency dignitaries. Heavy construction was expected to start in the fall of 1975.

The first hiccup came in October 1975, when Anne Arundel County decided that it did not want rapid transit after all. The entire southern half of the planned line, from Charles Center to Marley, had to be shelved — temporarily, it was hoped.

The infamous double-digit inflation brought a far worse problem, significantly boosting the project's cost. An acrimonious fight ensued in the Maryland General Assembly, and the "fall 1975" construction date came and went while the legislators argued over financing and the need for such an expensive project.

Metro stations won no prizes for grace and
elegance, but were built for efficiency and
economy. The Rogers Avenue station is typical of
those on the above-ground section of the line. This
scene dates to May 1985. (H. H. Harwood, Jr.)

After leaving the Mondawmin station,
northbound Metro trains roll over this impressive
concrete viaduct as far as Reisterstown Plaza.
This 1985 view at Rogers Avenue looks southeast
toward the city as an inbound train leaves the
station. At this point, the Metro route follows the
onetime Western Maryland Railway main line,
seen at the far left. (H. H. Harwood, Jr.)

Two sets of the austerely designed Metro cars meet just west of the Reisterstown Plaza station in April 1985. (H. H. Harwood, Jr.)

With Governor Mandel's support and active lobbying, the subway survived. Finally, serious digging started in December 1976, now with a hoped-for opening date of mid-1982. The delay brought its benefits, however. With more time to plan and with several cities opening new systems ahead of theirs, the MTA's engineers could study and heed the lessons of others — notably the successful Philadelphia-Lindenwold (New Jersey) line contrasted to the over-sophisticated, trouble-prone Bay Area Rapid Transit in California (which opened in 1972) and Washington, D.C.'s first subway line (1976). Baltimore designers determined to make their subway as simple, practical, and trouble-free as possible. They were wisely content to let others do the expensive pioneering and innovating, while they adopted those systems and equipment which had proven themselves.

The cars, ordered from the Budd Company in January 1979, reflected this aim. Often described as "spartan but efficient," they were rather boxy examples of conven-

tional subway car design, brightened by bodies of unpainted stainless steel. Each was seventy-five feet long and could seat seventy-six people, with standing room for ninety more. They were fast, with 175 hp motors geared for 70 mph. Like many contemporary rapid transit cars, they were built in semi-permanently coupled pairs, with underbody equipment split between the two cars and controls only in the outer ends of each set. To reduce the unit costs, Baltimore's car order was combined with an essentially identical group to be built for Miami's new system. The MTA calculated that it ultimately would need one hundred cars, but for "Section A" it took seventy-two of the initial 208-car order, with the balance going to Miami.

The "subway" itself actually combined underground, surface, and elevated construction. Beginning in a subway terminal at Baltimore and Charles Streets, it ran beneath the streets for 4½ miles, following Baltimore Street west and Eutaw Street north to the state office complex near Bolton Hill. Still underground, the line then cut

at an angle northwest through Bolton Hill and several cross streets to Pennsylvania Avenue, which it followed as far as the Mondawmin shopping mall. (Along the way between Charles Center and Mondawmin, it also passed beneath two railroad tunnels — CSX Transportation's 1895 Howard Street tunnel and the former Pennsylvania Railroad's so-called B & P tunnel, dating to 1873 and now owned by Amtrak.)

Three-quarters of a mile northwest of the Mondawmin station (and on the site of the long-departed Carlin's Park), the tracks emerged onto the surface alongside what was once the Western Maryland Railway's main line, now a CSX Transportation branch. For the remainder of the run to its temporary end at Reisterstown Plaza, the line was on a concrete viaduct sandwiched between the railroad track and Wabash Avenue — with a brief dip back to surface level by the shop and storage yard at Northern Parkway. Counting the two terminals there were nine stations, six in the subway and three above ground. These too were straightforward and functional — severe,

The Metro route included bits of virtually every type of rapid transit construction: underground, elevated, and several varieties of surface trackage. The final leg of the Owings Mills extension was located in the center of Interstate 795, built at about the same time. A mid-day two-car set heads into town at McDonogh Road in 1988. (H. H. Harwood, Jr.)

in fact — although each was embellished with original graphic art or sculpture. High-level center-island platforms were standard at all stations, simplifying construction and expediting train loading and unloading. As a necessary bow to the all-powerful automobile, the three outer stations included large park-and-ride lots.

In mid-1981, with construction well advanced, the previously anonymous rapid transit line was given an official name — Metro — and its own distinctive "M" logo to be used on signs and maps. The name had become more or less an international designation for urban subway systems, and subtly served to associate Baltimore with such big-league cities as Washington, Montreal, Paris, and Moscow — all of which had "Metros."

Further delays plagued the project, particularly a long strike at Westinghouse Air Brake, a subcontractor for the car fleet. The Budd Company itself suffered some management and quality control problems.

A year late, the first car arrived July 20, 1982, and only fifty-eight of the seventy-two-car initial order were on hand for the line's opening. (The first piece of Metro rolling stock on the property was a sixty-ton Plymouth diesel-hydraulic switcher, delivered in 1981.)

Opening day finally arrived on November 21, 1983. Nobody noticed it, and it certainly had not been planned that way, but Metro trains began carrying people almost precisely twenty years after the last streetcar ran. Thanks to its long gestation, however, the new incarnation of rail transit worked smoothly, with a minimum of teething troubles.

With its car fleet still limited, and lacking experience in day-to-day rapid transit operations, the MTA edged Metro slowly into a full-scale service pattern. Initially, only weekday service was offered, from 5 a.m. to 8 p.m., and it was not until the following June that bus routes in northwest Baltimore were redesigned to feed the line. Saturday

schedules were added in June 1985, and evening hours were later extended to midnight, but the system rested on Sundays until the spring of 1992, when 11 a.m. to 8 p.m. service was inaugurated.

Even before the silver-sided subway trains started running to Reisterstown Plaza, work was under way to extend the line six miles farther northwest to Owings Mills. Planning for this segment had begun in September 1981. (Both this and the later Johns Hopkins Hospital extension took advantage of a new and enlightened twist in government funding policy, and used money originally earmarked for expressway projects which subsequently were canceled.)

The Owings Mills route continued along the same ex-Western Maryland line through and under Sudbrook Park (by means of a short tunnel), crossed under the Baltimore Beltway, then occupied the median strip of Interstate 795 to its new terminal. Blessed with relatively easy con-

Metro passengers are treated to semi-rural woodlands between the Victorian suburb of Sudbrook and the Old Court Road station. An outbound train approaches Old Court station in 1987. (H. H. Harwood, Jr.)

struction on an all-surface right of way, the Reisterstown Plaza-Owings Mills extension opened ahead of schedule July 20, 1987. Again, the date marked an unremembered anniversary: Streetcar service to Owings Mills had ended July 3, 1932 — almost exactly fifty-five years earlier.

As before, the start of Owings Mills service was free of any unpleasant surprises, although a nasty one later appeared. It turned out that the concrete ties used on the new section were defective and had to be replaced as the line was operating. Once the new (and presumably permanent) terminal at Owings Mills was established, Metro operations became slightly more complex, with every other train turning back at the Milford Mill Road station. These cutback runs entered a "pocket" track just west of the station, where they changed ends and returned to Charles Center. By then, too, twenty-eight more cars had arrived, finally giving Metro its one hundred-car fleet.

The next step was eastward. In 1983, design work started on a 1 to 1½-mile extension from Charles Center to Johns Hopkins Hospital, one of the city's largest employers. The huge hospital complex and its nearby neighborhoods promised to be heavy subway traffic sources in themselves, but this line had a longer-range purpose too: Eventually it was to form the first leg of the long-deferred route through northeast Baltimore. From "The Hopkins," Metro would go next to Harford Road at Clifton Park — and, some day, perhaps complete the Overlea-Carney spoke of the now-ancient 1965 plan.

Unhappily the short Johns Hopkins Hospital line was the engineering opposite of the uncomplicated Owings Mills extension. It lay entirely underground, following Baltimore Street east and Broadway north, with much of the distance located below the water table. Along with the usual difficulties of tunneling beneath inner-city streets with their tangle of pipes and utility lines, Metro designers and builders had to cope with relocating the bed of the Jones Falls to accommodate an intermediate station, and also pass under several major sewer lines.

Construction could not begin until August 1989, and then was quickly beset with almost every problem known to tunnel building — cave-ins, flooding, fires, and finally the overpowering fumes from gasoline which had leaked into the ground from a long-abandoned service station at Broadway and Orleans Street. As of 1992, the job was well behind schedule, and no promises could be made for a planned mid-1994 opening.

Whenever it does open, this latest Metro extension possibly could be its last. For even as it was being planned, urban transit planners were becoming disenchanted with the bloodcurdling expense of subway tunneling and the time necessary to fund and build such projects. A new, cheaper, more flexible and pragmatic form of electric rail transport was then appearing in several United States and Canadian cities, and suddenly had become quite popular. Maryland's planners and politicians embraced it for their next project too. It was, in effect, the streetcar.

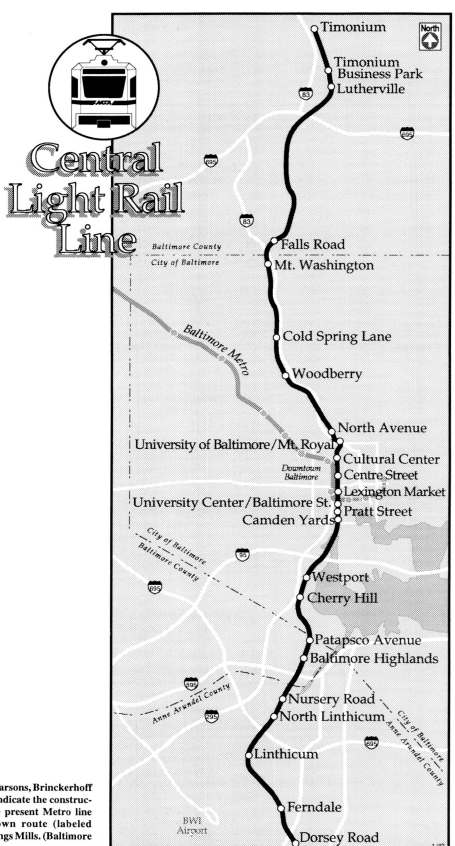

Central Light Rail Line

- Timonium
- Timonium Business Park
- Lutherville
- Falls Road
- Mt. Washington
- Cold Spring Lane
- Woodberry
- North Avenue
- University of Baltimore/Mt. Royal
- Cultural Center
- Centre Street
- Lexington Market
- University Center/Baltimore St.
- Pratt Street
- Camden Yards
- Westport
- Cherry Hill
- Patapsco Avenue
- Baltimore Highlands
- Nursery Road
- North Linthicum
- Linthicum
- Ferndale
- Dorsey Road

Baltimore County
City of Baltimore

Baltimore Metro

Downtown Baltimore

City of Baltimore
Baltimore County

Anne Arundel County

City of Baltimore
Anne Arundel County

BWI Airport

1/92

The original 1965 rapid transit plan proposed by the Parsons, Brinckerhoff engineering firm. The numbers shown for each line indicate the construction priority recommended by the consultants. The present Metro line roughly follows the "first priority" Randallstown route (labeled "Northwest Line" on the map), but terminates in Owings Mills. (Baltimore *News American* map; Robert L. Krueger Collection)

THE STREETCAR
COMES FULL CIRCLE

By Herbert H. Harwood, Jr.

In the new jargon of city transit planners and operators, Metro and its ilk became "heavy rail"; the alternate was named, not surprisingly, "light rail." Its basic aim was much the same as any rapid transit system — to move large numbers of people faster and more efficiently than automobiles or buses. But the technology and construction techniques were very familiar. Light rail tracks were laid mostly on the surface, usually on a reserved right of way, but, where necessary, on streets too. Electric power was delivered from an overhead wire, either a light simple catenary or traditional trolley wire. The cars themselves typically were low-platform, high-performance streetcars, often merely modified modern European tramcar designs. Station facilities were minimal — little more than open platforms with shelters, if even that.

To one degree or another, cities such as Boston, Cleveland, Pittsburgh, and Philadelphia have had light rail for many decades — although never called that. And indeed, some outer sections of Baltimore's old streetcar system had light rail characteristics, particularly the route of the "Red Rockets" to Sparrows Point. But the inspiration for what was inevitably dubbed as "the light rail renaissance" was the surprisingly successful San Diego system opened in 1981. San Diego's first line — which it shamelessly called "The San Diego Trolley" — was built primarily over the right of way of a freight railroad and frugally used off-the-shelf German streetcars and completely conventional overhead track and signaling. It had been built in a mere eighteen months, and without federal funds.

When Walter Addison planned Baltimore's first Metro line, he followed the expedient route outlined by the earlier consultants and headed northwest to Pikesville and Owings Mills. But one of the

heaviest, fastest-growing, and most congested corridors lay directly north. With the construction of the Baltimore Beltway and Interstate 83, business and residential development gravitated to Towson and the areas beyond — Lutherville, Timonium, Cockeysville, and Hunt Valley. Taken together, these had become an urban center easily rivaling downtown Baltimore. The 1965 Parsons, Brinckerhoff plan had included a rapid transit line from downtown to Towson and Timonium, following York Road. But this route required highly expensive subway or subway/elevated construction through a heavily built-up area. Even after Addison announced the first phase of the Metro project, the Towson-Timonium subway was a very distant and dubious hope.

So in 1972, Baltimore County Delegate Robert Stroble urged the state's new department of transportation to look into a quicker and cheaper alternative — restoration of some form of rail commuter service on the former Northern Central Railway line through the area. Once a main line route between Baltimore, York, and Harrisburg, Pennsylvania, the Northern Central roughly paralleled the Jones Falls Expressway/Interstate 83 corridor through Mount Washington, Ruxton, Lutherville, Timonium, and Cockeysville. While it lay considerably west of the center in Towson, the railroad line was well situated to serve several of the fastest-growing northern suburbs.

The Northern Central line dated to the early 1830s and was one of the country's earliest railroad projects. After 1861, it came under the wing of the powerful Pennsylvania Railroad and eventually was absorbed into the big eastern trunk line system. For many years, it had channeled Pennsylvania anthracite coal into Baltimore; through the first half of the twen-

tieth century, it also formed the PRR's primary passenger train link between the Baltimore/Washington markets and its own east-west main line at Harrisburg. Besides their heavy through limited trains between Baltimore and cities such as Chicago and St. Louis, the Northern Central and Pennsy also once offered extensive local suburban services along the line, terminating at Cockeysville and Parkton. In fact, the railroad was directly responsible for the development of many of Baltimore's northern suburbs, and the "Parkton Local" was once a revered part of Baltimore County's culture.

But the last Parkton locals died in 1959, and all through Baltimore-Harrisburg passenger service ended with the advent of Amtrak in 1971. By that time, the heavily built double-track line had been reduced to a single-track secondary branch. Tropical Storm Agnes severely damaged several sections of the route in June 1972, ending all operation north of Cockeysville.

Afterwards, all that remained of the Northern Central in Maryland was a low-speed local freight branch between Baltimore and Cockeysville, operating two or three days a week, to service several lumber dealers and the large Campbell (later Genstar) quarry at Texas, south of Cockeysville. By this time, too, the once-omnipotent Pennsylvania Railroad had disappeared into Penn Central, which in 1976 itself collapsed into Conrail.

Initially, the thought of reviving Northern Central passenger service was met with little enthusiasm from the MTA, which was then in the early stages of the Metro project, and was not sure how to accomplish it anyway. Community interest existed, but was not intense enough to develop sufficient political heat. So, from the early 1970s on, the idea struggled along for al-

The two fathers of the light rail line take a trial trip on November 20, 1991. MTA Administrator Ronald J. Hartman (at left) escorts Governor William Donald Schaefer aboard car 5002 at the Woodberry (Union Avenue) station for a trip south to North Avenue. (H. H. Harwood, Jr.)

most fifteen years in a sort of a twilight zone, not dead but not alive either. The MTA periodically conducted studies, held hearings, and pondered the pros and cons of converting the old railroad to a light rail line, paving it over as an exclusive busway, running a conventional railroad commuter service — or forgetting the whole thing and merely expanding express bus service on nearby Interstate 83.

In 1986, MTA planners restudied the proposal and settled on a minimal-expense light rail operation as the most feasible. Governor (and ex-Mayor of Baltimore) William Donald Schaefer became enthusiastic

The light rail line's railroad ancestry shows clearly in this view looking north from the 29th Street bridge. The tracks to the right and left of the car — and the crossing ahead of it — are part of an active Conrail freight branch operating over the south end of the old Northen Central. Conrail trains serving the light rail route to Cockeysville enter the transit line over the switch at the upper center of the photograph. Note that the light rail line goes from double to single track here too. (H. H. Harwood, Jr.)

about it and ordered the project started. In December 1987, he formally announced a twenty-seven-mile north-south light rail line which included not only the Northern Central route, but a southern leg to Glen Burnie — a partial revival of the aborted Metro plan which had been dropped in 1975. Although Anne Arundel County had spurned rapid transit twelve years before, new political leaders and growing congestion on such arteries as Route 3 and Ritchie Highway had changed many minds in the meantime. In addition to this main line, Schaefer included branches to BWI Airport and Amtrak's Penn Station in Baltimore.

Governor Schaefer's light rail route started in the North at the enormous Hunt Valley office/industrial park/shopping mall complex north of Cockeysville. From there it ran south to pick up the Northern Central right of way, which was used for fourteen miles as far as North Avenue in Baltimore. South of North Avenue there was no readily available right of way through the city's center, so the line was simply located along Howard Street for about sixteen blocks — part of it alongside the street, part in the center, and part off-center on one or both curbsides. Once a major north-south thoroughfare and the center of Baltimore's retail district, Howard Street had long since lost most of its commercial vitality and had slipped into an urban backwater; part of it already had been converted to a transit mall. (Ironically, an ideal ready-made light rail route through downtown — CSX Transportation's Howard Street railroad tunnel —

lay directly beneath. But this was still an active freight route and impractical to use.)

At the foot of Howard Street the rail line passed the Baltimore & Ohio Railroad's ancient Camden station, originally built between 1856 and 1865 and now restored to its late nineteenth century appearance (but no longer used as a railroad terminal). Directly south of the "old" Camden Station and adjacent to the new baseball stadium, Oriole Park at Camden Yards, light rail cars shared a minimalistic "new" Camden Station with MARC, the state's commuter rail operation.

South of the Camden complex, the light rail track hurdled several CSX Transportation railroad lines, the Ostend Street bridge, and the Middle Branch of the Patapsco River to reach Westport.

Typical of the curving, semi-bucolic Northern Central line is this scene inside Baltimore City near the old Mount Vernon textile mill. (H. H. Harwood, Jr.)

From Westport south, the Glen Burnie end of the line also used a railroad right of way, part of it long-abandoned and part still active. In this case, the line was that of the Baltimore & Annapolis and one of its predecessors. Commonly called the Annapolis Short Line in its earlier years, the B & A's route dated back to 1887, when it started steam-hauled service between Baltimore and the state capital. Between 1908 and 1950, the line was electrified and ran fast, heavy multiple-car interurban trains. B & A buses replaced the trains in February 1950; the electric wires came down, but the rails remained for diesel-powered freight runs. Gradually the freight business also withered, and by the early 1970s the track had been cut back to a six-mile stretch from a CSX Transportation (ex-B & O) freight connection at Baltimore Highlands (called Clifford by the

railroad) to Dorsey Road, north of the center of Glen Burnie.

The light rail right of way from Westport to Glen Burnie first crossed CSX Transportation's South Baltimore branch at Westport, then variously used the roadbed of two different former electric interurban lines which once ran through the area. From Westport to the B & A's existing track at Clifford, it was laid on a bed originally built by the Annapolis Short Line in 1908 and abandoned for passenger use in 1921. From Clifford to Linthicum, the B & A's line (and the new light rail) used the right of way of the legendary Washington, Baltimore & Annapolis Electric Railroad, a high-speed interurban line between Baltimore and Washington. (Between 1921 and its demise in 1935, the WB & A had owned the Annapolis Short Line.) And finally, from Linthicum to the

end of track at Dorsey Road in Glen Burnie, the light rail/B & A route followed the 1887 Annapolis Short Line alignment. It was a short and perhaps confusing trip through interurban history.

Since both the B & A and the old Northern Central lines were still active freight carriers, the light rail also had to accommodate railroad shippers and receivers, making it almost unique among urban rapid transit lines. (The San Diego "trolley" handles freight too.) The MTA contracted with outside railroads to serve these customers during the nighttime hours when passenger service was shut down. Conrail continued operating over the Northern Central, while the state-owned Canton Railroad handled the former B & A portion.

Thanks to Governor Schaefer's strong push, and because of relatively simple construction, light rail work moved swiftly —

On November 29, 1991, downtown Baltimore was introduced to its first light rail car, exhibited at Howard and Lexington Streets. Facing off with the new car was "Baltimore Transit No. 7398," actually a wooden replica of a Baltimore PCC car built for the movie *Avalon* and later donated to the Baltimore Streetcar Museum. (H. H. Harwood, Jr.)

despite the seemingly inevitable political and financial hurdles. To expedite the work, state and local funds were used in the initial phase of the line, twenty-two miles between Timonium and Dorsey Road in Glen Burnie. Extensions to Hunt Valley, BWI Airport, and Penn Station were to follow later. Engineering planning began in 1988; in February 1989, thirty-five two-unit articulated cars were ordered from ABB Traction, Inc., the North American subsidiary of the Swedish-Swiss partnership of ASEA-Brown-Boveri. On May 15, 1989, Schaefer formally broke ground at Howard and Lexington Streets in the company of Baltimore Mayor Kurt Schmoke and the county executives of Baltimore and Anne Arundel Counties.

Like Metro before it, the light rail project soon hit its own budget crisis. A re-study of cost estimates in late 1989 produced an amount 48 percent higher than the "high side" figure anticipated in 1987. Fortunately, light rail construction planning was flexible and some facilities could be deferred — enough, at least, to placate the General Assembly. The project was saved through some quick but reluctant cuts, including temporarily substituting several single-track sections, eliminating an overpass at busy Timonium Road, and reducing station amenities. As built, about 40 percent of the line's length was single track, although most of this was graded and prepared for eventual double-tracking.

Otherwise, construction was essentially uncomplicated, with only two significant engineering challenges. The first, and worst, was getting the line out of the Jones Falls valley at North Avenue and up onto Howard Street, at a considerably higher elevation. This had to be done within a short distance of several blocks over an alignment strewn with major obstructions and hemmed in by other structures. First, the tracks had to rise out of the valley floor and pass under both North Avenue and the adjacent Jones Falls Expressway; then, they immediately (and sharply) rose to cross CSX Transportation's Baltimore Belt Line tracks, and just as quickly, dropped to pass under the Howard Street Bridge. From there, they had to reach Howard Street over an alignment which would avoid passing too close to the Meyerhoff Symphony Hall, where it was feared that the noise and vibration might disturb the concerts. The problem was solved — but barely — by a series of sharp curves and steep ramps, which should keep passengers awake if not fully oriented.

Scenery and railroad interest abound on the light rail. Car 5001 skims beneath the 29th Street bridge in Baltimore. The two tracks nearest the camera are used by Conrail to reach its "Flexi-flo" bulk distribution terminal, located to the left and rear of the rapid transit car. (H. H. Harwood, Jr.)

The second problem was more straightforward, but required an even more elaborate structure. Leaving Camden Station on its way south to Westport, the light rail line had to cross over the CSX Transportation's main line just south of its Howard Street tunnel portal, then in quick succession pass over the Ostend Street bridge, a railroad junction immediately to its south, and the wide but shallow Middle Branch. These hurdles were solved by extending the Howard Street tunnel farther south and building a 3770-foot-long continuous concrete viaduct over the street, railroad tracks, and water.

Construction rolled ahead. In May 1990, fourteen miles of the former Northern Central were bought from Conrail for $17.5 million, and at the same time a

contract was let for rebuilding the line. By September of that year, the first new light rail track had been installed at the Timonium Road crossing. Afterwards, concrete ties, welded rail, and ballast went down rapidly. Conrail freight service was maintained throughout the work, although sometimes painfully.

Purchase negotiations for the Baltimore & Annapolis segment proved to be more lengthy and difficult. An agreement (for $9 million) was not formally signed until May 1991, putting the Glen Burnie end of the line behind schedule. To speed the work on this section, all freight service was suspended and the old track was completely removed before being replaced. During this time, freight shipments for the line's only customer were trucked in, and the B & A

remained in limited service switching the customer's warehouse.

On July 24, 1991, the first light rail car from ABB arrived by truck, and soon afterward, testing began on a 1½-mile section north of North Avenue. Not coincidentally, the new light rail fleet was given numbers in the 5000 series, the same numbers carried by the original group of Baltimore's beloved Brill semi-convertibles of 1905. (Also, coincidentally or not, these same original semi-convertibles were later rebuilt into articulateds.) The newcomers were three-truck articulateds measuring 95 feet long and a generous 9½ feet wide; they seated 84, could carry a total of 172 people, and could be coupled into two- and three-unit trains. Although they drew a conventional 750 volts DC through their single

The articulated light rail cars operate in trains of up to three cars. Here a three-car test run rolls over the single track section at Cedar Avenue in Baltimore. (H. H. Harwood, Jr.)

pantographs, they used a sophisticated AC propulsion system. Compared to their Metro cousins, they were somewhat more sedate, designed for a top speed of 55 mph and a normal operating speed of 50 mph.

On April 3, 1992, light rail cars took baseball fans to the first game at brand-new Oriole Park at Camden Yards and, after a May 12th dedication, commenced running a regular schedule between Timonium and Camden Station in mid-May, with service starting to Patapsco Avenue near Baltimore Highlands soon after. Glen Burnie operation was planned for early 1993. Final design work for the Timonium-Hunt Valley section and the branches to BWI Airport and Penn Station was still under way.

Other extensions may come. Back in 1988, an optimistic Governor Schaefer proposed a dramatic expansion of light

rail lines for both the Baltimore and Washington suburbs. Included were routes from Baltimore to Woodlawn, White Marsh, Dundalk, and a branch of the existing Northen Central line to Towson. Extension of the Glen Burnie line to Annapolis, over the abandoned but still-intact B & A right of way, was also a possibility. Since then, the economic and political climates have changed, making the probability and timing of more rail lines speculative.

But speculation is not the aim of this book; history is. And it seems that Baltimore's transportation history is coming full circle. After an absence of twenty-nine years, true streetcars were back in the city's streets; in fact, they had been gone from Howard Street for over fifty years. The Baltimore & Annapolis was electrified after forty-two years and again would carry

multiple-car trains. A former Annapolis Short Line underpass near Westport saw its first passenger trains again after seventy-one years. Double track had returned to parts of the Northern Central, just as in the days when doubleheaded K-4 Pacifics pounded over the line with the *Liberty Limited* for Chicago, and the Parkton locals carried their commuters. (And, as another ironic aside, electrification of this line fulfilled a plan made by the Pennsylvania Railroad seventy-six years before, but never carried out.)

And finally, the new light rail shop sits on the same site as the Northen Central's 1873 Mt. Vernon shop complex, dismantled in 1929 — a site which had been in continuous railroad service for over 160 years. The past has become the present, and the present become the past.

Car No. 3612, built by Brill in 1892, leads the parade of cars at the United's 1928 exhibition, which came to be known as the "Fair of the Electric Pony." This car, once preserved in the historical collection, was placed on display in a city park in 1957 due to limited storage space. Although vandals and the elements took their toll, its truck was salvaged for use on the BSM's overhead line car. (Louis C. Mueller Collection)

PRESERVING THE PAST

By Michael R. Farrell and Andrew S. Blumberg

George F. Nixon, curator emeritus of the Baltimore Streetcar Museum and also one of its founders, was instrumental in saving the United's original streetcar collection for posterity. (George F. Nixon Collection)

Not only has the streetcar reappeared in Baltimore in modern form, but parts of the past have been saved as well. Over a dozen vintage Baltimore streetcars have been preserved, and today most of these operate for the enjoyment of young and old at the Baltimore Streetcar Museum (BSM) on Falls Road, on the outskirts of downtown Baltimore. This organization is the culmination of planning, hard work, and periods of heartbreak, and merits a mention in any streetcar history.

The Museum harks back to an Association of Commerce luncheon and exhibition held by the United Railways and Electric Company in 1928. In addition to showing off its "modern equipment," the United spruced up a number of older cars that were still on the roster in work service. The display (dubbed by an inspired newspaper reporter the "Fair of the Electric Pony," in reference to the Baltimore & Ohio's renowned "Fair of the Iron Horse" the year before) started several company officers, notably Raymond Tompkins and A. T. Clark, thinking that representative cars should be preserved for a permanent museum. As a result, a group of cars was put aside in storage, but the United's bankruptcy several years later precluded any more definite action.

By the late 1940s, the United's successor, the Baltimore Transit Company, was under the control of pro-bus National City Lines. Baltimore Transit not only showed a lack of interest in the project, but desired to dispose of the collection. The wooden car bodies allegedly presented an unnecessary fire hazard.

Efforts spearheaded chiefly by indefatigable Baltimore transit historian George F. Nixon, plus a handful of other undaunted traction enthusiasts, convinced Baltimore Transit not to scrap the collection until arrangements could be made for its continued survival. In July 1954, largely through the efforts of the Baltimore Chapter of the National Railway Historical Society, the cars were presented to the Maryland Historical Society, which had agreed to act as "caretaker" until plans could be made to display them.

While an NRHS committee under Chairman Nixon was attempting to arouse public interest, Baltimore Transit decided to evict the cars from Irvington car house, where they had been stored. Now began an odyssey which was to see the cars housed at Edmondson Avenue car house, Cumberland Street car house, and even a Department of Sanitation garage, before it was announced that a permanent home had been found for them just north of the city at Robert E. Lee Park, along the banks of Lake Roland.

During the wandering, the local group had affiliated with a similar organization from the Washington, D.C. area. The situation looked promising when the combined collections were hauled by truck to a ravine at Lake Roland in September 1962. However, once the arduous task had been completed, not all of the neighbors were enraptured at the prospect of having total strangers venture into the formerly secluded area.

The details of the dreary years "at the lake" are now like water over the dam at Lake Roland. Suffice it to say that it was a disheartening experience to see hard work and financial contributions going for naught, as the cars rapidly began to disintegrate before the combined onslaught of weather and vandals.

The Washington group withdrew, taking its cars to another park in Montgomery County, where the present-day National Capital Trolley Museum was born. For a while, it looked as if the Baltimore cars would likewise have to be moved to a spot remote from the city where they belonged and for which they could be such an attraction.

Fortunately, the city administration recognized the potential of the collection, one of the best in the world at presenting a comprehensive view of the development of one city's transportation system. Just as his predecessor, Thomas J. D'Alesandro, Jr., had helped to find storage space for the cars, Mayor Theodore R. McKeldin actively sought a permanent location where an operating museum could function.

In 1966, it was announced that a site had been found: the old Maryland and Pennsylvania Railroad right of way along Falls Road, just north of the North Avenue bridge. Under the sponsorship of the Baltimore Streetcar Museum, Inc., which had been incorporated in June of the same year to save the cars for Baltimore, the cars were moved to a modern car house, built by the city in 1968 for long-term lease to the Museum.

The notion that an operating museum was an idle dream was soon dispelled once there was a suitable working place. The

Time was turned back on Sunday, July 11, 1954, as cars (left to right) No. 4732 (probably Baltimore City Passenger, 1880s); No. 1164 (Brill, 1902); and No. 264 (Brownell, 1900); all retired from service for decades, traveled west along Frederick Road, en route from Irvington car house to Irvington loop. The occasion was the presentation of the cars by the Baltimore Transit Company to the Maryland Historical Society. (BSM Collection)

scoffers saw the first cars so chosen restored to their former glories. Fortunately, the cars had been moved before the ravages of weather and vandals affected the structural soundness of the sturdy vehicles; still, upwards of three thousand hours of hard work were necessary before the first cars could pass the critical inspection of the all-volunteer BSM shop crew.

Crucial to these and other rehabilitative efforts throughout the Museum's history have been the shop facilities, located in the old Ma & Pa freight station along the line. Streetcar history played a role here, too — much of the shop equipment was donated by the Western Electric Company from its old Point Breeze plant, site of the United's famed Riverview Park until 1929.

Trackwork and overhead also required strenuous volunteer efforts, particularly in light of limited finances, which dictated that much of the work be done by hand rather than with expensive mechanical equipment. The electrical substation, named in honor of the Museum's then-Curator, George Nixon, was also largely constructed by the members.

Finally, on May 6, 1970, all was ready for a test, and streetcar wheels once again turned in Baltimore. Public operation followed on July 3rd, almost seven years after the end of revenue service on Baltimore's streets. During that holiday weekend, thousands of Baltimoreans thronged to the Museum to enjoy the novelty of a streetcar ride once more.

The original trackage was extended in the ensuing years, including 1976 and 1982, when loops were completed for the northern (28th Street) and southern (North Avenue) termini, respectively, of the line, bringing the round-trip distance to 1¼ miles. In addition, 1985 saw the start of double track being laid between a point just north of the BSM shop facilities and the North Avenue loop.

It is worthy of note that much of this trackage was salvaged from the streets of Baltimore itself. The Museum's 28th Street loop, for example, originally saw service as the West Baltimore Street loop of the No. 15 line, while the Sparrows Point loop of the No. 26 line now enjoys reincarnation as the BSM's North Avenue

Car No. 4732 is shown in the process of being moved to a Department of Sanitation garage on Greenmount Avenue in September 1957. In September 1962, it and its sisters were moved to the ill-fated museum site at Robert E. Lee Park. Despite rough treatment by weather and vandals, No. 4732 survived and now runs under its own power again at its Falls Road home, and under its earlier number — No. 417. (Baltimore Sunpapers)

Cars (back to front) No. 6119 (Brill, 1930); No. 7407 (Pullman-Standard, 1944); No. 3828 (Brill, 1902); and No. 3550 (Brill, 1904) are pictured at Robert E. Lee Park in 1964. The bucolic tranquility of the scene belies the many problems encountered at the site. (George J. Voith)

The steel framework is up for the BSM's car house, while rail, constituting future trackwork, collects in the foreground, in this early 1968 view, taken from the then-B & O Belt Line (today, CSXT) bridge. As work progressed, the cryptic billboard, right, would soon be removed. (Carl P. Hughes)

The same view as above was photographed twenty-three years later, June 23, 1991, during the Museum's 25th anniversary weekend. The visitors' center and North Avenue loop are to the left. (Andrew S. Blumberg)

When the Museum cars arrived at Falls Road, money was not plentiful, but volunteer workers were undaunted. Lever and fulcrum methods were more common than mechanical aids. Museum members Richard Obbink, left, and Clyde Gerald maneuver heavy specialwork into position. (Michael R. Farrell)

loop. Remnants of Eastern Avenue and Kelly Avenue (Mt. Washington) trackage, among other locales, also grace the Museum roadbed.

Baltimore trackage has also played a crucial role in keeping the collection, with just one exception, "pure" from a local standpoint. Museum cars travel on a prototypically correct, unique 5 feet 4½ inches track gauge, the widest that has ever been used in North America for street rail transit. Accommodating non-Baltimore rolling stock at the Museum would necessitate costly and cumbersome wheel

regauging. Although surely not known in 1859, Baltimore's decision to build a wide-gauge system contributed significantly to the BSM's preservational and promotional philosophy: to present as completely as possible the story of street rail transit for a single city, an approach unique in the rail-museum movement.

In 1978, with federal and city funding, a modern visitors' center was completed, featuring a dispatcher's office, auditorium, gift shop, display space, and archival facilities. It represents one of the finest such buildings of its kind.

The original collection of cars, first set aside by the United and later supplemented at the end of service by Baltimore Transit, continued to grow. The chief acquisition occurred in 1977, when the BSM filled a major gap in its collection by finally obtaining a Brill semi-convertible, a former Newport News & Hampton Railway, Gas & Electric Company car built in 1917, virtually identical to its Baltimore Brill sisters of the same period. In all, 885 Brill semi-convertibles, far more than any other type of local streetcar, clattered through the streets of Baltimore, the first ones entering service in 1905, with the last workhorses not retiring until 1955.

Not all was sublime in the BSM's first decade of operation, however. On September 5-6, 1979, Tropical Storm David ripped through the mid-Atlantic region. The Museum, which had escaped with minor damage in the wake of Hurricane Agnes in 1972, was not so fortunate this time. Nearly 6½ inches of rain fell those two days, including two inches within one hour from the evening of the 5th to the morning of the 6th. The normally docile Jones Falls became a torrent of water and debris. Rising over its banks, it flooded the car house, visitors' center, substation, and trackage. Water rose to a height of four feet in all Museum buildings.

Damage was extensive. Two twenty-five-foot sections of masonry were torn out of the car house's west wall. Streetcar trucks, vestibules, and interiors were immersed in fetid mud. In the visitors' center, low-level displays and gift shop merchandise were destroyed. Ten months and countless hours of labor later, the BSM reopened for business. Nearly $250,000 in damage was sustained by the property, for which new contingency measures were reviewed to address any future threats of flooding.

Happily, the years since the flood have seen overwhelmingly positive developments for the Museum. Besides the ongoing effort of preserving and promoting the history of rail transit in Baltimore through continuous public operation, car restoration and maintenance, community involvement, membership solicitation, and a myriad amount of other activities, the BSM

A Museum milestone was celebrated in August 1968, with the completion of car house construction. Cars No. 3550, No. 264, and, to the rear, No. 6119, are posed for the event. Conspicuous by its absence is the overhead to power the cars — the start of public operations remained nearly two years in the future. (A. Aubrey Bodine Collection, The Peale Museum)

Saturday, July 3, 1970, marked the first day of Museum operations. The parade of cars (left to right: No. 1164; No. 264; No. 3651, built by Brownell in 1898; No. 6119; and No. 3550) seemed to stretch nearly as far as the Museum's available trackage. That historic weekend remains the best-attended in Museum history. (Michael R. Farrell)

In December 1976, eight BSM cars were proudly posed on the just-completed 28th Street loop, northern terminus of the Museum trackage and formerly the West Baltimore Street loop of the No. 15 line. (Edward G. Willis, BSM Collection)

The Morning After — September 6, 1979, and the Museum confronts the destruction wrought by Tropical Storm David. Scattered masonry and gaping holes in the car house's west wall attest to the storm's ferocity. It would be ten months before the resumption of public operations. (Edward G. Willis, BSM Collection)

Newly restored No. 6119 (center, with bunting) was the star attraction at the BSM's 25th anniversary commemoration of the end of streetcar service, November 5-6, 1988. On Sunday, November 6th, the date of this scene, the Museum operated a five-car schedule and carried standing-room-only crowds. (Andrew S. Blumberg)

A streetcar that never was, poses on a street that never saw streetcars. The PCC mockup from *Avalon* sits on Rosebank Avenue, just west of York Road and the Senator Theatre in November 1989, prior to a full day of moviemaking. In the film, the car wore three numbers — Nos. 7062, 7383, and 7398. It also included many genuine parts supplied by the BSM. (Andrew S. Blumberg)

A nearly completely restored No. 7407 was on display at the Museum's 25th anniversary weekend, June 22-23, 1991. Six months of rewiring, testing, and other work remained before the car would reenter service. (Andrew S. Blumberg)

has witnessed a number of milestones and anniversaries along the way.

In November 1988, the Museum, along with the Mass Transit Administration (MTA), observed the 25th anniversary of the cessation of streetcar service in Baltimore. The BSM commemorated the occasion by reintroducing Peter Witt car No. 6119 back into service after a painstaking restoration that took fifteen years to complete. Fittingly, MTA exhibits afforded visitors their first look at the impending Central Light Rail project. The number of people visiting the Museum that weekend proved second only to the number attending the opening weekend festivities of July 1970.

The BSM even went "Hollywood" for an evening, in November of 1989. Hollywood director and Baltimore native son Barry Levinson shot several scenes at the Museum

for his movie *Avalon*, which depicted the history of his family in Baltimore. Peter Witt No. 6119 and PCC No. 7407 were recruited as the stars. The Museum also assisted the movie's production company in constructing a full-scale, diesel-powered Baltimore PCC mockup used in other scenes. The BSM became the proud owner of the "Hollywood" car, as it quickly became known, and has displayed it at special events.

The Museum marked twenty years of public operations in July 1990, while June of the following year saw a special weekend celebrating the BSM's first twenty-five years of existence. This time, PCC No. 7407, the last streetcar to operate in revenue service in Baltimore, and removed from Museum operation 1½ years earlier for a complete rebuilding, was "unveiled" to the public and officially returned to the

collection. The MTA, with which the BSM had developed close ties, helped greatly with the car's restoration. Visitors also enjoyed tours of the MTA's Central Light Rail yard and shop area, just across the Jones Falls from the Museum, and a visit by the "Hollywood" car.

In a very real sense, the Baltimore Streetcar Museum, in its first quarter-century, kept alive the concept of street railway transportation in Baltimore, through the tireless efforts of its all-volunteer membership. In 1992, with Metro operations nearing the ten-year mark and light rail — the streetcar technology of the 1990s and beyond — commencing service, the BSM's own future as an active, integral link between Baltimore's glorious street railway past and its promising future seemed more assured than ever.

THE BALTIMORE STREETCAR MUSEUM HISTORIC EQUIPMENT ROSTER

NO.	COMPANY*	BUILDER	YEAR	TRUCK(S)	MOTOR(S)	CONTROL EQUIPMENT	LENGTH	WEIGHT LBS.	SEATING CAPACITY	SE†/DE	ST‡/DT	TYPE
25	Baltimore City Passenger Railway Company	Poole & Hunt?	Ca. 1859	None	None	None	21' 1/2"		22	DE	ST	Horse Car (a)
129	Baltimore City Passenger Railway Company	John Stephenson Company	1880?	Pedestal	None	None	18' 10"	4,000	16	DE	ST	Horse Car
417	Baltimore City Passenger Railway Company	BCPR Co.?	1880s?	Lord Baltimore	(2) WH 49	K-10	24' 3"	16,300	20	DE	ST	Ex-Horse Car (b)
554	Baltimore Traction Company	Brownell Car Co.	1896	Lord Baltimore	(2) WH 49	K-10	31'	17,850	45	DE	ST	9 Bench Open (c)
1050	Baltimore Consolidated Railway Company	Brownell Car Co.	1898	Lord Baltimore	(2) WH 49	K-10	30' 8"	18,300	28	DE	ST	8 Window Closed (d)
264	United Railways & Electric Company	Brownell Car Co.	1900	Baltimore Maximum Traction	(2) WH 56	K-11	39' 6"	31,700	46	DE	ST	Convertible
1164	United Railways & Electric Company	J. G. Brill Co.	1902	Brill 22-A	(2) WH 306CV	K-36J	40' 5"	30,740	60	DE	DT	12 Bench Open
3828	United Railways & Electric Company	J. G. Brill Co.	1902	Brill 22-A	(2) WH 306CV	K-36J	39' 2"	31,030	36	DE	DT	10 Window Closed
4662	United Railways & Electric Company	J. G. Brill Co.	1904	Lord Baltimore	(2) WH 49	K-10	33' 11"	23,100	32	DE	ST	8 Window Closed (e)
4533	United Railways & Electric Company	J. G. Brill Co.	1904	Brill 21-E	(2) WH 101B	K-68B	35' 11"	26,600	35	DE	ST	One-Man Safety Rebuilt 4662 Type (f)
6119	United Railways & Electric Company	J. G. Brill Co.	1930	Brill 177-E1X	(4) GE 301	PC-19A1	46'	38,500	52	SE	DT	Peter Witt
4802	United Railways & Electric Company	J. G. Brill Co.	1922	None	None		23' 2 1/2"		22	SE	DT	Trackless Trolley (h)
7059	United Railways & Electric Company	J. G. Brill Co.	1920		None	None	48' 2 1/2"		60	DE	DT	Trackless Trolley
5885	Newport News & Hampton Railway, Gas & Electric Company	J. G. Brill Co.	1917				46' 7"		52	DE	DT	Semi-Convertible (a) (g)
2078	Baltimore Transit Company	Pullman-Standard Car Mfg. Company	1940	None	GE 1213D	GE-MRC	37'	21,780	40	DE	DT	Trackless Trolley (i)
7407	Baltimore Transit Company	Pullman-Standard Car Mfg. Company	1944	Clark B-2	(4) WH 1432H	WH-PCC	46'	37,900	54	SE	DT	PCC
1096	Baltimore Transit Company	General Motors	1945	None	671 Detroit Diesel	None	35'	17,000	41			Diesel Bus (i)
501	Baltimore Transit Company	The Autocar Company	1952	None	Autocar 377	None	13' 6"	6,370				Line Truck (i)
1962	Baltimore Transit Company	General Motors	1963	None	V671 Detroit Diesel	None	40'	21,000	51			Diesel Bus (i)

* All earlier Baltimore companies were combined into the UR & E on April 1, 1899; this was succeeded by the BTC on July 1, 1935. Eight cars were donated by the BTC for museum purposes on July 11, 1954: No. 6119 was added in 1955; and Nos. 4533 and 7407 were added after the end of rail service in 1963. Nos. 5885, 25, 129, and 7059, trackless trolleys Nos. 2078 and 4802, diesel buses Nos. 1096 and 1962; and Line Truck No. 501 were acquired subsequently.

(a) Body only.
(b) Previously listed as No. 4732; now being restored to its earlier number.
(c) Previously listed as No. 3390; now restored to its earlier number.
(d) Previously listed as No. 3651; now restored to its earlier number.

(e) Originally equipped with Brill 21-E trucks and WH 101B (2) motors.
(f) Previously listed as No. 3550; now being restored to its earlier number.
(g) Only non-Baltimore car. However, it is virtually identical to Baltimore semi-convertibles of the same period. Formerly identified in Virginia as car No. 90 and later No. 390.
(h) Body presently in storage off Museum property.
(i) Stored off Museum property.

(†) SE or DE: Single Ended or Double Ended
(‡) ST or DT: Single Truck or Double Truck

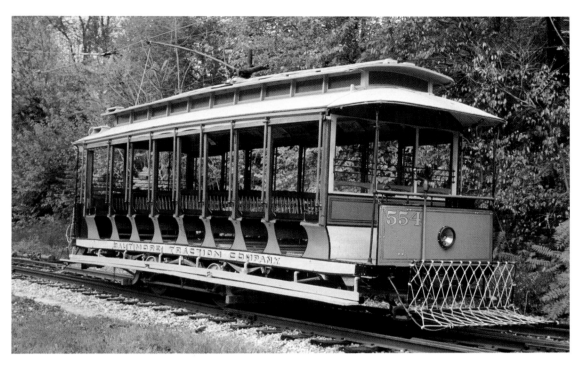

Baltimore Traction Company nine-bench open car No. 554, Brownell Car Company, 1896, Baltimore Streetcar Museum, November 1991. (Andrew S. Blumberg)

Baltimore Consolidated Railway Company eight-window closed car No. 1050, Brownell Car Company, 1898, Baltimore Streetcar Museum, November 1991. (Andrew S. Blumberg)

United Railways & Electric Company twelve-bench open car No. 1164, J. G. Brill Company, 1902, Baltimore Streetcar Museum, December 1991. (Andrew S. Blumberg)

United Railways & Electric Company convertible car No. 264, Brownell Car Company, 1900, Baltimore Streetcar Museum, November 1991. (Andrew S. Blumberg)

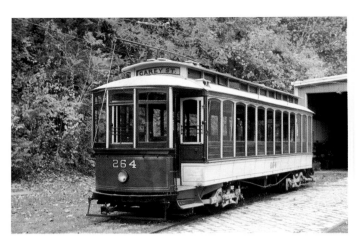

United Railways & Electric Company Peter Witt No. 6119, J. G. Brill Company, 1930, Baltimore Streetcar Museum, August 1991. (Andrew S. Blumberg)

Baltimore Transit Company PCC No. 7407, Pullman-Standard Car Manufacturing Company, 1944, Baltimore Streetcar Museum, January 1992. (Andrew S. Blumberg)

Semi-convertible No. 5460 entering Park Heights Avenue from Manhattan
Loop on No. 5 line. Note the wood-bodied station wagon, June 17, 1948.
(George J. Voith)

PCC No. 7372 in National City Lines "transition" color scheme on Park
Heights Avenue inbound on No. 5 line, June 17, 1948. (George J. Voith)

Green PCC on Huntingdon Avenue trestle outbound on No. 25 line. Note the Maryland & Pennsylvania Railroad ("Ma & Pa") tracks below in Wyman Park, ca. 1949. (Charles M. Wagner, Lee H. Rogers Collection)

Semi-convertible No. 5427 departs Park Terminal onto Fulton Avenue near Druid Hill Avenue on the No. 1 line, June 24, 1948. (George J. Voith)

PCC 7113 on service pit, Gardenville Yard on Belair Road No. 15 line, July 1963. (Richard R. Andrews)

Red semi-convertible leads two-car train outbound on Dundalk Avenue on No. 26 line, probably August 1950. (Charles M. Wagner, Lee H. Rogers Collection)

Red semi-convertibles Nos. 5181 and 5826 on Charles Street crossing Baltimore Street during the NRHS National Convention, September 6, 1948. The B & O office building is to the left and up Charles Street is visible O'Neill's department store. The tracks were not normally used. (George J. Voith)

"Red Rockets" Nos. 5181 and 5826 in front of the Edmondson Avenue car house on the No. 14 line during the NRHS National Convention, September 6, 1948. (George J. Voith)

PCC No. 7119 under brilliant fall foliage on the Catonsville private right of way inbound on the No. 8 line, October 20, 1963. (Thomas R. Buckingham)

Semi-convertible No. 5727 on Bethlehem Shipyard Loop on No. 26 line, Baltimore Chapter NRHS excursion, September 20, 1953. (Ara Mesrobian)

The last PCC, No. 7407, late at night on its final excursion at Charles and Fayette Streets passing under Hamburger's on the Nos. 8 and 15 lines, November 3, 1963. (Thomas R. Buckingham)

PCC No. 7359 on Belvedere Avenue at the Western Maryland Railway crossing during a Baltimore Chapter NRHS excursion on the day following closing of the No. 19 line, June 17, 1956. The operator is Carvey G. Davis. (George J. Voith)

PCC No. 7337 on Gwynn Oak at Liberty Heights Avenues, Gwynn Oak Junction, on an "almost last day" Baltimore Chapter NRHS excursion on the No. 32 line, August 28, 1955. As late as 1948, the No. 33 line terminated here. (George J. Voith)

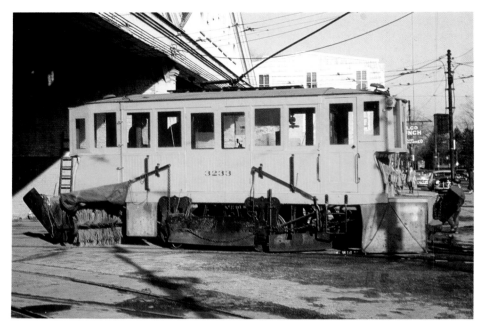

Snow Sweeper No. 3233 basks in the cold sunlight during a stopover at the Irvington car house on Frederick Avenue during an NRHS excursion, February 27, 1955. (Charles M. Wagner, Lee H. Rogers Collection)

Line car No. 3503 works on a new alignment at the Bethlehem Steel Sparrows Point plant on the No. 26 line, May 26, 1956. (George J. Voith)

PCC 7364 passes in front of a decorated City Hall on its way downtown on Holliday Street on the No. 8 line, October 14, 1962. (George J. Voith)

PCC 7021 passing Gwynn Oak Park on its way to Woodlawn on the No. 32 line during a Baltimore Chapter NRHS excursion, August 28, 1955. (George J. Voith)

Westbound PCC No. 7385 on Fayette Street turns north onto Eutaw Street
on the No. 15 line. Ford's Theatre is in the background, September 22, 1963.
(Thomas R. Buckingham)

Semi-convertible No. 5772 heads west toward Ellicott City on the bridge
over the Patapsco River on the No. 9 line, February 27, 1955. (Charles M.
Wagner, Lee H. Rogers Collection)

PCC No. 7089 crosses Orleans Street at Gay Street inbound on the No. 15 line, October 27, 1963. The tower of Enginehouse No. 6 overlooks the scene, which is about to disappear. (Thomas R. Buckingham)

Red, white, and blue semi-convertible No. 5728 poses for its picture in the fall of 1943 during World War II. Built in 1917 by Brill, it was a veteran of two wars. During the advertised appeal, it ran one day on each of the trolley routes that made up the system. (Transit Topics, BSM Collection)

It is wartime, and St. Louis PCC No. 7009, in all its glory, has its picture taken at the Carroll Park shops for summer 1943 issue of the company magazine. (Transit Topics, BSM Collection)

Looking south from the Pennsylvania Railroad overpass, PCC's 7126 and 7112 are operating on the No. 15 line on Gay Street, November 19, 1961. (Thomas R. Buckingham)

Rail Bond Test Car No. 3550 on last-day display at the Govans Loop spur at York Road, on the No. 8 line, November 2, 1963. Now part of the historic collection, it is being restored at the Baltimore Streetcar Museum as passenger car No. 4533. (Charles T. Mahan, Jr.)

Red semi-convertible No. 5193 heads toward Sparrows Point along the Bear Creek Bridge on the No. 26 line, June 30, 1948. (George J. Voith)

Central Light Rail car No. 5002 is shown on a test run opposite the 1877 Meadow Mill (later occupied by London Fog) in Woodberry, near where once the jerkwater cars from Falls Road ran, January 11, 1992. (Herbert H. Harwood, Jr.)

STREETCAR VIGNETTES

The track crews were among the unsung workers of the street railways. This gang is putting down girder rail on Baltimore Street in front of the Emerson Hotel around 1920. The pneumatic drill is only evidence of mechanical equipment in sight. A semi-convertible, bound for Gay Street, has a portable vestibule but still lacks platform doors. (Nixon/Gerding Collection)

IT TOOK MORE THAN CARS

To attempt to develop fully the story of the street railways of Baltimore, or any city, it is necessary to delve a little more deeply than merely to describe the routes, the corporate structure, and the equipment. The usual practice is to concentrate on such matters and only sketch in lightly other facets which really gave the breath of life to the industry.

Old-timers tend to reminisce about the soft clop of the horses' hoofs on the cobblestone streets or the quaintness of the bob-tailed cars. They overlook the fact that there was heard no clatter on the cobbles, no tinkle of horses' bells during the small hours of a winter's morning. There was, of course, no service after midnight.

Those quaint little cars were another matter, when one had to try to warm his or her feet under the moist straw piled on the floor during stormy weather. There was also the unhappy choice of keeping the windows open, while enduring the chilly blasts of the wintry air or raindrops of a summer shower, or keeping them closed and suffering the discomfiture of the foul air combined with the ever present odor of the rancid tallow used for illumination. Even in winter, this aroma, combined with the smell of heavily sweating horses, found its way into the cars. On a sultry summer's evening, the effect must have been overpowering. If one attempted to read a newspaper by the light of the one small lamp attached high on the bulkhead, he ran the risk of carrying on his clothing a splatter of oil as a memento of his journey.

This is not an attempt to destroy the romance of the industry. Rather, it is an attempt to bring into the proper perspective certain aspects of early operation that are overlooked by some present-day admirers, who gush adulation over the craftsmanship of a Stephenson, a Brill, or a Brownell. Let it be recorded that the same hands which write out this history have spent many a long hour in the dirty and messy job of restoring some of these vehicles to a semblance of their former glory. Have no fear, the cars themselves are fully appreciated, but what of the most colorful part of the whole legend — the men themselves?

Driving a horse car was not an easily acquired skill. An unidentified stable superintendent of "a leading (Baltimore) car line" was quoted in the *News,* July 28, 1887: "Experience has proven repeatedly that of the drivers employed fully nine out of ten fail to meet the requirements and have to be discharged before they have served as many days for pay as they have spent days in learning the road and rules of the company without pay."

In pre-vestibule days, the men taken on during the spring often sought other employment when the trees shed their leaves. Of those who stayed, the drivers wrapped themselves in horse blankets; the conductors added a suit or two of underwear, and both longed for April. Even the balmy days were not without their discomforts. The drivers had little protection from a drenching rain or broiling sun. When the men of one line offered to pay for the cost of adding a small awning, such as Bowie's men enjoyed, the general superintendent would not even consider the request.

On some of the lines, neither end had a layover point where the men could gain a few minutes shelter. On some routes that did, rules which required one of the crew to stay on the car at all times limited even this small respite. The small child standing on a corner clutching a lunch pail, while awaiting father's car to come along, was a familiar sight. This enabled a fortunate few to enjoy the semblance of a wholesome meal during the eight to fourteen minutes allotted for lunch or dinner.

The hours were incredible. Early research for this book unearthed some reminiscences of Cain Redican, who worked for over fifty years on the local cars; initially these were put aside as improbable. He stated that he had worked 18 hours and 20 minutes, day in and day out. Not only this, but if it was snowing, he took out a plow or salt car after his regular run. Incredible! There must have been a misprint or misquote, especially since the men worked on a schedule that called for only one day off every two or three weeks. But further research bore out his remarks. As late as 1886, one Towson run called for a driver to be on duty for 18 hours and 50 minutes. The men on the Govanstown cars had the shortest hours of all the crews in Baltimore County, a mere 15¾ hours. Needless to state, pay was not by the hour.

Many probably think that the pay-as-you-enter (P.A.Y.E.) cars of those halcyon times, just before World War I, were something new. Certain aspects of the operation were, yet the cars were actually a throwback to the earliest days of horse cars. The bob-tailed cars (so called because they had a platform only at the front) were in the charge of a driver whose duties also included seeing that fares were paid, making change, and opening and closing the rear open door by means of a contrivance of straps and levers. If a patron failed to walk up front, open the wicket door, and deposit his fare in the Slawson box, the driver would raise a clamor with his bell until this was accomplished.

On crowded cars, it was the practice to pass the fare forward. In time, chutes were placed in the vehicles to circumvent this practice. The coins could be inserted in convenient slots; gravity would carry them to the driver's farebox. Legend has it that this was less for the convenience of the patrons, than to ensure that all fares went into the company's coffers.

There were other employees besides the car crews, of course. According to one ac-

Special trackwork was required whenever tracks crossed or merged. Precision was essential, so the individual parts were bolted together at the Carroll Park shops to insure that no difficulties would be encountered during on-site installation. This layout for Light Street car house was fabricated from new and used components during World War II days. (Baltimore Streetcar Museum Collection)

count, City Passenger's Green Line (Pennsylvania Avenue to Canton), a typical busy line, required two stables to shelter its six hundred-odd horses. It took fifteen hostlers to feed, curry, and care for them. There were from eight to ten blacksmiths whose duties included reshoeing the animals every ten to twenty days. The harness was sturdy, rather than elaborate; still a half-dozen harnessmakers were kept busy with repairs.

By 1894, when the horses were well on the way out, their average value was $150, and they worked from three to eighteen years. On this line, seven miles in length, a horse made the round trip twice one day, and once the next. Newspaper comments on mistreatment of the animals were extremely rare, so it would appear that they were usually well treated.

At each steep hill, there was stationed a youth known as a "hill boy." His principal duty was to care for the "hill horse," which was attached to a car to assist it up the grade. In addition, the boy carried a bucket, which contained water for the regular team in hot weather or sand to sprinkle on the street during the icy season.

Wages varied, of course, but during the early nineties, drivers and conductors averaged about $12 a week, with the hill boys receiving $4. Low place on the scale was held by the clerical force, as indicated by the following advertisement in the *Sun* of December 19, 1891: "Wanted — a youth in an office, where it is necessary to work a portion of each Sunday; good references required; salary $3 per week."

What kind of men were they, these horse car drivers and conductors? A St. Louis paper, in 1895, defined them thus: "With some exceptions, of the lowest class. Their appearance and actions were calculated to convince the public that they were a little on the 'tough' side. The driver of those days was generally an uncouth and ill-mannered person, given to profanity that he would indulge in on the slightest provocation. The conductor was a grade higher. Yet, he too, lacked many of the instincts that go to make a gentleman."

Certain of these comments must have applied to the Baltimore men. One would scarcely expect a milquetoast on a job where the hours were many, the work by no means pleasant, and the pay small. Contemporary mention of them is rare, although Mayor Chapman's annual

John Karl and Kenneth Wagner renew paint and varnish on Brill semi-convertible No. 5854 at Carroll Park shops toward the end of car's four decades of service. Vehicles were beginning to show their age, but it is impossible to conceive of a bus running forty years. (George F. Nixon Collection)

Among the less glamorous jobs was that of keeping the cars clean. Shortly before abandonment, a shopman washes down a PCC with hose and mop. The BTC never did get around to installing automatic car washers. (James A. Genthner)

messages (1863-64) call them "polite and gentlemanly." The very lack of comment can be taken as favorable, because the editors were quick to speak out in caustic terms about any street railway shortcoming, real or imagined.

Although it would be naive to think that no fares were "knocked-down," there are few accounts of dishonesty. Until the big consolidation of 1899, many companies, including City Passenger, collected fares by hand. In the later years, there were registers as well as "spotters," but a little sleight-of-hand would have been easy.

The conductors had to be accurate, as any shortage came out of their own pockets. There is the story, probably apocryphal, of the Traction Company conductor who tried a clever play that backfired and cost him $10. It seems that a certain woman had boarded his car several times, on each occasion tendering a $10 note. As neither he nor anyone else on the car had change, each time she rode for nothing.

Vowing to stop the woman's trick, the conductor borrowed $10 in change from the company's office. Sure enough, several days later, the same woman got on his car and presented a ten-spot. Gleefully he took the note, giving a bag containing $9.95 in nickels in return. The lady emptied the bag gracefully, but without a smile, and got off at the next corner.

Our hero could not contain his mirth as he related the tale at the car shed. That night he turned in his money, with the $10 bill. The next morning, the bill was returned with a bit of paper attached marked "counterfeit."

One would suspect that, with the coming of "rapid transit," things would have begun to improve for the workers. This was true in some respects. However, they also found new problems to cope with. The fashion of the day called for much hirsute adornment of the face. The fad had particular appeal for the gripmen and motormen of the cable and electric cars, who found that a luxuriant growth of whiskers served more adequately to protect their faces and throats than an overcoat buttoned tightly around the chin. For the cold was felt much more keenly on a car whipping along at a snappy ten to twelve miles an hour, than it had been at

The conductor in neat blue uniform with shiny buttons, making change, dispensing transfers, and calling out street names, was the idol of many a small boy several generations ago. (UR & E Company, Willem Wirtz)

old Dobbin's pace. The men on the elevated line were said to have the coldest run. (This "honor" had previously gone to the Fort Avenue cars; by the turn of the century, the Shore Line would be known as the most frigid.)

In the summer, it was the conductors of the open cars who were exposed to a new problem. The handles at the end of each seat were of brass, and the perspiration from the conductor's hands reacted with the metal, coating them with verdigris. This invariably got into the eyes, eventually causing inflammation. The motormen could wear heavy leather or woolen gloves; but the conductor's duties of making change and punching transfers precluded his doing the same. The eventual solution

In July 1959, J. Brooke Duvall (left) of the BTC receives a plaque commemorating one hundred years of street railway operation from Charles W. Whittle, president of the Baltimore Chapter, NRHS. (George F. Nixon Collection)

Souvenir Ticket
100 Years of Street Railway Service
IN BALTIMORE
TROLLEY TOUR
SUNDAY, JULY 26, 1959
Baltimore Chapter
National Railway Historical Society, Inc.

Replica of ticket for 100th anniversary fantrip. (John S. Thomsen Collection)

was the substitution of wooden handles for the brass ones.

The legislature passed an act on April 1, 1886, which made it illegal to allow the men to work more than twelve hours a day. Still, there were exceptions — such as Christmas night of 1895 when a large fire forced more than half of the Baltimore City Passenger and Baltimore Traction motormen, gripmen, and conductors to stay on the cars all night because of the blockade. Despite the fact that they were protecting the companies' property, no concessions were made.

One kindly gesture on the part of the Central Railway seems rather ludicrous today. At Christmas time in 1897, it planned to give the men an eight-hour day at full pay. This was found to be impractical, so instead they gave each man a bonus. It consisted of a shiny fifty-cent piece!

The extra men had problems of their own. They had to collect their pay at the barns out of which they worked. One man on the City & Suburban reported collecting money at Roland Park, Huntingdon Avenue, Walbrook, and Waverly on a single payday.

There were all kinds of quirks in the regulations. For example, firemen in uniform could ride free on all of the lines except North Avenue. For some reason, City & Suburban refused the privilege on this route, and it was not granted until the next decade.

"Rapid transit" had eliminated the hill boys, but had produced other classes of outside workmen whose duties exposed them to the elements. A cable line required crews to keep the cable slot free of dirt and stones. These men worked at night, after the lines had stopped running. Their duties consisted of getting into the manholes and raking out the accumulation of trash and dirt with long handled tools. A wedgeman constantly patrolled the line in search of places where contraction or expansion had caused a crook in the slot. At two locations (at Paca and Fayette and at South and Lombard), an employee was on duty to manipulate the cable or turn the switch so that cars could proceed on the proper routes. Difficult as it may be to imagine, there were no traffic signals. The flow of traction ve-

hicles at busy intersections was controlled by signalmen, with flags or lanterns.

Probably the most uncomfortable job was that of grip inspector. He had to crouch in a pit about five feet deep and check the undergear of each passing car to see that the equipment was in order. At the Chinese Station (Fulton and Druid Hill Avenues), his location was under cover, but all other places required these men to face the weather.

The year just prior to the turn of the century saw the beginning of the end of the long struggle by the motormen to gain protection from the elements. As early as 1893, John F. Williams, a newly elected Maryland legislator, advocated a form of windshield to protect motormen and gripmen. As this would have meant an added expense for the companies, they opposed the bill vigorously. The companies even went so far as to present petitions against such protection, signed "voluntarily" by their men. The main argument was that in cold weather the glass would frost up so much as to present an actual visual hazard. (A little glycerine smeared on the panes would have prevented icing.)

Despite the fact that the Baltimore & Northern had successfully run vestibuled cars, it took the cruelly severe winter of 1898-99, to bring things to a head. At 8 a.m. on February 10, 1899, the temperature dipped to seven degrees below zero. There is still extant the following letter, written to William A. House, who, as the general manager of Consolidated Railway, was in a position to alleviate the problem. House had a reputation as a stern disciplinarian who had worked up the ladder the hard way; still one cannot help wondering what his reaction was upon receiving this note:

"How do you feel a morning like this when the thermometer is down below zero, sitting in your dining room reading the paper and smoking a good cigar, when only a few days ago you so heartlessly helped to condemn an ordinance that would have benefited your fellow man and made life more comfortable to thousands of homes and families, ain't there no God for you? A corporation Boss, you cannot enter their employ unless you sell your soul to the devil. I only hope you will burn in hell a thousand

years, in the same measure as your fellow man is now suffering from the cold and you helped their misery for a lousy money consideration.

Motorman"

Whether the letter helped or not is problematical, but windshields began to make their appearance shortly afterward; the convertibles purchased in 1900 came equipped with them, though it can be seen that they were an improvisation on the original plans.

The technical term for what was used at this time should be portable vestibule, rather than windshield. This unit consisted of a frame containing three panes of glass, the whole affair being removable in warmer weather. The first cars with completely enclosed platforms went into service in 1917, but it was not until the mid-twenties (about the same time that the summer cars were taken off) that the last unenclosed platform car disappeared.

The years prior to World War I saw the introduction of many features to ease the life of the motorman. Electric headlights replaced the pungent oil lamps; a stool to sit upon was placed on the platform; the closed vestibule enabled him to receive a modicum of warmth. Best of all was the introduction of air brakes in 1904.

The advancing technology was partly offset by modern problems; traffic congestion demanded greater skill; the faster speeds increased braking difficulties. Still, the operator of the 1940s could sit in his leather bucket seat with his foot resting lightly on a pedal to accelerate the PCC, fingering the console switches which automatically opened the front and center doors, switched on the lighting, dimmed the headlight, controlled the heating, even rang the gong. He was indeed a far cry from the motorman who formed the subject of a moving story which appeared in the *News* of February 3, 1899:

"Mr. House this morning gave the motormen who are to go before the (City) Council committee an object lesson on the futility of the vestibule. The men lined up by fours and marched out of the general offices and down Druid Hill Avenue. The first car that came along was stopped. On its front windows had collected considerable sleet that had to a great extent frosted the glass and made it impossible for it to be seen through.

" 'There,' exclaimed Mr. House. 'Can you see through that window? That's the way the windows of the vestibules would be. Could you see through them? You would have to have the windows down and would suffer just as much. Don't you see the uselessness of the vestibules?'

"The motormen saw.

"The motorman of the car being examined was a big, bearded fellow. His beard was literally a bunch of icicles. Sleet had collected all over his coat and face. He was a pitiable sight, and his movements were stiff, as if he were numbed by the cold. He said nothing. It was unnecessary."

NOTES AND COMMENTS:

Today's craftsmen do not build streetcars; they restore them. At the Baltimore Streetcar Museum, shop forces insist on a level of perfection that would surely please the artisans who originally constructed the vehicles.

Many facets of the difficulties faced by the men who ran the cars in the early years were extracted from an article "Problems of the Winter," which appeared in the *American,* January 15, 1893. References to rest periods, lunch and dinner allowances, and the like were found in the *News,* February 9, 1895.

Cain Redican recalled many experiences from his fifty years of service in *Trolley Topics,* June 1928.

Descriptions of the one-man, bob-tail cars are found in Janvier's *Baltimore In The Eighties And Nineties* and the *Baltimore County Union,* May 27, 1882.

The Slawson box, the invention of J. B. Slawson of the New Orleans horse railways, was a patented device into which passengers deposited their fare. John A. Brill, in his article, "The Development of the Street Car" in *Cassier's Magazine,* August 1899, describes the advantages of operating bob-tail cars. He praises the little car highly — "it made many a line successful commercially which would otherwise have been obliged to give up business."

The six hundred-odd horses credited to the Green Line appear out of line with actuality. (It is possible that some horses were stabled in Green Line barns, but used on other lines.) This figure, as well as the statistical breakdown of employees, is from the *American,* April 8,1894.

An outpouring of lofty praise for the men of the horse car era, in the form of poetry, appeared in the *Maryland Journal* (Towson), June 7, 1873. Entitled "The York Road Line," it is credited to "the Bard of Waverly."

"Tinkle, tinkle, little car.
How I wonder where you are!
Be you far, or be you nigh,
There are you and here am 1.
All along the dusty road,
Past the gate of my abode,
You go up, and you go down —
Baltimore and Towsontown.
Good conductor from afar,
Sees me stand and stops the car,
Greets me with a friendly grin,
Takes my hand and helps me in.

What a noble man was he,
Built this pretty car for me!
Not to call him great and good,
Would be base ingratitude."

The *Baltimore County Union* of March 12, 1887, reported another little trick played by the "sharpies." A gang was reported to be working the bob-tailed cars, which operated without a conductor. Members would politely collect the fares of lady passengers, palm the good money, and deposit a lead imitation in the Slawson box.

The cultivation of whiskers is reported in the *Herald,* March 10, 1894; the verdigris problem in the *Sun,* May 29, 1896.

A report of the Christmas night blockade appears in *News,* December 26, 1895; of the Central's fifty-cent bonus, *American,* December 20, 1897.

The *American,* February 11, 1899, verifies the minus-seven-degree temperature of the previous day. The original of the letter to House still is in existence. Somewhat tattered, it is pasted in volume seven of the United Railways and Electric Company scrapbooks preserved at the Enoch Pratt Library.

During the last days of operation the sight of an immobilized sweeper was not unusual. Unlike olden days, abandoned private vehicles on the tracks often caused more difficulties than snowdrifts. Sweepers carried a crew of three — motorman, conductor, and a shopman to handle the brooms. No. 3202 was one of the "modern" sweepers, bought from Brill in 1900. (George F. Nixon Collection)

THE STORM

Despite its location to the south of the Mason-Dixon line, Baltimore is not unfamiliar with snow. Though the winters cannot compare in severity with, say, those of Chicago or Buffalo, occasional storms have paralyzed the city.

Of fairly recent memory are the big tie-ups of 1951 and 1958, as well as the Palm Sunday storm of 1942. Old-timers never forgot the blizzard of 1888; but for several reasons the storm that was the most significant in streetcar history in Baltimore was the one that hit town on February 12-13, 1899.

The month had gotten off to a snowy start with twelve inches falling between the 5th and the 8th. This was followed by a bitter cold spell, with temperatures dropping to six and seven below on the tenth and eleventh; therefore much of the accumulation still lay alongside the tracks where it had been pushed by the sweepers when a new fall began on the evening of Sunday, February 12th.

As was the common practice, sweepers were kept running all night long over most of the lines. Come morning, the regular cars were sent out, as usual, to carry the patrons into the city. The sweepers, which had been given a brief respite, were returned to service, and no unusual difficulties were foreseen.

Things changed, however, as the wind picked up in intensity. The snow, which was of the "light" variety, consequently began drifting back as fast as it could be pushed aside. The sheer bulk of the white stuff was so great as to cause the commutators of some sweepers to burn out while they struggled through the hilly portions of town. The Central Railway in particular was crippled by this problem and was able to make no real effort to run on the 13th.

The other companies experienced their own difficulties. A passenger car, a mail car, and a sweeper were all that managed to battle their way to Catonsville by 8:30 a.m.; but after struggling to Irvington on the return trip, they were put into the barn and service on that line was abandoned. The same situation prevailed on the Towson line, and, when a sweeper broke down, everything halted on the York Road north of Waverly.

Elsewhere on the Consolidated, it was much the same. North Avenue, Edmondson Avenue, Maryland Avenue, and Highlandtown all shut down well before noon. Some cars made it back to the barns; others were left where they stalled, caught up in the whirling storm. By noon, only the company's Druid Hill Avenue, Carey Street, and Gilmore Street lines were operating at all.

City Passenger was not without its troubles. The Green Line was forced to stop running when a water main broke on Pennsylvania Avenue, resulting in a solid sheet of ice, eighteen inches thick, across the breadth of the street. The Red and White Lines were still being run by cable, and before long the snow had clogged the slots, putting both out of commission. The overhead was in place for the coming electrification of these two lines, but attempts to run trolley cars over them met with failure. The Yellow Line was next to go, and by early afternoon, the Blue Line was City Passenger's only route still in service.

By 1 p.m., about twelve inches of new snow had fallen, so that a total accumulation of two feet was on the ground and being driven into drifts by winds reaching thirty miles an hour. The temperature hovered at about eight above zero.

On the few lines still running, even the sweepers could hardly move. The tracks were like troughs between the ever increasing banks of snow. Most of what was brushed to the top slid back down, and the rest was soon redeposited on the tracks by the gale.

The Consolidated tried coupling two cars together and running them behind a sweeper. Despite the combined eighty horsepower, the cars could not make it through the storm, and by 3 p.m. only their Gilmor Street line was still open. Even this was cut back at City Hall, the elevated portion having been shut down hours earlier. Before long, the remainder was forced to give up.

The people who had ventured downtown had no way to get home. Little knots of them huddled on the street corners late in the afternoon, refusing to believe that the cars had been brought to a halt. Things were different with public transportation in those days; but, despite the heroic attempts of the various companies, it eventually became apparent to the waiting crowds that the streetcars had lost the battle. The people then turned to the carriages on the stands, only to find outrageous prices being asked for a relatively short ride.

The Blue Line did manage to maintain some service until about 6:30 p.m., but after that hour not a wheel was turning on Baltimore's entire streetcar system.

The various companies had, during the day, augmented their maintenance forces, which normally handled the snow fighting work, by hiring whatever additional help could be obtained. The new recruits were given brooms and shovels and put to work clearing the busier intersections. As the night wore on, the snow finally ceased, but this was not until a total of eighteen inches had fallen on February 12th-13th, which, combined with that previously on the ground, meant more than thirty-two inches to deal with. Men were constantly added to the work force until, by the morning of the 14th, there were fully two thousand of them attempting to open the lines.

Unlike the streamlined cars, whose low-slung motors could be shorted by a heavy, wet snow, the semi-convertibles were most vulnerable to derailment. On January 28, 1922, the rear truck of a No. 3 route car was thrown off the track on Linden Avenue by packed snow. At least a dozen cars were soon stalled behind it. Do not feel too sorry for the riders; most had only to walk two blocks to continue their trips on paralleling lines. (The Peale Museum)

In one of a series of paintings depicting Baltimore's streetcars, Leonard Levee caught a wintry mood with this vivid representation of sweeper No. 3221 at Clifton and Garrison (Walbrook Junction). The car was built by Brill in 1902. (Baltimore Sunpapers)

The day the streetcars almost stopped. An unseasonably late blizzard, which hit town on Palm Sunday, March 29, 1942, seriously slowed but did not halt the cars. During the 1950s, a number of storms almost immobilzed the city. Was it a coincidence that most streetcar lines had been discontinued, and the elderly sweepers and plows were no longer around to clear the streets? (A. Aubrey Bodine Collection, the Peale Museum)

During a heavy snowfall in December 1948, Sweeper No. 3217 swings its wing plow to clear the rails on Maryland Avenue at North. (Robert W. Janssen, Herbert H. Harwood, Jr. Collection)

The snow removal cost to the street railway companies was between $10,000 and $15,000 a day, with the loss of revenues approximating the same amount. According to the City Code of 1893, they were responsible for half of the expense of cleaning the streets on which their tracks ran.

With the sweepers having proved ineffectual, the general managers began to improvise equipment. City Passenger's Hart attached a scraper to a flatcar, coupled it ahead of a pair of sweepers, and added a Pennsylvania Avenue passenger car as a trailer. The latter was filled with men armed with picks and shovels to dig out the spots where ice had accumulated over the rails. Slowly the procession made its way along the Madison Avenue line to Patterson Park.

By 9 a.m. on the 14th, this route and the Blue Line were again running. The blockade was broken, and by nightfall most of the city lines were open. It had not been without a struggle, though. The sun had broken through, with the resulting rise in temperature changing the snow from the light, feathery stuff that had fallen to a heavy, clinging mass that made its removal a cumbersome process.

The suburban lines were still out, of course. The Gilmor Street cars did not run over the elevated, and the ice on Pennsylvania Avenue blocked the Green Line, but by midnight the situation was getting back to normal.

There was considerable apprehension when more snow was predicted for the 17th. However, the precipitation took the form of heavy rain. It poured from 11 a.m. to 11 p.m. This downpour, combined with the melting snow, turned the streets into rushing torrents. However, the high-wheeled cars took the water in their stride. Except for the Maryland Avenue line, which was detoured from Pratt Street to Fayette when the harbor overflowed, there was no disruption of service.

For all the suffering caused by the storm, it did have one beneficial result. It crystallized the growing concern for the suffering of the motormen, who had long been exposed to the elements, with the low dasher as their only protection against cold, wind, and snow. By the next winter season, portable vestibules had been installed. But it

Wet snow begins to accumulate as No. 5552 picks up a passenger at 24th and St. Paul on January 16, 1945. (Louis C. Mueller Collection)

Snow Sweeper No. 3215 is making the loop on North Avenue at Charles Street on January 16, 1945. (BSM Collection)

was well into the 1920s, before completely enclosed platforms became standard on the Baltimore cars.

Snow sweepers had an exceptionally long life, even by street railway standards. According to data compiled by George Nixon in his notes, six sweepers which had fought the 1899 blizzard were still in active service sixty years later. The oldest was former Baltimore City Passenger Railway No. 2, which had been built by Brill in 1894. The others, with their original owners, builders, and dates built are as follows: Baltimore City Passenger Railway No. 1 (Brill, 1895); City & Suburban No. 11 (Brill, 1895); Baltimore Traction No. 349 (J. W. Fowler, 1896); City & Suburban No. 849 (Brill, 1897); and Baltimore Consolidated Railway No. 850 (Brill, 1898).

Conductor observes a plume of snow being thrown out by this sweeper as it proceeds eastwardly along Pratt Street toward Market Place. The large buildings looming in the background are the railway company's power house, right, and the Candler Building. (A. Aubrey Bodine Collection, the Peale Museum)

NOTES AND COMMENTS:

The account of the snowstorm was pieced together by gleaning information from all available Baltimore papers covering the period February 7-17, 1899, especially the *Sun* and *American*.

Mention of snow-fighting equipment goes back at least as far as May 1860, when the Baltimore City Passenger Railway Association was formally organized as a partnership; the listing of its equipment included two salt cars. Land Records of Baltimore City, Liber G.E.S. 190, folio 266.

A later reference appears in the *Sun* of February 3, 1874. At the time, City Passenger was double-teaming and salting its tracks (this latter practice was soon to be banned). Citizens' Railway, however, was sweeping its line with a "snow-scraper."

An invention of the company's president, James Hagerty, it consisted of a three-foot arm terminating in a steel scraper, with the opposite end being attached to an iron socket under the platform of the car.

Fighting the snow was usually a cold, tiring job, but it could have its lively moments. Such an occasion was reported in the *American,* January 2, 1893, and *News,* January 15, 1893. According to the law of the time, the street railway companies were required to keep their tracks — and a space two feet on each side — clear of snow and ice. But, according to the newspaper accounts, the Baltimore Union Passenger Railway, at Pratt near Charles, had merely piled the snow along the side of the street. Passing wagons and drays pushed it back

onto the tracks, disrupting horse car service. Soon, a crew of twenty-five men was sent by the Union Passenger management to throw the snow off the track again. The merchants on the south side of Pratt Street decided that this would make the street impassable for their wagons. So, they armed their employees with shovels and ordered them to toss the snow back on the railway track. A crowd of spectators gathered and spurred the men of both sides on with applause. As a number of policemen were on hand, there was no trouble except some lively snowball battles and the contest ended in a draw. The result was a new ordinance which required the street railway companies to pay half of the expense of removing snow from streets on which tracks were laid. *American,* April 16, 1899.

Do not be fooled by that "Direct to Curtis Bay" hangsign; car No. 615 is actually resting in the Patapsco River after plunging off the Long Bridge on April 8, 1913. (George F. Nixon Collection)

Pity the poor motorman when an accident wrecked a car like this. While the passenger section was solidly constructed, platforms of early electric cars offered little protection to the crew in case of an accident. In this instance, the dasher is crumpled, portable vestibule completely collapsed, yet car body is almost unscathed. This particular victim is a Brill single-truck convertible built in 1898. (Louis C. Mueller Collection)

THE ACCIDENT

At 8:06 on the morning of November 21, 1897, car No. 34 of the Baltimore & Northern Railway passed switch No. 3 on a southbound trip to Mt. Washington. At almost the same moment, car No. 21, northbound, thumped across the points of switch No. 2, at the Pikesville turnout, on its way to Owings Mills. The most frightening occurrence which could take place on a single track line had just happened. There were now two cars on the one set of rails, heading toward each other, with no way for the motormen to know it.

Add a patchy fog, rolling countryside, and an inexperienced motorman, and you have all the ingredients of a harrowing tragedy. This was precisely what happened at 8:07 a.m. in a little valley at what is now the intersection of Reisterstown Road and the Baltimore Beltway. The small open single-truck No. 34 and the heavy double-truck closed car No. 21 came together with such force that the front sections of both were lifted from the track, locked in an inverted "V" like two primeval beasts engaged in mortal combat.

Since neither motorman survived the accident, the precise reason why it occurred remains as obscure as the visibility in Councilman's Hollow on that misty November morning. However, the events that led up to it point out clearly how easily one mistake in judgment could result in disaster. That there was no recurrence of the tragedy is a tribute to the skill of the men who ran the Baltimore streetcars.

The wreck came little more than a month after the Baltimore & Northern had begun operations between Emory Grove and Charles Street in Baltimore. But the stretch on which it happened was a part of the affiliated Pikesville, Reisterstown & Emory Grove, where cars had been running about four years. The railway followed alongside the Reisterstown Turnpike, duplicating its dips and rises. It was one of those not unusual mornings which come to rural Maryland in the fall — mornings when one can drive along in beautiful clear sunshine and then suddenly come upon a patch of fog so dense that objects can scarcely be seen an arm's length ahead. This is particularly true of rolling terrain, such as that just north of Pikesville.

Theodore Merrick was taking car No. 34, as an extra movement, from the car house at Owings Mills to Mt. Washington, where it would be used as a tripper to carry the expected crowds to Electric Park. He was thirty-eight and had worked as a lineman for several different street railways in the city over the past few years; however, he had never motored before joining the Baltimore & Northern, upon its completion just four weeks previously.

Orders posted by Dispatcher Luther Maddox at the Owings Mills car house called for Merrick to wait at McDonogh, switch No. 3, for the arrival of the northbound car. Due to the absence of signaling on the single-track line, such orders were the only method of controlling conflicting movements. For some reason, car No. 34 passed the switch without waiting, while car No. 21 was proceeding toward it, totally unaware that anything was amiss.

The 21 had passed through Mt. Washington at 7:40 a.m. and was due at switch No. 3 at 8:10. It was a half minute late in passing Pikesville, but this posed no problem as the southbound car was supposed to wait at least five minutes before proceeding. The motorman of the northbound car was W. F. Horner, twenty-eight; unlike novice Merrick, he was a four-year veteran and was considered one of the most reliable men in the company's employ.

The perplexing question is — why did Merrick run by the switch? His unfamiliarity with the territory could easily account for failing to recognize its exact location in the fog and semidarkness. However, the company had specific orders that all switches would be left open so that either the car would have to enter the turnout, or the switch would have to be thrown for it to proceed on the main line.

In light of the weather conditions and his inexperience, it seems incredible that Merrick would have deliberately tried to make Pikesville ahead of the scheduled northbound car, though he was reportedly about four minutes early for the meet. Therefore, the most plausible explanation is that the switch was missed in the fog because it was aligned incorrectly or had been tampered with by vandals.

The actual collision can be reconstructed from the recollections of the trio of passengers and the conductor on the northbound car, all of whom survived, as well as the other information in the company's investigative report.

Motorman Horner must have seen the oncoming southbound car looming in the fog just before the impact. He applied his brakes hard and set the controller to the "off" position. On the other hand, there was no sign, according to the company investigation, that Merrick had set his brakes at all, and the controller was reported to be "turned on at full speed."

Merrick was killed instantly in the wreck, so no one heard his story; possibly he had died still unaware that he had missed the meeting point. Or, it may be that, upon belatedly realizing this fact, he was desperately racing toward Pikesville, a mile to the south. In any event, he became a victim in foggy Councilman's Hollow. Strangely, his conductor, who survived serious injuries from flying glass, seems to have made no public statement as to what had preceded the accident.

Horner was alive but gravely injured when help reached the rather isolated scene. A message was sent to Pikesville to

This single-truck yard crane was shop-built in 1907. Originally numbered 6018, it became No. 3734. The bumpy cobblestone road became busy Washington Boulevard. (Louis C. Mueller Collection)

bring up car No. 24, still waiting at the switch for the southbound car that never arrived. The motorman, conductor, and two injured passengers were laid on extemporized stretchers made of boards placed between the car seats. As the car sped toward the city, Horner passed away just beyond Mt. Washington.

Two hours later, the line had been reopened, and the wrecked cars reposed in the Owings Mills car house awaiting disposition. The small open car, No. 34, was scrapped, but car No. 21 eventually was put to another use. Several years later, by which time it had become the property of the United Railways through the consolidation, the United decided that it was worth salvaging.

Once this gaily painted yellow car had carried frolicking picnickers to the dells north of Reisterstown and elegant trolley parties for which the Baltimore & Northern had become famous. Now it was redone in a dark red hue and after extensive remodeling became an express car.

No statistical record can be found pertaining to the number of accidents on the Baltimore system. However, a perusal of newspapers and literature covering the span of the existence of the street railways fails to uncover any account of accidents resulting in a fearful loss of life, such as were not uncommon in some other places. Minor collisions were, of course, from the beginning one of the hazards of operation. The main source of danger in such accidents was from broken window glass. Most of the deaths and serious injuries in horse car days, though, occurred to persons who fell while trying to get on or off a moving car or to unwary pedestrians. In both cases, the danger came from being thrown beneath the car and mangled by the wheels.

The coming of faster electric and cable cars increased the chances of an accident. According to the *News,* September 21, 1893, an average of one person a month had been killed by "rapid transit" vehicles, and two persons injured in the same span of time. Quite a few of these were young children, who delighted in such "games" as placing sulphur matches on the track to be ignited by the passing cars. Steps were taken, both by the companies and the City, in an effort to reduce the number of accidents. Fenders of various types were attached to the cars, all of which prominently displayed the warning: "Boarding or leaving the car while in motion is forbidden. Employees cannot waive this rule" — or some similar notice.

NOTES AND COMMENTS:

The main basis for the account of the Baltimore & Northern accident is the *Sun,* November 22, 1897.

A city ordinance was enacted in 1893 requiring all streetcars to stop for passengers at the near side of an intersection. *Sun,* May 5, 1893.

In special situations, such as the Guilford Avenue elevated and the Huntingdon Avenue viaduct, various signaling systems described elsewhere were used. Many of the single-track suburban routings were likewise protected by automatic signals, beginning in the World War I period. Track-circuit block signals were installed on the Bay Shore and Sparrows Point routes in August 1917. At about the same time, Nachod trolley contactor signals were put in use on the Halethorpe line. These were replaced by track-circuit block signals, effective June 7, 1931. *Electric Railway Journal,* vol. 50, pp. 292, 336 (1917); *News,* February 5, 1920; Kenneth Morse notes.

In 1921, United Railways purchased two of these tower trucks, featuring solid rubber tires, warning bell, motorized tower, and provision for towing and firefighting equipment. Their cost was about $3,500 each. (Louis C. Mueller Collection)

A reel car loading wire at Retreat Street car house. The hand brake prevented a runaway if the coupling broke. Around the turn of the century, several serious accidents were caused by inability to halt utility vehicles not so equipped. (Louis C. Mueller Collection)

This view of the elevated shows a northbound semi-convertible No. 5584 in March 1947. To the rear is the Orleans Street Viaduct. Note barrier in foreground between platforms. The span carried the street railway over the yards of the Northern Central Railway, later the PRR. It was 4000 feet in length, spanning between Chase and Lexington Streets, and lasted from 1893 to 1950. Today's Jones Falls Expressway (I-83) lies directly to the left. (Leonard W. Rice, Herbert Harwood, Jr. Collection)

THE TRESTLE

The boy was young, about six or seven, and he was restless. Idly, he gazed out of the fourth-story rear window of the venerable dwelling on North Calvert Street, where his grandmother had taken him to visit an aunt. Their talk was dull to him, and he was bored.

The view from the top-floor kitchen encompassed a wide area. Calvert Street perched on a bluff, the land rolling rapidly downhill away from the tiny yard at the foot of a series of stairs and landings which served as a fire escape route. To say that the scene which spread out before him was magnificent would be untrue. The few trees visible in the gloom of the late fall afternoon were leafless, and a block and a half away loomed the massive fortresses that were the Maryland Penitentiary and the Baltimore City Jail.

Stretching between the back yards and the dismal stone walls were railroad yards. These presented some relief from the dreary gray tones, filled as they were with dark red boxcars and interspersed with a yellow refrigerator car here and there. Still, there was not much activity in evidence. Though a grimy yard engine periodically sent a plume of smoke high into the air, its movements were pretty well obscured by the intervening railroad cars and a steel structure which ran high above the railroad tracks.

The boy could see neither end of this structure and vaguely wondered its purpose. Suddenly, into his line of vision came a car riding on top of it. Of course, this was the streetcar trestle. He had often seen it from another angle as the No. 8 cars, one which he usually rode, turned from Hillen Street into Holliday. How he had longed to ride over it. The route was an alternate way to town from his home, but grandmother "didn't think it was safe." The view from beneath had not been nearly as impressive. All one could see was iron beams and a partial glimpse of the cars as they passed by the Pleasant Street station.

From here it was different, though. The cars seemed to be miniatures, but every detail was visible. For the first time, he noted that they had two trolley poles, one raised to the overhead wire, the other secured against the car roof, where it would be invisible from the ground. These cars were more colorful than the ones to which he was accustomed on the York Road line. They were a bright yellow, set off by touches of red striping, with silver-colored wire mesh window screens.

Far in the distance he could just make out one of the stations, with its long, long stairway leading up to the wooden platform, with sides sheathed in corrugated iron, the whole painted a rather dreary olive drab. On rare occasions someone would mount the stairs and a car would stop. It seemed strange to see the person board the front of the car and equally strange to see passengers leaving by the rear doors. Just the reverse was the case on his familiar red cars.

Every few minutes a car passed by. The names on the destination signs meant nothing to him — Bedford Square, Guilford Avenue, Gilmor Street. But he could read the numbers that they carried, mostly "1"s, with a smattering of "11"s. Enchanted, he watched until it grew to be dusk. Now the whole panorama took on a different complexion. The interior of each car stood out against the steadily darkening background. The bright headlight could be seen approaching from far in the distance, and the tiny red marker lamps at the rear looked like two shimmering rubies after the car had passed.

As he grew older, there were many other sights of the street railway which he would remember — some vividly, others only vaguely. At times he would transfer at Greenmount and Preston. The yellow No. 27 car against the bright yellow paving bricks, polished almost as shiny as tiles, reminded him of a photograph in his geography book of an ancient town in Holland.

When he began to ride the No. 29 line out to Roland Park, the fascination was of a different sort. Coming up the hill from 39th Street toward Roland Avenue, the semi-convertible would begin to roll and writhe until he thought it would shake apart. But the cars were built to be flexible, and, though they swayed so much that the straps hanging from the rafters would be thumped first against one side and then the other, the cars continued merrily on their way.

Other recollections were not so clear. Thinking back over a few rides to Bay Shore conjured up only the memories that one seemed always to be riding on a bridge of some sort and that the conductor was continually collecting fares. The few memories of the Ellicott City line consisted chiefly of the long ride on private right of way along Edmondson Avenue and the leisurely jaunt through the woods, before clattering across the truss bridge spanning the Patapsco River and venturing up narrow Main Street to the terminus alongside the firehouse.

Still, the elevated proved to be the favorite over the years. Most of the people he knew talked of it as the trestle or viaduct — "vidock" in the local parlance. He naturally sought it out as soon as he was old enough to ride the cars alone. The experience was not a disappointment.

Graphically recalled is the magic moment when one approached the incline, slowly began to mount the structure at what seemed to be a 45 degree angle, and then majestically crested the elevated to ride far above the automobiles and trucks on Guilford Avenue below. While not as fearsome, it was truly more of a thrill than the first ride on the Mountain Speedway at Carlin's Park. A mental note was made to find out more about this elevated. As is the usual case, this research was put off, and not until over thirty years later, when the trestle had long been torn down, were the facts ferreted out.

A PCC on the No. 8 line has just departed the Pleasant Street station its way northbound on the Guilford Avenue Elevated, in the late 1940s, during final years of operation on the trestle. There were three stations altogether. The one pictured was the only one to have a single stairway with a walk across the track between platforms. The elegant Baltimore Trust (Maryland National Bank) building, tallest in the City at one time, looms high in the background. (Mettee Studio photo, BSM Collection)

The trestle, viaduct, or elevated had its inception in the plans of the North Avenue Railway Company to gain access to downtown Baltimore. Before construction began, this company had come under the control of the Lake Roland Elevated Railway, which actually built the structure. The contract was awarded to the Pennsylvania Steel Company in June 1892. It was double tracked and about three-quarters of a mile in length. December saw work commence on the elevated itself, the stone piers having been placed earlier. On the lower end it was necessary to drive piles to secure a solid base. The tracks were placed on steel girders, except at the lower halves of the two inclines, which were solid masonry.

The first trip was made on May 3, 1893, with the car carrying company officials leaving North Avenue at 5 p.m. When the first public rides were offered several days later, Baltimoreans became enraptured with the "sky-ride." The cars were soon so crowded that police had to be called to restore order. Though one man tried to have the police marshal arrested for refusing to allow him to squeeze on a crowded car, the mood was generally festive, with a Salvation Army band arriving at nightfall to add to the merriment.

In time, the Lake Roland became part of the Consolidated Railway, which made plans to improve the structure. As originally built, it was a series of dips and rises, caused by the fact that all of the columns were of the same height with no allowance for the contours of the land. Again, the Pennsylvania Steel Company was selected to level off the elevated, which at its steepest dip had to be raised 5½ feet. The work was completed by May 21, 1898, on which date open cars were run across it for the first time. As a safety measure, footways with handrails were constructed along the outer edges, and the center pole arrangement was changed to side-pole span wire construction. The rebuilding of the station platforms was also necessary to accommodate the open cars.

Things remained much the same until 1910, when a rather complicated set of Kinsman signals was installed, and the structure thoroughly overhauled and reinforced, in preparation for operation of the heavy double-truck semi-convertible cars over it. (As far as can be discovered, the earliest use of track-circuit block signals on the local street railways was on the elevated. In 1898, the Baltimore Consolidated Railway had installed a red light at each station, as well as at the double curve near Chase Street; on the inclined plane leading down from the south end of the structure, a green light had been placed as a warning to go slowly.)

During all of 1935 and most of the following year, the viaduct was out of service, due not to any internal defect, but to reconstruction work on the nearby Guilford Avenue bridge which isolated it.

In June 1947, the No. 11 line was discontinued, and the No. 1 cut back at City Hall, with its Guilford Avenue leg eliminated; but the elevated was retained for use by the No. 8 cars. It was necessary to modify the platforms again to handle the PCCs.

On September 10th of the following year, a switching mishap occurred on the Pennsylvania Railroad below; a gondola car derailed and was pushed into one of the supporting columns, taking the elevated structure out of service for about a month. After repairs, the future of the elevated looked fairly secure; but on January 1, 1950, the last car rumbled across it, the company having decided to return the No. 8 line to its former Greenmount Avenue routing.

The elevated was pulled down the following May. Ironically, the scrap was sent to the Bethlehem Steel Company at Steelton, Pennsylvania, where much of it had been fabricated fifty-seven years previously, when this plant was the property of the Pennsylvania Steel Company.

NOTES AND COMMENTS:

Even as recently as 1940, the streets on which the cars ran were provided with a variety of surfacing materials. While I seem to remember a few cobblestone stretches on Guilford Avenue near Monument Street, evidences of this method of piecing together stones of random size to make a durable, if bumpy, roadbed had almost completely disappeared. On the other hand, Belgian blocks (granite blocks hewn to a standard size) were still much in evidence even in the downtown area, including the stretch of Fayette Street between Charles and Howard. Red brick paving was common all around town, and yellow brick roads stretched away from Greenmount Avenue at both Preston and 25th Streets. Even wooden blocks, impregnated with creosote, still remained on a small portion of Guilford Avenue above Baltimore Street. Concrete extended from curb to curb on long stretches of Belair Road. Still, then as now, the ubiquitous asphalt and macadam were the most common coverings for roadways.

The elevated structure was sometimes blamed for depressing property values along its route, but in earlier times it had one redeeming social value. The *Sun* reported on October 24, 1895: "The building and operation of the elevated railway on North Street resulted in the removal of all the disorderly houses on North Street by order of the police department." (North Street was the former name of Guilford Avenue.)

In December 1910, six elaborate Kinsman track-circuit signals were put in use between the Madison and Centre Street stations. A white light indicated proceed, track clear; a green light meant caution; a red light, stop. These signals were replaced in January 1920 by Union track-circuit block signals. This system was still in use at the end; its lights showed a red aspect for stop and orange for caution. *Electric Railway Journal,* January 7, 1911; *News,* February 5, 1920.

By 1897, Traction Company cars were running through to Gwynn Oak Park. With most everyone making the trip on the electric cars, the parking problem was minimal. No. 23, behind the two "sports" with derbies and handkerchiefs around necks, was a rebuilt Druid Hill Avenue cable car. (Louis C. Mueller Collection)

OF PARKS AND PARTIES

As has been frequently noted, Druid Hill Park played a most important role in the early story of the Baltimore street railways. City Passenger always had the edge in the competition for the traffic to the park, though Citizens', and later Baltimore Traction and Central Railway, managed to get a foot in the gate during the 1880s and 1890s. With the coming of the electric cars, the street railway companies began really to play up to the public's desire for picnicking. If the people enjoyed the public park so much, why not have their own company parks? Located properly, these would not only bring in a profit through the rental of concessions, but would also lure passengers to places that were accessible only by one's own streetcars. Once committed, the street railway operators proceeded to lay out parks with wild abandon.

There is some question as to which was the most popular over the years. Depending on one's interpretation, it may well have been Riverview. Certainly this was to become the epitome of trolley amusement parks at the turn of the century. It came into being as a beer garden, probably in the early 1880s. At first, it was known as Lowrey's place on Colgate Creek. The Highlandtown & Point Breeze soon laid horse car tracks to the park. Rechristened Point Breeze, the place was not an immediate success; the horse cars ceased to operate that far, though the tracks were left in place.

But better days were ahead. In 1897, when all of the companies except City Passenger were acquiring parks, City & Suburban (which had absorbed the Point Breeze line) brought the old beer garden to life with a vengeance. Although food remained one of the prime attractions of the place, amusement devices and rides were added and expanded until it was referred to as the "Coney Island of the South" as often as its official name of Riverview. (It had been given that name in 1898 after the City

& Suburban was merged into the Consolidated Railway.)

Alas, as with so many things, changing times took their toll. Having survived fires and other misfortunes, the park was razed in 1929 so that the plant of the Western Electric Company might be erected on the site. Curiously enough, the industrial complex took the name of Point Breeze, the designation used back in the days when Frank Lowrey had his beer garden there. The plant, in turn, has since been closed.

Yet Riverview of wondrous memory was not the first. That honor goes to the park of the Baltimore, Catonsville & Ellicott's Mills, located northwest of Frederick Road and Paradise Avenue as early as 1865. Another early park that few have even heard of today, much less recall, was Ridgewood Park. This is not strange since Ridgewood, an offspring of the North Avenue Railway Company, had a very brief span of existence. Started about 1892 by the company, which was likewise the instigator of the first overhead electric road in this area, it was located near where the Mount Holly Casino stood at a later date. Though having an amusement ride or two, it was most notable for its almost inaccessible location. One first had to walk across a trestle spanning a deep ravine and then climb a long flight of steps to reach the park. Its fate was sealed, when the developers of some land a bit to the north arranged for a car line to be built into their area. Near the end of this line was established a new park, Gwynn Oak.

In its earliest days, Gwynn Oak attempted to compete against the better established parks with a boast of genteel respectability. The lake was an attraction, along with the recitals and musicals given on Sundays. No alcoholic beverages were permitted, and its advertisements subtly looked down upon some of the goings on at rival parks.

Things could not have been too sedate even in the earliest days, though. A

newspaper item reports that during the first year the band was discharged a few days before the seasonal closing of the park. It seems that the members, who had acquired a reputation for "sky-larking," had begun amusing themselves by pitching acorns at each other. (This was Gwynn OAK, you remember.) Then some of the boys became agitated and began tossing rocks instead of acorns.

In any event, while the other places burned or closed down one by one, Gwynn Oak kept going year after year until it finally closed in 1974, outliving the streetcar era. This was a Traction Company park, the original line serving it (the Walbrook, Gwynn Oak & Powhatan) having been absorbed soon after it began operating.

A strong competitor for most popular would have to be Bay Shore. The last to be established (it was always served by the United Railways, having been built after the big consolidation), Bay Shore proved to be a hit, and, except for purchase of the property by Bethlehem Steel, might have given competition to Gwynn Oak for many more years.

Bay Shore had its formal opening August 11, 1906. It contained thirty acres of land, with a half-mile frontage on the Chesapeake. A concrete pier extended several hundred feet into the water. The band concerts and the midway, with its roller coaster, flying horses, and shooting galleries, as well as dining in the hotel, drew many to the park; but the big attraction was swimming and sunning on the white sandy beach.

Bay Shore was served by an extension of the Sparrows Point Line, with cars running straight through. The ride was an exceptionally interesting one, there being long trestles over Bear, Jones, and North Point Creeks, as well as over Shallow Creek on the Fort Howard part of the loop. Passengers had the impression that the conductor was constantly collecting fares once Highlandtown was left behind, as at

A twelve-bench, screen-sided open car posed for its photograph at the bridge over Gwynn's Falls, just east of Gwynn Oak Park about 1903. (Enoch Pratt Library, Armistead Webb)

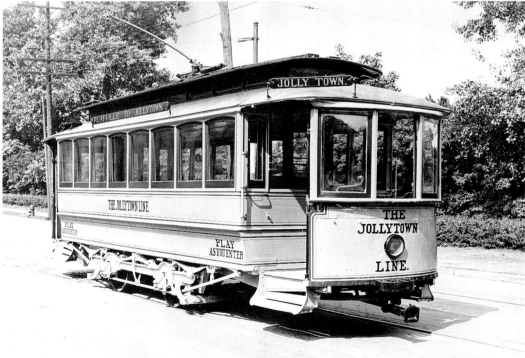

During the 1920s, the United Railways placed surplus cars at company parks and several neighborhood playgrounds for the amusement of youngsters. "Jollytown" car, pictured at Gwynn Oak Park, was a former Consolidated Railway car built by Brownell in 1898. Signs, "Play as you enter," etc. were a take-off on actual messages. (George F. Nixon Collection)

The Bay Shore Park Terminal, looking west. This may have been the only place in the country where a streetcar line passed under a roller coaster. (Charles Houser Collection)

On an NRHS fan trip on April 28, 1946, No. 5843 pauses at Bay Shore Park station. Dimly visible behind car is the roller coaster shown above. (Louis C. Mueller Collection)

So far, we have covered only parks with a direct connection with one of the railway companies. There were also several very successful places independent of railway control, to which the cars hauled many passengers. One was Electric Park, which stood almost opposite the Belvedere car house in what is now Pimlico. Originally a trotting track, it was bought by August Fenneman in 1895. There were many plans for its development, including one in which the Baltimore Orioles would play baseball, INDOORS! Alas for Baltimore's premature Astrodome, it was actually made into a conventional amusement park, featuring bright lights in keeping with its name. It was first served by Baltimore Traction, though later on it became one of the objectives of the Baltimore & Northern. Hit by severe fires on occasion, it nevertheless survived in part until about 1916, when it was torn down and replaced by houses.

"Spend a day at Gwynn Oak, you will enjoy it." Founded by the Walbrook, Gwynn Oak & Powhatan Railroad in 1894, this was to be the last survivor of the parks operated by the United, not closing until 1974, long after its ownership had ended. This 1926 ad extolled its virtues. (UR & E Company, Willem Wirtz)

various times there were three and four zones. The cars were always crowded in the summer months, and on this line the multiple-unit cars were used to the end.

The park got off to an unforgettable start, when on the evening of its official opening there was a power failure on most of the United's lines in the east Baltimore area. Thousands of people were stranded all along the line until the wee hours of the morning.

United Railways was particularly proud of its station at Bay Shore. There had long been much complaining about the pushing and shoving of passengers attempting to return home from Riverview after a day's outing. Particular pains were taken to avoid this at Bay Shore, and they worked well. There was a loop, with a platform fenced in so as to segregate incoming and outgoing crowds, making it possible to load the cars in an orderly manner.

Despite the inauspicious beginning due to power failure, the lure of the Chesapeake made the place immediately and immensely popular. As time went on, rides were added to the initial attractions of ballroom, bowling alley, and restaurant. The park was to become a rival of Riverview, only to meet the same fate, industrial expansion about 1948, when it was sold to a nearby steel mill. That expansion never took place and the land is now a state park, with the goal of reversion to a natural state.

Carlin's Park of a later date was a similar proposition. Its location at Park Circle in northwest Baltimore made it feasible for the railway company to run extra cars to the entrance during the summer season, but it was never affiliated with the United.

So much for the successes. With so much competition, it was inevitable that there would also be failures. The Lake Roland Elevated tried its hand at promoting a park located near the lake from which it took its corporate name. The time was about 1894. While many improvements were made, this park never was really popular. Though

offering similar, or better, attractions than Gwynn Oak had boasted during a comparable time in its development, Lakeside Park was abandoned several years after the big consolidation of 1899.

In its advertisement in the *News*, July 4, 1897, Lakeside Park offered a magnificent car ride through beautiful scenery and refreshing breezes on the way to the park "on the banks of Lake Roland." Once there, one could enjoy the merry-go-round and a few other amusements, have refreshments on the first floor of the pavilion, or dance on the upper floor. The Consolidated Railway added forty-eight acres to the original property; but the park was closed sometime prior to 1909; apparently even "the finest drinking water in the state" was not sufficient attraction to keep it open. The two-story pavilion, though, survived as an anachronism until it was destroyed by fire in the 1960s.

A more spectacular failure was Shore Line Park. It was located near the site of the present Harbor Park Hospital Center. Launched by the company which built the Shore Line Railway, the park was promoted widely. Certainly it offered patrons a memorable ride along what is now Waterview Avenue, between a high bluff and the Patapsco River. Yet there was quite a bit of rowdyism on the part of passengers bound for various recreation spots along the river. The southern terminus was usually referred to as Shore Line

"Salt water bathing and amusements for all." Bay Shore Park was a favorite of Baltimoreans who wanted to swim in the Chesapeake Bay and sample the delights of the amusement park. Streetcars ran to, and through, the United-owned park. This 1926 ad advertised its advantages.(UR & E Company, Willem Wirtz)

Parks (plural), for, in addition to the railway company's resort, both Meeter's Park, one thousand feet distant, and Klein's Park up on the bluff (now called Cherry Hill) were considered a part of the complex. The combined attractions provided dancing pavilions, billiards, boating and crabbing, musical concerts, excellent cuisine, and picnic groves. The Shore Line Park never did reach anything like the potential that was predicted for it, but nearby Meeter's Park became an attraction.

After Meeter's went up in flames and the Middle Branch silted up, the cars traveling along Fish House Road (now Waterview Avenue) carried few passengers. It was not even popular with the conductors and motormen — who declared that, whatever the advantages of the line in the summer, the cold breezes off the Patapsco in the wintertime made it one of the least desirable of runs.

As previously noted, Riverview began as a beer garden; the cars also carried many patrons to similar retreats which abounded around Baltimore. Especially were these places numerous along the Belair and Harford Roads, with Darley Park being merely one of the better remembered. To the southwest, there was Arion Park, which perched on its hill, high above the Halethorpe line. There were also many places catering to the family trade (bring the wife and kiddies for a picnic and a swim) along the Back and Middle Rivers.

So far, the successes and failures, the well-known and little-remembered parks have been mentioned; but it would not be right to leave out one of the best known of all "watering places" that the streetcars served. Any old-time Baltimorean must be wondering by now if it will be passed over. Jack Flood's! The very mention of the name still evokes the argument — what kind of place was it?

As it closed down about 1914, there are now few with first hand knowledge of its operation. Yet, its history has been recorded and passed on. Jack Flood's was in operation as early as 1893. By 1897, he was running a general hotel, vaudeville theater, and cafe. The theater burned that fall, but a replacement rose phoenix-like from the ashes before the next season. Flood's became readily accessible to Baltimore when the Curtis Bay line was built, crossing the Patapsco by means of the trestle-like Long Bridge at the foot of Light Street.

There were several other similar places in the area across the river in Anne Arundel County, but John T. Flood's was by far the most popular. Basically, it was a beer garden, featuring good food at moderate prices. This made it popular with the working men of south Baltimore. In addition, Flood offered drinks on Sundays, along with vaudeville attractions and stage shows. These shows were considered a bit risque at the time, but they could not have been too offensive as they were reportedly attended by some of the street railway men, who valued their reputations.

One thing is sure, Flood maintained order on his premises. This, and a certain tendency to be tight-fisted, are facts that are seldom disputed. When a crowd arrived, he is reported to have locked all the water pumps on the place. If you did not care to drink alcoholic beverages, you could buy lemonade, but there was no free water to slake the thirst.

The bad name that his place received was largely because, when the last car left for Baltimore at about 2:30 a.m., there was no one aboard to control those who had over-indulged. The Traction Company did not employ private policemen, and usually the few Anne Arundel deputies were far away. Maintaining law and order was in the hands of the conductor and motorman. This run was not one for the faint-hearted.

The usual practice was to force the troublemakers to leave the car to find their way home afoot. One unfortunate conductor was reprimanded in the press for making a bully get off his car, rather than bringing him into the city where he might have been turned over to the police. This late car could always be depended upon to have some passengers who delighted in singing all the way up through south Baltimore, much to the chagrin of the early-to-bed stay-at-homers. However, this levity could not be charged only to the partakers

Cars of the No. 20 line also ran to Curtis Bay. Here we see a packed, open-bench summer car, No. 2059, ostensibly bound for Jack Flood's. One wonders how the conductor ever managed to collect fares. (BSM Collection)

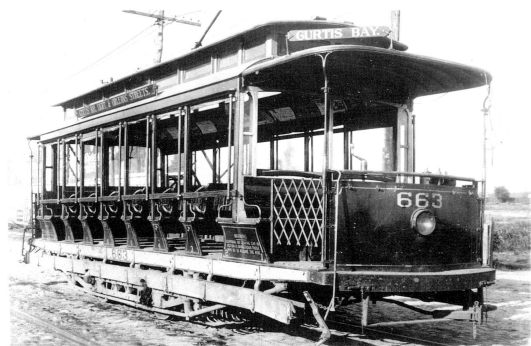

Open cars were tremendously popular for trips to the parks and trolley parties. A minor accident to its running board caused No. 663, a ten-bench Laclede, to be captured on film. Benches on platforms of open cars were not at all common in Baltimore. (Louis C. Mueller Collection)

of liquid refreshments returning from the Arundel shore, as the story of the trolley parties which follows will show.

As another means of adding to their revenues, the companies began to charter cars to private parties. It became fashionable about 1894 to hire a car for an evening's entertainment, either to journey to and from one of the amusement parks, or just to ride around the countryside, ofttimes with a piano or organ aboard. Most of these affairs were rather sedate, but at times there were enough young bloods riding along, singing lustily or shooting off skyrockets and firecrackers from the cars, to cause the *News* to editorialize on June 16, 1896, "It is time that public sentiment and public officials should together put forth an effort to bring about a change in the state of affairs."

Some of the excursions were elaborate. On October 8, 1895, over fifty cars were run in a baseball trolley parade to honor the Orioles, who were playing Cleveland in the Temple Cup Series. The following August, the Star of the Sea Council No. 33, Catholic Benevolent League, sponsored what the *Herald* described as the grandest trolley party ever held in Baltimore. At least sixteen hundred people crowded on the twenty-five cars which were festooned with red, white, and blue lights, as well as American flags and bunting.

The fad gradually declined with the arrival of the automobile, but the United promoted chartered cars well past the World War I era. Some idea of how much the streetcars were used for recreation at the turn of the century is contained in the statement that in July of 1900, on any warm evening, 4,000 people journeyed to Riverview, 2,500 to Electric Park, 2,000 to Gwynn Oak, 2,500 to Back and Middle Rivers, 5,000 to the city parks, and 5,000 to the resorts across the Patapsco. And, of course, they all went by streetcar.

NOTES AND COMMENTS:

An advertisement inserted in the *News* of July 4, 1897 extolled Riverview Park as "the Coney Island of the South." Inducements for spending the Fourth there included: Pindell's Veteran Corps Band; dancing in the pavilion; fireworks display; boating, bathing, and fishing; fish, crab, and chicken suppers; bowling alleys. *News,* July 29, 1897; *Sunday Herald,* May 20, 1898; *Herald,* June 18, 1898; *Evening Sun,* August 20, 1947.

Ridgewood Park is sketched in the *Sun,* May 22, 1947 and *North Baltimore Home News,* July 6, 1939. Mt. Holly Inn burned December 7, 1920, and some details of its history appear in the *Sun* of the following morning.

Frank Brown, president of Baltimore Traction, is mentioned in the *Sun,* March 29, 1895, as sending a letter to the County Commissioners which included the following: "You are no doubt aware that it is the intention of the Traction Company to keep this park (Gwynn Oak) as a resort for ladies and children, and we will not allow any spiritous or fermented liquors to be sold on the property." Its July 4, 1897 (*News*) advertisement promised the following: "Baltimore's most beautiful summer resort. Professor White's Circus and trained animals. Balloon ascension every day of the week. Finest dancing floor in Maryland. Lawn tennis grounds, boating, and bathing. Gwynn Oak falls. Merry-go-round. Farson's Orchestra. Meals and refreshments in the restaurant." Isaac Rehert's columns in the *Sun,* July 15 and 22, 1971, contain an interesting account of the past fifty years of the park's operation and a colorful description of the thrills of a streetcar ride on a suburban line many years ago.

References to Bay Shore in the *Sun,* August 4, 1906; *Street Railway Journal,* July 27, 1907; *Evening Sun,* August 20, 1947; and *Sunday Sun Magazine,* May 1, 1966.

Those interested in Electric Park will find articles in the *American* September 1, 1895; *Sun,* January 10, 1904 and August 11, 1936; *Sunday Sun,* August 14, 1949.

Gilbert Sandler brought back memories of Carlin's in his article in the *Sunday Sun Magazine,* May 5, 1968.

References to Lakeside Park in the *American,* February 6, 1898; *Sun,* September 10, 1900; *Sun,* July 25, 1909.

During the Gay Nineties, the west side of the Middle Branch of the Patapsco, all the way from Spring Gardens down to where Broening Park is located today, was a popular place for swimming, boating, and gunning. Janvier, in his *Baltimore In The Eighties And Nineties,* recalls renting a rowboat from Cutaire's place at Ferry Bar for a Saturday of camping along the shore. There were a number of small parks along the waterfront. These were not amusement parks in the usual sense, rather they were more like the "shores" of a later era. Janvier mentions Meeter's which dated to 1883 (*American,* September 2, 1898) and Acton's, where one could still witness the cruel live-pigeon shooting matches.

It did not take long for the street railway managements to perceive the advantages of a route along Fish House Road (now Waterview Avenue). An independent company, the Shore Line Electric Railway, built the line, which began operation May 31, 1896, from the crossing of the Baltimore & Ohio Railroad and Ridgely Street to a point opposite Ferry Bar. However, about two weeks previous to this event, the Traction Company had entered into a perpetual agreement to operate the trackage. *Sun,* May 14, 1896. References to the shoreline parks in the *American,* July 29, 1897; *Sun,* June 1, 1896; *World,* August 20, 1896.

Early references to Flood's in the *News,* July 29 and November 10, 1897. Flood's establishment was the subject of at least two articles in the *Sunday Sun Magazine* — by Theodore Bowkleman on November 26, 1950 and William H. Mariner on May 20, 1962. Bowkleman, as a former conductor on the Curtis Bay line, gives details on the problems the streetcar crews faced. Mariner, who worked for Flood, records many facets of the resort's last days. He supports the theory that opposition by Billy Sunday, the Anti-Saloon League, and others to Sabbath sales of liquor on the premises ultimately led to the closing in 1916.

In addition to trolley parties, streetcars of the period were sometimes rented for advertising purposes. In May 1896, a Traction Company open car, bright with electric lights and carrying a brass band, roamed

NRHS special car poses for photographers at Cochran's Pond on the Lakeside line in April 1946. (Baltimore Sunpapers, BSM Collection)

the streets promoting the races of the Arlington Jockey Club. Details of this and the trolley parties appeared in the *News,* October 8, 1895, May 11 and June 16, 1896, and the *Herald,* August 18, 1896.

Some seem to have the impression that the latter years of the Victorian era were peopled exclusively by young suitors, all of whom were prim and proper. This was not the case, of course. Any research will come across much to show the seamy side of life. Still, I was so fascinated by the following, taken from the *Baltimore County Union,* July 13, 1895, that I cannot resist including it in some detail:

"The trolley car party is as popular in other cities but it remained for Baltimore to invent an attractive novelty for the trolley ride. Last week, a party of forty, comprising a due proportion of youths and maidens, properly chaperoned, started for a ride to Glyndon. On the return trip, a member suddenly left his

seat and had a long whispered consultation with the motorman, whose subject he refused to divulge to his curious companions, although, stimulated by the mischievous twinkle in his eye, they plied him with questions. On merrily went the car until, all at once the motorman sang out: 'At the top of this hill look out for the tunnel.' The mystified members of the party looked at him in amazement for no tunnel could they remember on the road. But, when the top of the hill was reached, they shot into quick darkness, for the motorman had turned off the electric lights. A peal of laughter rose as the joke was seized and then all over the cars arose sounds of osculatory nature, which the perplexed chaperones could not locate but were pacified when told the girls were only kissing their hands in deference to tunnel customs. Six tunnels were passed, and finally the motorman called out: 'Last tunnel before we reach the city.' And the tunnels were unani-

mously voted the best part of the trolley party."

The attendance statistics quoted for the various amusement parks are taken from an article in the *Herald,* July 29, 1900.

After World War II, chartered car trips on Baltimore Transit were essentially reduced to those of individuals and organizations interested in street railways. The Baltimore Chapter of the National Railway Historical Society sponsored numerous trips between 1946 and 1963. In 1948, it acted as host for the annual convention of the Society and chartered a two-car train for a part of the weekend activity. In later years, a number of farewell trips took place on various lines — in some cases on the day following formal abandonment of rail service. On the final night of operations, November 2-3, 1963, the Chapter ran a trip with PCC No. 7083, covering all parts of the remaining trackage.

CARRYING THE MAIL
AND EXPRESS

In a day when the emphasis is on speed, few people realize that almost one hundred years ago at least one item moved much more rapidly. That was the local mail. In the Victorian era, one could post a letter in, say, Roland Park in the morning, and it would quite probably be delivered to the addressee in Catonsville the same day! Nor was it necessary to memorize the string of digits in a zip code — Catonsville was Catonsville, not 21228.

It was the street railway which to a large extent made this possible. As early as 1863, the Baltimore & Yorktown Turnpike Railway had carried pouches of mail from the post office in Baltimore to Waverly, Towson, and other outlying towns. A few other routes later offered the same service, but it was not until October 1895, that Postmaster Warfield proposed having a railway postal car service. In that month, he made a trip to Philadelphia, New York, and Brooklyn to investigate similar service being offered in those cities. The arrangements were not completed until May 1897, when, on the 6th, two cars were placed on display. These were to be used on the routes of Baltimore Traction. They were rebuilt Lewis & Fowler passenger cars. The Traction Company would soon add an additional Lewis & Fowler car, as well as a Stephenson carried over from the Lake Roland Elevated days, to complete its mail fleet.

These cars were painted white, with blue striping and gold lettering, and carried the legend "U. S. Railway Post Office." For night identification, the words "U. S. Mail" were etched into the front clerestory glass. They were 24 feet long overall, 16 feet inside, and about 7½ feet wide. Interiors were fitted with sorting tables, pouch racks, and filing cases, as well as such conveniences for the two clerks as washing and drinking water and an electric heater. The

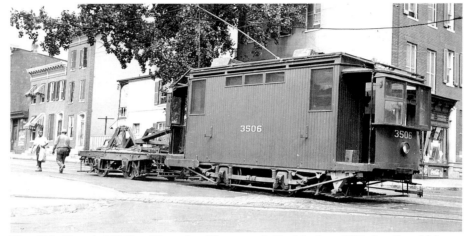

The odd-looking windshield on this overhead line car probably dates from 1906 when the vehicle was rebuilt in company shops from an older car. Overhang of window frame was necessary to allow room for cranking the gooseneck hand brake. Trailer is reel car, sans roll of wire. (Louis C. Mueller Collection)

Traction Company furnished the motorman and conductor.

Service was inaugurated by the Traction Company when car No. 220 left the Brooklyn car house at 5:11 a.m. on May 17, 1897. Nineteen minutes later, its southbound counterpart left the Druid Hill Avenue barn. The full route extended from Arlington to Curtis Bay, about fourteen miles. Intermediate post offices served included Fairfield, Brooklyn, the main office, Walbrook, and Powhatan.

No factor was overlooked in speeding delivery. Collection districts were laid out on either side of the car line, with carriers picking up mail from boxes in the contiguous area and depositing this mail in special receptacles along the car routes. These special receptacles were the pride of Postmaster Warfield and had two compartments, one for packages and one for letters. Canvas bags were hung in each compartment. When the postal car approached a mailbox, the clerk jumped off while it was still in motion, opened the box, took out the canvas sacks, replaced them with empty

ones, and hurried back to jump aboard the car. The collected mail was sorted, canceled, and either transported to the main post office or transferred to another car for direct distribution.

City & Suburban had two routes, and likewise ran four cars. These were also former Lewis & Fowler passenger cars, but had, however, been rebuilt by Jackson & Sharp, rather than in the company's own shops. All eight cars were similar in appearance with regard to their interior appointments.

Due to a delay in receiving its reconstructed cars, C & S did not begin mail service until a short time after Baltimore Traction. One of its routes ran from Towson to Catonsville, serving Govans, the main post office, and Carroll during its seventeen-mile trip. The other connected Roland Park and Dundalk, passing the main post office and Highlandtown. (The southern terminal was actually St. Helena post office, as the town of Dundalk did not exist at that early date.) Initially, the cars transferred mail to horse-drawn wagons in the

Baltimore Traction's Druid Hill Avenue cable power plant and attached car house are only a half dozen years old here, but already electric power has replaced the rope. Mail car served until 1929; the buildings still stood in 1992 and were but little changed outwardly. (Louis C. Mueller Collection)

vicinity of the main office; the tracks into that building were not constructed until 1910.

The United Railways built six new cars in its Carroll Park shops in 1903, and, although car No. 219 (later renumbered No. 200) was burned in the Waverly car house fire in 1906, the remainder stayed on the roster until after the service was discontinued on November 9, 1929. By then, it was the last remaining street railway mail operation in the country. The income from the mail cars, street railway companies claimed, was of no great consequence, particularly since they sometimes slowed regular service. Still they offered, at least in the early days, some benefits which are often overlooked. Teamsters balked at

obstructing the tracks on which the mail cars ran, for fear of being brought before a U. S. District Judge. In case of a strike, interference with the movement of the cars by strikers invited the intervention of United States troops or marshals. The same source giving these statements continues ". . . the employees would hesitate about inaugurating a strike, or would not strike . . . at all. To put it plainly, they would be afraid to strike for trivial causes. In this manner, a mail line would work a benefit to the men as well as the company."

While the postal cars handled the mail, there was another service to take care of package freight. The first recorded attempt in this direction was made by the Baltimore and Northern in March 1898, when it began

running one of its combines as a "market car." By October this had been expanded to a regular express service between Baltimore and Glyndon. Rates varied according to weight, and most of the nine agencies were located in general stores along the route.

Nothing much came of this, but after the consolidation a rather extensive express service began operating to Ellicott City, Towson, and Glyndon. It was incorporated on May 29, 1900 as Gaither's City & Suburban Express Company. Always closely allied with the United Railways, it was managed by James A. Gaither.

The original equipment consisted of two rebuilt Lake Roland Elevated cars, with a Baltimore & Northern combine car being

Chattolanee Bottled Water was among the many items handled by Gaither's Express cars. Crew is unloading carboys of water, brought in from the Green Spring Valley, on Franklin Street, near Howard. The Provident Bank building — second from left — later was used by the United as waiting room, lost and found department, and employee recreation facility. (Louis C. Mueller Collection)

added in 1900. Business increased to such a degree that two more cars were built in the company's shops in 1903, and an additional pair in 1904. Among the consignments were dressed hogs, lumber, ice by the ton, and barrels of cement, flour, and whiskey. The United furnished the cars and the power; the express company handled the rest of the operation. Business declined with the advent of the motor truck competition, and the service was discontinued on December 31, 1912.

NOTES AND COMMENTS:

On August 20, 1863, the first car of the Baltimore & Yorktown Turnpike Railway arrived in Towson. Within two weeks, the mail contractor had withdrawn his omnibus and made arrangements to have the mail carried on the horse cars. *Baltimore County Advocate,* August 22 and September 10, 1863. As of July 1, 1868, the B & YT was awarded the mail contract, which called for service twice daily between Baltimore and Towson via Waverly and Govanstown. The pact paid $400 per annum. *Baltimore County Union,* March 28, 1868.

Warfield's trip was reported in the *American,* October 24, 1895, which also noted that Baltimore Traction had been carrying pouch mail to suburban points for

some time past. Details of the early mail service and cars were obtained from the *Sun,* February 15 and May 18, 1897; *Herald,* May 6, 1897; *News,* May 17, 1897; other data is from the notes of A. T. Clark and L. C. Mueller. The postal cars were able to gain direct access to the post office for the first time in 1910 when, in the construction of an annex to the building, a space was provided for loading and unloading mail cars. *United Railways Annual Report,* 1910. Wrightson Chambers, who had worked as a clerk on the mail cars circa 1902-10, recalled many incidents of the service in the *Sunday Sun Magazine,* November 16, 1958.

The remarks concerning the peripheral benefits of operating mail cars are attributed to an unidentified president of one of the St. Louis street railway companies. *St. Louis Globe-Democrat,* May 4, 1896. Baltimore companies were singularly blessed with a minimum of management-labor disputes in the early days, just the opposite of St. Louis.

A good, detailed reference on Baltimore streetcar mail operations is the monograph *The Street Railway Post Offices of Baltimore,* by Douglas N. Clark and F. Edgar Ruckle (Mobile Post Office Society, Omaha, Nebraska, 1979).

Specific references to the operation of Gaither's Express are given in the notes and comments on the chapter, "Built to Last."

Serving the exclusive Guilford community, lines Nos. 1 and 11 made their way on separated tracks along St. Paul Street to Bedford Square at Charles Street south of Coldspring Lane. Northbound No. 5591 arrives at Bedford Square Station (still preserved in 1992) as another semi-convertible departs. (George J. Voith)

"THE HOODOO CAR"

During the 1940s the *Sunday Sun* contained a comic book supplement featuring a detective-like character called "the Spirit." One episode, vaguely recalled, was based on some weird happenings which occurred during a streetcar ride on a foggy evening. The trip was over a private right of way line with many trestles, reminiscent of the No. 26 route between Dundalk and Bay Shore. The resemblance was probably not a coincidence, as Will Eisner, creator of the strip, apparently spent some time in the vicinity.

Since the street railway business was by nature one of precise schedules and careful cost accounting for all operations, there is little of the mysterious in its real life story. One exception, apparently with some basis in fact, is the tale of the "Hoodoo Car." This was a single-truck convertible used on the Druid Hill Avenue route; it seems natural that the car should have been numbered "13." (However, the 1313 of the North Avenue line, which might be expected to have been doubly jinxed, had no such reputation.) According to the story, car 13 had been involved in an unlikely number of accidents during the ten years between its delivery and its sudden disappearance in 1908.

In that year, the car just dropped from the company records. No mileage reports were turned in, and a check of the shop reports failed to show that it had been taken out of service. A search of paperwork and storage facilities failed to offer any clue. No renumbering of cars could be found which affected car 13. Apparently, it had just vanished.

The mystery was only deepened when the missing vehicle turned up again in late 1909. It was found by workmen of the Ways & Structures Department who, in removing a large quantity of roofing material stored in the Owings Mills car house, found it chained to the track behind the building supplies.

Available evidence indicates that the car showed signs of having been in some sort of accident. However, who concealed the car and why remains a mystery to this day.

Another seemingly strange event having a connection with the company has a logical explanation. It begins with a boy of fourteen and his new bike. He soon found a favorite place to ride — out St. Paul Street, from University Parkway to Bedford Square and back again.

After a time the return trip assumed a pattern. The youth would wait by the concrete station alongside the layover point at Bedford Square until the streetcar was about ready to leave on its trip to downtown Baltimore.

Just as the motorman released the brake and notched up the controller, the boy began to pedal furiously down the St. Paul Street hill. Within a block or so he had attained a speed of between ten and fifteen miles an hour. Since there was relatively little traffic on St. Paul during the hours in which he rode there, and street crossings were protected by stop signs, this "furious speed" presented a minimum of danger to the cyclist.

Meanwhile, the motorman had notched his controller up a few points, and was rapidly closing the gap between his car and the boy on the bike. Though the men at the controls of the trolleys probably never suspected it, there now began a contest, the memory of which remained vivid some thirty-two years later.

As the boy pumped the pedals, he became increasingly aware of the car creeping closer and closer. For those who do not remember St. Paul Street circa 1938, it consisted of a macadam roadway maybe three lanes wide. To either side, the streetcars ran on private right of way, separated from other traffic by neat green hedges, perhaps six feet high. On the other side of the tracks, there was almost a solid wall of

stately trees, intertwined with large, bushy shrubs.

The wall of greenery served to deflect the noise of the streetcars outward from the residences. This, combined with the hedge alongside the roadway, resulted in the sound of the car's passage (which was intensified by the unpaved right of way) being channeled upward and outward onto St. Paul Street. Therefore, on a quiet summer morning, an approaching streetcar often seemed to have a decibel rating equal to a freight train.

At least, so it seemed to the boy. As the car approached from the rear, he could hear the squealing of the wheel flanges as they rode along the head of the "T" rails, the creaking of the wooden body of the semi-convertible, the thumping of the heavy trucks as they jounced across a depressed rail joint or slammed through a section of trackwork which needed maintenance, and the clanging of the gong as the motorman signaled his approach to a cross street.

It is a difficult thing to explain, but as the streetcar pulled almost even with the rear wheel of the bike, a sensation came over the youth that he was being pursued by something unreal. The racket pouring over the hedge seemed to drown out everything else. As the shrieking, groaning thing crept closer and closer, he was consumed with an overwhelming compulsion to look back to be sure that it was really a streetcar approaching.

This was the contest. He, of course, knew that it was a streetcar. The sounds which carried to his ears were familiar. What made it so strange was the fact that, when there was no automobile traffic, the streetcar drowned out all other noises. The whirr of the bike tires, the chirping of the birds, the rustling of the trees in the gentle breeze — all the soft sounds ordinarily audible in Guilford were overwhelmed.

Try as he might, the compulsion to look back could not be overcome. Of course,

Semi-convertible No. 5572 rests between runs in March 1947 at the picturesque Bedford Square terminal waiting station. (Leonard W. Rice)

The "Hoodoo" car was built by Brill in 1898. Photo is thought to show its condition in 1909, shortly after car was "found" at Owings Mills car house. In any event, standing at Carroll Park shops, the car is defintely the worse for wear. (Louis C. Mueller Collection)

when he did give in and turned his head, it was only to see the familiar yellow streetcar, and, as often as not, the motorman had a friendly wave for the boy.

Summer turned to autumn. The bike rider returned to school. The races with the streetcars on St. Paul Street were relegated to the remoter regions of his memory. The transfers which he had collected (along with bubble gum cards and postage stamps) were filed away in the attic. Somewhat later, the streetcar photographs which he had taken were scattered among collectors across the country when his camera turned to other subjects.

As the years flew by, the incident was forgotten completely, until one early evening in the fall of 1968. The boy, now in his early forties, was late in getting home from work. His route, after leaving the bus, required a walk of about a mile. Usually, he took a short cut along the route of the old Ellicott City car line, then gone over a dozen years.

On the evening in question, there was more than a trace of scattered fog. It was not enough to hinder vision to any great extent, but, as sometimes happens in the area, the fog created an atmospheric condition in which sounds played strange tricks.

As the man strode along the old streetcar right of way, he could hear a freight train droning along the tracks of the Baltimore & Ohio, which ran along the Patapsco River, half a mile away. The land between his path and the railroad tracks was divided by a high hill. At times, particularly in autumn, sounds from the B & O trains, rising from the bowl of the Patapsco valley, rebounded from an overhanging fog and spilled over the top of the ridge to roll down across the old streetcar line.

On this particular evening, the sounds were unusually distinct. The diesel locomotives could be heard clearly as they threaded their way alongside the river, pulling their heavy load.

In a few minutes, the engines entered the tunnel at Union Dam, and the noise of their roaring exhausts was lost to the man's ears. A new rhythm took over. Rolling out of the valley came the muted rumble of 125 or so freight cars. Sometimes, he could make out individual sounds like the squeal of protesting flanges screeching around the tight curves; again, the banging of trucks across a bad rail joint was the predominant theme. At times, it might be the creaking of some ancient refrigerator cars or the thump, thump, thump of a flat wheel that the car inspectors had overlooked. But usually it was not any one sound that was distinguishable, just a melding of the dozens of squeaks, bangs, and rattles produced by a fast-moving train of cars.

Gradually, at first, then more and more quickly, the sound intensified manyfold. Soon the train actually seemed to be right on the abandoned right of way. Fantastic as it seems in the retelling, the sound seemed to be coming from close behind the man. After thirty-odd years, his mind flashed back to the old contest with the streetcars on St. Paul Street.

He laughed to himself. He had no bike; he was walking. There were not even any tracks on the old right of way — no ties, no trolley wires, hardly any ballast. Still, the sound seemed to be growing in intensity. The car was catching up — but he knew that there could not be any streetcar. The old impulse to turn his head was almost irresistible.

He knew the sound that he heard was that of a freight train; he knew the train was at least a half a mile distant. Still, as the illusion seemed to come closer and closer, the noises of nature were drowned out, and the sounds which he could hear tended to blend into the old irresistible siren call that he had heard on St. Paul Street in his youth.

Regardless of the logic of the situation, the old impulse was just too strong. The train (or streetcar) seemed almost on top of him. He knew that there would be nothing on the path if he gave in and turned his head; it would be the same old story, would it not? Still, the sound was so near, the rhythm so well recalled.

Again, he lost the contest. Slowly, ever so slowly, he turned his head to face back in the direction from which he had come.

NOTES AND COMMENTS:

The story of the "Hoodoo" car is based in large part on an article by Frank Badart, which appeared in the *Sunday Sun Magazine,* September 30, 1951. For this and many other interesting anecdotes the author is indebted to Fred Scharnagle.

A nine-bench Brownell-built open car at Fort McHenry gate about the time of the Spanish-American conflict. Late one night in 1898, a streetcar ran off the end of track into the gate house, causing the alarmed guard to turn out the garrison with a report that the enemy was advancing down Fort Avenue from Locust Point. (Louis C. Mueller Collection)

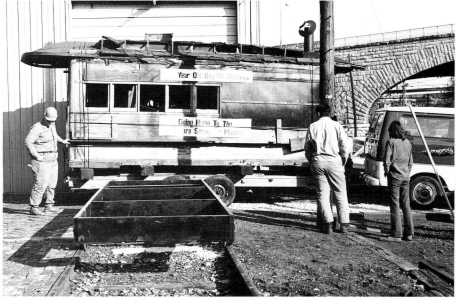

A Baltimore City Passenger Railway horse car, which dates from before the Civil War, is a tangible bit of folklore. It last ran on the Gay Street line in the 1890s, but origin is obscure. After being made obsolete by more modern cars, it served various purposes on a Baltimore County farm for half a century. Discovered by Robert W. Janssen of the NRHS and documented by BSM members, it was presented by the owners, the Garrison family, to the museum. The car is shown arriving at the Falls Road car house in 1970. (Michael R. Farrell)

THE FOLKLORE OF
THE STREET RAILWAY

Anything so closely associated with the daily activities of a large group of people must invariably leave in its wake certain stories which fall into the category of folklore. The horsecars and streetcars were no exception.

The horse car companies made use of some very unusual equipment. During extremely heavy snowfalls, the Baltimore & Yorktown Turnpike Railway substituted sleighs for their horse cars. The Baltimore & Powhatan Railway went one step further and mounted two or three cars on runners. A correspondent for the *Baltimore County Union* took a ride on one of them in January 1881 and found that the jolting was so severe "that it was all he could do to keep himself together, and his hat on his head."

A tale of the Baltimore & Hampden comes from the days when the Daft third-rail system was in operation. After one light snowfall, an official of the line (the story has it none other than Nelson Perin) chanced to see two of his men tied to the front of one of the electric motor cars, furiously brushing snow from the power rail. The official expressed the fear that the men would be run over should they fall in front of the car; he was reassured that if that ever happened, the car would stop short. Apparently, the question remained an academic one.

One practice, still prevalent on the buses today, was the dangerous sport of hitching a ride on the rear of the vehicles. The Baltimore & Hampden reportedly handled this problem in a rather drastic way. A battery was carried on the front platform of the car, and when the freeloaders climbed aboard, it was connected with a wire leading to the metal dasher and handrail at the rear of the car. Once they gripped the rail, the culprits could be dealt

with at leisure, for the voltage made it impossible for them to loosen their grip.

The street railway companies engaged almost constantly in bitter controversies over franchises and other rights. As a general rule, these involved only the various corporations and the city and state governing bodies; the average citizen, while directly concerned, usually had little to say about the outcome. However, in the fall of 1898, a druggist, Charles Moore, proved to be an exception. The Consolidated Railway wanted to slice off a piece of the sidewalk in front of Moore's drug store at Patterson Park Avenue and Fayette Street, in order to put in a curve connecting its tracks at this point.

"No," said druggist Moore to this proposal and, when the workmen arrived, he seated himself on a chair placed on the disputed pavement so as to prevent any digging. For almost two months, Moore, his family, and friends sat on the small portion of concrete, keeping at times a twenty-four hour vigil. Once there was an actual skirmish which saw the defenders driven off, and the workmen began to dig up the disputed section. Moore's young daughter saved the day, however, when she jumped into the hole and defied the Consolidated's men to drag her out.

Finally, the dispute was settled, with the railway company reportedly paying Dr. Moore $300. Ironically, before the work was completed, the competing companies were combined into the United Railways, which had no use for the trackage on that block of Patterson Park Avenue; hence no regular service was ever run over the disputed curve.

Though not on a scale with that waged by the Santa Fe and the Denver & Rio Grande Railroads, Baltimore had its own "railroad battle" in 1889. In that year, the

York Road Railway Company, which also owned the turnpike of the same name, was indicted for permitting a nuisance to exist on that road. The complaint cited the piers supporting the trestle of the narrow gauge steam railroad which crossed it just south of Towson. These, it was claimed, interfered with the passage of farm wagons. Since the steam road refused to put up a new bridge, the manager of the horse railway company sent a gang of men to tear out the offending piers. The steam railroad superintendent, having anticipated this action, had placed two gondola cars filled with stone on the overpass. When the York Road men began their work, a fusillade of rocks sent them scurrying.

The horse car people had the sympathy of the large crowd which had gathered, and public opinion possibly had an effect in settling the affair peacefully. In any event, within a month, the narrow gauge railroad put up a wooden truss bridge which required no supports in the roadway. The narrow gauge line later became the standard gauge Maryland & Pennsylvania (the "Ma & Pa"). Although the railroad was abandoned in 1958, the abutments of the successor bridge still survived in 1992.

William Scott, a lineman for the Lake Roland Elevated Railway, merits a special mention for being among the most courageous (or foolhardy) men in Baltimore street railway history. His actions were precipitated by a trolley wheel catching in an overhead frog at Guilford and Lexington. This wrenched the trolley pole and base from the car, very effectively tying up the line during the evening rush hour.

Scott procured a piece of insulated wire, stripped the ends bare, ran one end into the car, and stood atop the vehicle, holding the other end, which he had attached to a wheel, against the wire. He maintained this position as the car traveled over the elevated section and all the way to Walbrook. In the words of the *Baltimore County Union,* "Scott's position was a novel one and startled persons unused to electricity as he stood on top of the car amid myriads of sparks and illuminated by lightning-like flashes from the trolley wire."

While there are numerous reports of private vehicles entering upon structures such as the Huntingdon Avenue viaduct and the Bear Creek bridge, only one automobile is known to have made it completely across any of them. The incident happened on the most unlikely one of all, the Guilford Avenue elevated. This structure seems to have had an affinity for attracting trespassers.

Within a year or so after its completion, a patron, having climbed the long stairway to the station platform, found himself on the side where only southbound cars stopped. The man, who was reportedly more than slightly under the influence, decided that it would be easier to make his way across a foot-wide girder to the opposite platform, rather than going to the trouble of descending and reascending all those steps. Part way across, he lost his balance and fell to his death on the cobblestones below. Though there are a number of reports of cars colliding on the elevated, this is the only known instance of a fatality connected with the structure.

Several years later, a gentleman from Baltimore County, after a bit of celebrating in the big city, attempted to drive his rig onto the elevated. The horse had almost made it to the top when it lost its footing; horse, buggy, and driver all landed in a heap alongside an abutment. Charges were dismissed the next morning by a judge who decided that the man had suffered enough.

Not more than half a dozen years before the demise of the elevated, which was torn down in 1950, a similar attempt was more successful. This time it was on a New Year's Eve and a taxicab was involved. Investigating reports that automobile headlights had been seen moving along the structure early in the morning, police found a stolen cab parked adjacent to the northern ramp. After checking, they confirmed that the vehicle had indeed been driven up the

There was just enough room for the streetcars to squeeze between parked automoblies on Lexington Street between Charles and Liberty Streets in 1926. The company ad in which this drawing appeared stated that everyone who had ridden to town in the autos could have been carried by the streetcars pictured. This stretch of Lexington Street is now part of Charles Center, where the automobiles are concealed in underground parking garages. (UR & E Company, Willem Wirtz)

ramp at Lexington Street and had successfully negotiated the entire elevated line. The driver was not identified, so it will probably never be known who performed the feat.

All things must end; so a clever trick employed by motormen who used the elevated might be a good note on which to conclude this chapter. The elevated, it may be remembered, was built for most of its length above the tracks of the Northern Central Railway. In the days of steam engines on the railroads, this was not an unmixed blessing. Particularly in the vicinity of the Centre Street elevated station, the railroad engineers seemed to delight in waiting until a streetcar had stopped almost

PCC emblazoned with Red Cross slogans turns from Falls Road onto the Kelly Avenue bridge at Mt. Washington. The concrete bridge replaced the old Baltimore & Northern trestle in 1927. (Robert W. Janssen)

directly overhead before releasing a veritable cloud of smoke, cinders, and steam — much to the discomfiture of the motorman, conductor, and passengers of the car above. This practice came to a sudden end when the motormen of the electric cars took to opening their well-filled sandboxes, which action, as the structure had no flooring, allowed the fine grit to sift down between the ties and find its way into the cabs of the yard engines below.

NOTES AND COMMENTS:

A. D. Sanks, superintendent of the York Road line, had constructed in the fall of 1886 "a large, covered sleigh with double runners." It was put in service on December 7th of that year, carrying passengers between Towson and Govanstown. *Baltimore County Union,* December 11, 1886.

The tale of snow sweeping on the B & H was included in the memoirs of one of the men who had run the Daft cars. These appeared in *Trolley Topics,* August 1927 — some forty years after the actual event.

The incident of the battery on the horse car platform was recounted in the *Maryland Journal* (Towson), May 23, 1885.

Doctor Moore's struggle with the Consolidated Railway received widespread coverage in all the Baltimore papers during the fall of 1898. The disuse of the track was reported in the *News,* February 17, 1900.

The *Maryland Journal* (Towson), July 13 and August 31, 1889, carried accounts of the "railroad battle."

William Scott's exploit attracted the attention of a reporter for the *Sun,* June 9, 1893.

The sources for the incidents relative to the Towson trestle are as follows: Man falling from structure, *American,* July 17, 1900. Baltimore County man and his rig,

American, November 25, 1901. Automobile driven across the trestle, personal recollection of reading about the event. George F. Nixon recounted this, as well as many other aspects of the operation of the elevated, in the *Sunday Sun Magazine,* January 17, 1963. In George's version, though, the driver was apprehended, and, as the police led him to the patrol wagon, his only comment was, "It was a pretty rough ride." The *News,* August 3, 1901, carried an account of the sand dumping which ended the pastime of sending up clouds of smoke and steam by the PRR (Northern Central) crews.

The United minted metal tokens or "car checks" beginning in 1919. The were usually sold at a modest discount. Small metal dispensers would hold a larger quantity for frequent users. (UR & E Company, Willem Wirtz)

Festooned with American and Maryland flags, the state seal, and posters advertising Bay Shore and Gwynn Oak Parks, the United Railways building at Franklin and Howard is decked out to celebrate the 50th anniversary of the Baltimore street railways in July 1909. (George F. Nixon Collection)

RANDOM NOTES FROM BYGONE DAYS

Though the horse car operators were required to buy out the stagecoach line owners within the city by the terms of the franchise granted in 1859, the stagecoach, or omnibus, did not entirely disappear from the streets of Baltimore. Omnibuses continued running to such outlying places as Bel Air, Pikesville, and Randallstown from downtown hotels.

On June 24, 1878, the old-time omnibuses entered into direct competition with the horse cars when the Harlem Stagecoach Company began running a line from Fulton Station to Exchange Place (Lombard and South Streets). This company survived for several years. However, the spectacularly-named Baltimore Chariot Company (from South Baltimore to Broadway and Gay Street), established February 10, 1880, and a line of Herdic coaches (between Eutaw Street and Exchange Place), started in May 1881; each lasted only a few months.

The "dummy line" in Druid Hill Park was among the earliest street railways to be constructed for use by Baltimoreans; yet all three of its stations, constructed in 1864 at a total cost of about $7,500, are in existence today. Two of the "dummy line" stations stand on their original sites, the Chinese station at the northwest corner of Fulton and Druid Hill Avenues and Council Grove station, adjacent to the western boundary of the zoo. Orems (or Rotunda) station was moved many years ago to a knoll overlooking the north side of Druid Lake.

Vandalism was not unknown in the old days. The boy who unceremoniously dropped the Monumental Railway's first horse car into a turntable pit did not realize the consequences of loosening the hand brake, but other youths were more purposeful. Some made it a practice to mar the beautiful piano finish of the early cars by standing close beside the passing vehicle with a nail that would leave a scratch along the entire side panel. The unfortunate conductor was held accountable for the resulting damage.

The platform of an early electric car could prove to be a hazardous location as motorman Leonard Nicholson discovered one March day in 1899. He was at the controls of car No. 740 of the Consolidated's Saratoga Street line. While crossing the specialwork at Gilmor Street, where Saratoga makes a 45 degree jog, Nicholson lost his balance due to the jolting of the car. He grasped the lattice gate at the side of the platform but was thrown to the street when the gate was wrenched from its fastenings. As this was before the days of the deadman controller, which would have automatically cut off the power and applied the brakes, the car continued eastward along Saratoga, with Nicholson vainly chasing after it.

To make the scene even more like an early Hollywood comedy, the conductor abandoned the car as it picked up speed going down the hill toward Stricker Street. There was no hilarity in the situation for the lone passenger, a 35-year-old woman. With the controller still on and the terrain either level or downgrade, the runaway car continued to pick up speed.

She finally jumped off at Fremont Avenue, by which time the car was going rather rapidly. The injuries which she sustained were serious enough for her to collect $1,500 in damages, a large amount for the time. She picked a poor moment to jump because Saratoga begins to run upgrade just beyond Fremont. The hill slowed the car enough to allow a passerby to jump aboard and bring it to a halt without further incident.

The Long Bridge across the Patapsco was the scene of another freak accident. This bridge was actually a trestle of low pilings, with a draw in the center. The legend is that there was some fast running across the span, especially with the trippers operated by men from the No. 20 line. There had been several derailments, but no serious damage prior to April 8, 1913, when a car heading toward Ferry Bar derailed at a joint, continued along the ties for sixty feet, and then lurched through the three planks serving as guardrails and on into the murky Patapsco.

The fortunate circumstance that the water was only about 4½ feet deep at this point prevented a more serious tragedy. Nevertheless, one passenger was killed and many others injured. To salvage the car, the company had it lifted onto a barge and floated around the harbor to the Pratt Street power house, which was located at Dugan's Wharf.

While the two electric car accidents cited could be traced to human failings, the cable lines had an inherent safety hazard that was never solved. Though there were some safeguards, on rare occasions the grip would become caught on a broken strand of the cable wire. It would then be impossible to release the grip, so the car would continue on until some outside force intervened.

Gripman Thomas Donahue found himself in such a predicament just as he eased car No. 3 away from the Traction Company's terminal at Patterson Park on May 18, 1894. By a coincidence, there was only one passenger aboard, a woman. As soon as Donahue discovered his dilemma, he began sounding his gong continuously to warn traffic out of the way.

The woman did not perceive anything was amiss, until they had swept down the

The crew of a line car pauses from repairing trolley wire on the elevated structure above Guilford Avenue to pose for photographer. When a PCC car lost the wire on the trestle, the motorman had to perform some contortions to put it back on. The usual procedure was to kneel on rear seat with upper portion of torso thrust through the window. A brilliant flash of blue flame burst over the scene every time the trolley wheel made contact with the wire. (Charles R. Lloyd)

East Baltimore Street hill and swooshed around the corner into Ann Street without slackening their pace. She began to grow panicky as, still accompanied by the constant clanging of the gong, the cable car whizzed around another corner onto Pratt Street. She started for the rear platform, intending to jump off, but was restrained by the conductor, who assured her that the car had to stop at the Pratt Street power house, less than a dozen blocks away, as the cable ended there. He failed to mention that he had no idea of what would stop it, as this was a new experience to him, too.

Meanwhile, Donahue, on the front platform, was still vainly trying to free the grip, at the same time keeping up the incessant ringing of the bell. Fortune was smiling on him as a policeman, hearing the racket, managed to clear the busy Broadway intersection in time, and there was no electric car to contest the Caroline Street crossing. He had only a brief moment to relax before the car was bearing down on Central Avenue.

Just before the yellow car reached this corner, he heard what sounded like the bellow of a foghorn. It seemed that their luck was about to run out. The sound, he knew, was a signal by a man mounted atop a freight car, warning that a team of horses was approaching the intersection with a number of freight cars attached and expected the right of way.

The threatened crash never came. At the last moment, the driver, quickly realizing what was happening, pulled his teams sharply around to one side. The gripman,

conductor, and frenzied woman saw the heavy freight cars bearing down on them, but the cable car just cleared the closest one, with a railroad man on top screaming something unintelligible at them. The woman screeched, then sank back into her seat.

Donahue now faced the last crisis; the brick power house loomed just ahead. He believed that the grip assembly would be torn loose by the sudden ending of the cable slot. His brakes were useless, having been damaged in the uneven contest which had pitted their puny effort against the enormous pull of the cable, designed to be strong enough to move a dozen cars at one time.

As the car swung around a slight curve before passing in front of the power house, there was the terrible shriek of rending metal as the grip tore loose; but, as fate would have it, there was another car ahead on the same track ready to start downtown on the next cable.

Donahue was still clanging for all he was worth, and fortunately the gripman on the other car, No. 66, realized what was amiss. Immediately he started his car, but No. 3 had too much momentum. Donahue made a quick dash inside the car just as the two vehicles came together. Luckily, no one was injured, as the impact was slight, and damage to the cars was relatively minor.

Many will remember a safety ritual that continued into the post-World War II period. Each evening, the conductors on some of the wooden semi-convertibles

would, an hour before dusk, light a pair of oil lanterns and hang them from the rear corners of the cars.

This precaution was the outcome of an accident that happened around the turn of the century. A group of merrymakers were on their way to Riverview Park. Just after rounding a curve on the private right of way south of Eastern Avenue, someone on the crowded rear platform evidently pulled the trolley from the wire as a lark.

The loss of power left the car immobile and dark. Before the pole could be replaced, a following car came round the bend. Its feeble headlight failed to pick out the stopped car in time to prevent a collision.

There were many changes in lifestyle during the 104 years that streetcars roamed the city streets. To help set things in perspective, it might be recalled that only a couple of years before the dawn of the twentieth century, the City & Suburban Railway wanted to put down tracks on Mount Street in west Baltimore. One of the objections presented was that this would interfere with the driving of cattle down the thoroughfare.

On the other hand, at the same period in time, a proposed electric railway between Baltimore and Washington was contingent on an appropriation by Congress for construction of a "national boulevard," which the cars would parallel. Although such arrangements are not uncommon today, this particular project foundered, as the Interstate Highways System was far in the future.

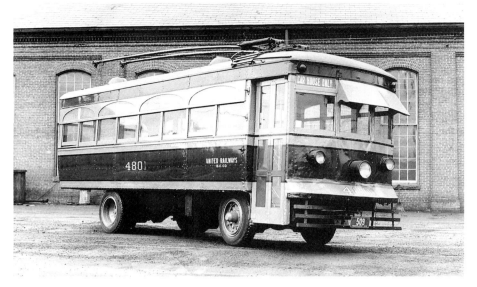

A Randallstown trackless trolley as it looked in the last days of operation. About a year before the line was discontinued, the vehicle emerged from the Carroll Park shops with a new paint scheme, pneumatic tires, and an extra headlight. (Robert W. Janssen Collection)

An offspring of this projected line to Washington later proposed an operating procedure which would have to rank as one of the most bizarre schemes in electric traction history. On April 20, 1901, the company entered into a contract with the United Railways which would have permitted a through service from Washington into downtown Baltimore by means of the United's trackage east of Ellicott City.

There was one major problem — the interurban was building to a gauge of 4 feet 8½ inches, while the United's was 5 feet 4½ inches. The new company planned to switch trucks under its cars at Ellicott City in the manner later used by the narrow-gauge East Broad Top Railroad in Pennsylvania. No one seems to have questioned all the problems posed by switching trucks on which traction motors were mounted.

The choice of the name United Railways and Electric Company for the corporation, which resulted from the final street railway consolidation of 1899, indicates that the company planned to enter the power field, as well as operate electric railways. Indeed, Alexander Brown was the moving spirit in unifying all of the Baltimore electric light corporations into the United Electric Light and Power Company, which came under the control of the UR & E by an exchange of stock in November 1899.

Yet, the street railways and the power companies always remained separate entities. In light of subsequent events, the relative values of the companies as presented in the following excerpt from a financial report put out by Wilson, Colston and Company in February 1900 is quite interesting: "The earnings of the electric light companies are sufficient to pay all fixed charges, interest on bonds, dividends on stock, and it is not a burden on the railway company, but an advantage."

In addition to the North Street (now Guilford Avenue), Stony Run Valley (at the present Sisson Street), and Huntingdon Avenue viaducts, Baltimore had another impressive trestle in the southeastern section of the city. This had been built by the Structural Iron Erecting Company of Baltimore for the Baltimore, Middle River and Sparrows Point Railway. It was of iron, twenty-five feet high where it crossed the tracks of the Philadelphia, Baltimore & Washington Railroad (a Pennsylvania Railroad subsidiary), and extended 713 feet from the end of Lombard Street to the vicinity of what is now the Francis Scott Key Medical Center. It was built in 1896 at a cost of $20,000.

The public was quick to chastise the transportation companies for any faults, real or imagined. The fare structure was under almost constant attack.

This is not an economic treatise, but the following may provide an interesting insight into one man's idea of bettering the plight of the working man. It is a portion of an endorsement published in the *Sun* during March 1898 in support of a bill then being pushed in the state legislature to reduce streetcar fares from five cents to six tickets for a quarter. It quotes the manager of a large establishment engaged in the manufacturing of overalls and drawers, which had about two thousand employees on the payroll, of whom eight hundred did work at their homes.

"All of them, especially the latter, are compelled to use the streetcars frequently. While many of them make fair wages, there are in most cases others dependent upon them for support, and (they) can ill afford streetcar fare which it becomes necessary for them to spend. . . .

"Whenever the weather is inclement, the firm sends to each department a supply of nickels which can be borrowed by any of the hands who have overlooked bringing carfare with them when they left home in the morning. The hands are thus provided with the means to avoid walking home in disagreeable and inclement weather, and perhaps saved from contracting sickness, as when the day's work is done they are tired and not in condition physically to withstand hardship. If the street railway company would sell six tickets for 25 cents the firm would buy them in large quantities, and more of the hands would use the cars than at present, as they would then be charged only four cents."

Such an arrangement would have increased the peak load in bad weather and worked havoc with the companies' ability to properly utilize their cars and manpower. It was good news to the railway companies when the bill failed to be adopted.

Beginning in the mid-1930s, a fare reduction arrangement known as the "two-trip slip" was placed in effect. This continued for a dozen or so years, and offered a second ride at half fare during off-peak hours. Like so many other things in the street railway field, a reduced off-peak fare was nothing new. In March 1887, the Baltimore, Catonsville & Ellicott's Mills had begun charging a fare of ten cents between its terminals on weekdays, as opposed to a fifteen-cent fare on Sunday, the company's busiest day.

Strangely, a building once owned by the Baltimore and Northern, a company considered by some to be the meanest of the local street railway properties, rose higher in the social scale than any other street railway structure. In the late 1920s, an old frame spring house on its Falls Road property was moved to the Baltimore Museum of Art in order to preserve it as an example of pure Grecian Revival architecture.

Until the arrival of the electric cars, which allowed the use of resistance grids for warming the interiors of the vehicles, the search for a satisfactory method of heating during the cold months led to some novel experiments. Possibly the most unusual attempt was made by the Citizens' Railway during the winter of 1886-87. This called for a stove on the front platform, under the watchful eyes of the driver; the warm air was piped into the car by means of ducts much in the manner of a hot air furnace.

Citizens' also seems to have been the first to offer open cars with cross seating. This happened in 1889, the same year that the company installed fare registers.

Some items overlap almost the entire period of street railway history. As early as the 1860s, the York Road Turnpike Railway was selling paper tickets, which gave passengers a slight saving in return for

buying them in advance of boarding the cars, thus speeding up fare collections.

More than half a century later, the United Railways also used paper tickets. Metal car checks, or tokens, were put in use after a year, and were found to be more practical. (However, tickets survived for zone fares for suburban riders.)

Tokens were usually sold at a modest discount. Originally minted for the United as early as 1919, they were still in use (with, of course, the appropriate fare increases) by the BTC and the MTA until they were withdrawn in 1992.

Still, tokens provided an unexpected complication. The great influenza epidemic of 1918 made patrons so aware of the spreading of germs that the railway company was forced to bathe in a chemical solution all car checks dropped into their fareboxes. For a while this was done on a daily basis.

NOTES AND COMMENTS:

The listing of omnibus lines appeared in *Trolley Topics,* June 1926. The last omnibus line known to have operated in the city, whose name has been lost in the mists of time, began running from Preston and Broadway to the lower end of Broadway December 9, 1895. *American,* December 8, 1895.

The runaway car on Saratoga Street was reported in the *American,* March 17, 1899; the award of damages, September 22, 1900.

An account of the car falling into the Patapsco can be found in the *Sun,* April 8, 1913.

The *Herald,* May 19, 1894, related the wild ride of Traction Company cable car No. 3.

Mention is made of the "national boulevard" and its paralleling electric railway in the *World,* March 4, 1893. As to the transfer of trucks, the *News,* August 21, 1903, said, "that if the new road should decide to do so, it could change at Ellicott City the truck used under its cars, substituting a truck of the gauge used by United Railways, and then the cars could be run through Baltimore to Washington without requiring passengers to change." The interurban had two other options, simply having patrons transfer between cars at Ellicott City or having a third rail laid inside the United's wide gauge trackage.

For details concerning the acquisition of the Baltimore electric light companies, see *Sun* and *American,* February 1, 1899, as

well as King's *Consolidated Of Baltimore,* 1950.

Grover C. Shipley recalled some interesting details about the Huntingdon Avenue viaduct in the *Sunday Sun Magazine,* November 19, 1967, though he errs in several facts about the structure. It spanned Stony Run, not Western Run, and was built by City & Suburban two or three years prior to the 1897 date mentioned in the article.

On October 1, 1918, the "traditional" fare of five cents on the streetcars was increased to six cents. Because of the awkward amount. the company tried using paper tickets. These were unpopular with the riders; so, on February 1, 1919, metal tokens or "car checks" were substituted. *Sun,* January 31, 1919; *Star,* January 31, 1919 and October 27, 1919.

Like all good railway companies when traction was at its zenith, the United Railways had a number of elegant private cars. This office car, the *Eloise,* had been converted from a former Central Railway passenger car in 1900. (Its name was a combination of the names of then-General Manager House's daughters, Ella and Louise.) It was fitted out with wicker chairs for official inspection trips; built-in desks could be lowered from the car sides when needed. (Louis C. Mueller Collection)

The configuration of the land required the Baltimore companies to construct some impressive bridges, but little cut and fill was necessary. One exception was on the former Columbia & Maryland between Catonsville and Ellicott City. This was the "deep cut," where the line passed under the Westchester Avenue bridge. (John S. Thomsen)

During the summer months, Queen Anne's lace and black-eyed Susans practically obscured the old right of way, but when the frost killed off the vegetation, and especially with a frosting of snow, the old line to Ellicott City could be easily traced for years after abandonment. (Michael R. Farrell)

THE ART OF ABANDONMENT

At precisely ten minutes to six on a bitingly cold December evening during 1953, a streamlined car turned into the loop at Rolling Road and Edmondson Avenue accompanied by the sound of squealing flanges. A man stopped reading, rose from his seat, grasped the handholds at either side of the aisle, and maneuvered his way toward the front doors. A strong grip, combined with a certain amount of dexterity, was necessary to prevent his being flung back into a seat by the centrifugal force as the rigid car body pivoted on its kingpins while negotiating the sharp curve.

There was no necessity for his haste. The act was a reflexive one, the result of long years of commuting on the Ellicott City line. It was only a matter of seconds before the car halted in front of the little waiting station, where there would have been ample time to finish reading his article.

However, for over a year, since September 1952, he no longer folded his newspaper under his arm, paid the zone fare to the conductor as he alighted from the red-painted semi-convertible (which had carried him directly from downtown Baltimore on the No. 14 line), and found himself a mere block from his home. Now, Rolling Road was the turnback for through service on the line. He grumbled to himself as he pulled up his coat collar against the stiff wind blowing directly into his face as he stood on the graveled platform; it was necessary to take a No. 9 shuttle car for the remaining mile of his journey.

This car ran between Catonsville Junction and the fire station on Main Street in Ellicott City on a schedule which ranged from fifteen-minute to hourly intervals. Some of the trips made close connections with the cars from town, others did not. The man knew from experience that he would have a twenty-five-minute wait. As he cupped his hands to light a cigarette, he noticed the first big flakes of a wet snow by the glare of the cluster of bare light bulbs

the company had attached high up on the wooden pole in front of the waiting station.

After a moment or two of shivering, the man made a decision. Stepping with care to avoid the grease which coated the web and base of the curving rails and had also spattered on the ties and ballast, he left the loop and crunched his way along the cinder pathway beside the track. Ten minutes later, just as he turned away from the tracks for the short trek up the hill to his home, the headlight of the car from Ellicott City could be seen approaching on its way to the Junction. It would not be back past his stop on its return trip for another fifteen minutes.

The man seldom rode the No. 9 cars thereafter. Thus, he joined many of his neighbors who had found ways to avoid the inconvenience of changing cars in making the trip to and from downtown. Not many walked, but it was a simple matter to obtain a lift to Catonsville Junction if one did not care to drive his own automobile to a point where it was possible to board a through No. 8 or No. 14 car, leaving his own automobile parked for his return. Others found it more convenient to form a car pool, and the Transit Company lost three fares in each direction for every person who chose this option.

It is of little wonder then that, when the company took a rider count on the Ellicott City line in January 1954, it found an average of only 6.3 riders on fifty-one weekday round trips. On Saturdays and Sundays, when only thirty-five runs were scheduled, 6.5 and 3.3 fares respectively per trip were dropped into the box. With figures such as these to present to the Public Service Commission, the Baltimore Transit Company had a strong case for abandonment, and even the most optimistic railfan realized that the end of the No. 9 line was rapidly drawing near.

What most did not comprehend though, in blaming the Fitzgerald brothers and their National City Lines for this turn of events, was that NCL was merely the instrument

(and a willing one) for ending streetcar service to Ellicott City and many other places. The sequence of events had actually begun in the World War I era.

It has been noted in the narrative portion of this story that the street railway company got into the bus business only to offset the loss of passengers to independent operators. In this it had the strong backing of the Public Service Commission. As far as can be ascertained, both the railway company and the PSC maintained this posture until the early 1920s, when, after investigative trips both in this country and abroad, members of the Commission began to push for the adoption of trackless trolley lines as a means of expanding the transportation system of Baltimore.

Gradually the idea of using buses (mainly on auxiliary lines) gained acceptance. By the time that the United Railways & Electric Company had emerged from bankruptcy in 1935 as the Baltimore Transit Company, both the company and its public overseers agreed in principle that streetcars should be used on the routes with the heaviest traffic, trackless trolleys on those of medium density, and buses on feeder lines.

From an objective viewpoint, one can find little to fault with this arrangement, except that it was proposed to convert the outer extremities of some heavily traveled car lines to bus operation when the investment in track and overhead had been depreciated. This arrangement would result in persons who had purchased homes in the vicinity of these lines, with the expectation of enjoying a through ride to the downtown area, being forced to change vehicles at some point on their journeys. In theory, this may not have seemed a great inconvenience; in practice, it undoubtedly provided an impetus for many persons to purchase automobiles. Thus mobile, these erstwhile patrons found it convenient to ride the streetcars only on rare occasions such as when heavy snowfalls engulfed the

Just prior to World War II, all except rush-hour service on the Ellicott City route was cut back at this crossover on Edmondson Avenue, opposite Catonsville Junction. Windows of semi-convertible slid upward into roof pockets, giving riders plenty of fresh air. (Louis C. Mueller Collection)

Though this scene is not on the Ellicott City line, it underlines the fact that some routes were written off years ahead of actual abandonment. In advance of taking up the No. 29 line tracks in June 1947, this pit was dug at Lake and Roland Avenues in order that the BTC could service the lone car assigned to the No. 24 Lakeside Shuttle line, which would then be isolated from the rest of the system. The "orphan" was locked at night in a cage built around the pit for over two years until the route was discontinued. No such luxury was afforded the No. 9 line; its three cars were merely secured to the track at Rolling Road loop. (Henry S. Wells, Jr., photo)

The United promoted the modern "kiss 'n' ride" idea as early as 1926. In this advertisement, the company advised commuters to leave their autos with their wives and take the streetcar from the Bedford Square station to town. (UR & E Company, Willem Wirtz)

city — times when the company least appreciated them.

During the 1930s and 1940s, a number of these cutbacks were made, for instance, on the No. 5 line at Manhattan loop, the No. 19 at Parkville, and the No. 23 at Back River.

The cutback of the No. 23 line was precipitated by "an act of God." In August 1933, a hurricane severely damaged the bridge over Back River. Rather than go to the expense of repairing the span, the United simply put a shuttle car on the isolated portion of the route between Back and Middle Rivers. This jerkwater operation began August 24, 1933, and was replaced by a bus almost exactly one year later. The same storm washed away much of the fill in the vicinity of Shallow Creek on the portion of the loop between Bay Shore Park and Fort Howard. The company never repaired this damage either, and, though No. 26 cars still ran to both places, the former practice of making a circuit of the loop was no longer possible.

The Ellicott City line, however, saw service cut by a most unusual method. As far back as December 1, 1927, the Ellicott City route had been assigned two numbers. One line, designated No. 14, operated from Charles and Lexington Streets to Rolling Road. The other, given the route number 9, duplicated this run, but continued past Rolling Road to Ellicott City.

This arrangement continued until 1941, when the Baltimore Transit Company petitioned the Public Service Commission to allow it to cut back the No. 14 line at the city boundary (North Bend) and continue service on the remainder of the 9-14 route as a shuttle operation. (It should be stressed that this was long before National City Lines entered the local picture.) The object of this proposal was to allow the use of the modern PCC cars on the city portion of the line. Double-ended semi-convertibles would continue to serve the county segment. The PCCs could not be operated all the way through, as there was no loop at Ellicott City, and the configuration of the land precluded locating one there.

There was considerable opposition to the plan; on May 20, 1941, the PSC announced its decision, which required the railway company to loop the No. 14 line at Rolling Road, rather than at North Bend. In addition, the Commission told the BTC that during rush hours, including Saturdays, the older No. 9 cars must be operated through to downtown Baltimore. Curtailment of service occasioned by the manpower shortage during World War II resulted in the elimination of Saturday service; but the old cars of the No. 9 line continued going downtown during rush hours, Monday through Friday, until August 8, 1952, when they were cut back to a shuttle running between Ellicott City and a crossover on Edmondson Avenue at Catonsville Junction.

This setup lasted until September 18, 1954, at which time the streetcars on the No. 14 line were replaced by buses. Several weeks earlier, on July 22nd, the Transit Company had petitioned for total abandonment of the No. 9 line, which would be

The Ellicott City line was a favorite haunt of railfans. Many chose to photograph cars from the B & O overpass. Until the late 1940s, one could reach Ellicott City by both streetcar and train. The railroad survives today for freight service. (John S. Thomsen)

completely isolated from the rest of the company's trackage when the No. 14 line was taken up. (The term Catonsville Junction was by then a misnomer, as there had been no physical connection between the tracks on Edmondson Avenue and the loop of the No. 8 Catonsville line for many years.)

In light of the small number of patrons who were now being carried on the cars, there is no doubt that the company was losing money on the No. 9 line. However, if considered as part of an integrated system, i.e., combined with the No. 14 line as was the former practice, the route was admittedly operated at "a substantial profit," according to the PSC.

Open to question were the company's claims of operating losses of $58,640 in 1953, and $46,660 in 1954. As was the usual railway practice, these totals included allocations of system costs, many of which would not be affected by the discontinuance of the No. 9 route. Among the items of expense reported in 1954, which appear questionable, was a charge of $4,342 to way and track. After an inspection of the three miles of double-tracked

right of way, the Public Service Commission's Director of Transportation reported "that the ties throughout the route are generally in poor condition and that more than 75 percent of them should be replaced; ballast is badly needed in many places; some rail joints are depressed; rails are in need of realignment; practically all the curves require replacement."

At the same time, he found the three semi-convertible cars on the line, all more than thirty-five years old, to be "antiquated and in very poor condition." Therefore, the Commission could not understand the item of $4,799 for maintenance of vehicles. Even stranger was the inclusion of a figure of $2,440 for shop expense, as the cars were locked to the track at Rolling Road when not in service, and there was no means of transporting them to any shop or car house. Likewise, the PSC felt that the charge of $9,468 for depreciation to the route seemed "out of line with actuality." While there is no way to determine how the line would have fared if it had been properly maintained and modern, double-ended cars provided, it seems obvious that the company had deliberately let it run down for at least two decades.

It would also appear that the Public Service Commission must bear some of the blame for the deterioration of service, yet that body now came forth with the following profound rhetoric:

"If, for the ostensible purpose of effecting operating economies . . . the company is permitted to terminate through service at an outlying point short of the end of the route, and it then sets up that small segment of the line as a separate operating unit, it probably could show, in almost every instance, that the short segment is operated at a loss. If, after the separation occurs, the company fails to maintain the rail line and the equipment used thereon, it might well make out what would appear to be a strong case for total abandonment of service on the outlying portion of the line.

"By this process the company could, in effect, ultimately terminate its service on almost any of its suburban lines at any selected point.

"But the Commission does not believe that this is something that the company can itself do, or something that the Commission should permit. As we said

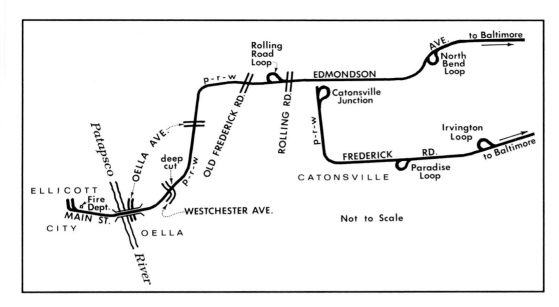

The Ellicott City-Catonsville area in 1952-54. At this time, No. 9 Ellicott City shuttle cars terminated at Catonsville Junction, opposite the No. 8 Frederick Road line.

in a case concerning another transit company:

'On any transit system it is only reasonable to expect that, as the end of the route is approached, traffic will become lighter. If we were to carry the jurisdictional division one step further, it might be argued that each zone . . . should be treated as a separate and distinct entity. That such treatment would inevitably militate against the best interests of the bus riding public is readily seen. (43 PSC Md. 153, page 156.)"

The report went on to state that, if rail service was to be continued, the line must be practically rebuilt and new cars provided. At the same time, the Commission pointed out, the present volume of traffic and future prospects did not justify spending the large sum of money that this would require.

The solution, as might have been expected, was to take off the streetcars and substitute bus service. A serious drawback to this plan was that the Ellicott City line operated almost exclusively over private right of way, and few of the existing county roads ran in close proximity to it.

Nevertheless, the bus line began running June 19, 1955, on a six-month trial basis,

and the streetcar tracks were taken up. Many of the patrons who had depended on the streetcars were now isolated from convenient public transportation. At the same time, the bus service along the county roads failed to attract many passengers. Its little Ford buses made poor time over the hilly and circuitous routing, and potential riders in the area circumjacent to the former rail right of way saw little reason to abandon their automobiles merely for the sake of getting to Catonsville Junction. Accordingly, after a brief trial period, the bus line was withdrawn on February 2, 1957.

NOTES AND COMMENTS:

The "three fares" that the company lost for each rider who deserted the cars, consisted of the base fare plus two zone fares. Commuters could buy books of tickets at a reduced price. Thus, in 1941, for example, a regular rider could make the one-way trip from Ellicott City to downtown Baltimore for a total of 19½ cents.

Much of the statistical material, as well as the quotations, cited in "The Art of Abandonment" is from Case 5360, Order 51390, which is chronicled in *Maryland Public Service Commission Report,* 1955, pp. 78-83.

"The (Public Service) Commission has suggested that the United, following the precedent that it established with the Charles Street buses, be itself the opera-

tor of the supplementary bus service." *American* December 20, 1921.

With reference to the types of vehicles to be used, *Baltimore Transit Annual Report, 1940* (issued in the spring of 1941) explained its current policy: "In former reports we have stated that in the present state of the art, we believe that modern rail cars are most efficient for heavily traveled lines, trackless trolleys for medium, and buses for lighter traffic. Nothing has occurred in the past year to change that principle." After a paragraph setting forth reasons why the company favored streetcars for carrying heavy traffic, the report went on: ". . . our present policy is to work towards supplying our base city service as quickly as possible with new cars. If war-

time conditions do not become too severe, that goal is now in sight. After that has been accomplished, if future conditions seem to justify a gradual change to other forms of vehicles, we can begin to concentrate the present new cars on certain lines to make them 100 percent with this type and introduce the other forms on certain other lines." (Note to those too young to remember this period and who sense an ambiguity in the words "if wartime conditions do not become too severe" in a report prepared almost eight months before Pearl Harbor — most of Europe and Asia had been at war since 1939, and much of the industry of the United States was overwhelmed by war production for "our allies" and "in the national defense.")

The streetcar pictured could seat fifty-two passengers. To handle the same number of commuters, at an average of one and a half bodies per automobile (the figure often cited at the time), would require thirty-four automobiles. This ad stated that, in 1925, more than 3,280,000 students were carried to and from city public schools in safety, using school tickets costing five cents each. Those under twelve rode for four cents each. (UR & E Company, Willem Wirtz)

THE LEMMING STRAIN WAS STRONG

Such a detailed overall history of the street railways of Baltimore has never been presented previously. Therefore, it undoubtedly contains errors of commission and omission despite the thousands of hours of research done by dozens of people which have gone into it. While it has been presented as objectively as is possible, still the manner in which the facts have been brought out basically represents the sentiments of one person; for serious students of railway history, a few paragraphs of subjective comments may give an insight into what made the words fall into place as they did.

In the five years or so spent in putting this book together, one was constantly struck by the fact that what appeared to be the most practical way of transporting the city's population from here to there and back was almost constantly teetering on the brink of disaster.

It was difficult to put one's finger on a theme which would tie the complexities of the diverse situations into a discernible pattern. Finally, the thought occurred that the street railways had a predilection toward the ways of the lemming — that distant Arctic relative of the field mouse — which has an innate tendency toward self-destruction.

Take the acceptance of the park tax. At a time when all comparable cities had a fare of five cents, the local applicants for a franchise made no objection to a park tax. Since they had already agreed to accept a fare of four cents a passenger, this meant that any increase would result in a fare of an awkward amount.

A suspicion persists that in reality they expected to have this tax abated, but they overlooked the tenacity with which a governmental agency holds on to any source of revenue. As to the contention that the grantees of the franchise were sincere in asking only a four-cent fare in their petition for a franchise — it took less than five years before they were asking permission for an increase.

Colleague John Thomsen hastens to point out that it is far from clear that the company could not have survived marginally on a four-cent fare under normal conditions. It must be admitted that the Baltimore City Passenger Railway was soon beset with the inflation caused by a long war; that in about five years costs apparently more than doubled, while the base fare went up only 40 percent; and that, while an additional charge for transfers was put into effect, only about 10 percent of the passengers used these.

On the other hand, patronage can be expected to increase markedly during wartime periods. Such a situation occurred during World War II when the Baltimore Transit Company earned a profit which confounded at least some of the experts. Of course, the two cases are not completely analogous — City Passenger's patronage continued to rise after 1865, while Baltimore Transit's postwar business took a nosedive as many of its patrons returned to their automobiles.

Another way in which the company failed to protect its future interests was in its acquiescence in allowing the establishment of competing lines. At first blush, it would appear that the company could have done little to combat the decrees of the City Council which allowed other companies into the field. However, they in part brought the problem on themselves. The Baltimore City Passenger Railway drew constant criticism for its failure to develop fully the franchises which it did hold, especially the South Baltimore and Canton lines, and it built the Charles Street line only under threat of charter revocation.

Another weakness was the failure of the railway companies as a whole to prevent the encroachment upon their private domain by other types of vehicles. They cannot be faulted for building their tracks to a wide gauge (5 feet 4½ inches) that would allow their use by other vehicles on the city streets. After all, they were in a sense interlopers and had to accept the gauge as a franchise requirement, which incidentally gives some idea of the condition of the city streets.

However, as early as 1887, the Baltimore, Catonsville & Ellicott's Mills Passenger Railway allowed its tracks on the city portion of Frederick Road to be moved to the center of the street in order to widen the roadbed. Beginning with this incident, the companies continually permitted their private rights of way to be eroded by the moving of the streetcars into direct confrontation with other traffic. This, more than anything else the companies did, contained the seeds of self-destruction. As the automobile became more and more a factor in the overcrowding of the streets, the fact that much of the width of the present roadways had resulted from the addition of the streetcars' private rights of way to the paved highway was ignored.

Again Thomsen suggests that this carries too strong an implication that the United Railways could have successfully resisted street widening and that it would have been likely to lose important governmental goodwill in the attempt.

It is a moot question whether the company could have actually blocked the street widening advocates; the point is that they made no real try. Several decades earlier, various companies had waged successful

View of Harford Road at Erdman Avenue on October 9, 1910 shows conditions that prevailed on many of today's broad thoroughfares in earlier days. In light of the fact that the railway companies' private rights of way were taken over for use by automobile and truck traffic, condemnation of the trolleys as interlopers by city officials in later years seemed incomprehensible to supporters of the streetcars. (Nixon/Gerding Collection)

fights, against strong opposition from city officials, to overcome opposition to the use of electric propulsion and to the operation of cars on certain streets. With regard to governmental goodwill, the company claimed in the 1920s that it was paying the highest taxes of any street railway in the country, so what great effect could the loss of governmental goodwill have had?

One of the fundamental reasons for the course of self-destruction practiced by the lemmings is a proclivity to panic when encountering an obstacle in their paths. Consider then the course of action taken by Baltimore Traction and City Passenger at the time both were unable to convert to electric operation. In the face of statements from all and sundry officials that they did

not want to run cable lines, they promptly put in the expensive systems. The prohibitive costs were passed on to future generations, as these investments were part of the $64 million capitalization inherited by the United Railways in 1899, by which time the cable systems were all but a memory.

How could the course plotted by the big consolidation of 1899 be called anything but self-destruction? In 1900, the United was committed to paying out 46 percent of its gross revenues for the purpose of meeting the interest on its debts. An additional 9 percent went to the city fathers in the form of the park tax, leaving only 45 percent of total income to meet operating expenses, finance improvements, and, with luck, pay dividends.

But the potential of the street railway operation overcame even this obstacle, and after some adroit financial maneuvering in 1906, the company climbed to the highest point of its checkered career. During the half-dozen years preceding the entry of the United States into World War I, the United paid regular 4 percent dividends, while at the same time acquiring new cars annually and erecting numerous car houses and power stations. However, even in this prosperous period, one phase of the business was sliding backward. In contrast with the old days, when track extensions were constructed against the hope of future patronage, from about 1915 on, the United pursued a policy of laying new rails into an area only after the landowners agreed to

A scene that was repeated with variations many times a day. The motorman was not always so patient. This incident took place on Park Avenue and Clay Street, just south of Saratoga Street. (UR & E Company, Willem Wirtz)

reimburse the railway for the losses incurred during the period in which the subdivisions were developing.

Needless to say, few promoters were willing or able to do this. With the exception of some trackage on Liberty Heights Avenue, built under prodding by the Public Service Commission, only the relatively short line to Guilford (at Bedford Square) and the even shorter Idlewylde Railway on Regester Avenue were constructed during this period. After the war, the rapid rise in wages and the cost of materials again pushed the company into a financial position where it was unable to extend its lines even if it had had the desire to do so.

In the early 1920s, the United was again in extreme disfavor with the general public. It was caught in a squeeze between the inflation of the postwar period and its inability to raise fares to a degree which would keep pace with the rising pay scales.

To mitigate this difficulty, the company took the logical step of reducing the number of "platform" men (motormen and con-

ductors) needed to run the cars. Among the first moves was rebuilding about thirty of the older single-truck cars into one-man vehicles. This had become practical with the development of safety devices which would stop a car automatically in the event that the motorman became incapacitated.

The arrangement worked fairly well on jerkwater lines, but was not thought practical for more heavily traveled routes. For these, one hundred trailers had been bought in 1920. These were without motors and were intended to be pulled behind motor cars already on the property. While the multiple-unit trains had worked well on the Sparrows Point line, the trailers proved a dismal failure. Even though the pulling cars were remotored, the two-car units were still underpowered and slow. Braking ability was likewise deficient, if not downright unsafe. But, worst of all, from the public's viewpoint, the spartan wooden seating arrangements were definitely lacking in comfort.

Next the company turned to the single-truck Birney cars. They were even worse

than the trailers. While these standardized cars could travel more rapidly, overall speed was held down by the one narrow doorway used for both entrance and egress. Especially during rush hours, this greatly increased what, in rapid transit parlance, is termed "dwell time" — that portion of a trip spent in picking up and discharging passengers.

By the mid-1920s, it was realized that the trailers and the Birneys were not the answer; neither was a pair of experimental cars of the Peter Witt design built by Brill in 1924. All of these cars had the same flaw. Rather than speeding up schedules, they actually slowed them down. It was then decided to reconstruct and modernize older cars already owned by the company. The first try was to rebuild two older semi-convertibles into a permanently-coupled train. However, the savings from the experiment were almost completely offset by the expense of making the alterations.

The next attempt consisted of splicing older semi-convertibles and obsolete open summer cars into articulated units. At the same time, management went back to its

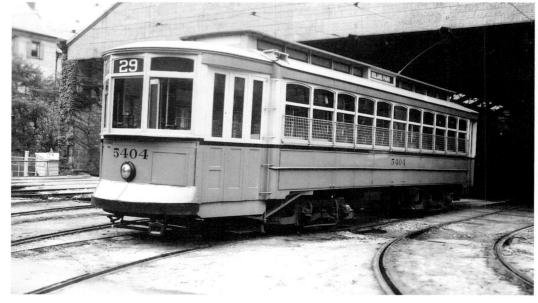

A car crossing the bridge over Gwynn Falls at Wetheredsville Road, just east of Dickeyville. While the railway company had a fair amount of such private right of way in the suburban areas, once the cars got close to town, at least in the later days, they had to take to the center of public roadways and became slowed in the tangle of traffic. (Robert W. Janssen Collection)

An obviously newly-painted and refurbished semi-convertible sits outside Roland Park car house. Despite the company's oft-repeated statistics that the public could save money by riding such vehicles, its patrons had fallen in love with the automobile, and no amount of wooing would win them back to streetcars. (Robert L. Krueger Collection)

original approach — to convert older cars to one-man operation. This time, it used double-truck cars and developed a versatile vehicle.

It must be admitted that these articulated cars and rebuilt double-truck, one-man cars did their jobs well. Many remained in service for twenty more years, but there is no getting around the fact that many of the public considered them to be obsolete and old-fashioned. Rationalize as you will, the evidence is irrefutable that patrons rapidly drifted away to ride brand-new buses or to purchase styled-right-to-the-minute automobiles.

Probably the most compelling reason for the demise of the streetcars in Baltimore

was that they came to be regarded as intruders on the very roadways, which in many cases, had originally been their own private domain. Again, the behavior of the street railways resembled that of the lemming, which at times during migration periods pushes blindly on with little regard for consequences — to end its existence by drowning in the sea. Time after time, the companies agreed to sacrifice their private rights of way so as to enable the roadbeds to be widened, thus surrendering the advantages of operating on unobstructed pathways.

As time went on, the manner in which many of the broad highways had originated was forgotten, and the motorists began to

resent the curse of slippery rails, safety pylons, and ponderous articulated units. With the rise of the expressway syndrome during the 1950s, this type of roadway was hailed as the salvation of the city from its traffic problems. Already the proliferation of the automobile had led to several one-way streets, with the rail vehicles effectively barred from them. If only the remaining two-way arterial streets could be made one-way, this stopgap measure would suffice until the expressways could be built. With this kind of thinking prevailing, the last streetcar lines were abandoned in November 1963. In 1992, however, many of the inner-city expressways remained unbuilt, and two modes of rail rapid transit have appeared. All, it seems, is not lost.

NOTES AND COMMENTS:

The matter of the acceptance of the park tax is covered fully in the opening pages of this book.

One classic example of a street railway company "fighting City Hall" is the legal battle between the Lake Roland Elevated and the city authorities of Baltimore over the right to lay double tracks on Lexington Street between North (now Guilford Avenue) and Charles Streets. This case was appealed all the way up to the United States Supreme Court. The railway proved that a double-track line had been permitted between Baltimore and Saratoga on Charles Street, a narrower thoroughfare. Nevertheless, the Court upheld the single-track restriction on Lexington Street, although it did reject the City's attempt to require a new franchise application for even this single track. Mayor and City Council of Baltimore v. Baltimore Title & Guarantee Co., *Supreme Court Reporter,* vol. 17, pp. 696-701 (1896-97).

In 1930, the United Railways engaged in a more successful effort. The Supreme Court upheld its request for a ten-cent fare against the opposition of the Public Service Commission. United Railways v. West, *Supreme Court Reporter,* vol. 50, pp. 123-139 (1929-30).

During 1926, the United Railways launched an advertising campaign in the newspapers to acquaint the public with its contributions to the city. One of these,

among many of the ads reprinted in *Trolley Topics* during the year, includes the sentence, "Your street car company is the highest taxed street railway in America."

The 46 percent debt service figure appeared in the *Electric Railway Journal,* vol. 57, pp. 1053-1054 (1921).

The Idlewylde Railway commenced operation on or about August 31, 1916, on a route extending eastward from York Road on Regester Avenue. The line was about two-thirds of a mile long. The United Railways provided men and cars under an operating arrangement. Service was apparently discontinued as of December 31, 1921, and the company's franchise revoked by county order the following August 1st. *Maryland Public Service Commission Report,* 1916 and A. T. Clark notes.

According to George F. Nixon notes, the one hundred steel trailers purchased in 1920 were used on the Nos. 2, 4, 6, 7, 10, 15, 26, and 31 routes and as far as Howard Park on the No. 32 line.

The following account from the *Evening Sun,* November 10, 1920, though lacking in technical eloquence, provides an insight into the layman's evaluation of the trailer experiment, which lasted until 1930. "We arrived at Calverton at 5:40, fifteen minutes late, a (2600 series) car came pulling one of the new trailers. The United Railways acquired the new (2600 series) cars rather recently for the Sparrows Point

line. It was found that they were slower than the old (2400 series), because the motors were built for stronger current [*sic*]. Now they have transferred a number of these cars to the Edmondson Avenue line with an even weaker current, and loaded them with trailers."

To pull the trailers, the United used the following semi-convertibles: Nos. 2401-2480, purchased 1907, later renumbered 5301-5379 (one was destroyed before renumbering); 401-426, purchased 1913, later renumbered 5500-5525; 2601-2650, purchased 1919, later renumbered 5825-5874. The 2600 series cars came equipped to handle trailers, but the 400 and 2400 series cars were remodeled with enclosed platforms and fitted with rear electric marker lamps and Tomlinson couplers. In light of the previous quote from the *Evening Sun,* it would appear that the company assigned cars from the Bay Shore line to other routes in the off season.

Details on other cars mentioned will be found under the notes on the chapters entitled "Brill Semi-Convertibles" and "Articulated Units and Permanently-Coupled Trains."

Traffic Director Henry Barnes devoted much of his autobiography, *The Man With The Red And Green Eyes,* to his days in Baltimore.

On the eve of World War II, Baltimore's main shopping district intersection looked like this. Though streamlined cars were making inroads, the semi-convertibles were still much in evidence. A No. 4 line car is turning onto the single block of North Howard Street which still contained tracks. By the summer of 1941, the Windsor Hills cars would be routed up Park Avenue and the red and yellow bricks in foreground would be extended to meet similiar paving on Saratoga Street. (Enoch Pratt Library, Wendell Phillips photo)

BRILL SEMI-CONVERTIBLES

The time — early afternoon in late October of 1905. The place — any of a number of terminal points of the United Railways. The attraction — the car which was to become the backbone of streetcar service in Baltimore, a Brill semi- convertible.

In those days, innocent of movies and television, a new type of trolley passing along the streets could create tremendous excitement. The ending of October or the first part of November often coincides with Indian summer in Baltimore. On a Sunday, this weather would draw quite a multitude to Druid Hill Park, who, strolling leisurely homeward, could have seen one of the brand new cars as it clattered across the special work at the Fulton Avenue entrance.

The time and the scene might well have been symbolic. Fall then, as now, often came with a vengeance in the Monumental City. One awakened to a nippy morning, the grass covered with hoarfrost, the trees tinted with red and yellow. The days rapidly became colder. Soon the brisk autumn winds were swirling leaves around the elegant brownstone fronts on Park Avenue and the trim row houses with the inevitable marble steps which stretched in almost unbroken ranks eastward from Frederick Avenue to beyond Patterson Park, and from above North Avenue south almost to Ferry Bar.

Then, suddenly, there was Indian summer. The bitter-sweetness of this last balmy spell, tempered by an occasional chilly breeze, was mindful of the long winter just ahead.

So it was with the United. Born of the consolidation of 1899, when all was sunshine and brightness, United now embarked upon lean times. Much of the anticipated savings of consolidation had proved illusive, a long-range hope at best. Yet, these new cars held a promise that all might work out well, though there were to be many dark, dreary days ahead for the company.

The cars were bright and big. The warm red of the body contrasted with cream above the sills and liberal silver striping. This was something of a throwback to the days of yore, when Baltimore cars glistened in rainbow hues of green, blue, salmon, and — honestly — shocking pink. With consolidation, all cars were repainted a somewhat melancholy dark red, relieved only by the single word "United" inscribed in black along either side.

The semi-convertibles represented the ultimate compromise of the problem that had long been perplexing traction companies — whether to use open or closed cars. For years, managements in areas with a changeable climate had run open cars during the warm months and closed cars in the cold ones. This was never a really successful solution, as in spring and fall there were invariably periods when unseasonably cool weather caused complaints about the use of the open vehicles. Even during the summer months, the open cars, while a pleasure during fair days and nights, were a source of irritation during driving rains, as it was impossible to keep the interiors even reasonably dry.

As an initial gambit, two sets of bodies — open and closed — were employed, allowing the same trucks and motors to serve all year long. These cars were subject to the same objections as the separate ones; with the additional time-consuming task of transferring the bodies twice a year. The next development was the convertible car. These were basically closed bodies with the entire window panels removable during warm weather. This design still failed to solve the basic problems: rapid conversion in cool weather and weathertightness.

The J. G. Brill Company came up with a clever solution in its semi-convertibles. In these cars, raising the lower sashes carried the uppers into pockets in the side roofs. This produced almost the same effect as completely removing the side panels of a convertible, with the added convenience of

instant conversion in bad weather. Brill's 1905 models included, according to the company, "the recent improvements which eliminate the sash trunnions and runways, formerly used, and (the window system) simplifies the method of connecting each pair of sashes."

This feature could be readily seen, yet there were other innovations which would not be noted by the casual observer. Among these was a cantilever arrangement by which angle irons reinforcing the knees at the center of the platforms were brought 4 feet 8 inches back of the center of the body bolsters. This carried a portion of the platform load directly back to the trucks without strain to the bottom framing. The cars were mounted on Brill's model No. 27-GE-1 trucks, short base double trucks, with solid forged side frames.

Boarding the cars brought a pleasant surprise, especially to the fair sex. Many of the previous cars presented a real challenge for those who were not dexterous. Especially was this true of the summer cars. One of the local papers had quipped "the running boards of the open cars are one of those high and mighty things which must come down." Another carried this commentary, "Too many (women) say that the high step is simply impossible; all of them say it is troublesome and dangerous." From the rail to the platform step of the semi-convertible was 15¾ inches; from the step to the platform, 14 inches; from the platform to the car floor, 9 inches.

The platform itself seemed strangely enclosed, as the cars were equipped with portable vestibules. The name "vestibule" is actually a misnomer in light of the general use of the term. The sides of the platform were open; the vestibule merely consisted of a frame, containing three panes of glass, mounted on the front of the vehicle between the dasher and the hood.

The platforms themselves measured five feet long. This, combined with a car body of 30 feet 8 inches, made the cars 40 feet 8

A three-car train races across the
Bear Creek bridge in 1920, when
the cars were only a year old. All
of the cars have motors, although
only two poles are raised. In later
years, two-car trains were the
maximum; often the rear car was a
trailer. (Nixon/Gerding Collection)

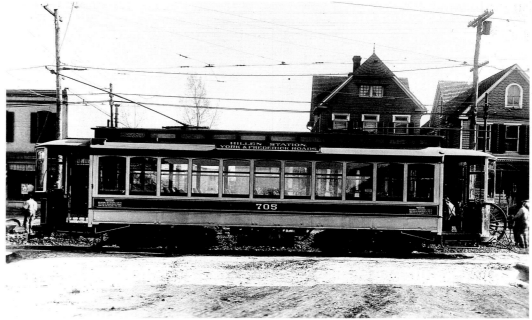

One of the first group of semi-convertibles sits in front of Irvington
car house. Among the changes
made over the years were the addition of platform doors and window screens and replacement of
wooden destination signs with the
roller-type sign in the clerestory.
This car was rebuilt into an articulated unit about 1925. (Louis C.
Mueller Collection)

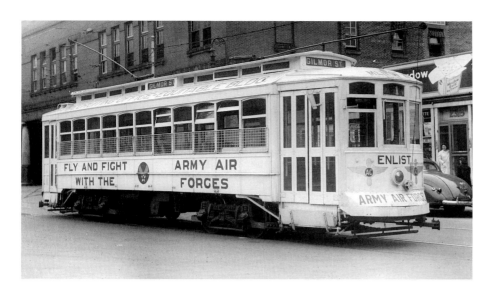

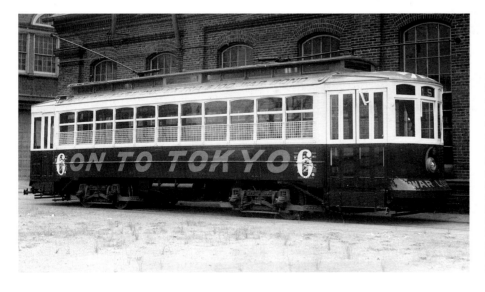

During World War II and the years immediately thereafter, the Transit Company "helped the cause" by providing painted semi-convertibles (and also PCCs) to advertise various patriotic or worthy community causes. Here we see three typical examples of the painter's talent. Bold lettering and brilliant colors were always used, hence the term "billboard cars." The double-ended semi-convertibles could run on any line in the system; at least sixteen cars were provided and carried such messages during this trying period. Top: No. 5632 promotes enlistment in the Army Air Forces. Center: No. 5664 (shown with Majors David T. Raisen and Edward X. Hallenberg) advertises for civilian help at Fort Meade. Bottom: "On To Tokyo" was popular post-Pearl Harbor theme. (BSM Collection)

Charles F. Buschman, who has prepared a series of scale drawings for the Baltimore Streetcar Museum, drew No. 5201, one of the first semi-convertibles, especially for this book.

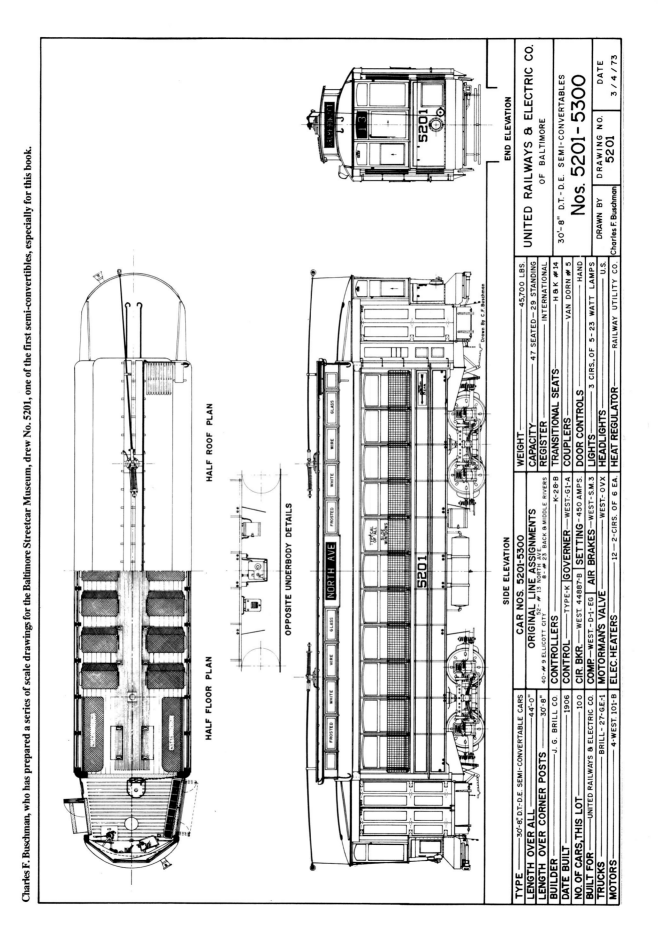

HALF ROOF PLAN

HALF FLOOR PLAN

OPPOSITE UNDERBODY DETAILS

END ELEVATION

SIDE ELEVATION

UNITED RAILWAYS & ELECTRIC CO.
OF BALTIMORE

30'-8" D.T.-D.E. SEMI-CONVERTABLES

Nos. 5201 - 5300

DRAWN BY	DRAWING NO.	DATE
Charles F. Buschman	5201	3/4/73

TYPE	30'-8" D.T.-D.E. SEMI-CONVERTABLE CARS	
LENGTH OVER ALL	44'-0"	
LENGTH OVER CORNER POSTS	30'-8"	
BUILDER	J. G. BRILL CO.	
DATE BUILT	1906	
NO. OF CARS, THIS LOT	100	
BUILT FOR	UNITED RAILWAYS & ELECTRIC CO.	
TRUCKS	BRILL-27-GE-1	
MOTORS	4-WEST. 101-B	

CAR NOS. 5201-5300		
ORIGINAL LINE ASSIGNMENTS		
40-# 9 ELLICOTT CITY	52-# 13 NORTH AVE.	18-# 23 BACK & MIDDLE RIVERS
CONTROLLERS	K-28-B	
CONTROL	TYPE-K	
CIR. BKR.	WEST. 44887-B	
COMP.	WEST.-D-1-EG	
MOTORMAN'S VALVE	WEST.-OVX	
ELEC. HEATERS	12-2-CIRS. OF 6 EA.	

WEIGHT	45,700 LBS.	
CAPACITY	47 SEATED-29 STANDING	
REGISTER	INTERNATIONAL	
TRANSITIONAL SEATS	H & K # 14	
COUPLERS	VAN DORN # 5	
DOOR CONTROLS	HAND	
LIGHTS	3 CIRS. OF 5-23 WATT LAMPS	
HEADLIGHTS	WEST-S.M.3	
HEAT REGULATOR	RAILWAY UTILITY CO.	
GOVERNER	WEST-G1-A	
SETTING	450 AMPS.	
AIR BRAKES	WEST-S.M.3	

NORTH AVE

5201

inches overall, the largest cars yet to operate in Baltimore. The width over the sill, including the panels, was 8 feet 2 inches. The spaciousness of the cars allowed for a seating capacity of forty-four.

A few years earlier, the company had plumped for longitudinal seating. This was obviously a ploy to accommodate more standees. The company's explanation was that this type of car aided in rapid entrance and egress. A further explanation was "that women frequently object to occupying one of the double seats with low-bred men."

These statements notwithstanding, a new seating arrangement was to become familiar. Seven transverse double seats were placed on either side of a center aisle. Longitudinal seats at each corner accommodated four passengers each. The once familiar seat covering of plush was replaced by the more practical rattan, though woodwork of the interior still extolled the splendor of an earlier day. It consisted of solid cherry, contrasting with ceilings of birch veneer.

For all of the designing ability of the Brill Company, its cars in Baltimore were furnished with several refinements developed by United Railways, of which the local company was quite proud. One, very obvious to anyone, was the flooring of the platforms. This consisted of ¾-inch by 2¼-inch boards, with a ¾-inch space between each. These boards were placed transversely and the flooring underneath raised slightly in the center, so that in rainy weather the water ran off either side through the troughs, thus keeping the platforms relatively dry. Another innovation, praised by the *Street Railway Journal* as an "interesting and novel device," was a means of oiling the truck center plates by a pipe leading from the floor of the car through the upper plates. This obviated the common difficulty of getting oil into the central portion between the plates.

It was early in December 1905, when the company decided that it had received enough of the cars to place them in regular service. Thus, just in time for the first snowfalls of the winter, the Brill semi-convertibles went forth to begin their thirty-five-year reign as the backbone of the Baltimore streetcar fleet. Similiar (though progressively improved) versions of this basic design would be built through 1919. By then, the Brill semi-convertible fleet would total an awesome 885 units.

A No. 10 line car lays over at Roland Park not long before being replaced by trackless trolleys. The door adjacent to the Red Cross placard was sealed when the car was made into a single-end vehicle in 1932. (Henry S. Wells, Jr. photo)

NOTES AND COMMENTS:

Unlike many other phases of this work, there was a plethora of information readily available on the semi-convertibles. For those interested in specific details on any particular group of these vehicles, the best single reference is the book, *Baltimore Streetcars, 1905-1963: The Semi-Convertible Era,* by Bernard J. Sachs, George F. Nixon, and Harold E. Cox (Baltimore Streetcar Museum, 1982). Space limitations here do not permit a complete rundown of all the changes incorporated in the vehicles over the years. While many facts were verified in the trade journals and elsewhere, I acknowledge my indebtedness for much of the material included on the semi-convertibles (both in this chapter and elsewhere in the book) to the following individuals: Henry S. Wells, Sr., Henry S. Wells, Jr., John S. Thomsen, George F. Nixon, Edward White, Louis F. Meyer, Robert W. Janssen, and Louis C. Mueller.

The following summary shows the years in which semi-convertible cars were delivered, the last numbers which they carried (assigned in 1922), and some of the distinguishing features (all cars built by Brill unless otherwise noted):

1905 (5001-5160) b, d, f

1905 (5161-5200) b, d

1906 (5201-5300) b, d

1907 (5301-5379) a, b, d, f

1910 (5380-5439) b, d, the first cars with roller signs on sides

1912 (5440-5499) b, d

1913 (5500-5559) b, d, the first cars to have lighted glass route numbers

1914 (5560-5644) c, d

1917 (5645-5744) c, d

1918 (5745-5824) c, e

1919 (5825-5884) a, c, e

a — This list totals 884, one less than the total number of cars purchased. The explanation is that one car of the 1907 delivery burned prior to the last renumbering and no allowance was made for it.

b — Originally open platform, enclosed with doors and folding steps, 1916-22.

c — Built with enclosed platforms.

d — eleven windows

e — thirteen windows

f — Forty of each group built by a Brill subsidiary: 1905, Stephenson; 1907, Kuhlman.

Despite its financial troubles, the United was able to float $1 million worth of car trust certificates in 1905. These bore 5 percent interest and were, of course, secured by the vehicles. The Safe Deposit & Trust Company was the trustee; the banking houses of Hambleton & Company and Baker, Watts & Company purchased the certificates. *Sun,* October 24, 1905.

The J. G. Brill Company emphasized the advantage in the design of its semi-convertible windows, which slid upward into the roof rather than downward into side pockets. Its carefully worded advertisement noted that "Having the window pockets in the roof rids the car of places that a certain class of passengers keep filthy." The American Car Company put the matter a bit more bluntly, explaining that "One of the worst features of the wall window pockets is that careless passengers use them for cuspidors."

ARTICULATED UNITS AND PERMANENTLY-COUPLED TRAINS

The standard Baltimore car was clearly the Brill semi-convertible. There were modifications and improvements in the 885-car fleet over the years, but all were variations on a basic design of the J. G. Brill Company. The PCC and even the Birney fell into a similar category. Although many specifications for all of these cars were designed to meet certain peculiarities of the operation in Baltimore, the basic design was one developed for the entire industry. Not so with the articulated cars, though. These represented a type of car design specifically adapted to local conditions and built at the Carroll Park shops of United Railways.

This is not to say that the idea originated in Baltimore. Articulated vehicles had operated in Boston and Richmond, but these were essentially two single-truck cars joined together, with no truck under the center articulated section — the so-called "two rooms and a bath" affairs. The United rejected this design because of the possibility of its breaking open when a switch was split. Other versions called for trucks located at the extreme ends of the cars to reduce overhang and allow covered passageways or the use of end doors interlocked with the control circuits so as to allow passenger movement between cars only when at rest. In the end, it was felt that the United's best prospects lay with the articulated two-car, three-truck combination, at that time used only by Milwaukee in this country.

Indeed, at first glance, the Baltimore cars did look strikingly similar to those being used in Milwaukee. A closer inspection would show, however, that there were many differences. Though the center drum — which was the key to the combination — was common to both, the Wisconsin cars looked more like early Peter Witts, joined front to back.

The first Baltimore articulated appeared on the streets in late 1924, but it is necessary to cast back a bit earlier to understand the reason for its adoption. Since the close of World War I, wages and material costs had risen drastically; people had moved farther out into the suburbs, and private automobiles had become serious competition for patronage, particularly the off-peak variety. Even the elimination of "all-day" parking in the downtown area had worked to the railway company's disad-

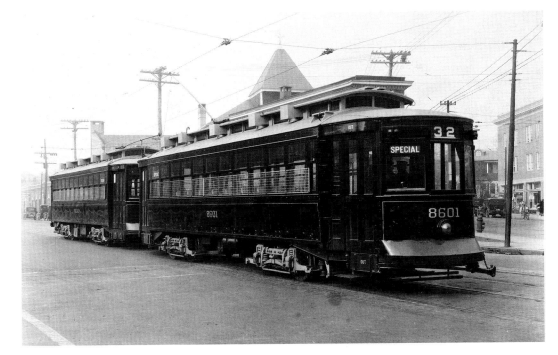

The first of the permanently-coupled trains built up from the 1902 open cars, No. 8601-8602, waits at Berwyn Avenue shortly after construction in 1924. Unlike the articulated units, each car of train had its own number. (Louis C. Mueller Collection)

Conductor stands on Druid Hill Avenue to warn oncoming traffic that this articulated unit is backing from Fulton Avenue into Park Terminal. The view is looking east. (George J. Voith)

vantage. The workers were thrown back on the streetcars when their all-day parking spots were eliminated, thus adding to the rush-hour peaks. The places thus left open drew the automobiles of many who formerly traveled by rail in the off-peak hours. Thus, at the same time, the rush-hour problem was aggravated, while traffic in off-peak hours declined markedly.

The United met the situation by installing some "skip-stop" operation and purchasing some lightweight Birney cars, as well as by remodeling some older two-man units to one-man operation. These steps were initially successful in halting the advance of expenses. But, it soon became imperative to effect still greater economies. The logical answer was greater use of one-man operation; in one fell swoop this would halve platform expense.

Upon studying the situation, the company decided to take one further step — in the words of Assistant General Manager S. E. Emmons: "Why not one-man operation, but in the form of two men to two cars?" A great advantage of this would be the elimination of the need for the motorman to handle the additional duties of collecting fares, issuing transfers, making change, etc. (Many will recall the notice

posted above his head on the two-man cars stating: "Please do not talk to the motorman when the car is in motion. Traffic demands his full attention.")

This was the reasoning behind the articulateds, for which the company claimed five major advantages:

(1) Reduced first cost. Less equipment, trucks, couplers, and other costly parts were needed. The elimination of one truck on each combination made construction simpler.

(2) At the same time, the unmotored center truck and the elimination of two vestibules reduced the weight per seat (or per passenger).

(3) The operating cost was reduced, not only by the obvious need for fewer men, but by a smaller consumption of energy. With fewer trucks and lighter weight, maintenance costs were reduced on the track as well as the cars.

(4) As the adjacent ends of each body were carried on one truck center, there was no overhang of the bodies beyond the trucks. This improved riding qualities, as the most comfortable ride in any car body is obtained midway between the truck centers, where there is a minimum amount of lateral

movement when entering curves and passing over crossings. In comparison to ordinary coupled cars, there was no nosing or rolling.

(5) The placement of electrical installations was more convenient, and wire connections were much simpler.

The company admitted one serious drawback to the cars, which was to prove a fatal flaw. They were not as flexible as the multiple-unit cars. "Were it possible to fill all the available space of the cars during a larger portion of the day, the problem would be solved." But the problem never was solved; as the differences between the peaks and valleys of the rush and non-rush hour service increased, the articulated units became correspondingly less efficient.

The question naturally arises — would it have been better instead to have spent the money used in their construction to buy more modern cars then under development, such as the two Peter Witts purchased from J. G. Brill in 1924? The answer will be left up to the reader. (It is certain that for some the response will be colored by sentimental recollections.) There is no doubt that the company was proud of its creations. And justly so. Not only did the articulateds solve the problem at hand; at the same time they

Formal portrait of an articulated unit. Differences in construction resulted in two different types. The 8100s consisted of two semiconvertibles butted end to end and had wooden bodies. The 8500s utilized two open cars plus salvaged material from the semis. The latter group had steel sides. (Louis C. Mueller Collection)

Anatomy of an articulated unit. Torn asunder to await the scrapper's torch, No. 8119 clearly shows that it was once two individual cars. Dark cylindrical object to right of bodies is rusted drum which once allowed passage between the sections. (George J. Voith)

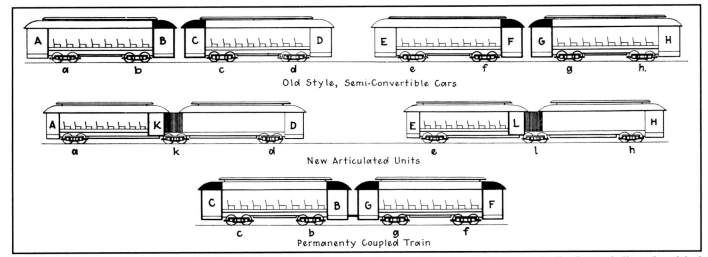

One permanently coupled train and two articulated units are made from four semi-convertible cars and two open car bodies. Letters indicate the original and final positions of trucks and vestibules. K and L are new center-exit doors; k and l are new trucks. Cross seats are removed from the first cars of the articulated units and placed in the open car bodies of the permanently coupled train.

allowed the United to reclaim surplus equipment which otherwise would have necessarily been written off.

Once the decision had been made to experiment with the articulated construction, two older semi-convertibles were selected. One vestibule and the adjacent truck were removed from each car. They were then joined by a hollow drum, which formed a covered passageway. This was set directly upon an unmotored third truck. Rubber buffers between the drum and car bulkheads completed the weatherproof arrangement. The cross seats in the forward car were replaced by longitudinal ones. Little change was made in the seating plan of the rear car, except that a semi-circular seat was installed on the back platform. Total seating capacity was eighty-seven.

The motorman was placed, as usual, at the center of the platform of the leading car; the conductor was positioned at the front, right, and side of the following section, adjacent to one set of doors. The only other doors were located in the front, at the motorman's right, where all passengers entered, with the option of obtaining a seat in the front portion or passing directly to the rear section. Loading and unloading were speeded tremendously as fares were collected only when passing the conductor, regardless of the point at which one boarded the car. Exit, of course, was only through the door controlled by the conductor. For reverse movements in switching and emergency situations, a control and air

brake were placed behind the semi-circular rear seat.

This experimental car was placed in service on September 29, 1924. Since it was pronounced entirely successful, plans were made to construct 110 of the units eventually.

There was considerable salvage from the two semi-convertibles used in the construction, including two vestibules, two trucks, cross seats, controllers, motors, and miscellaneous parts. It so happened that the company had on hand 110 twelve-bench summer car bodies, which had been lying idle since the company had removed open cars from service. These bodies had no equipment, sharing trucks, motors, controls, etc. with an equal number of closed bodies, which had been purchased as a set in 1902. The articulated program suggested a use for these. Combining the surplus parts from the semi-convertibles with a comparatively small amount of additional material to close in the sides, build windows, etc., the company could turn the open bodies into closed cars not unlike the standard Brill units.

One such car was remodeled at the same time the first articulated was being constructed and put in service, December 8, 1924. It was later decided that these units could be better utilized as two-car, permanently-coupled trains, and succeeding conversions followed this pattern. The accompanying diagram shows how the parts left over in building the articulateds were

utilized to construct the permanently-coupled cars.

Both the articulateds and the permanently-coupled cars required new motors, the old GE 80 type being replaced by Westinghouse model 306-CV4 motors. On the articulateds, two motors were mounted on each of the end trucks, the one under the center drum being an idler. On the permanently-coupled cars, one motor was placed on each truck. In addition, multiple-unit control replaced the type K controllers on the trains. The first permanently-coupled, two-car train went into service February 28, 1925.

In actuality, experiments with the permanently-coupled trains had preceded any consideration of the articulateds. The original plan had been to rebuild the closed cars which were the mates to the twelve-bench open ones. These were hand-braked, two-motor cars with Maximum Traction trucks. Two of them were rebuilt into a permanently-coupled train and provided with multiple-unit equipment and air brakes. In addition, the two central platforms of the unit had to be lengthened to provide double doors for entrance or exit. This experimental train was put in service on November 24, 1924. The company stated that this permanently-coupled train would not be duplicated as the expense involved offset the limited savings in platform labor (a train required a crew of three — a motorman and two conductors). While the technique of combining summer car bodies with salvaged vestibules and other parts was at first used principally in constructing permanently-coupled units, it was later applied to building articulated ones. Sixteen articulated cars of this type were eventually added to the United roster.

Available records indicate that there were a total of fifty-four articulated cars built between 1924 and 1931. Thirty-eight were from semi-convertibles and sixteen from 1902 open bodies. All were scrapped by 1948. Also, there were twelve per-manently-coupled trains built in 1925. One (scrapped in 1939) was from 1902 closed bodies and eleven from the 1902 open-body mates of the closed cars. All were retired in 1931 and scrapped in 1936.

NOTES AND COMMENTS:

In addition to the references which follow, much information on the cars described in this chapter came from conversations with David M. Novak, Henry S. Wells, Jr., George F. Nixon, and Col. John E. Merriken, the latter an authority on the Washington, Baltimore & Annapolis and other interurban lines in the area.

An abundance of material on these cars is contained in two articles in the *Electric Railway Journal* — "Rush-Hour Train Operation in Baltimore," vol. 65, pp. 577-580 (1925), and "Articulated Units Are Useful for Mass Transportation," vol. 70, pp. 482-484 (1927).

Some have questioned the statement that the articulated cars had a fatal flaw due to the impossibility of uncoupling the vehicles and operating them as individual cars, as could be done with single (powered) cars joined in multiple-unit trains. The latter *Electric Railway Journal* article cited above mentions that the articulated units and permanently-coupled trains had the advantage of simplicity and lower equipment cost. But, the piece went on to say, "There is no question about the greater flexibility of the multiple-unit train in its ability to meet varying traffic conditions and in the ease with which it can be modified as conditions change." The ar-ticle, which is credited to S. E. Emmons, assistant general manager of the United Railways, continues — "The choice . . . largely depends on original costs, the possibility of utilizing older equipment as trailers and whether the line under consideration is of major or secondary importance." One wonders about the last statement of the sentence in light of the fact that, in 1930, the local company was running cars with trailers attached between Highlandtown and Dundalk Junction on a 1¼ minute rush-hour headway. *Sun,* February 25, 1930. But, that is what the man said.

This 1930 Peter Witt car has not been slowed by the passing of time. Here it races along the private right of way at the Baltimore Streetcar Museum, much as it once ran alongside Gwynn Oak Avenue on its way to Woodlawn, when the car's speed captivated newspaper feature writers. "Golden-Glow" headlight illuminates lower front of car to a degree equal to that provided by interior dome lights. (Michael R. Farrell)

A car for any season. A Peter Witt heads up Garrison Boulevard near Liberty Heights Avenue with at least two feet of snow piled on top, during Palm Sunday blizzard in March 1942. (Roland Nuttrell)

THE PETER WITT CARS

Baltimore's original horse cars, way back in 1859, were reportedly obtained secondhand from one of the Philadelphia street railway companies. The first equipment built specifically for service in this city by Poole & Hunt of Woodberry seems to have been patterned very closely upon vehicles already in use elsewhere.

Thus was established a trend which continued for almost seventy years. Prior to 1899, the various independent Baltimore street railways spread their car orders among many builders in the North Atlantic and Midwestern states. Except for fifty-five convertibles purchased from Brownell in 1900, the United Railways gave all of its business to the J. G. Brill Company or its ancillaries, Stephenson and Kuhlman.

However, until 1930, whether the car orders were spread out among the various builders or concentrated with Brill, no real attention was given to creating a specific Baltimore car. Even the articulated units did not completely meet this criterion, as they were not only based largely on a Milwaukee design but were restricted in originality by the basic dimensions of the old bodies which were being converted.

The arrival, in the spring of 1929, of Lucius Storrs to head the United Railways changed all of this. Just at the time of the stock market crash, representatives of most of the streetcar builders descended on the Carroll Park shops to present specifications for what was to be called the "Baltimore Car." For several weeks, tests were made, which resulted in the elimination of many proposed features and the retention of others. Previous to this, several officials of the local company had made a tour of Cleveland, Detroit, Boston, Pittsburgh, Cincinnati, Philadelphia, Montreal, and Toronto to obtain first-hand information on the types of modern streetcars being used in North America.

A. T. Clark, superintendent of rolling stock and shops for the United, described the projected cars as "the show window of the transportation industry," when 150 vehicles were ordered on March 17, 1930. One hundred were to be built by Brill, fifty by the Cincinnati Car Company, at a total cost of $2,550,000.

Despite the United's attempt to label the vehicles "Baltimore Cars," they have been usually referred to over the years as "Peter Witts." The name honored a Cleveland politician and former city traction commissioner, who had designed the cars' interior layout.

Exteriors were painted a brownish-yellow color with touches of red and black. The numbering was 6001 to 6150. The interiors of the new cars were painted a reddish-brown from floor to window sills, then a lighter brown (almost tan) on the window posts, with cream from the top of the windows across the headliner (ceiling). The ceiling panels were finished off with pin-striping around the edges. The two-tone brown interior, together with the brown leather bucket seats and window shades, made for a most effective and pleasing combination.

The Peter Witts were also the first order of Baltimore cars to have dome lamp globes completely covering all bare bulbs. These were thirty-six watts at first. While the company claimed that the interior lighting at night was comparable to that during daylight hours, the bulbs were later changed for ones of fifty-six watts.

As can be seen in photographs of the cars, all were similar in appearance. They measured forty-six feet in length. An important but not obvious difference was the twenty-two-inch diameter wheels on the last thirty Brill cars (6121-6150), as compared with the twenty-six-inch wheels on the others. The Cincinnati cars, without exception, had GE 301 motors and Brill 177E1 trucks. So did most of the Brill-built vehicles, but a few had Westinghouse 516, GE 1154, GE 298, and Westinghouse 1426 motors; at least one was reportedly mounted for a time on a set of Cincinnati trucks.

Particularly interesting is the fact that thirty cars (6121-6150) were reputed to be suitable for multiple-unit operation, though there is no evidence that they were ever used as such in actual service.

Despite the apparent variety of controllers, authorities agree that all functioned basically in the same manner. They were known as PC (pneumatic cam) controllers, indicating that the controller was advanced automatically by air in each of the three points switching, series and parallel. On the other hand, "operators" (the proper term for those motoring one-man cars) claim that the four-inch variation in wheel diameter made a distinct difference. The small-wheeled cars were claimed to be terrors to brake on wet or leaf-covered tracks.

Though the cars have gone down in history as Peter Witts, there is much disagreement among old-timers as to whether the Peter Witt system of fare collection (which called for a conductor stationed next to the center door well) was ever actually used on them. The majority opinion seems to be that it was not. However, the following item from the *Baltimore Post* of February 27, 1931, would seem to indicate that memories get a trifle hazy over the years. "Most of them (the new cars) are on a one-man basis of operation, now that the company's motormen have had sufficient training in handling them. During rush hours, however, a few of the cars still carry both a motorman and a conductor." Indeed, Peter Witt No. 6119 at the Baltimore Streetcar Museum is equipped, at the center door, with a base on which to mount a farebox, a conductor's bell, and a key-operated control for opening and closing the center doors.

When the cars went into operation in August 1930, many a motorist was in for a big surprise. The new type of controller enabled them to accelerate from a dead stop at a rate of three miles per hour per second,

All Baltimore single-end cars had emergency controls at the non-operating end. These were particularly useful in car house switching. In Peter Witts, the back of center rear seat dropped to reveal a controller and brake valve. Here, Charles R. Lloyd applies the brake during BSM operations. (Michael R. Farrell)

leaving many an Essex, Reo, and Whippet in their wakes.

An impartial newspaper reporter clocked one at 43 mph shortly after delivery, and another was hitting 25 mph within one hundred yards from a dead stop. The latter incident took place on Gwynn Oak Avenue, which, along with Falls Road above Cold Spring Lane, was one of the favorite speedways for the Witts. It is doubtful, however, if these accomplishments were anywhere near the cars' utmost capabilities.

NOTES AND COMMENTS:

Though a rather extensive file on the Peter Witt cars was available, many of the technicalities of the vehicles were clarified by Edward White, David Novak, Robert Krueger, and, especially, the man who since is largely responsible for restoring car No. 6119 to like-new condition at the Baltimore Streetcar Museum literally inch by inch, Carl P. Hughes.

Work on designing a modern car, which had been in progress for a year prior to Storrs' arrival in the spring of 1929, came to a climax with a series of tests in March 1930. *Post*, March 18, 1930.

A special four-page issue of *Trolley News* was devoted exclusively to the new cars in August 1930. Technical details on these cars appeared in the *Electric Railway Journal*, vol. 74, pp. 248-250, 354, 599 (1930). The comments on the braking characteristics of the small-wheeled Witts are

based on conversations with several retired motormen visiting the Museum.

A further documentation of two-man operation is provided by Kenneth Morse, who quotes a Transportation Department Bulletin dated October 31, 1930. "Helpers on the new cars on (routes) Nos. 6, 16, 17, 25, 29, and 31 must stand at center doors on position provided for conductors unless otherwise instructed, to direct persons to step down on door treadle to alight, announce all streets, etc."

The *Post* article of February 27, 1931 is the basis for recalling newspaper accounts of the speed of the cars. Entitled "Plenty Fast, These New Street Cars," it was reprinted in large part in the *E.R.A. Headlights*, April 1947 issue.

The choice of the words "street car" by the *Post*, rather than the combined form "streetcar" which is the style used throughout this book makes this as good a

time as any to point out several of the peculiarities of terms used by local railfans. Although such diverse sources as M. H. Forney's 1879 *Dictionary Of Terms Used In Car-Building*, the *Electric Railway Journal*, and both the United Railways and Baltimore Transit Company all go along with the use of "street car," the pundits at the local street railway museum insist upon "streetcar" as the proper term.

A somewhat similar situation occurs in the use of the word "trolley" to describe an electric street railway vehicle. Though I have resorted to this usage several times when no other synonym appeared convenient, Baltimore railfans declare that the word "trolley" applies only to the wheel which rolls beneath the overhead transmission wire — despite the fact that the United Railways' employees' publication was called *Trolley Topics* and that the little informative folders placed in the "take-one" racks were known for many years as *Trolley News*.

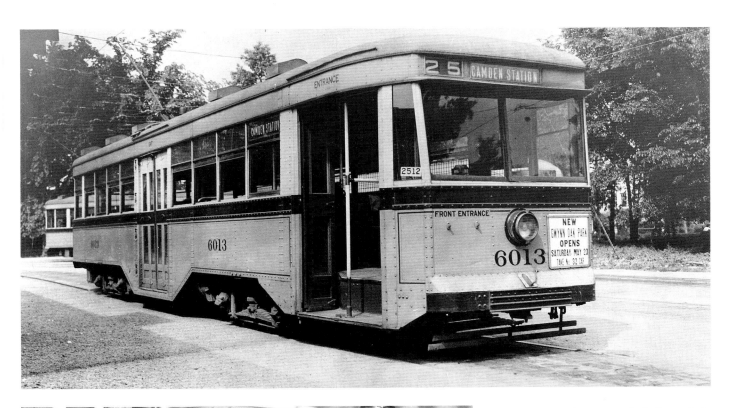

It seems appropriate to conclude these photo pages with two pictures of the "Baltimore car." No. 6013 (above) was caught at Belvedere loop by Burridge Jennings; posed interior shot (left) is a company photo. (Both, Enoch Pratt Library)

PASSENGER CAR ROSTER
UNITED RAILWAYS & ELECTRIC COMPANY / BALTIMORE TRANSIT COMPANY
1922-1963

Space limitations preclude a fully detailed all-time Baltimore streetcar roster in this book. The subject is awesomely complex, not only because of the variety of equipment of the UR & E's predecessors, but also because of the UR & E's own early practice of numbering its cars by route rather than in common number blocks. But the year 1922 marked the beginning of order. In that year, the UR & E adopted a systemwide common car numbering system; also by that date, virtually all cars built before the UR & E's formation had been retired from passenger service. Thus this summary roster arbitrarily begins in 1922 and carries the city's streetcar history through 1963 — the peak years, the decline, and the end.

Specifications, mechanical and electrical equipment shown are those of the cars as original-ly delivered, or as they existed in 1922. Many cars subsequently were modified in various ways — particularly the Brill semi-convertibles (Nos. 5001-5884). Various individual semi-convertibles were rebuilt as one-man cars (some single-ended, some not); multiple-unit controls were added or removed; motors and controls were replaced. These details, along with individual retirement or scrapping dates, may be found in *Baltimore Streetcars, 1905-1963: The Semi-Convertible Era*, by B. J. Sachs, G. F. Nixon, and H. E. Cox (The Baltimore Streetcar Museum, 1982). Full data on cars built before 1905 are contained in *Early Electric Cars of Baltimore*, by H. E. Cox (H. E. Cox, Forty Fort, Pennsylvania, 1979). The material in this roster is derived primarily from these two sources and from a 1930 UR & E car inventory.

Nos.	Type	Builder Date	Body Length	Motors	Truck(s)	Control	Seats	Comments
1101-1165	DT Open	Brill 1902	31' 9"	—	—	—	60	Bodies only; see note (a)
1651-1695	DT Open	Brill 1902	31' 9"	—	—	—	60	Bodies only; see note (a)
3801-3910	DT Closed	Brill 1902	28'	(2) WH 306C	Brill 22	K-36J		3909-3910 RB as PC train,1924; 3828 at BSM; all others scr. 1931
3909-3910	PC Train	RB 1924	28'	(2) WH 306C	Brill 22	MU HL	81	Scrapped 1939
4001-4023	ST SD Birney	Brill 1920	28' ½"*	(2) GE 264	Brill 79-E-1	K-63	32	Sold 1925-28
4024-4033	ST SD Birney	Brill 1920	28' ½"*	(2) WH 508	Brill 79-E-1	K-63	32	Sold 1925-28
4034-4065	ST DD Birney	Brill 1921	30' 1"*	(2) WH 508	Brill 79-E-1	K-63BR	33	Sold 1929
4501-4552	ST OM Safety	Brill 1904	22' 11"	(2) WH 101B	Brill 21E	K-68B	35	RB 1922-23 for OM; scrapped 1931-33; 4533 at BSM
4601-4698	ST Closed	Brill 1904	22' 11"	(2) WH 101B	Brill 21E	K-10	30	Scrapped 1929-33; 4662 at BSM
4701-4714	ST OM Closed	Brownell 1897-98	20' 9"	(2) WH 49	Lord Baltimore		26	Originally Balto. Traction & Balto. Consol., RB 1916-20; scr. 1933
4715-4744	ST Closed	Brownell 1897-98	20' 9"	(2) WH 49	Lord Baltimore		26	Originally Balto. Traction & Balto. Consolidated; scr. 1922-29
5001-5160	DT Semi-Conv.	Brill 1905	30' 8"	See note (b)	Brill 27-GE-1	K-28B	44	See note (c)
5161-5200	DT Semi-Conv.	Steph. 1905	30' 8"	(4) GE 90	Brill 27-E-1	K-28F	47	"Hi-Speed" suburban cars; remotored 1926-27; scr. 1940-50
5201-5300	DT Semi-Conv.	Brill 1906	30' 8"	(4) WH 101B	Brill 27-GE-1	K-28B	47	Scrapped 1945-48
5301-5379	DT Semi-Conv.	Brill, Steph. 1907	30' 8"	(4) WH 101D	Brill 27-E-1	MU AB	47	"Hi-Speed"; all MU; remotored 1927; scrapped 1937-44
5380-5439	DT Semi-Conv.	Brill 1910-11	30' 8"	(4) WH 101B	Brill 27-GE-1	K-28R	47	Scrapped 1946-50
5440-5499	DT Semi-Conv.	Brill 1912	30' 8"	(4) GE 246	Brill 27-GE-1	K-35G	47	Scrapped 1946-50
5500-5559	DT Semi-Conv.	Brill 1913	30' 8"	(4) GE 246	Brill 27-GE-1	K-35G	47	Scrapped 1945-50
5560-5644	DT Semi-Conv.	Brill 1914	30' 8"	(4) GE 200-I	Brill 27-GE-1	K-35U2	47	Scrapped 1947-50
5645-5744	DT Semi-Conv.	Brill 1917	30' 8"	(4) GE 200-I	Brill 27-GE-1	K-35U2	47	Scrapped 1947-50
5745-5824	DT Semi-Conv.	Brill 1917-18	33' 6"	(4) GE 200-I	Brill 27-GE-1	K-35U2	55	Scrapped 1948-55; 5748 preserved
5825-5874	DT Semi-Conv.	Brill 1919	33' 6"	(4) WH 532B	Brill 76-E-1	K-28E	55	Scrapped 1947-50; see note (d)
5875-5884	DT Semi-Conv.	Brill 1919	33' 6"	(4) GE 247	Brill 76-E-1	K-35U2	55	Scrapped 1949-50; see note (e)

Numbers	Type	Builder/Year	Length	Motors	Trucks	Control	Seats	Remarks
6001	Peter Witt	Brill 1924	35' 1"	(4) GE 265	Brill 76-E-1	C-28E	53	Renumbered 6991, 1930
6002	Peter Witt	Brill 1924	35' 1"	(4) WH 510	Brill 76-E-1	C-28E	53	Renumbered 6992, 1930
6001-6050	Peter Witt	Brill 1930	32' 1"	(4) WH 516	Brill 177-E-1	WH-29A4	52	Scrapped 1949-56
6051-6100	Peter Witt	Cinci. 1930	32' 1"	(4) GE 301	Brill 177-E-1	GE-PCM	52	Scrapped 1949-56
6101-6120	Peter Witt	Brill 1930	32' 1"	(4) GE 301	Brill 177-E-1	GE-PCM	52	Scrapped 1949-56; 6119 at BSM
6121-6150	Peter Witt	Brill 1930	32' 1"	(4) WH 1426	Brill 177-E-1	WH-29A4	52	Scrapped 1949-56
6991	Peter Witt	Brill 1924	35' 1"	(4) GE 265	Brill 76-E-1	C-28E	53	Ex-(1st) 6001; scrapped 1947
6992	Peter Witt	Brill 1924	35' 1"	(4) WH 510	Brill 76-E-1	C-28E	53	Ex-(1st) 6002; scrapped 1947
7001-7100	DT CE Trailer	Brill 1920	48' 2½"*	—	Brill 53-F	—	60	Sold or scrapped 1935-37; body of 7059 at BSM
7001-7022	PCC	St. Louis 1936	46'*	(4) GE 1198	Clark B-2	GE-17K-13E	54	Sold or scrapped 1956-63
7023-7027	PCC	St. Louis 1936	46'*	(4) WH 1432	Clark B-2	XM-48	54	Renumbered 7301-7305, 1938
7023-7147	PCC	Pullman 1939-44	46'*	(4) GE 1198	Clark B-2	GE-17-KC73A5	54	Sold or scrapped 1956-63
7301-7305	PCC	St. Louis 1936	46'*	(4) WH 1432	Clark B-2	XM-48	54	Ex-(2nd) 7023-27 (1938); scrapped 1956
7306-7428	PCC	Pullman 1939-44	46'*	(4) WH 1432	Clark B-2	XM-148	54	Sold and scrapped 1956-63; 7407 at BSM
7501	Brilliner	Brill 1939	46'*	(4) GE 1198G1	Brill 97-ER-1	GE-17KM3E	54	
8101-8118	Articulated	UR & E 1924-25	61' 4"	(4) WH 306 CV4	(2) Brill 27-GE-1 (1) Brill 77-E-1	480-28-N	87	RB from Nos. 5001-5036; scrapped 1944-48
8119-8128	Articulated	UR & E 1930-31	61' 4"	(4) WH 306 CV4	(2) Brill 27-GE-1 (1) Brill 77-E-1	480-28-N	87	RB from Nos. 5093-5112; scrapped 1943-48
8137-8146	Articulated	UR & E 1925-26	61' 4"	(4) WH 306 CV4	(2) Brill 27-GE-1 (1) Brill 77-E-1	480-28-N	87	RB from Nos. 5073-5092; scrapped 1947-48
8521-8526	Articulated	UR & E 1926	62' 5"	(4) WH 306 CV	(2) Brill 27-GE-1 (1) Brill 77-E-1	480-28-N	89	RB from Nos. 1141-1152; scrapped 1947-48
8527-8536	Articulated	UR & E 1930-31	62' 5"	(4) WH 306 CV	(2) Brill 27-GE-1 (1) Brill 77-E-1	480-28-N	85	RB from Nos. 1119-1136, 1153-1154; scrapped 1947-48
8601-8618	PC Train	UR & E 1925	2 x 31' 9"	(4) WH 306 CV4	Brill 27-GE-1	MU	97	RB from Nos. 1101-1118; R 1931; scrapped 1936
8637-8638	PC Train	UR & E 1925	2 x 31' 9"	(4) WH 306 CV4	Brill 27-GE-1	MU	97	RB from Nos. 1137-1138; R 1931; scrapped 1936
8639-8640	PC Train	UR & E 1925	2 x 31' 9"	(4) WH 306 CV4	Brill 27-GE-1	MU	97	RB from Nos. 1139-1140; R 1931; scrapped 1936

ABBREVIATIONS:

BSM — Baltimore Streetcar Museum
CE — Center entrance and exit
DD — Double-door (Birney)
DT — Double-truck
MU — Multiple-unit controls
OM — One-man operation
PC — Permanently coupled two-car train
PCC — President's Conference Committee design

R — Retired
RB — Rebuilt
Scr. — Scrapped
SD — Single-door (Birney)
ST — Single-truck
Steph. — John Stephenson Co. (Brill)
* — Total length

NOTES:

(a) Open car bodies 1101-1165 and 1651-1695 shared motors and trucks with closed cars 3801-3910. As of 1922, the open bodies were stored out of service. Many were rebuilt into articulateds and two-car PC trains between 1925-31; see Nos. 8521-8536 and 8601-8640 above. All remaining bodies scrapped by 1934 except 1164, preserved at BSM.

(b) Cars 5026-5075 equipped with (4) WH 101B motors; all others built with (4) GE 80.

(c) Cars 5001-5036 RB to articulateds 8101-18 in 1924-25. Cars 5073-5092 RB to articulateds 8137-8146 in 1925-26. Cars 5093-5112 RB to articulateds 8119-8128 in 1930-31. Others scrapped in 1937-40.

(d) Cars 5825-5874 originally purchased and owned by U.S. Emergency Fleet Corp.; bought by UR & E about 1922. All built as MU cars.

(e) Cars 5875-5884 orginally purchased and owned by U.S. Housing Board; bought by UR & E in 1924. Originally ordered for Newport News but diverted to Baltimore. MU installed 1941-42.

GLOSSARY

Anticlimbers: ribbed metal strips applied to the front and rear of cars, which were designed to prevent telescoping of the car bodies in case of a collision.

Arlington Junction: point on Kelly Avenue and Cross Country Boulevard at which the old Baltimore & Northern tracks divided, just west of Mt. Washington.

Articulated units: two cars connected by a hollow drum which rested on an idler truck. Operated from front end of first unit.

Baltimore car: name applied by the United Railways to the Peter Witt cars.

Baltimore Coach Company: bus subsidiary of the second Baltimore Transit Company.

Baltimore & Potomac Railroad: steam line which extended from a point just west of Union Station, through a tunnel under Wilson Street to Fulton Station, and on to Washington. Originally a Pennsylvania Railroad subsidiary. The B & P line is now part of Amtrak's Northeast Corridor route.

Baltimore Streetcar Museum: a non-profit corporation founded in 1966 to preserve the collection of historic Baltimore streetcars. Presently operating a variety of electric cars on trackage adjacent to Falls Road, north of Lafayette Avenue.

Baltimore Transit Company (1st): a bus subsidiary of the United Railways.

Baltimore Transit Company (2nd): a name chosen for the successor to the United Railways & Electric Company.

Battery electric operation: a means of powering streetcars by storage batteries carried on the vehicles. In theory, the best system, but never proven very practical. Size and weight limited the number of batteries and hence severely restricted the distance the car could travel without recharging.

Bay Shore Park: an amusement park which was located southeast of Sparrows Point on the Chesapeake Bay at the mouth of the Patapsco River.

Bicycle railway: a type of monorail seriously proposed, but not built, by the Gwynns Falls Railway.

Birney car: single-truck economy car, mass produced by various builders in the 1920s. Spartan accommodations and rough-riding characteristics made it unpopular.

Bob-tailed car: horse car with a platform at one end only.

Bolster: cross timber or trussed beam on the underside of a car body and in the center of a truck. The body bolster rested on a truck bolster.

Boulevard Line: colloquial name for the Columbia & Maryland Railway. Also, route designation of the No. 29 line from Roland Park to Pratt and Calvert Streets.

Brill, J. G. and Company: a Philadelphia car builder, once the largest in the industry, which furnished many of the Baltimore streetcars.

Bulkhead: the end framing of a streetcar between the body proper and the platform.

Cable conduit: a heavy tube of cast iron encased in concrete. It was located between the running rails. Through this conduit, the cable ran on a series of pulleys.

Cable railway: a street railway on which cars were propelled by gripping a cable running in a conduit beneath the streets.

Cable slot: a narrow opening at the top of the cable conduit through which the grip was admitted to take hold of the cable.

Calverton: a station on the Baltimore & Potomac Railroad, just west of the Franklin Street crossing in west Baltimore.

Car barn: while the term car house refers to any structure in which streetcars are stored, car barn technically applies only to those buildings used by the horse railway companies. However, in popular usage the term car barn was generally employed for any car house.

Car checks: a term used by the United Railways to designate car tokens. Also used by some of the early companies instead of transfers.

Carlines: the timbers which extended from one side of the car body to the other and supported the roof boards.

Carlin's Park: was located on Reisterstown Road in northwest Baltimore adjacent to Park Circle and Druid Hill Park.

Catonsville Junction: Edmondson and Dutton Avenues in Baltimore County.

Catonsville Railway Park: was located northwest of Frederick Road and Paradise Avenue and extended north to Edmondson Avenue in Baltimore County.

City Hall Loop: Routing on Holliday Street, Guilford Avenue, South Street, and Fayette Street, over which various horse car companies had trackage rights.

City Passenger: Baltimore City Passenger Railway.

Clerestory: portion of a car roof which rose above the main roof and contained windows or ventilators. Also called monitor roof.

Collection cars: obsolete streetcars converted for use in carrying cash receipts between car houses and banks.

Combine: a car divided into passenger and freight sections.

Controller: a device located on the front platform of electric cars, by which the amount of current fed to the motors was varied, thus regulating the speed of the cars.

Convertible car: a type of streetcar popular around 1900. It could be operated as a closed car in cold weather and, by removing the window frames and glass, could be converted to a semi-open car in warm weather.

Daft Electric Operation: system pioneered by Professor Leo Daft on the Baltimore & Hampden in 1885-89. Main difference from conventional electric operation was the use of an electrified third rail between the running rails, though at crossings a crude overhead pickup was employed.

Darley Park: was located on the east side of Harford Road, north of present intersection with Broadway.

Dasher: the curved metal plate or wooden panels enclosing the end of a car platform or vestibule above the floor and below window level.

Devilstrip: space between the inner rails of a double-track line.

Dolores: car built by the United Railways especially for funerals. It had a special compartment for the casket and a secluded area for immediate family, in addition to conventional seating arrangement for other mourners.

Double deck: a vehicle with a second story. In Baltimore there were double-deck horse cars and buses, but not electric cars.

Double-truck car: a vehicle mounted on two sets of four wheels each.

Drab: color of some early cars. Light drab approximated milk chocolate in shade, dark drab resembled slate.

Dugan's Wharf: site of the United Railways main power house, southwest of Pratt Street and Market Place — sometimes called O'Donnell's Wharf.

Dummy engine: small steam locomotive often used by street railways on which the boiler and moving parts were covered by a false car body so that horses would not be frightened. The term was often used to denote any small steam engine.

Dundalk Junction: was at Broening Highway and Dundalk Avenue in Baltimore County.

Early Peter Witt cars: two experimental cars bought by the United Railways in 1924, somewhat similar to later Peter Witt purchases. The early cars, which could be operated singly or as a multiple- unit train, were handicapped by slow speed.

Electric Park: an amusement park which was located on the south side of Belvedere Avenue, just east of Reisterstown Road in northwest Baltimore.

Ellicott's Mills: present-day Ellicott City, located on the Patapsco River in Howard County.

Epizootic: a respiratory disease affecting horses which seriously hampered operations in late 1872 and early 1873.

Express runs: an experiment of the 1920s in which certain cars were supposed to run without stops on portions of some routes.

Fenders: a device of ropes on an iron framework attached to the front of a car, designed to scoop up unwary pedestrians and thus prevent them from being dismembered by the car wheels.

Fremont Street: designation of the present Fremont Avenue until about 1900.

Frick Lines: originally the Baltimore, Peabody Heights & Waverly Passenger Railroad; later the North Baltimore Passenger Railway.

Fulton Station: temporary terminus of the Western Maryland Railroad steam line, beginning in 1873; it was located on Laurens Street, west of Fulton Avenue near the west end of the B & P tunnels, which the WM used to reach Union station and its own Hillen Station.

Gaither's Express: the company which, from 1899 to 1912, operated a delivery service for packages and light freight along the lines of the United Railways.

Girder rail: a type of rail for use in city streets. It had a cup-like section attached to the head of the rail to allow wheel flanges to extend below the surface of the street.

Grip: a device mounted under the front platform or center of cable cars which could be opened and closed to grasp cable in conduit.

Gripman: the employee who operated the grip on a cable car.

Gwynn Oak Junction: the intersection of Liberty Heights and Gwynn Oak Avenues in northwest Baltimore.

Gwynn Oak Park: located on Gwynn Oak Avenue between the present, western city line and Woodlawn in Baltimore County.

Hackneys: horse-drawn cabs of the last century.

Hall's Springs: located on Harford Road just west of the north end of the bridge over Herring Run in northeast Baltimore.

Hangsigns: metal destination signs hung from brackets on the dasher — sometimes covered with paper signs showing either destination or public service announcements.

Hayward, Bartlett and Company: the predecessor of Bartlett-Hayward Division of Koppers Company, which in the 1860s manufactured steam engines.

Headliner: streetcar ceiling.

Hetty Green: a financial wizard of the nineteenth century of legendary reputation.

Hill Horse: an extra horse that was kept in readiness to assist horse cars up steep grades.

Hollywood Park: was located at Eastern Avenue and Back River in Baltimore County.

Hookstown: the original name of Arlington, in northwest Baltimore.

Hunter signs: cloth destination signs used from about 1900 onward. They were mounted on rollers to facilitate changing and were translucent so that interior lighting would make them visible from the street at night.

Huntingdon Avenue Viaduct: extended from the north end of Huntingdon Avenue across the Stony Run valley to 33rd Street.

Idler truck: an unmotorized truck.

Interurban: an electric railway connecting different cities or towns. In the vicinity of Baltimore, the best remembered are the Washington, Baltimore & Annapolis and the Hagerstown & Frederick.

Jack Flood's: beer garden which was located on Curtis Creek in south Baltimore.

Jerkwater: a branch line or shuttle connecting with or extending from a main route. In later years, especially, they were sometimes physically disconnected.

Jim Crow car: a vehicle in which the passengers were segregated by race.

Jitney: earliest type of motor bus, consisting of crude benches mounted on a truck chassis.

Knocking down fares: withholding of revenue from the company.

Lakeside Park: was located near the eastern bank of Lake Roland in Baltimore County in the vicinity of the dam now part of Robert E. Lee Park.

Lifeguard: safety device located under front platform of the car. If a person was missed by the fender, his body struck a wooden frame hung from the car body; this impact actuated a lever attached to a wooden slat platform, causing the latter to drop to the track in front of the car wheels.

Light Rail: a low-cost type of rapid transit operation, using essentially streetcar technology in modernized form.

Long Bridge: trestle-like affair which connected the southern end of Light Street with Brooklyn in south Baltimore.

Lorraine Cemetery: located between Woodlawn and Franklintown in Baltimore County. Car service was provided to the Dogwood Road gate.

Mail cars: cars especially outfitted so that the interior was suitable for processing mail collected en route.

Monument Square: the block of North Calvert Street between Fayette and Lexington, in which the Battle Monument is located.

Multiple unit (MU) operation: method of connecting two or more motored cars together so that the motors and brakes of the trailing cars could be operated from the leading one.

Nachod signals: a type of color light signaling in which a contactor on the trolley wire counts the number of cars into and out of a protected section of track.

Northern Central Railway: steam railroad between Baltimore, Harrisburg, and Lake Ontario. It operated from Calvert Station (Franklin and Calvert Streets) northward out of Baltimore, roughly paralleling Interstate 83. Controlled by the Pennsylvania Railroad after 1861, then successively operated by Penn Central and Conrail. The Central Light Rail line currently operates over a portion of the NC line between North Avenue and Cockeysville.

Omnibus: type of vehicle similar to a stagecoach used for intracity transportation in the nineteenth century.

Open and closed sets of cars: streetcars popular around the turn of the century. Two sets of bodies were purchased but only one set of trucks and electrical equipment. Bodies were transferred in the spring and fall. (Examples are car Nos. 3828 and 1164 in the BSM Collection.)

Open cars: cars on which the sides were unenclosed from the roof to the floor. Canvas curtains provided some protection from the elements when needed. (Examples are car Nos. 554 and 1164 in the BSM Collection.)

Overhead electric operation: the conventional electric streetcar system, in which current is collected from an overhead wire by the trolley wheel and transmitted through the controller to the motors. The tracks form the return circuit.

Owl cars: provided all-night service.

Park tax: a unique tax levied against the Baltimore street railways, originally calling for 20 percent of the gross revenues to be paid to the City for acquiring and maintaining a park system. It was lowered to 12 percent in 1874 and 9 percent in 1882, remaining at this rate until 1932, when it was cut to 3 percent.

Pay cars: older passenger cars altered to provide facilities for paying the men while on duty. The pay car was usually parked at the end of a line, and motormen and conductors picked up their pay during layovers.

P.A.Y.E. cars: abbreviation for pay-as-you-enter cars put into service just prior to World War I, in which a fixed conductor's station was provided. Passengers paid fares immediately upon passing this station, rather than being sought out by the conductor.

PCC cars: the streamlined cars of the last years. Basic concept was the result of a cooperative effort by officials of the leading street railway companies; hence the name, Presidents' Conference Committee car.

Peabody Heights: a community in the vicinity of Charles Street and 26th Street in north Baltimore; this general area is known as Charles Village today.

Permanently coupled (PC) trains: pairs of cars, rebuilt in the 1920s from obsolete vehicles. The front car was repowered with more powerful motors to haul the second as an unpowered trailer and the vehicles permanently coupled to simplify electrical and brake connections.

Peter Witt car: type of car with front entrance and center exit, designed largely to the specifications of the United Railways. Despite the company's efforts to label the vehicles "Baltimore cars," the 150 streetcars purchased in 1930 are almost universally recalled as Peter Witts after the inventor of the interior layout and proposed fare collection system.

Platforms: extensions to the car body on which conductors and drivers or motormen were stationed. The brakestand and controller of the electric cars were located here.

Poole and Hunt: large machinery and metalworking plant complex located in Woodberry, immediately north of Druid Hill Park. Constructed first orders of horse cars for the Baltimore City Passenger Railway and the Baltimore and Yorktown Turnpike Railway; later manufactured cable car equipment.

Portable vestibule: framework containing three panes of glass mounted on the dasher of a car — really a windshield.

Powhatan: a mill village located on what is now Woodlawn Cemetery in Baltimore County. About 1900, some houses were moved across the road to become the nucleus of Woodlawn.

Private right of way: a track located on private property owned or leased by the railway companies.

Rapid transit: term used in the last century, circa 1890, for any form of transit which was faster and more efficient than animal power, primarily cable or electric cars.

In modern usage it denotes a system in which the cars (usually rail vehicles equipped for multiple-unit operation) travel exclusively on private right of way, such as subway or elevated.

Reserved trackage: similar to private right of way. As used in this book, it indicates rails laid alongside of or in the center of a road and usually separated from other traffic by a hedge or other barrier.

Ridgewood Park: located on Windsor Mill Road, east of Gwynns Falls in west Baltimore.

Riverview Park: formerly located on the present site of the now-closed Point Breeze plant of the Western Electric Company and bounded by Broening Highway, Colgate Creek, and the Patapsco River.

Roberts noiseless motor: a car run by compressed air which proved to be less than a success due to its inability to travel for any prolonged period of time without replenishment of its air supply.

Root scraper: car equipped with a kind of chisel used for removing ice which formed in the groove of the girder rail.

Rope: a synonym for the cable of a cable system; it was composed of strands of wire wrapped around a core of hempen rope.

St. Denis: a station on the Baltimore & Ohio Railroad, just east of Relay on the Patapsco River in Baltimore County.

St. Helena: the first community in the Dundalk area. Located on the west side of Dundalk Avenue, just south of the present city limits.

Semi-convertible car: a further development of the convertible car concept, in which the windows and their frames, instead of being removable, could be raised into pockets in the car roof.

Shore Line Parks: a group of amusement parks which were located in the vicinity of the present Broening Park and Cherry Hill in south Baltimore.

Single-truck car: the truck is a structure composed of beams or bars, to which journal boxes, axles, springs, etc. are attached. A single-truck car rode on two pairs of wheels, mounted in a single unit.

Skip-stop: a system of improving schedule time by omitting some stops, usually alternate streets.

Slawson box: a late-nineteenth century patented fare box invented by an official of a New Orleans horse railway company.

Snow scraper: a small portable plow attached to a utility car for snow removal in the horse car era.

Snow sweeper: special car for removing snow from tracks by means of revolving brooms under the car body. Baltimore practice was to operate both front and rear sets of brooms at all times. Some sweepers had small plows attached.

Soffit board: a board which formed the underside or ceiling of some subordinate part or member of a car. Similar to eaves.

Specialwork: in street railway terminology, a complex arrangement of trackage, such as a junction with switches and/or crossings.

Spotters: men employed by the railway companies to observe the conductors to make sure that all fares were turned in.

Standard gauge: in the early days, street railways of the country were built to whatever gauge was deemed expedient. Later, many were built to a gauge (distance between inside edges of rails) of 4 feet 8½ inches, which had already been adopted by many steam roads. The Baltimore street railways were built to a gauge of 5 feet 4½ inches, as specified in the original 1859 ordinance, and retained this wide gauge to the end.

Stoddard's Hotel: terminus of the Baltimore, Catonsville & Ellicott's Mills Passenger Railway, it was located at the point where the Catonsville line swung north from Frederick Road, near Montrose Avenue.

Tallow lamps: the headlights of many horse cars used rancid tallow, a mixture of refined animal fats, for fuel.

Third-rail system: Railway system in which current is picked up from an electrified third rail on or in close proximity to the ground.

Trackage rights: an arrangement by which the cars of one company were allowed to use the tracks of another.

Track-circuit signals: a system of lighted signals which are activated by the presence of a car on the section of track ahead of the signal or on adjacent sections.

Trackless trolleys: electrically-powered vehicles which ran on ordinary roadways and used rubber tires, rather than steel wheels. As there were no rails for return current, two overhead wires were necessary.

Traction Company: the Baltimore Traction Company.

T-Rail: type of rail ordinarily used on private right of way. It had no cup or flange, as did girder and tram rail.

Tram rail: an early type of rail used in city streets, which was provided with a flange to accommodate the wheels of horse-drawn buggies and wagons.

Tramway: street railway.

Transfer: a colored printed slip of paper, punched as required by conductor or operator (who had an individualized punch), which allowed a change of connecting cars and buses at usually, but historically not always, no additional charge. Perforated, two-piece versions allowing an

additional "re-transfer" were introduced in the 1930s after a fare increase to ten cents.

Transfer cars: shuttle cars used in the early days, similar to jerkwater cars.

Trestle ("The Trestle"): colloquialism for the elevated section of railway above Guilford Avenue.

Tripper: an extra car not listed on the schedule.

Trolley: originally the small wheel at the end of a pole which collected current from the overhead wire. In time, the term was extended to include the car itself.

Trolley parties: parties for which a private group rented a car for an evening's outing.

Turnout: a track switch; in street railway parlance, also a passing siding.

Two-trip slip: a small, colored and symbolized slip of paper entitling a rider to a second ride at half-fare during off-peak weekday hours and all day on Sundays.

Union Passenger Railway: Baltimore Union Passenger Railway.

Vestibule: an enclosed streetcar platform.

Walbrook Junction: the intersection of Clifton Avenue and Garrison Boulevard in west Baltimore.

Western Maryland Railroad (later Railway): a steam road running from Baltimore to western Maryland. Originally, it entered the city by way of a connection with the Northern Central Railway at Lake Roland. In 1873, the company finished a new line connecting with the Baltimore & Potomac at Fulton Station.

Windshield: same as portable vestibule.

Yellow Line: a route of the Baltimore City Passenger Railway, unusual in that it had two branches. One, the old Baltimore & Hall's Springs Railway line, ran out Harford Road; the other extended into east Baltimore past the Johns Hopkins Hospital to Patterson Park.

Yorktown Turnpike: the early name for the present Greenmount Avenue and York Road in north Baltimore.

Zone fare: supplemental fare charged for riding longer distances than the base fare would allow, such as beyond the city line. They were deposited in the fare box upon departure. On one-man cars, the center or rear doors were kept closed.

BIBLIOGRAPHY

Books

Alexander, Edwin P. *Down At The Depot* (Clarkson N. Potter, New York, 1970).

Arnold, Ian. *Locomotive, Trolley, and Rail Car Builders; An Alltime Directory* (Trans-Anglo Books, Los Angeles, ca. 1965).

____ *Baltimore City Code,* Editions of 1869, 1879, supplement 1885, 1906.

____ *Baltimore City, Maryland — The Book Of Its Board Of Trade* (George W. Engelhardt, Baltimore, ca. 1895).

Clark, Douglas N. and Ruckle, F. Edgar. *Street Railway Post Offices Of Baltimore* (Mobile Post Office Society, Omaha, Nebraska, 1979).

Coyle, Wilbur F. *The Mayors Of Baltimore* (Reprinted from Baltimore Municipal Journal, 1919).

Cox, Harold E. *Early Electric Cars Of Baltimore* (H. E. Cox, Forty Fort, Pennsylvania, 1979).

____ *The Early Eighties* (Mercantile Trust & Deposit Company, Baltimore, 1924).

Forney, Matthias Nice. *A Dictionary Of The Terms Used In Carbuilding* (1879).

Frey, Jacob. *Reminiscences Of Baltimore* (Baltimore, 1893).

Hall, Clayton Cofman, Editor. *Baltimore — Its History And People* (Lewis Historical Publishing Co., New York, 1912).

Harwood, Herbert H., Jr. *Baltimore And Its Streetcars* (Quadrant Press, New York, New York, 1984).

Hilton, George W. *The Cable Car In America* (Howell-North Books, Berkeley, California, 1971).

Hilton, George W. and Due, John F. *Electric Interurban Railways In America* (Stanford University Press, Stanford, California, 1960).

____ *History Of The City Of Baltimore — Its Men And Institutions* (Baltimore American, 1902).

Janvier, Meredith. *Baltimore In The Eighties And Nineties* (H. G. Roebuck, Baltimore, 1933).

Kelker, DeLeuw & Company. *Report Of The Routings Of The Street Railway Lines And The Methods For The Improvement Of Street Railway Conditions* (Waverly Press, Baltimore, 1926).

King, Thomson. *Consolidated Of Baltimore* (Consolidated Gas Electric Light & Power Company of Baltimore, 1950).

____ *Laws Of Maryland* (1860-1906).

____ *Maryland And District Of Columbia Gazetteer And Business Directory* (R. L. Polk & Co., Baltimore 1899-1901).

____ *Maryland Public Service Commission Reports* (1914-1961).

____ *McGraw-Hill Electric Railway Dictionary* (McGraw-Hill Co., New York, 1911).

____ *Memoirs Of John Mifflin Hood* (Baltimore, ca. 1911).

Middleton, William D. *The Interurban Era* (Kalmbach Publishing Co., Milwaukee, 1961).

Richardson and Bennett. *Baltimore — Past And Present* (Baltimore, 1871).

Sachs, Bernard J.; Nixon, George F.; Cox, Harold E. *Baltimore Streetcars; 1905-1963 The Semi-Convertible Era* (Baltimore Streetcar Museum, 1982).

Scharf, J. Thomas. *History Of Baltimore City And County* (Louis H. Everts, Philadelphia, 1881).

Semmes, Raphael. *Baltimore As Seen By Visitors 1783-1860* (Maryland Historical Society, 1953).

Shannon, Fred Albert. *The Centennial Years* (1967).

Shepherd, Henry Elliott. *History Of Baltimore 1729-1898* (S. B. Nelson, 1898).

____ *Souvenir Album Of The East Baltimore Business Men's Association* (1897).

Stockett, Letitia. *Baltimore — A Not Too Serious History* (Norman, Baltimore, 1928).

Wainwright, Nicholas B. *History Of The Philadelphia Electric Company 1881-1961* (Philadelphia Electric Company, 1961).

Wirtz, Paul W. (Editor). *Baltimore And Streetcars — 1926* (Baltimore Streetcar Museum, 1982).

Journals

The American Philatelist, January 1939

American Railroad Journal

Architect's Report, Spring 1962

B & O Magazine

Baltimore City Directories

Baltimore Engineer

Baltimore Magazine, July 1915; August 1930

Baltimore Methodist, July 19, 1900

Baltimore Sun Almanacs

Baltimore Transit Company Annual Reports

Brill Magazine

Capital Traction Quarterly, 1965

Cassier's Magazine

Electric Lines

Electric Railway Journal

Electric Railway Review

Electric Traction Weekly

Electrical Engineer, May 26; June 30, 1898

Headlights, Electric Railroaders' Association

Headway Recorder, December 1949; Autumn 1963; Spring 1964

Locomotive And Railway Preservation

Industrial Philadelphia, Girard Trust Company

Interchange, Baltimore Chapter NRHS

Live Wire, Baltimore Streetcar Museum

Manufacturers Record

Motor Coach Age, 1988

Municipal Journal (Baltimore)

National Railway Historical Society Bulletin

New Electric Railway Journal

Philadelphia Stockholder, 1895-96

Poor's Directory Of Railroads

Railfan & Railroad

Railroad Magazine

Railway Age

Read As You Ride, Baltimore Transit Co.

Reports Of The Park Commission, 1862-94

Street Railway Gazette

Street Railway Journal

Street Railway Review

Sunday Sun Magazine, Baltimore

Traction And Models

Traction Heritage

Transit Topics (Baltimore Transit Co.)

Trolley News (UR & E Co.)

Trolley Topics (UR & E Co.)

Newspapers

Annapolis *Evening Capital*

Baltimore *American*

Baltimore *Daily Commercial*

Baltimore *Daily Exchange*

Baltimore *Daily Gazette*

Baltimore *Evening Sun*

Baltimore *Herald*

Baltimore *News*

Baltimore *News-American*

Baltimore *News-Post*

Baltimore *Patriot*

Baltimore *Post*

Baltimore *Star*

Baltimore *Sun*

Baltimore *Sunday Herald*

Baltimore *Sunday Sun*

Baltimore *Weekly Sun*

Baltimore *World*

Catonsville *Herald-Argus*

Catonsville *Times*

Kansas City *Star*

New York *Times*

North Baltimore *Home-News*

St. Louis *Globe-Democrat*

Toronto *World*

Towson *Baltimore County Advocate*

Towson *Baltimore County Democrat*

Towson *Baltimore County Union*

Towson *Jeffersonian*

Towson *Maryland Journal*

Washington *Sunday Star*

Pamphlets and Booklets

An Analysis Of The United Railways And Electric Company, Makubin, Goodrich & Co., February 16, 1931

Baltimore Streetcar Routes, Kenneth Morse, 1960

Baltimore Transit Company Operations, Baltimore Chapter, NRHS, 1959

Brownell Car Company Advertisements, ca. 1895

Hampden-Woodberry Souvenir Book, 1938

Lorraine Park Cemetery Brochure, ca. 1904

Mail Delivery By Trolley, David B. Ditman, Baltimore Streetcar Museum, 1979

Maryland Historical Society, First Showing Of The Historic Street Cars, July 11, 1954

Maryland's Homecoming Week, October 1907

A Plan For The Extension Of The North Avenue Railway, 1890

Souvenir Of The Last Day Of Operation, National Capitol Historical Museum of Transportation, November 2, 1963

Wilson Colson and Company, circular, February 1900

Maps

(listed in chronological order)

1857, *Map Of The City And County Of Baltimore,* Robert Taylor (1857)

1872, *New And Enlarged Map Of Baltimore City,* J. F. Weishampel (Baltimore, 1872)

1873, *Map Of Baltimore,* F. Klem

1876, *Atlas Of Baltimore, Maryland And Environs,* vol. 1, G. M. Hopkins (F. Bourquin, Philadelphia, 1876-77)

1877, *City Atlas Of Baltimore, Maryland And Environs,* vol. 2, G. M. Hopkins (F. Bourquin, Philadelphia, 1877)

1884 (circa), *Map Of The City Of Baltimore And Suburbs,* Sheriff and Taylor's Baltimore City Directory (A. Hoen, Baltimore, 1885)

1894 (circa), *City Of Baltimore Topographical Survey*, H. T. Douglas (A. Hoen, Baltimore, 1894-96)

1898, *Atlas Of Baltimore,* Bromley

System maps and individual route guides published by the United Railways and the Baltimore Transit Company from about 1915 through the end of service

Manuscripts and Notes

Individuals over the years have been collecting material concerning the street railways of Baltimore. A number of these collections were made available to the author.

Copious notes and unpublished manuscripts came from the late A. T. Clark, R. W. Janssen, the late L. C. Mueller, G. F. Nixon, J. S. Thomsen, and the late R. S. Tompkins. In addition, J. R. Kean, R. Krueger, W. Mangold, J. E. Merriken, the late K. Morse, F. Scharnagle, H. S. Wells, Jr., and the late H. S. Wells, Sr. gave generously of notes collected over the years.

A number of United Railway & Electric Company scrapbooks containing newspaper clippings and other items from the years 1886 to 1902 supplied a wealth of information. Several scrapbooks covering various portions of time from about 1918 to 1930, which had been put together by the company's Transportation Department, aided in filling in the period between the semi-convertibles and the Peter Witts. Precise information on route changes during the mid-1950s was obtained from a collection of BTC operating bulletins. Other important sources of information were the files of the Baltimore Chapter,

NRHS and the Baltimore Streetcar Museum. Many of the above collections are filed in the archives of the Joint BSM/NRHS Library at the Museum and are available to serious historians and researchers by appointment.

The Maryland Room of the Enoch Pratt Library is the repository for much data on the street railways, including, in addition to the aforementioned scrapbooks, such diverse items as old maps and schedules and even a collection of ancient transfers.

Illustrations

The black-and-white drawings found throughout the book were abstracted from a series of drawings done in 1926 by a Baltimore artist, Willem Wirtz. They ap-peared originally in a series of full-page institutional newspaper advertisements published during that year by the United Railways and Electric Company. They were reprinted in the U R & E employee magazine, *Trolley Topics*, at that time and, more recently, in *Baltimore and Streetcars — 1926.*

INDEX

Bold page numbers indicate illustrations or pertinent information in captions as well as text.

Abandonments, 153, 154, 155, **158-173**, **266-271**, 277
    Cartoon, **162**
ABB Traction, Inc., 187, 188
Abell, A. S., 101
Accidents, 118, 122, 228, **232-235**, 253, **256-259**, 261, 262, 264
Acton's Shore, 247
Addison, Walter J., 176, 183
Air brakes, 130, 224
Alex. Brown & Sons (Alex. Brown combine), 91, 97-101
All-Night cars, 23, 24, 219
"All-service" vehicle, **149**, 153
American, Baltimore, 16, 81
American Car Company, *see* Cars by builder
American City Lines, 155
American Electric Railway Association, 131
Amtrak, 179, 183, 185
Amusement parks, *see* Parks
Annapolis, 189
Annapolis Short Line, 186, 189
Anne Arundel County, 47, **136**, 177, 185, 187, 245
Anti-saloon League, 247
Arion Park, 245
Arlington, Maryland, 45, 50, 87, 166, 249
Arlington & Pimlico Railroad, 45, 50, 57
    Map, **34**
Arlington Junction, 87, 89
Articulated bus, **149**
Articulated units (cars), *see* Cars, revenue
Automobiles, **123**, **127-130**, **136**, **139**, **142**, **143**, **150**, 159, **258**, 259, 267, **272-277**, 285, 286
Avalon, **187**, **198**, 199
Back River, 91, 154, 245, 269
Baetjer, Edwin C., 108
Baier, George M., 50
Baldwin & Pennington, 106
Baldwin, Francis E., 113
Baltimore *American, see American,* Baltimore
Baltimore & Annapolis Railroad, 175, 186, 188, 189
Baltimore & Curtis Bay Railway, 47, 50, **65**, 69
Baltimore & Delta Railroad, 46
Baltimore & Frederick Turnpike Company, 116
Baltimore & Hall's Springs Railway, **10**, 35, 40, 91, 94
    Map, **34**
Baltimore & Hampden Railway, 35, 50, **52-59**, 257, 259
    Map, **52**
    see also Daft line and motors
Baltimore & Jerusalem Turnpike Company, 80, 82
Baltimore & Laurel Electric Railway, 49
Baltimore & Lehigh Railroad, 70
Baltimore & Loreley Electric Railway, 75, 80
Baltimore & Northern Railway, 41, 75, 77, 82, 83, 84, **86-90**, 97, 98, 103, 113, 116, **157**, 160, 224, 233-234, 244, 250, **259**, 264
    Map, **86**
Baltimore & Ohio Railroad (now CSX Transportation), 13, 14, 20, 50, 75, 81, 87, 103, 113, 134, 164, 185, 186, 191, 194, **206**, 247, 255, **270**

Baltimore & Pikesville Railroad, 84
Baltimore & Potomac Railroad, 21, 23, 33, 41, 45, 46, 48, 172, 179
    Tunnel, 179
Baltimore & Randallstown Railroad, 45, **49**
Baltimore & Reisterstown Turnpike Company, 50, 84
Baltimore & Washington Turnpike & Tramway Company, 45
Baltimore & Yorktown Turnpike Railway, 35, **38**, 39, 50, 57, 71, 73, 169, 225, 249, 251, 257, 259, 264
Baltimore, Calverton & Powhatan Railway, 35, 37, 40, 41, 45, 48, **51**, 91, 169, 257
Baltimore, Canton & Point Breeze Railway ("Rams Horn Railway"), 48, 50
"Baltimore car," 291, **293**
    see also Cars, revenue, Peter Witt
Baltimore, Catonsville & Ellicott's Mills Passenger Railway, 35, **36**, 40, 45, 49, 50, **54**, 55, 241, 264, 273
Baltimore, Gardenville & Belair Electric Railway, 82
Baltimore Chapter, NRHS, **158**, **165**, 169, 191, **206**, **207**, **209-211**, **223**, **243**, **248**
Baltimore Chariot Company, 261
Baltimore City Council, *see* City Council (Baltimore)
Baltimore City Passenger Railway, **10**, **13-25**, 27-29, 32, 33, 35, **39**, 41, 57, 59, **60**, 61, 63, 65, **68**, 71, **83**, 88, 91-94, **97-99**, 143, 155, **157**, 169, 220, 222, 224, 227, 230, 231, 241, 273
    Acquired by Baltimore & Northern, 97-101
    Acquisitions of other companies, 35, 40, 81-82, 84, 91, 94, 101
    Cable cars, **60**, **66**, **79**, 91
    Cable operation, **60**, 65, **68**, 71, 75, 76, **79**, 80, 91-94, 274
    Car barns, **66**, **67**, 91
    Cars, *see* Cars, by owner
    Competition, 23-24, 64, 273
    Electrification, 63, **74**, 75, **79**, 91-94
    Fares, 13-20, 21, 23, 24, 273
    Finances, 23, 24, **60**, 61, **66**, 91, 94, 273
    First car, **14**, 20
    Formation, 13-18
    Incorporation, 13, 18, 20, 27
    Injunction (Baltimore Street), 20
    Last horse car, 91
    Legal cases, 20, **74**, 91, 94
    Map, **22**
    Ordinance, 13-18
    Route identification by color, 20, 21
    Routes, *see* Routes, Baltimore City Passenger Railway
Baltimore City Passenger Railway Association 20, 231
    see also Baltimore City Passenger Railway
Baltimore Coach Company, **119**
Baltimore Consolidated Railway Company, 45, 48, 49, **83**, 84, 97, 101, 103, 106, 109, **111**, 116, 224, 227, 239, 241, **242**, 244, 257, 259, 261
    Formation, 81, **83**, 91
    Merged into United Railways, 98, 101
Baltimore County, 27, 41, 43, 50, 80, 87, **136**, 169, 183, 187, 219, 247, 256, 258, 259
Baltimore Fire (1904), **102**, 106, 110, 131
Baltimore, Gardenville & Belair Electric Railway, 75, 80
Baltimore Gas & Electric Company, 115, **146-147**

Baltimore gauge, 21, 45, **110, 112**, 195, 273
Baltimore, Halethorpe & St. Denis Railway, 107
Baltimore, Hampden & Lake Roland Railway, 60, 69
Baltimore Highlands, 186, 189
Baltimore mayors, *see* Mayors (Baltimore)
Baltimore, Middle River & Sparrows Point Railroad, 81, 84, 91, 97, 263
Baltimore Museum of Art, 264
Baltimore, Peabody Heights & Waverly Railroad (Frick lines), 23, 33, 41, 43
    Map, **42**
Baltimore, Pimlico & Pikesville Railroad, 37, 40, 43
    Map, **34**
    see also Pimlico & Pikesville Railroad
Baltimore Security & Trading Company, 49
Baltimore, South Baltimore & Curtis Bay Railway Company, 50
Baltimore Streetcar Museum, 110, 143, 151, **155**, 173, **190-200**, 225, **256, 282, 290-292**
    Car collection, **39, 99, 106, 107, 133, 155, 187, 190-202, 208, 215, 223, 256, 290-292**
    Trackage
        North Avenue loop, 192, **194, 195**
        28th Street (West Baltimore Street) loop, 192, **197**
Baltimore Terminal Company, 49
Baltimore Traction Company, 20, 37, 40, 41, 43, 45, 47, 48, 50, 58, 61, 63, 65, **67**, 71, **77**, 84, 87, 91, 94, **105**, 106, 143, 222, 224, **240**, 241, 244-247, **249-251**
    Acquisitions of other companies, 75, 77, 87
    Cable cars, **61**, 63-64, 65
    Cable operation, **61, 62**, 63-65, **67**, 68, 76, **77**, 80, 261-262, 264, 274
    Cars, *see* Cars, by owner
    Electric operation, 65, 75, 76, 94
    Finances, 60, 61, 66, 91, 94, 131
    First car, 63
    Formation, 61, 66
    Mail route, 249, 251
    Map, **28**
    Merged into Baltimore Consolidated Railway, 81, **83**
    Power houses, **62, 63**, 65, **67**
Baltimore Transit Company (first BTC — bus subsidiary of United Railways), 118, **119**
Baltimore Transit Company (second BTC — successor to United Railways), 99, 113, **122, 137-173**, 175, 176, 191, **192**, 195, **223, 266-271**
    Acquired by National City Lines, 155, 159, 161
    Cars, *see* Cars, by owner
    Conversions to bus, 153, 155, **158-167, 267-271**
    Fares, 163, 264, 267, 271, **272**, 275
    Finances, 137-140, 270, 273, 274
    Formation as successor to UR & E, 113, 137-138
    Last car, 169, 173
    Last day of rail operation, **169-173**
    Legal case, 161
    Operated by State (after strike), 163
    Routes, *see* Routes, United Railways and BTC
    Trackless trolleys, **133, 149, 150**, 153, 155, 159-160, 163, 166, 267, 271
Baltimore Union Passenger Railway, 35, **36, 38**, 40, 41, 45, **46**, 48, 50, 53, 57, 61, 71, **73**, 80, 231
Baltimore-Washington International (BWI) Airport, 175, 185, 187, 189
Barnes, Henry A., 159, 277
Barnum's Hotel, 14, **18-19**
Base, Robert, 50
Battery cars, 57-58, 59, 71
Battle Monument, *see* Monument Square
"Battles," 169, 231, 257, 259
Baxter & Company, 64, 241
Bay Shore Park, 109, **156**, 234, 237, 241, **243-245**, 247, 253, **260**, 269, 277
Bear Creek, 163, **280**

Bedford Square, 122, **158-160**, 237, **252-254, 269**, 275
Belgian block paving, **128**, 169, 239
Bellport, Long Island, New York, 50
Belt Line, *see* Baltimore & Ohio Railroad
Bentley & Knight, 53
Bethlehem Steel Corporation, **210**, 239, 241
"Bicycle railway," 48, 50
Birney (one-man) cars, *see* Cars, revenue
Bishop, George T., 110
Blakistone, George, 48, 69, 75, 82, 85
Block numbers, **145**
Blue Line, *see* Routes, Baltimore City Passenger Railway
"Bob-tailed cars," **15**, 33, **38**, 169, 219, 225
Bolton Hill, 179
Bonds and interest, 103, 108, 110, 131, 137-139, 274
Boston, Massachusetts, 68, 285
Boundary avenue proposal, 16
Bowie, (Gov.) Oden, 14, 23, 24, 25, 41, 59, 63, 64, 68, 74, 75, 80, 81, 88, 91, 175, 219
Bowkleman, Theodore, 247
Boynton electric railway system, 50
Bridges, trestles, and viaducts, 18, 40, **46**, 47, **51**, 58, 70, **73, 79**, 88, 91, 109, 113, **117**, 118, **134, 140**, 153, 159, 163, 169, 173, 185, 187, 191, **194, 204, 212, 214, 215, 232**, 234, 236-239, 241, 245, 257, 258, **259**, 261, 263, 264, **266, 276, 280**
    see also Guilford Avenue elevated
Brill, J. G. Company, *see* Cars, by builder
Brilliner, *see* Cars, revenue
Broadway (Fells Point), 18, 20, 21, 33, 82, 91, 166, 262, 264
Brock, Jonathan, 18-20, **27**
Broening, (Mayor) William, 118, 127
Brooklyn, Maryland, 47, 118, 249
Brooklyn, New York, 143, 249
Brooks, Chauncey, 13, 27
Brooks, Robert S., 109
Brooks-Barnum bill, 13-14
Brown, Alexander, 97, 101, 103, 159, 263
    see also Alex Brown & Sons
Brown, (Gov.) Frank, 14, 61, 247
Brownell Car Company, *see* Cars, by builder
Browning, William G., 13
Buschman, Charles F., **282**
Buses, 118, **119**, 120, 122, **128, 136**, 143, **149**, 153-155, 176, 267, 271
    Competition from, 115, 117-118, 120, **136**, 277
    Double-deck, **119**, 120, 122, **128, 139**, 154
    First United Railway service, 118, **119**, 267
    Substitution, 120, 153, **158-165, 267-271**
"Cable cocktail," 68
Cable systems, 29, 40, **59-68**, 75, 76, 80, 91, 94, 98, 103, 127, 131, 222, 224, 227, 261-262, 274
    Abandonment, 76, 91-94
    Cars, **60, 61**, 63-64, 65, **66**, 91, **99**, 127, **240**
    First car, 63, 64
    Grips, 64, 91
    Power houses, **62**, 64, 65, **67**, 91, 94, **250**, 261, 262
Calvert Station, 21, **60**, 69, 160
Camden Station, 21, 114, **134**, 153, 160, 185, 188, 189
Canton, 13, 18, 48, 91, 101, 143, 220, 273
Canton Railroad, 186
Car barns, *see* Car houses
Car checks, **261**, 264
Car houses (barns)
    Belvedere, 113, **141**, 159, 160, **167**, 244
    Brooklyn, 249
    Cumberland Street, 91, 191
    Darley Park, 35, **39**, 40, 91
    Druid Hill Avenue, 63, **67**, 68, **77, 83, 105**, 106, 249, **250**
    Edmondson Avenue (Frick lines), 113

Edmondson Avenue (United Railways), **104**, 113, **116**, 191, **206**, **210**
Falls Road, **88**, 89
Falls Road (BSM), 191, **194**, **196**, **197**, **256**
Greenmount Avenue, 191, **193**
Howard Park, **80**
Irvington, 169, **172-173**, 191, **192**, **210**, **280**
Light Street car house, 91, **220**
Lombard Street, 113
Madison Avenue, **78**, 89, 91, **92-93**, **94**
McMechen Street, **40**, 58
Montebello, 113
North Avenue (and Gay), 91, 113
Oak Street (and 25th, now Howard Street), **53**, **54**, 55, **57**
Owings Mills, 234, 253, 254
Park Terminal, **108**, **109**, 113, **158**, 163, **204**, **286**
Potomac Street, 82
Pratt Street, 63
Preston Street (near Jones Falls), 69, 82
Retreat Street, **84**, 235
Roland Park, **111**, 153, 276
Smallwood Street, **66**, 91, 169
Walbrook, 69
Waverly, **104**, 107, 113, 169, 250
York Road, 113, **161**, **167**, 169
Carlin's Park, 179, 237, 244, 247
Carney, 131, 134, 166, 181
Carroll (Carroll Station), 172, 249
Carroll Park shops, 106, 110, 113, **129**, **166**, **214**, **220-221**, 250, **254**, **263**, 285, 291
Cars, by builder
  ABB Traction, Inc., **184-189**, **216**
  American Car Company, **108**, 284
  Baltimore City Passenger Railway, **99**, **192**, **193**, **194**, **256**
  Baltimore & Northern Railway, **90**
  Brill, J. G. Company, **49**, 57, 58, 60, **63**, **73**, **79**, **85**, **95**, **105-107**, 109, **111-114**, 116, 118, 120, **121-126**, **128-130**, 131, 132-136, **138-139**, **142**, 143, **145-148**, 150, 153, **156-158**, 163, **165**, **167**, 188, **190**, **192**, **193**, 195, **198**, **201-207**, **212**, 213, **215**, **218**, **221**, **226**, **228**, 230, **232**, **236**, **243**, **248**, **252**, **254**, **266**, **268**, **270**, 275, **276**, **278-286**, **290-293**
  Brownell Car Company, **83**, 118, 122, 134, **201**, **202**, **242**, **256**, 291
  Budd Company, **177-181**, **216**
  Cincinnati Car Company, 131, **134**, 291
  Fowler, J. W. Car Company, 230
  Jackson & Sharp, 249
  Kuhlman Car Company, 284, 291
  Laclede Car Company, **88**, **89**, 90, **94**, 116, **246**
  Lewis & Fowler Car Company, **65**, 76-78, **84**, 116, 249
  Poole & Hunt, 20, 35, **38**, 89, 291
  Pullman Car & Manufacturing Company, 70, **71**
  Pullman-Standard Car & Manufacturing Company, **143**, **145**, 151, **153-155**, 159, **161**, **164-165**, **167-172**, **193**, **199**, **202-203**, 205, **207-209**, **211-214**, **221**, **238**, **259**
  St. Louis Car Company, **104**, **143**, **144**, **148**, 151, 159, 161, **214**
  Stephenson, John Car Company, **29**, **31**, **38**, **40**, **47**, **64**, 69, **76**, **223**, 249, 284, 291
  United Railways & Electric Company, **234**, 251
Cars, by owner
  Baltimore & Curtis Bay Railway, **65**
  Baltimore & Hampden Railway, **54-57**, 257
  Baltimore & Northern Railway, **88-90**, 97, 224, 233-234, 250
  Baltimore & Randallstown Railroad, **49**
  Baltimore & Yorktown Turnpike Railway, 35, **38**, **39**, 257
  Baltimore, Calverton & Powhatan Railway, **51**, 257
  Baltimore, Catonsville & Ellicott's Mills Passenger Railway, **36**, **54**
  Baltimore City Passenger Railway, **10**, **14**, **15**, 20, 21, **24**, **25**, **36**, **39**, **60**, **66**, **68**, **79**, **83**, 91, **94**, 97, **99**, **100**, **101**, 230, 231, **256**
  Baltimore Consolidated Railway, **83**, 97, 109, **111**, **201**, 230, **242**

Baltimore Traction Company, **61**, 63-65, **72**, **78**, **81**, **201**, 230, **240**, **250**
Baltimore Transit Company, **122**, **134**, **141**, **142**, **173**, **192**, **203-215**, **221**, **223**, **226-231**, **236-238**, **243**, **248**, **252**, **254**, **259**, **262**, **266**, **268**, **270**, **276**, **278**, **281**, **283**, **284**, **286**, **287**, **290**
Baltimore Union Passenger Railway, **36**, **38**, **46**
Central Railway, **31**, **46**, 48, 69, 72, **73**, **85**, 101, **265**
Citizens' Railway, **18-19**, **26**, 231
City & Suburban Railway, **76**, **83**, **84**
"Dummy line" (Druid Hill Park), **26**, **29**
Frick lines, **40**, **43**
Lake Roland Elevated Railway, **71-73**, **76**, 249, 250
Loudon Park Cemetary, **36**, 172
MTA, **177-181**, **184-189**, **216**
Newport News & Hampton Railway, Gas & Electric Company, 195
North Avenue Railway, 60, **63**, **64**, 66
North Baltimore Passenger Railway, **40**, 57-58
People's Railway, **81**
Pikesville, Reisterstown & Emory Grove Railroad, 87, **88**
Pimlico & Pikesville Railroad, **37**
Towson & Cockeysville Railroad, 58
Walbrook, Gwynn Oak & Powhatan Railroad, **44**
United Railways & Electric Company, **39**, **78**, **79**, **89**, **90**, **92-93**, **95**, **96**, **98**, **100-118**, **120-140**, 190, 191, 195, **218**, **228**, **232**, **234**, **235**, **242**, **246**, 250, 251, **253-255**, **265**, **274**, 275, 277, 279, **280**, **282-293**
Cars, non-revenue, by type
  Crane, 150, **234**
  Dump, **151**
  Flat, **45**, **90**
  "Jollytown," **242**
  Line, **47**, **105**, **160**, **210**, 249, **262**
  Office car "Eloise," **265**
  Pay, 120
  Rail bond test car, **215**
  Reel, **151**, **235**, 249
  Salt, 219, 231
  Shifter, **101**
  Snowplows, 109, 219
  Snow sweepers, 109, **121**, **141**, **210**, **226-231**
  Sprinkler, **90**
  Weed sprayer, **151**
Cars, revenue, by type
  ABB Traction, Inc., *see* Cars, by builder
  Articulated units, 127, **128**, 130, 131, **141**, 154, **157**, 159, 169, 172, 184, 188, **189**, 275, 276, **280**, **285-289**, 291
  Baggage combine, **88**, 89, 90, 250
  Birney (one-man), **118**, **124**, **125**, 127, 134, 143, 275, 285, 286
  Brilliner, 143, **145**, **148**, 151, 169
  Budd Company, *see* Cars, by builder
  Cable, **60-66**, **79**, 91, 127, **240**
  Closed, **46**, **63-65**, **73**, **76**, **78**, **83**, **89**, **99**, **101**, **106**, **201**, **242**, 279, 288
  Convertible, **79**, **96**, **105**, **108**, **192**, **202**, 224, **232**, 253, **254**, 279
  Express, 90, 103, 116, **140**, 224, 250, **251**
  Funeral, **36**, 90, **100**, 103, 109, 120, 172
  Light rail, **184-189**, **216**
  Mail (RPO), **64**, 77, **84**, 103, 120, **249-251**
  Market, 250
  Master units, 143
  Metro, **177-181**, **216**
  Multiple-unit trains, 109, 130, 131, 141, 159, 275, **280**, 286, 289
  One-man (*see also* PCC and Peter Witt), 15, 20, **40**, **124**, **129**, 130, 131, 134, **136**, **146-147**, 150, 152, 156, 157, 158, 165, 203, 204, 207, 212, 225, **230**, **236**, 252, 254, 268, 275, **276**, **278**, **283**, 284
  Open, 44, 76, 78, 91, **92-93**, **95**, 104, 108, 111, 120, **123**, **192**, **201**, **240**, **242**, **246**, 247, **256**, 264, 275, 279, **285**, **287**, 288
  Open and closed sets, 279, 288

P.A.Y.E. (pay as you enter), 115, 116, 219
PCC, 139, **143-145**, 148, **151-156**, 159, **161-173**, **187**, **198**, **199**, **202-205**, **207-209**, **211-214**, **221**, 224, **238**, 239, **259**, **262**, **269**, **285**
Permanently-coupled trains, 275, **285**, 288, 289
Peter Witt (Baltimore car), 127, **130-134**, 137, 139, 143, 159, 171, 173, **198**, 199, 202, **290-293**
Peter Witt (experimental), 121, 131, **132**, 275, 285, 286
Private (parlor) cars, **88**, 90, **111**, **117**, 118, **265**
Semi-convertible, **107**, 109, **112-116**, **122**, **123-126**, 127, 131, **135-136**, **138-139**, **142**, **146-147**, **150**, **152**, **156**, **157-158**, 159, 161, 163, **165**, **167**, 169, 172, 188, 195, **203-207**, **212**, **213**, **215**, **218**, **221**, **228**, **230**, **236**, 237, 239, **243**, **248**, 252, **254**, 262, **266**, **268-270**, **275-284**, 285, **287**, 288
    Trailers, 118, **121**, 122, 127, 130, **132**, 143, 169, 275, 277, 280, 289
Cartoon (Edmund Duffy), **17**, **162**
Cathcart, Robert, 13
Catonsville, 35, 40, 49-50, 109, 116, 159, 169, **171**, 173, 175, **207**, **208**, 227, 249
    Map, **271**
Catonsville Junction, 103, 109, 163, **168-169**, **171**, 173, **267-271**
Catonsville Railway Park, 173, 241
Catonsville Short Line Railroad, 45, 49, 50, 107
Central Light Rail Line, **126**, 127, **136**, 173, **182-189**, 199, **216**
Central Railway, **31**, 33, **46**, 48, 50, **67**, 75, 82, 84, **85**, 88, 90, 94, 131, 153, 166, 224, 225, 227, 241
    Acquired by Baltimore City Passenger Railway, 81-82, 84
    Cars, *see* Cars, by owner
    Electric operation, 65, 69, 72, **73**, 94
    Map, **70**
Chambers, Wrightson, 251
Chapman, (Mayor) John L., 220
Charles Center, **146-147**, 150, 169, **176**, **177**, 179, 181, 258
Chartered cars, 109, **158**, **165**, 169, **171**, 173, **206-209**, **211**, **243**, **247-248**
Chattalanee Bottled Water, **251**
Chicago, Illinois, 59, 72, 183, 227
Chinese station, 29, **30**, **61**, 224, 261
Cincinnati Car Company, *see* Cars, by builder
Citizens' Railway, **18-19**, 23, **26**, 28, 29, 32, 33, 41, 61, 63, **67**, 231, 241, 264
    Map, **32**
    Merged into Baltimore Traction Company, 61
    Steam motor test, **26**, 32-39, 59
City & Suburban Railway, 71-72, 75, **76**, 77, **84**, 87, 94, 116, 224, 241, 249, 262, 264
    Cars, *see* Cars, by owner
    Electric operation, 71-72, 75, 94
    Formation, 71
    Mail routes, 249
    Map, **82**
    Merged into Baltimore Consolidated Railway, 81, **83**, 84, 91, 241
City Council (Baltimore), 13-16, 21, 23, 24, 33, 41, 68, 120, 224, 273
City Hall, **15**, 33, 35, 41, 48, 60, 69, 71, **154**, 169, **211**, 227, 239
City Motor Company, 118
City Park Railway, 27, 29, 33, 37
City Passenger, *see* Baltimore City Passenger Railway
"City passenger railways," 45, 169
Civil War (War Between the States), 18, 23, 35, 273
Clark, A. T., 191, 291
Clark Equipment Company trucks, **149**
Clifford, 186
Clifton Park, 181
Cockeysville, 183, **185**
Colors, designation of routes by, 20, 21, 81
    see also Paint schemes
Columbia & Maryland Railway, 45, **46**, 48-49, 103, 107, 109, **266**
Compressed air propulsion, 57, 71
Conductorettes, *see* Employees

Conductors, *see* Employees
Conrail, 183, **185**, 186, **188**
Consolidated Gas, Electric Light & Power Company of Baltimore, 115
Consolidated Railway, *see* Baltimore Consolidated Railway
Consolidations, 41, 45, 61, 75, 81-84, 90, 97-101, 103, 159, 166, 241, 263, 274, 279
Conversions to bus, 153-155, **158-166**, 267, 269, 271
Convertible cars, *see* Cars, revenue
Council Grove station, **26**, **29**, **31**, 261
Councilman's Hollow, 233
Court of Appeals of Maryland (cited in *Maryland Reports*), 43, 94, 116, 131, 134, 161
Cowen, John K., 50
Crews, *see* Employees
Cross, E. J. D., 50
Cross, Thomas A., 116, 127
CSX Transportation, 179, 185, 186, 187, 188, 194
Curtis Bay (Curtis Creek), 47, 113, 118, **134**, 154, 160, **232**, 245, **246**, 247, 249
Daft, Leo, 35, **54-56**, 58, 59
Daft line and motors, 35, 36, 52-58, 122, 257, 259
D'Alesandro, (Mayor) Thomas J., Jr., 191
Darley Park, 35, **39**, 40, 91, 245
Davis, Carvey G., **99**, **209**
Dead-man controls, 130, 261
"Deep cut," 173, **266**
DeGoey, William, 13
Destination signs, 20, 81, **104**, 114, 155, 159, **166**, **232**, **280**
Dickeyville, 163, 276
Dividends, 24, 41, 59, 94, 103, 110, 263, 274
Dolores, **100**, 103, 109, 120
Donahue, Thomas, 261-262
Double-deck buses, **119**, 120, 122, **128**, **139**, 154
Double-deck horse cars, 35, **38**, 39, 169
Drivers (horse car), *see* Employees
Druid Hill Park, 21, 23, **26-33**, 37, **61**, 64, 67, **94**, 97, 241, 261, 279
    Railway, *see* "Dummy line"
Duffy, Edmund, 162
Dugan's Wharf, 106, 261
"Dummy line" (railway in Druid Hill Park), **26-32**, 261
Dundalk (Dundalk Junction), 113, **164**, 175, 189, 249, 253, 289
Duquesne Railway (Pittsburgh, Pennsylvania), 71
Duvall, J. Brooke, **223**
Duvall, John Brooke, Sr., 155
East Broad Top Railroad, 263
East Fayette Street bus lines, 120
Edmondson Avenue, Catonsville & Ellicott City Electric Railway, 45, 49
Eisner, Will, 253
Elections, **17**, 18
Electric Light & Railway Company, 84
Electric light companies, 101, 263, 264
Electric operation, 66, 75, 76, 94
    Baltimore City Passenger Railway, 61, 75, **79**
    Baltimore Traction, 75, **77**, **78**
    Central Railway, 69, 72
    City & Suburban, 71, 75, **76**
    Dangers and objections, 59, 68, **74**
    First conventional trolley car, 60, **63**, 65, 66
    First operation (Daft motor), **53-58**
    Lake Roland Elevated Railway, **71-73**, 75, **76**
Electric Park, 41, 87, 89, 233, 244, 247
Electric Storage Battery Company, 58
Elevated railways, **69-73**
    see also Guilford Avenue elevated
Elkins, William, 61, 64
Ellicott City (Ellicott's Mills), 35, 40, 45, 49, 103, 109, 116, **140**, 163, **171**, 173, **212**, 237, 250, 263, 264, 267, 268, 269, **270**, **271**
    Map, **271**

Ellicott's Mills, *see* Ellicott City
Emergency controls, 173, 288, **292**
Emmons, Charles D., 116, **121**, 127, 131
Emmons, S. E., 286, 289
Emory Grove (campground), 87, 116, 233
Employees, 107, 120, 127, **140**, **158**, **218-222**, 224, 225, **226**, 253, 275
   Conductorettes, 120, **122**
   Conductors, 20, 21, **25**, 38, 39, **44**, 69, 88, 130, 131, 219, **220-222**,
     225, **226**, **231**, 233, 234, 237, 241, 245, **246**, 247, 259, 261, 262,
     275, 288
   Crew changes, 88
   Drivers (horse car), 20, 38, 219, 220
   Extra men, 118, 224, 227, 230, 231
   Grip inspector, 224
   Gripmen, 64, 222, 224, 261-262
   Motormen, **44**, 69, 89, 115, **122**, 130, 154, **158**, 222, 224, 225, **226**,
     230, 232, 233-234, 245, 248, 249, 253, 258, 259, 261, 262, **275**,
     286, 288
   Operators, **144**, **145**, 224, 291
   Stable workers, 219-220
   Track crews, **218**
End of streetcar service, *see* Last day of rail operation
Engleman, John V., 173
"Epizootic" (epidemic among horses), 23, 25
Epworth Independent Methodist Church, 65
Exact change required, 21
Express service (package), 103, 115-116, **140**, 234, **251**
Express service (passenger), 127
Expressways, 159, 180, 183, 233, **236**, 277
Extra men, *see* Employees
Fairfield, 134, 154, 249
"Fair of the Electric Pony," **190**, 191
"Fair of the Iron Horse," 191
Fairy Grove Park, 91
Fairview Inn, 172
Falls Road Electric Railway, 75, 77, 82, 84, 87
Fareboxes and collections, 88, 90, 219, 225, 264, 291
Fares, 13-16, 20, 21, 23, 35, 50, 69, 73, 109, 122, 127, 131, 134, 137,
     153, 166, 169, 219, 241, 263, 264, 267, 271, 273, 277
   Special rates, 137, 153, 264, 271, **272**
Fayette Street (E. Fayette) bus lines, 120
Fells Point, *see* Broadway
Fenders, 120, 134
Fenneman, August, 244
Ferry Bar, 18, 33, 47, 134, 247, 261, 279
Fields, John W., 23
Fiftieth anniversary (of rail operation), **92-93**, **260**
Finances, 23, 25, 75, 81, 82, 91, 94, 97-101, 103, 107, 108, 109, 110,
     113, 118, 127, 131, 137-140, 155, 175, 187, 188, 270, 274, 277,
     284
Fires, 113, 118
   Car house, 40, **63**, 103, **104**, 107, **108**, 113, 169, 250
   Baltimore Fire (1904), **102**, 106, 108, 110, 131
First cable car, 63, 64
First day of operation (horse car), **14**, 20, 166, 169
First electric car (conventional trolley), 60, **63**
First electric operation (Daft motor), **53-58**
Fitzgerald, Roy, 155, 161, 267
Flood's (Jack Flood's), 47, **245-247**
Ford's Theatre, **12**, **212**
Forest Park, 166
Fort Howard, 163, 241, 269
Fort McHenry, 33, 64, **158**, **256**
Fowler, J. W. Car Company, *see* Cars, by builder
Franchises (ordinances and charter provisions), 13, 14, 16, 18, 21, 23,
     32, 33, 35, 41, 48, 50, 69, 91, 94, 101, 108, 120, 257, 261, 273,
     277
Francis, Edward T., 58

Franklin, Walter S., 81, 88, 91, 97
Franklin Street waiting station, 120, 251, **260**
Franklintown, 35
Freight, 250
Frick, George, 41
Frick lines, 20, 33, **41-43**, 61, 113
   Map, **42**
Friendship Airport, *see* BWI
Fulton Depot, 33, 261
Funeral cars, *see* Cars, revenue
Gaither, James H., 116, 250
Gaither City & Suburban Express Company, 115-116, **140**, 250, **251**
Gardenville, 82, 121, **145**, **205**
Garrison family, 256
Gauge, 48, 49, 87, **110**, 112, 195, 263, 264, 273
   Origin of Baltimore gauge (5 feet 4½ inches), 21
   Standard (4 feet 8½ inches), 45, 48, 49, 177, 263
General Assembly (Maryland), *see* Legislature (Maryland)
General Electric Company, 137, 171
General Motors Corp. (GMC), 153
Genthner, James A., **170**
Gerald, Clyde, **195**
Glen Burnie, 175, 176, 185, 186, 187, 188, 189
Glenn L. Martin Company, 154
Glyndon, **79**, 248, 250
"Golden-glow" headlight, **290**
Govans(town), 35, 71, 169, 219, 249, 251, 259
Green Line, *see* Routes, Baltimore City Passenger Railway
Greenmount Cemetery, 169
Grip Inspector, *see* Employees
Gripmen, *see* Employees
Grove, Conrad, 18
Guilford (Bedford Square), 122, **252-254**, 275
   see also Bedford Square
Guilford Avenue bridge, 239
Guilford Avenue elevated, **69-72**, 73, 127, 159, 160, 169, 234, **236-239**,
     257-259, **262**
   Abandoned, 160, 239
   Stations, **237-239**
Gwynns Falls, 37, 48, **242**, **276**
Gwynns Falls Railway, 40, 48, 50
Gwynn Oak Junction, 122, 160, **209**
Gwynn Oak Park, **44**, 48, 113, 211, **240-242**, 244, 247, **260**
Hackneys, 13
Hagerty, J. S., 41, 61, 63, 231
Halethorpe, 113, 131, 234, 245
Hall's Springs, 35, 40, 75, 91, **100**
   Map, **34**
Hambleton, Frank S., 108
Hambleton, T. Edward, 41, 58, 61, 63, 81, 84
Hambleton and Company, 61, 97, 284
Hampden, *see* Baltimore & Hampden Railway; Daft line and motors
Hanover Street bridge, **117**, 118, 134
Harford Road Turnpike Company, 91
Harlem Stagecoach Company, 261
Hartman, Ronald J., **184**
Harundale, 176
Hayward, Bartlett & Company, 28
Heating of cars, 131, 264
Herdic coaches, 261
Highland Park, *see* Walbrook
Highlandtown, 48, 50, 75, 81, 91, 113, 123, **136**, 153, 154, 160, 161,
     163, **164**, 227, 241, 249, 289
Highlandtown & Point Breeze Railway, 48, 50, 61, 241
   Map, **61**
Hill, Bancroft, 139
Hill boys, **24**, 220, 224
Hillen Station, 48, 50

Hill horse, 35, 220
Hilton, George, 63, 66, 68
Historic car collection, *see* car collection, Baltimore Streetcar Museum
Holland, J. C., 50
"Hollywood" car, 199
Hood, John Mifflin, **103**, 106, 110
"Hoodoo car" (No. 13), **253-255**
"Hooking rides," 257
Horner, W. F., 233
Horse cars, **13-15**, **18-21**, **23-25**, 28, 33, **35-41**, **43**, **45-51**, 52, 64, **68**, **81**, **85**, 91, **99-101**, 122, 169, 219-220, **223**, 225, **256**, 257, 261, 291
    Early proposal for lines, 13
Horses, 23, 219, 220, 225
Hours, working, 38, 219, 220, 224, 225, 227
House, William A., 30, 64, 87, 106, 113, 115, 116, 224, 225, 265
Howard Street extension, 153
Howard Street tunnel, 127, 134, 179, 185, 188
Hughes, Carl P., 292
Hundredth anniversary (of rail operation), **223**
Hunt Valley, 183, 185, 187, 189
Huntingdon Avenue viaduct, 159, **204**, 258, 263, 264
Hurricane Agnes, 195
Idlewylde Railway, 275, 277
Inflation, 23, 127, 273, 275, 285
Injunctions, 20, 89, 90, 161
Interest (debt service), 103, 110, 137, 139, 274
Inter Mural Railway (Chicago, Illinois), 72
Interstate highway system, **180**, 183, 184, 187, 262
Interurban railways, 45, 48, 49, 87, 107, 262-263
Irvington, **99**, **172**, **192**, 227, 280
Jackson & Sharp, *see* Cars, by builder
Janssen, Robert W., **256**, 284
Jenkins, George C., 50
Jenkins, Michael, 97-98
Jenkins family, 81
Jerkwater lines, 20, 40, 130, 153, 160, 163, 269, 275
Jitneys, 115, 117, 118, 119, 122
Johns Hopkins Hospital Metro extension, 180, 181
Jones Falls, 195, 199
Karl, John, 221
Kean, J. Randolph, 94
Keck, J. L., 50
Keene, John Henry, Jr., 69, 72
Kinsman signals, 239
"Kiss 'n' ride," **269**
Klein's Park, 245
Know-Nothing (Native American) party, 13, 14, 16, **17**, 18, 21
Krueger, Robert, 292
Kuhlman Car Company, *see* Cars, by builder
Laclede Car Co., *see* Cars, by builder
Lake Roland, 21, 75, 191, 244
Lake Roland Elevated Railway, 41, 48, 50, 60, 61, **64**, 69-70, **71**, **72**, **73**, 75, **76**, **112**, 122, 166, 239, 244, 249, 257, 277
Lakeside (Park), 134, **158**, 159, 160, 244, 247
Last car (electric), **155**, 169, 173, **199**, **208**
Last day of rail operation, 155, 163, **167**, 169, **170**, 173, 248
Last horse cars, 37, **85**, 91, 169
Latrobe, (Mayor) Ferdinand, 32, 68, 69
Latrobe, John H. B., **27**
Laurel, 45
Legal cases, 20, 43, **74**, 90, 94, 99, 116, 131, 134, 161, 173, 277
Legislature (Maryland), 13, 20, 21, 23, 41, 109, 177, 187
Levee, Leonard, **228**
Levinson, Barry, 199
Lewis & Fowler Car Company, *see* Cars, by builder
Lexington Market, 68
"Lifeguards," **85**, 120

Linthicum, 186
Lloyd, Charles R., **292**
Long Bridge, 47, **232**, 245, 261
Loops, *see* Routings and trackage
Loreley, Maryland, 75
Lorraine (Cemetery), 37, 40, **85**, 91, 134, 163
Lorraine Electric Railway, 163
Loudon Park Cemetery, **36**, 49, 109, 172
Lowrey, Frank, 241
Lowrey's place, 241
Lutherville, 183
Mack (Mack Trucks, Inc.), 153
Mackenzie, John T., 39
Maddox, Luther, 233
Mail service, 50, 77, 84, 103, 120, **249-251**
Maintenance-of-Way Department, **47**, **90**, **115**, **121**, **140**, 141, **145**, **150**, **151**, **215**, **218**, **226**, 228, **229**, **230**, **231**, **235**, **249**, **262**
Mandel, Governor Marvin, 177, 179
Maps, **22**, **28**, **32**, **34**, **42**, **52**, **59**, **62**, **70**, **82**, **86**, **174**, **182**, **271**, **end sheets**
MARC, 185
Mariner, William H., 247
Marley, 176, 177
Martenet, Simon J., 80
Martin, Glenn L. Company, 154
Maryland & Pennsylvania Railroad, **46**, 70, 169, 191, 192, **204**, 257
Maryland & Washington Railway Company, 45
Maryland Electric Railways, 81, 107, 108, 110, 113, 131
Maryland Historical Society, **99**, 191, **192**
Maryland Institute of Art, 148
Maryland Legislature, *see* Legislature (Maryland)
Maryland Traction Company (successor to Columbia & Maryland), 45, 107
Maryland Traction Company (Baltimore & Northern constituent company), 84
Mass Transit Administration, *see* MTA
Maximum-traction trucks, **107**, **111**, 288
Mayors (Baltimore), 14, 16, **17**, 18, 21, **27**, 32, 41, 68, 69, 118, 127, 159, 177, 187, 191, 220
McDonough, 233
McDonough Road, **180**
McGuire Manufacturing Company, 69
McKeldin, (Mayor) Theodore R., 191
McLane, James L., 61, 69
Meese, William H., 137
Meeter's Park, 245, 247
Memorial Stadium, 154, 173, 175
Mencken, H. L., 134
Merrick, Theodore, 233
Merriken, (Col.) John E., 49, 289
Metro ("Heavy Rail" subway), 127, **174-181**, 183, 187, 189, 199, **216**
Metropolitan Transit Authority, *see* MTA
Meyer, Louis F., 284
Miami Metro, 179
Middle River, 81, 91, 154, 247, 269
Millington, 169
Milwaukee articulated units, 285
Monorail, *see* Bicycle railway
Monumental Railway, 48, 261
Monument Square (Battle Monument), 13, 14, 15, 16, 18, 21
Moore, (Dr.) Charles, 257, 259
Morrell Park, 153
Morse, Kenneth, 161, 292
Motormen, *see* Employees
Mount Holly casino, 60, 241, 247
Mount Olivet Cemetary, 172
Mount Royal Station, 103

Mount Washington, 87, 88-89, 103, 113, 143, 160, 183, 195, 233, 234, 259
MTA (initially Metropolitan Transit Authority, now Mass Transit Administration), 84, 106, 110, 175, 179, 180, 183, 184, 199, 264
Mueller, Louis C., 134, 284
Mules, 53, 58
Multiple-unit trains, 109, 130, 131, **141**, 159, 275, **280**, **285**, 286, 291
Municipal Stadium, *see* Memorial Stadium
Munnikhuysen, Howard, 61
Murray, J. D. Company, 69
Museums, *see* Baltimore Streetcar Museum; Baltimore Museum of Art; National Capital Historical Museum of Transportation; Seashore Trolley Museum
Nachod signals, 234
National Capital Historical Museum of Transportation (Washington area streetcar museum), 191
National City Lines, 155, 159, 161, 163, 191, **203**, 267, 269
National Railway Historical Society, *see* Baltimore Chapter, NRHS
Nelson Cook & Company, 131
News, Baltimore, 224-225
Newsboys, **118**
New York, New York, 70, 249
Nicholson, Leonard, 261
Nixon, George F., 120, 155, **191**, 192, 259, 277, 284, 289
North Avenue Market, **143**, **230**
North Avenue Railway, 59, 60, 61, **63**, **64**, 66, 69, 116, 239, 241
  Map, **59**
North Baltimore Passenger Railway (Frick lines), 37, **40**, 41, **43**, 57-58
  Map, **42**
North Bend, 269
Northern Central Railway, 46, **60**, 69, **72**, 87, 88, 98, 134, 183, **185**, 186, 188, 189, **236**, 258-259
Novak, David M., 284, 292
Obbink, Richard, **195**
O'Donnell's Wharf, 113
Oella, 109, 173
Omnibuses (Stagecoaches), 13, **16**, **17**, **18-19**, 40, 261, 264
One-man cars, *see* Cars, revenue
Open and closed car sets, *see* Cars, revenue
Open cars (summer cars), *see* Cars, revenue
Operating costs, 23, 24, 58, 127, 134, 175, 177, 187, 270, 273
Oriole Park (29th Street), 169, 173
Orioles (Baltimore baseball team), 244, 247
Orleans Street viaduct, 153, 155, **236**
Overhead lines, **105**, **134**, **156**, 229, 257, **262**
Overlea, 163, **172**, 181
Owings Mills, 176, **180**, 181, 183, 233, 234, 253, **254**
Paint schemes, 20, 21, 63, 64, 65, 69, 81, **107**, **111**, 120, **129**, **132**, **138**, 148, 151, 154, 163, 167, 169, **203**, **213**, 234, 237, 249, 279, **281**
Park Railway, 27, 33, 41
Parks, 173, **240-248**
  see also names of specific parks
Park tax, 16, 18, 21, 23, 24, 25, 27, 108, 137, 139, 273, 274, 277
Park Terminal, *see* Car houses
Parkton, 183
Parkville, 269
Parlor cars (private cars), *see* Cars, revenue
Parr, Henry, 87, 97, 103
Parsons, Brinckerhoff, Quade & Douglas, **174**, 175, 176, 183
Parties, **240-248**
Part-time operators, 154
Patapsco River, 18, 33, 35, 77, 109, 118, **140**, 163, 173, 185, **212**, **232**, 237, 244, 245, 247, 255, 261, 264
Patronage (ridership), 127, 134, 152, 245
Patterson Park, 32, 64, 65, 261, 279
Paving, **112**, **128**, 159, 169, 239
P.A.Y.E. (pay-as-you-enter) cars, *see* Cars, revenue
PCC (Presidents' Conference Committee) cars, *see* Cars, revenue

Peale Museum, **15**, **154**
Penn Central Railroad, 45, 183
  see also Pennsylvania Railroad
Penn Station light rail branch, 185, 187, 189
Penniman, George D., 50
Pennsylvania Railroad, 45, 49, 118, **123**, **130**, 153, 160, 169, 179, 183, 189, **214**, **236**, 239, 259, 263
  see also Penn Central Railroad; Baltimore & Potomac Railroad; Northern Central Railway
Pennsylvania Station, *see* Union Station
Pennsylvania Steel Company, 69, 239
People's Passenger Railway (later People's Railway), 33, 38, 41, 81, 106
  Merged into Baltimore Traction Company, 61
Perin, Ella (Keck), 80
Perin, Nelson, 41, 45, 49, 50, 53, 71, 75, 80, 81, 83, 84, 87, 97-98, 103, 106, 159, 169, 175, 257
Permanently-coupled trains, *see* Cars, revenue
Peter Witt cars, *see* Cars, revenue
Peter Witt fare collection system, 130, 131, 291
Philadelphia, Baltimore & Washington Railroad, 263
Philadelphia, Pennsylvania, 20, 48, 64, 98, 249, 291
Philadelphia Traction Company, 64
Philadelphia, Wilmington & Baltimore Railroad, 32
Pikesville, 35, **37**, 45, 87, 90, 175, 183, 233, 260
Pikesville & Reisterstown Turnpike Company, 75, 84
Pikesville, Reisterstown & Emory Grove Railroad, 75, 79, 82, 84, 87, 88, 89, 90, 233
Pimlico, 35, 50, 153, 154, 294
Pimlico & Pikesville Railroad, **37**, 45, 50, 69, 87, 90
  see also Baltimore, Pimlico & Pikesville Railroad
Pindell's Veterans Corps Band, 247
Poems, 81, 225
Point Breeze, 50, 137, 154, 160, 241, 247
Poole, Robert, 89, 90
Poole & Hunt, *see* Cars, by builder
Portable vestibules, **218**, 224, 230, **232**, 279
Postal service, *see* Mail service
Power houses, cable
  Baltimore Street, 91
  Charles Street, 91
  Druid Hill Avenue, 63, **67**, 68, **250**
  Eutaw Street, 91
  Gilmor Street (Epworth Church), 65
  Pratt Street, 63, 64, 261-262
Power houses, electric
  Baltimore Streetcar Museum, 192
  Carey Street, 115
  Falls Road, 69, 113
  Gilmor Street, 115
  Light Street, 91, 94
  Pratt Street (Dugan's Wharf), 106, **110**, 113-115, **231**, 261
  Preston Street, 69, 82, 115
  Stony Run (Falls Road), 70, 113
Powhatan, *see* Woodlawn
Pratt, Enoch, 24, 33
President Street Station, 32
Private cars, *see* Cars, revenue
Private right of way, 87, 127, 159, 160, 163, **165**, **170**, **171**, **207**, **208**, **212**, 237, 253, 262, 271, 273, **274**, **276**, 277, **290**
  see also Reserved right of way
Proposed rapid transit system, *see* Rapid transit (modern)
PSC, *see* Public Service Commission
Public Service Commission (PSC), 90, 115, 118, 120, 134, 153, 161, 267, 269, 270-271, 275, 277
Pullman-Standard Car & Manufacturing Company, *see* Cars, by builder
"Railroad battles," *see* "Battles"
Railroad riots (1877), 21

Randallstown, **120**, 122, 175, 261, **263**
Rapid transit (modern), *see* Central Light Rail Line and Metro
Rapid transit (street railway terminology), 21, 45, 60, 61, 222, 224, 234
Receivership (United Railways), 137
Redican, Cain, 219, 225
Red Line, *see* Routes, Baltimore City Passenger Railway
"Red rockets," **152**, **156**, 164, 183, **205**, **206**, **215**
Regional Planning Council, 175
Reisterstown, 87
Reorganization (of United Railways as BTC), 137-140
Rerouting, 153, 155, 159-161, 163, 166-167
Reserved right of way, 127, 153, 164, **205**, **211**, **213**, 253, 273
    see also Private right of way
Richmond, Virginia, 57, 285
Ridgewood Park, 60, 241, 247
Riverview Park, 77, 113, 120, 169, 192, 241, 244, 245, 247, 262
Robbins, T. C., 50, **54**, 55, 57
Robert E. Lee Park, 191, **193**
Roberts Noiseless Motor, 57, 71
Roland Avenue Electric Company of Baltimore City, 69
Roland Park, 70, 72, 75, **111**, 113, 122, **136**, 153, **158**, 160, 224, 249,
    276, **284**
Rotunda station, **30**, 261
Route numbers, **138**, **155**
Routes, Baltimore City Passenger Railway, 18, 20, **22**
    Ann Street cars, 91
    Blue Line (Charles Street), 15, 21, 35, 65, **79**, **83**, 88, 91, 113, 227
    Green Line (Pennsylvania Avenue), 20, 21, 75, 91, **94**, 220, 225,
        227, 230
    Fulton Station connection, 33
    Hall's Springs (branch of Yellow Line), **10**, 75, 76, 94
    Red Line (Gay Street-W. Baltimore Street), 20, 21, **25**, 35, 65, 79,
        91, 227, **256**
    South Baltimore line, 21
    White Line (Madison Avenue), 20, 75, 76, 77, 79, 91, 227, 230
    Yellow Line (Orleans Street branch), **24**, 75, 91, 227
Routes, miscellaneous older companies
    Arlington & Pimlico Railroad (steam), 45, 50
    Baltimore & Curtis Bay Railway, 47, 50
    Baltimore & Hall's Springs Railway, **10**, **34**, 35
    Baltimore & Hampden Railway, **52-58**
    Baltimore & Northern Railway, **86**, 88-90
    Baltimore & Yorktown Turnpike Railway, 35, 39, 71
    Baltimore, Calverton & Powhatan Railway, 35-37, 40, 41, 48, **51**, 91
    Baltimore, Catonsville & Ellicott's Mills Passenger Railway, 35, 40
    Baltimore Consolidated Railway, 45, 103, 109
    Baltimore, Middle River & Sparrows Point Railroad, 81, 91
    Baltimore, Peabody Heights & Waverly Railroad (Frick line), 41, **42**
    Baltimore, Pimlico & Pikesville Railroad (later Pimlico & Pikes-
        ville Railroad), **34**, 37, 40, 45
    Baltimore Traction Company, **28**, **61-65**, 75, 261-262
    Baltimore Union Passenger Railway, 35, 50, 71
    Central Railway, **31**, 33, 69, **70**, 82, 88, **101**
    Citizens' Railway, 28, 29, **32**
    City & Suburban Railway, 71-72, 75, **82**, 84, 87, 262
    Columbia & Maryland Railway, 45, 103
    Gwynns Falls Railway, 48
    Highlandtown & Point Breeze Railway, 48, **62**
    Idlewylde Railway, **277**
    Lake Roland Elevated Railway, 69-70
    Monumental Railway, 48
    North Avenue Railway, **59**, 60
    Park Railway, 41
    People's Passenger Railway (People's Railway), 33
    Pikesville, Reisterstown & Emory Grove Railroad, 87, 90
    Pimlico & Pikesville Railroad (formerly Baltimore, Pimlico & Pikes-
        ville Railroad), **34**, **37**, 40, 45, 50
    "Rams Horn Railway," 48, 50

Shore Line Railway, 247
Towson & Cockeysville Railway, 58
Walbrook, Gwynn Oak & Powhatan Railroad, 47
Routes, United Railways and BTC
    #1 (Gilmor Street-Guilford Avenue), 122, 127, **156**, 159, 160, 161,
        204, 237, 239, **252**
    #2 (Carey Street-Fort Avenue), 118, **158**, 160
    #3 (Linden Avenue-Halethorpe), 113, 131, 153, **228**
    #4 (Edmondson Avenue-Windsor Hills), 106, 142, **146-147**, 153,
        155, 163, 169, **278**
    #5 (Druid Hill Avenue-Emory Grove), 153, 160, **203**, 269
    #6 (Curtis Bay), 113, 118, **130**, **134**, 154, 160
    #7 *see* #8
    #8 (Towson-Catonsville), 109, 127, **148**, 153, **154**, 159, 160, 163,
        167, **169-173**, **207**, **208**, **211**, **215**, 237, **238**, 239, 267, 270, **271**
    #9 (Ellicott City), 103, 109, 163, 173, **212**, 237, 267, **268**, 269, **270**,
        271
    #9 (Preston Street), **125**
    #10 (Roland Park-Highlandtown), **115**, **136**, **150**, 153, 154, **284**
    #11 (Bedford Square), 122, **158**, 159, 160, 237, 239, **252**, 253, **269**
    #12 (John Street-Westport), 113, 118, 153, 155
    #13 (North Avenue), **112**, **114**, **141**, **143**, 163, 167, **230**
    #14 (Rolling Road), 103, **150**, 163, **206**, 267, **268**, 269, **270**
    #15 (Gay Street-W. Baltimore Street), **124**, **128**, **145**, 159, 160, 163,
        165, **167**, 169, **172**, **205**, **208**, **212**, **213**, **214**
    #16 (Madison Avenue), 160, 166, 167
    #17 (St. Paul Street-Gorsuch Avenue), 96, **102**, **114**, 122, 153, 159, 173
    #18 (Pennsylvania Avenue), 116, 160, 163
    #19 (Harford Avenue), 131, 160, 161, 163, **165**, 166, 167, **209**, 269,
        274, **287**
    #20 (Point Breeze), 154, 160, 241, **246**, 261
    #21 (Preston Street-Caroline Street), **129**, **133**, 153
    #22 (Wolfe Street), **101**
    #23 (Back and Middle Rivers), 153, 154, 269
    #24 (Lakeside), 153, 159, 160, **165**, **248**, **268**
    #25 (Mt. Washington), 143, 153, 159, 160, **204**, **259**, **293**
    #26 (Sparrows Point-Bay Shore), 109, 113, 118, **123**, 131, **136**, 153,
        156, 160, 161, 163, **164**, **205**, **207**, **210**, **215**, 237, 241, 253, **280**
    #27 (Federal Street-Washington Boulevard), **124**, 153, 237
    #28 *see* routes #24 and #33
    #29 (Boulevard-Roland Park), 113, 122, 153, 154, 155, 159, 160, 237, **268**
    #30 (Fremont Avenue), 113, **157**, 160, 166
    #31 (Garrison Boulevard), 120, 143, **148**, 159, 163, 166, 167
    #32 (Woodlawn), 113, 153, 160, 163, **209**, **211**
    #33 (West Arlington), 160, **209**, **286**
    #34 (Highlandtown Short Line), 81, 160
    #35 (Lorraine), 163
    "Jerkwaters"
        Belvedere Loop-Mt. Washington, 160, 167
        Fort Howard shuttle, 163, 269
        Key Avenue shuttle, 160
        Union Avenue Line, 160
Routings and trackage
    Belvedere Loop, **141**, **148**, **243**
    Car storage yards, **108**, **121**, **135**, **157**, **166**, **179**, **205**
    Catonsville "cut-off," 103, 109, **207**, **208**
    City Hall loop, 41, 48
    East Monument Street extension, 113
    Fairfield loop, 154
    Govans loop, **215**
    Irvington loop, **99**, 169, **171**, 172
    Lexington Street trackage, 277
    Mail car routes, **249-251**
    Overlea loop, **172**
    Paradise loop, 154, 172
    Pearl Street Loop, 160
    Post office tracks, 250, 251
    Rolling Road loop, **269-271**

Shipyard branch (Sparrows Point), 118, 122, **123**, **207**
Stadium spur, **154**, 173
West Baltimore Street Loop, **145**
    see also Routes
Rowdyism, 13, 16, 18, 21, 241, 244, 245
Ruxton, 183
Safe Deposit & Trust Company, 284
Safety precautions, 161, 262, 275
Safety zones, **130**, **136**, 164, 277
St. Helena, 249
St. Louis Car Company, *see* Cars, by builder
San Diego "Trolley," 183, 186
Sandler, Gilbert, 247
Sanks, A. D, 259
Schaefer, Governor/Mayor William Donald, 177, **184**, 186, 187, 189
Scharf, Thomas, 21, 41, 45
Scharnagle, Fred, 255
Schmoke, Mayor Kurt, 187
Scott, William, 257, 259
Seashore Trolley Museum, 163
Seating, 20, 283
Segregation on cars, 23, 24, **38**, 39
Semi-convertible cars, *see* Cars, revenue
Shoemaker, William S., 18
Shops, 91, 179, 192, **221**
    see also Carroll Park shops
Shore Line Park(s), 77, 244, 245
Shore Line Railway, 77, 80, 222, 244, 247
Shortest line, **94**
Signals, 88, 118, 224, 234, 239
Sioux City Elevated Railway, 70, 72
Skip stops, 120, 154, 286
"Skybus," 175
Slattery, C. J., 122
Slawson, J. B., 225
Slawson farebox, 23, 219, 225
Sleighs, 257, 259
Smallwood Street turnback, 169
Smith, E. D. and Son, 64
Snow, **40**, **141**, **142**, 159, **208**, 219, 225, **226-231**, 257, 259, 267, **290**
    see also Cars, non-revenue, salt, snow sweepers, snowplows
South Baltimore Company, 80
Spanish-American War, **256**
Sparrows Point, 91, 106, 109, 113, 131, 156, 159, **160**, 161, 163, 175, 183, **210**, **215**, 234, 241, 275
Shipyard branch, 118, 122, **123**, 192, **207**
Specialwork, **220**
"Spotters," 222
Sprague, Frank, 53, 55
Sprague system, 53, 59, 66
Stable workers, *see* Employees
Stadium spur, **154**, 173
Stagecoaches, 72, 261
Standard gauge trackage, 45, 49, 177, 263
State Roads Commission, 115
Stations, Light rail
    Camden Yards, 185, 189
    Dorsey Road (Glen Burnie), 186, 187
    Oriole Park at Camden Yards, 173, 185, 189
    Woodberry (Union Avenue), 184, **216**
Stations, Metro
    Milford Mill, 181
    Mondawmin Mall, 178, 179
    Old Court, **181**
    Reisterstown Plaza, 177, **179**, 180, 181, **216**
    Rogers Avenue, **178**
Stations, Streetcar, *see* Waiting stations
Statler, Edward, Jr., 33

Steam engines ("dummies"), **26**, 28, **29**, **32**, 33, 48, 50, 57, 70, 71
    see also "Dummy line"
Stephenson, John Car Company, *see* Cars, by builders
Stoddard's Hotel, 35, 103, 173
Storms, 159, 183, 195, **226-231**, 269
Storrs, Lucius, 126, 131, 137, 139, 292
Street listings
    Ashland Avenue, **165**
    Baltimore Street, 98, 102, 123, 124, **176**, 218
    Belvedere Avenue, **209**
    Berwyn Avenue, **285**
    Calvert Street, 18-19, 60
    Charles Street, **83**, 119, 128, **139**, **142**, 206
    Druid Hill Avenue, 30, 61, 77, 108, **109**, 250, **286**
    Dundalk Avenue, 164, 205
    Eastern Avenue, 164
    Edmondson Avenue, 116, **206**, 268
    Eutaw Street, **68**, 96
    Falls Road, 88, 194, **196**, 197
    Fayette Street, 10, 12, 18-19, 170, 212
    Fort Avenue, 158
    Franklin Street, 251
    Frederick Road and Avenue, 36, 171, **192**
    Fulton Avenue, 109, 204, **286**
    Garrison Boulevard, **290**
    Gay Street, 213, 214
    Greenmount Avenue, **193**
    Gwynn Oak Avenue, 80, **209**, 211, 242
    Hanover Street, **134**
    Harford Road, **39**, 274
    Holliday Street, 211
    Howard Street, **126**, **136**, 150, **187**, 278
    Interstate 795, 180
    Kelly Avenue, **259**
    Lafayette Avenue, **157**
    Lexington Street, 15, 146-147, 150, 258
    Liberty Heights Avenue, **209**
    Linden Avenue, **228**
    Lombard Street, 105, 150
    Madison Avenue, 78, 92-93
    Maryland Avenue, **229**
    McMechen Street, **40**
    North Avenue, 112, 113, 114, 141, 143, **230**
    Park Avenue, **275**
    Park Heights Avenue, 203
    Pratt Street, **95**, 110, **231**
    Preston Street, **129**, 149
    Redwood Street, **130**
    Reisterstown Road (Pikesville), **37**
    Remington Avenue, 54, 56
    Retreat Street, **84**
    Roland Avenue, **56**, 115
    St. Paul Street, **230**, 252, 254, **269**
    33rd Street, **54**, 55
    25th Street, **156**
    Washington Avenue (Towson), **168**
    Washington Boulevard, **234**
    Windsor Mill Road, **51**
    York Road, **161**, 170
Strikes and labor disputes, 20, 163, 250
Stroble, Robert, 183
Structural Iron Erecting Company, 263
Subway (trolley), proposed, 134
Subway system, Metro, 174, **181**
Sudbrook Park, 180, **181**
Summer cars, *see* Cars, revenue, open
Sumwalt, Joshua G., 13
Sunday, (Rev.) Billy, 247

Sunday operation, 23, 143, 166
Supreme Court (U.S.), 131, 134, 277
Swann, (Mayor) Thomas, 14, 16, **17**, 18, 21, **27**, 159
Sweepers (snow), *see* Cars, non-revenue
Sweet Air shuttle, 58
Taney Place, **143**
Taxes, 23, 140, 175, 274, 277
   see also Park Tax
Thomas-Latrobe bill, 13
Thomsen, John S., 21, 68, 273, 284
Thomson-Houston system, 73
Tickets, 263, 264, **272**
Timonium, 58, 175, 183, 187, 189
Tokens, *see* Car checks
Tompkins, Raymond, 191
Tower trucks, **235**
Towson (Towsontown), 35, 58, 71, 73, 116, 159, 168, 169, 175, 183, 189, 219, 227, 249, 250, 251, 257, 259
Towson & Cockeysville Railway, 58
Towson State University, **170**
Trackless trolleys, **120**, 122, **133, 149, 150**, 153, 159, 160, 163, **166**, 263, 267, 274, **284**
Trackwork, cable, 63, 65
Trackwork, electric, **218, 220**, 270
Traction Company, *see* Baltimore Traction Company
Trailers, *see* Cars, revenue
"Transfer cars" (jerkwaters), 20, 35, 40
Transfers, 23, 24, 87, 103, 109, 163, 166, 273
Travers, William H., 13
Travers ordinance, 13-14, 16, 18, 21
Trestles, *see* Bridges, trestles and viaducts; Guilford Avenue elevated
Trippers, 261
"Trolley" (first car), 66
Trolley parties, **246**, 247-248
Tropical Storm David, 195, **197**
Trucks, maximum-traction, **107, 111**, 288
Tunis, Edwin, 48
Two-trip slips, 153, 264
Tyson, Henry, 20, 23, 24, **27**
Uniforms, 120, **144, 222**
Union Passenger Railway, *see* Baltimore Union Passenger Railway
Union Station (Pennsylvania Station), 21, 33, **46**, 49, 69, **83, 114, 123, 139**
   see also Penn Station light rail branch
United Electric Light & Power Company, 263
United Railways & Electric Company, 49, 82, **98-140**, 163, 166, **190**, 191, 195, **260**, 263, 264, 269, 271, 273
   Advertisements, 12, 125, 222, 244, 245, 258, 260, 269, 272, 275, 277
   Bankruptcy, 137, 267
   Bus operation, 118, **119**, 120, **128, 136**
   Capitalization, 99-101, 131, 274
   Car houses, **80**, 89, 104, 107, 108, **109**, 113, **116, 161**
   Cars, *see* Cars by owner
   Finances, 75, 131, 134, 137, 274, 284
   Formation, 97-99
   Legal cases, 131, 277
   Mail and express service, **249-251**
   Map, **end sheets**
   Offices, 106, **260**
   Parks operated, 109, 120, **240-245**, 247
   Power plant, 106, **110**, 113, 115

   Reorganization (as BTC), 137, 139
   Shops, 106, 110, **221**
   Trackless trolley operation, **120**, 122, **263**
U.S. Emergency Fleet Corp, **156**
United States Light & Power Company, 58
U.S. Supreme Court, *see* Supreme Court (U.S.)
Valuation case (rate of return — United Railways), 99, 131, 134
Vandalism, 191, 261
Vestibules, 89, 115, 219, 224-225, 230, **232**, 279, 288
Viaducts, *see* Bridges, trestles and viaducts; Guilford Avenue elevated
Wages, 20, 127, 163, 220, 224, 275, 285
Wagner, Kenneth, **221**
Waiting stations, streetcar, 26, **29-31**, 49, 70, 118, 120, **123, 168, 236**, 237, **238**, 239, **243**, 244, 251, **252-254, 260**, 261, **269**
Walbrook (Walbrook Junction, Highland Park), 35, 37, 40, 41, 48, **51**, 60, 70, 75, 83, 106, 163, 166, 167, 224, **228**, 249, 258
Walbrook, Gwynn Oak & Powhatan Railroad, **44**, 47, 50, 75, **80**, 241, **244**
Walker, P. H., 40
War Between the States (Civil War), 18, 23, 35
Warfield, (Postmaster) S. Davies, 249, 251
Washington, D.C., 45, 48-49, 107, 173, 179, 191, 262
Washington, Baltimore & Annapolis Railway, 48-49, 110, 134, 186
Washington Boulevard (Columbia Avenue), 90, **92-93**, 106, 153, **234**
"Watered" stock, 99-101
Waterfront, **95, 110**
Water Tower loop (Roland Park), 153
Waverly, 33, 41, **104**, 107, 113, 224, 227, 249, 251
Webb, George, 75, 87-88, 90, 97, 103, 106, 159
Wells, Henry S, Jr., 284, 289
Wells, Henry S. Sr., 284
West Arlington, 166
West Baltimore Street repaving (1948), 160
Western Electric Company, 120, 137, 192, 241
Western Maryland Railroad (later Railway), 33, 47, 50, 87, **103**, 106, **178**, 179, 180, **209**
Westinghouse Electric & Manufacturing Company, **171**, 288, 291
Westport, 49, 77, 80, 118, 134, 153, 159, 185, 186, 188, 189
Wharton, William, Jr., 48
White, Edward, 284, 292
White, J. G. Company, 69
White Line, *see* Routes, Baltimore City Passenger Railway
White Marsh, 189
Whittle, Charles W, **223**
Whitton, A. D., 64
Widener, P. A. B., 61, 64
Williams, John F., 224
Wilson, Colston & Company, 263
Windshield wipers, 148
Windsor Hills, 106, **142**, 163, **278**
Women operating employees, 120, **122**, 154, 159
Woodlawn (Powhatan), 37, 48, **51**, 91, 113, 154, 163, 184, 249, **290**
Work equipment, *see* Cars, non-revenue
Working conditions, 38, 89, 115, **144, 218-225**, 227, 230, 231
World War I, 58, 118, 120, **122, 123**, 154, 234
World War II, **122**, 137, 140, 151, **152**, 153, 154, **167, 213, 214**, 269, 271, 273, **281**
Wyman Park, **204**
Yellow Line, *see* Routes, Baltimore City Passenger Railway
York Road Railway, *see* Baltimore & Yorktown Turnpike Railway
York Road reconstruction, 71, 169
Zone fares, 244, 264, 267, 271

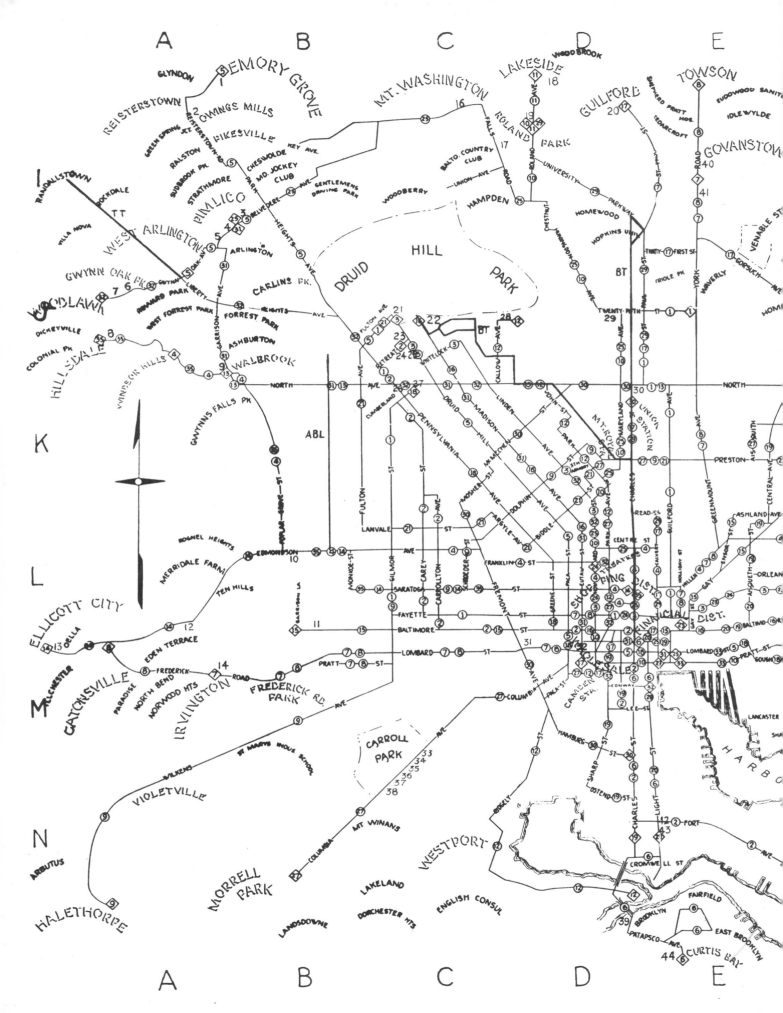